FREEDOMS GAINED
AND LOST

RECONSTRUCTING AMERICA
Andrew L. Slap, series editor

# Freedoms Gained and Lost

*Reconstruction and Its Meanings 150 Years Later*

Adam H. Domby and Simon Lewis, Editors

FORDHAM UNIVERSITY PRESS
NEW YORK  2022

Copyright © 2022 Fordham University Press

All rights reserved. No part of this publication may be reproduced, stored in a retrieval system, or transmitted in any form or by any means—electronic, mechanical, photocopy, recording, or any other—except for brief quotations in printed reviews, without the prior permission of the publisher.

Fordham University Press has no responsibility for the persistence or accuracy of URLs for external or third-party Internet websites referred to in this publication and does not guarantee that any content on such websites is, or will remain, accurate or appropriate.

Fordham University Press also publishes its books in a variety of electronic formats. Some content that appears in print may not be available in electronic books.

Visit us online at www.fordhampress.com.

Library of Congress Cataloging-in-Publication Data

Names: Domby, Adam H., 1983– editor. | Lewis, Simon, 1960– editor.
Title: Freedoms gained and lost : Reconstruction and its meanings 150 years later / Adam H. Domby, and Simon Lewis, editors.
Other titles: Reconstruction and its meanings 150 years later
Description: First edition. | New York : Fordham University Press, 2022. | Series: Reconstructing America | "The essays gathered in this volume derive from a conference convened in Charleston, South Carolina, in March 2018 by the program in the Carolina Lowcountry and Atlantic World (CLAW)." | Includes bibliographical references and index.
Identifiers: LCCN 2021037945 | ISBN 9780823298150 (hardback) | ISBN 9780823298167 (paperback) | ISBN 9780823298174 (epub)
Subjects: LCSH: Reconstruction (U.S. history, 1865–1877) | United States—Politics and government—1865–1877. | United States—Social conditions—1865–1918. | United States—Race relations—History—19th century.
Classification: LCC E668 .F74 2022 | DDC 973.8—dc23
LC record available at https://lccn.loc.gov/2021037945

Printed in the United States of America

24 23 22    5 4 3 2 1

First edition

Dedicated to all the champions of freedom,
equality, and equity, sung and unsung,
wherever and whenever they have operated.

*Contents*

Introduction
*Simon Lewis and
Adam H. Domby* | 1

Whom Is Reconstruction For?
*Bruce E. Baker* | 17

Implementing Public Schools:
Competing Visions and Crises in
Postemancipation Mobile, Alabama
*Hilary N. Green* | 39

Reconstruction Justice: African
American Police Officers in
Charleston and New Orleans
*Samuel Watts* | 57

1874: Self-Defense and Racial
Empowerment in the Alabama
Black Belt
*Michael W. Fitzgerald* | 78

"They Mustered a Whole Company
of Kuklux as Militia": State Violence
and Black Freedoms in Kentucky's
Readjustment
*Shannon M. Smith* | 96

A Woman of "Weak Mind": Gender,
Race, and Mental Competency in the
Reconstruction Era
*Felicity Turner* | 121

Idealism versus Material Realities:
Economic Woes for Northern
African American Families
*Holly A. Pinheiro, Jr.* | 143

"Works Meet for Repentance":
Congressional Amnesty and
Reconstructed Rebels
*Brian K. Fennessy* | 159

Toward an International History
of Reconstruction
*Don H. Doyle* | 181

The Dream of a Rural Democracy:
US Reconstruction and Abolitionist
Propaganda in Rio de Janeiro,
1880–1890
*Sergio Pinto-Handler* | 212

Lessons from "Redemption":
Memories of Reconstruction
Violence in Colonial Policy
*Adam H. Domby* | 232

Remembering War, Constructing
Race Pride, Promoting Uplift:
Joseph T. Wilson and the Black
Politics of Reconstruction
and Retreat
*Matthew E. Stanley* | 249

Fact, Fancy, and Nat Fuller's Feast
in 1865 and 2015
*Ethan J. Kytle* | 276

| | |
|---:|---|
| *Acknowledgments* | 305 |
| *List of Contributors* | 307 |
| *Index* | 309 |

## Freedoms Gained and Lost

# Introduction

*Simon Lewis and*
*Adam H. Domby*

The essays gathered in this volume derive from a conference convened in Charleston, South Carolina, in March 2018 by the program in the Carolina Lowcountry and Atlantic World (CLAW). Coinciding with the 150th anniversary of South Carolina's 1868 Constitutional Convention, the conference was the latest in an arc of conferences convened by the CLAW program probing two of the central issues of Lowcountry, American, and Atlantic World history: the relationship between the eighteenth-century revolutionary ideals of liberty and the practice of slavery, and the variety of ways in which emancipation was achieved.[1]

Conferences hosted by CLAW have long been a place where freedom has been examined. As long ago as 2000 during CLAW's conference on manumission, Orlando Paterson had made the provocative argument that manumission was actually one of the tools used by slave societies to help maintain the system of slavery. By providing a kind of safety valve in the possibility of manumission, slave owners diminished the risk of rebellion. Manumission, therefore, according to Paterson, far from threatening or undermining the system of slavery, was actually an integral and active part of it. When freedom from enslavement is "given" by the enslaver rather than taken by the formerly enslaved, it is, in the art historian Marcus Wood's phrase, "the horrible gift of freedom"; self-congratulatory representations of manumission, emancipation, and abolition are thus part of white slave owners' "extended archive of liberation fantasy." This archive prevents a recognition "that freedom, in a terribly real sense, was never something they had the power to give the slave populations they had created."[2]

Similarly critical of a simple teleological narrative moving from slavery to freedom, the 2008 CLAW conference on the abolition of the international slave trade drew attention to the ambiguities of the US and UK bans of 1807 and 1808, ambiguities that might be summed up by Nancy Stepan's memorable formulation that in the nineteenth century "just as the battle against slavery was being won by abolitionists, the war against racism was being lost."[3] Conferences on the Haitian Revolution (in 1998 and 2005), on marronage (2016), and on the Denmark Vesey

Conspiracy (2019) explored what happens when the enslaved claimed—or attempted to claim—freedom on their own terms: The revolutionary ideal of liberty was not to be tolerated when espoused by the formerly enslaved. So when Reconstruction began to make good on President Abraham Lincoln's promise of a "new birth of freedom" in the United States following the formal end of the Civil War, it is not surprising to see the backlash and the various efforts to control the newly emancipated.

Whether we think of Reconstruction in terms of Lincoln's phrase "re-birth of freedom" or Eric Foner's "Second Founding," it was "a period of extraordinary social, political, and constitutional change, when the United States abolished slavery and remade the Constitution to create birthright citizenship, equal protection, and due process, and to ban racial discrimination in voting."[4] As Foner's *The Second Founding: How the Civil War and Reconstruction Remade the Constitution* makes clear, the Reconstruction amendments fundamentally changed how the Constitution defined freedom. Despite the fact that "the amendments were compromises" that allowed "conflicting constructions," their potential was far more radical than their subsequent eclipsing by Jim Crow laws might imply. Indeed, Foner is correct that in the mid–twentieth century when Civil Rights activists were pushing for "the Second Reconstruction," they did "not need a new Constitution; [they] needed the existing one enforced."[5] Furthermore, the amendments had national, not just sectional, implications. Some northern and border states resisted confirming the Fifteenth Amendment because it would provide African Americans with rights that had not yet been granted in those states. The Fifteenth Amendment's first articles, for example, prohibiting limits on who could vote, some affected northern states more than southern.[6]

This volume, however, is not limited to rehashing what legal rights were promised and what legal rights are protected.[7] Rather, its unifying theme is the expansion and contraction of the many and varied manifestations and meanings of freedom. The essays explore the frequent "gaps" between legal and political gains supposedly secured in the statute books and people's actual lived experience. Even after legal emancipation, formerly enslaved people faced a lack of economic freedom dependent on equal educational access and employment opportunity. George Fredrickson wrote that Reconstruction can be seen as "the most radical experiment in political democracy attempted anywhere in the nineteenth century,"[8] but, as essays in this book also make clear, there were limits to that radical experiment, and many aspects of it were delayed if not entirely stymied. As just one example, Holly Pinheiro, Jr. argues that many Black northern Union soldiers who had risked their lives fighting for the emancipation of their enslaved brethren found themselves not only treated in discriminatory ways but actually losing ground economically as a consequence of their service.

Struggles over freedom were central to understanding Reconstruction even while the period played out. One Tennessee newspaper declared in July 1865 that "the great question of our day is the suffrage question."[9] Even historians of the overtly racist Dunning School saw freedom as central to the struggles of Reconstruction—albeit not in the fashion a modern scholar might consider. Describing the conflict in the first years after the war, J. G. de Roulhac Hamilton, for instance, recognized that the exercise of freedom was a key fight in the Reconstruction era. The freedmen's "first instinct upon emancipation," he opined, "had naturally been to move about and put their freedom to a test." Hamilton's conclusion, however, that "freedom in their minds, meant freedom not only from slavery but from work," is not a narrative a reputable historian would push today.[10] Even while rejecting Hamilton's interpretation of African American demands to control their own labor W. E. B. Du Bois, in his classic 1935 history of the period, agreed that fights over the meaning of freedom were the central battles of Reconstruction. Indeed, he wrote that "the decisive battle of Reconstruction" was over whether to give African Americans "physical freedom, civil rights, economic opportunity and education and the right to vote."[11]

Discussions of freedom have remained central to studies of Reconstruction, as Bruce Baker's essay in this volume describes, tracing the historiography backward from the present day to the Dunning School.[12] In recent years, one of the most critical debates has been over the issue of whether Reconstruction was, as Eric Foner argued in 1989, an "unfinished revolution" or, as Greg Downs has argued, part of a completed and successful Second American Revolution "that culminated in four million people's freedom."[13] Despite their disagreement over whether a revolution was unfinished or completed before being overthrown, both focus on issues of freedom, especially as manifested in contests over "visions of freedom and citizenship."[14]

This volume does not attempt to settle the perhaps unsettleable debate over Reconstruction's success or failure. In fact, rather than looking at the contest between slavery and freedom in these overarching terms, the essays in this volume probe the multiple forms various freedom struggles took in the period, from macro-scale freedoms embodied in economic independence, the ability to vote, access to education, the ability to work, freedom to own land, and freedom from police harassment to more micro-scale freedoms such as freedom to occupy space in a theater or on a sidewalk. Even the way freedom and freedom struggles were remembered reveals insights into how Reconstruction occurred, was undone, and in many cases continued after the traditional periodization.

Freedom was not just a question of being enslaved or not enslaved; nor was it just about access to the ballot. Whether freedom was gained or lost in any particular place and time was variously influenced by any number of specific factors, including friendships and associations, violence, gender, race, and class. None of those factors were restricted to the former Confederacy; consequently, the analyses in this book reach beyond just the former Confederacy to probe struggles over freedom in the North, in border states, in South America, and around the world, all the way to Australia. The essays in this book thus cover a broader range of social and political struggles than is typical and extend the geographical and temporal coverage to include the international impact of Reconstruction and its legacy into the twentieth and twenty-first centuries.

As seen in the following essays, again and again, the issue of the day was freedom—but not always in the way we might expect. Black Americans, who had most to gain through emancipation and the subsequent entrenchment of political rights, also had the most to lose in the fight and after the war took very different routes to attempt to safeguard their gains—gains that, though legally granted, could not always be guaranteed in practice. Among other insights of this collection, the essays gathered here highlight the distinctly local nature of Reconstruction. Communities experienced Reconstruction differently according to their particular location, and in each individual place the experience varied over time in relation to rapidly changing circumstances. African Americans were not the only group trying to gain freedoms. As the various essays show, there were many struggles over freedoms. One might even say that there were multiple Reconstructions. The experiences of both whites and Blacks in Kentucky, a slave state that had remained in the Union and therefore did not require federal Reconstruction, were very different from the experience of people in Alabama, which experienced federal occupation. There was no one experience for Republicans in the South or one solitary narrative for conservative Democrats. Similarly, African Americans from South Carolina had a very different experience from those from New York.

Alongside this call to differentiate among the various different experiences of Reconstruction, a second implication of this volume—perhaps tangential at times—is that what happened in the US case is not totally unique but at least to some degree instructive in relation to postconflict situations elsewhere in the world where compromises made in the name of stability come at the expense of real reform.[15] In this latter regard, the period we know as Reconstruction and that period's historiography may stand as a general example for what to do and what to avoid in future situations that may be comparable: for example, in how to come to terms with the history/memory of the conflict; how to teach about it; how to balance the needs for punishment, amnesty, and reabsorption; how to establish and maintain new institutions; and how to monitor and enforce acquiescence with new laws. The particular racial context of the US Civil War, however, means that the Reconstruction-era dispensations and the way those arrangements were recorded, reported, and, frankly, "spun" had uniquely baleful influences elsewhere in the world in relation to race and race making. This volume is not comprehensive in addressing the international impact of Reconstruction but does make some forays into how Reconstruction was not just of regional or even national importance. If in no other regard than this, these essays show that the legacy of Reconstruction remains deeply significant not only in the United States but internationally, too.

This book also takes an expansive view of the periodization of Reconstruction. Implicitly supporting Eric Foner's contentions that "Reconstruction can also be understood as a historical process without a fixed endpoint," and so "in a sense, Reconstruction never ended," these essays vividly portray that the key political, social, and cultural battles over the meaning and limits of freedom did not simply cease in 1876.[16] Indeed, a third major insight of this book is that Reconstruction has had a lasting legacy extending far beyond 1876 and American shores. Not only did Reconstruction shape the economic lives of an entire generation, but memories of Reconstruction and the legal changes brought about during the period have helped shape American and world politics ever since. And although the Dunning School narrative of Reconstruction as an ill-conceived failure is no longer dominant, it is still possible to encounter historians whom we might characterize as belonging to a neo–Dunning School.[17] Contested memories of the era are still used and abused for political ends.

When asked in January 2016 which former president most inspired her, Democratic presidential candidate Hillary Clinton named Abraham Lincoln. She explained her rationale as follows:

> You know, he was willing to reconcile and forgive. And I don't know what our country might have been like had he not been murdered, but I bet that it might have been a little less rancorous, a little more forgiving and tolerant, that might possibly have brought people back together more quickly.

But instead, you know, we had Reconstruction, we had the re-instigation of segregation and Jim Crow. We had people in the South feeling totally discouraged and defiant. So, I really do believe he could have very well put us on a different path.[18]

Clinton's inclusion of "Reconstruction" *alongside* "the re-instigation of segregation and Jim Crow"—rather than in counterdistinction to the two latter terms—gave the impression that far from viewing Reconstruction as a valiant attempt at establishing multiracial democracy in the United States, she saw it simply as a failure, presumably marred by a lack of the willingness she ascribes to Lincoln to "reconcile and forgive."

The attitude implied by her statement appears to have been bipartisan. Following Clinton's defeat and Republican success in the 2016 election, Speaker of the House Paul Ryan used the term "redemption" to describe his party's regaining of control of the US government. While Ryan's phrasing may have been accidental, as Adam Serwer wrote in the *Atlantic*, "however hopefully the speaker meant it, the idea that America needs to be redeemed, like the notion that it needs to be made great again, rests on the notion that something has gone horribly wrong." However these statements were received by the American public, to many professional historians, they provided evidence of at least one thing: that Reconstruction remains misunderstood by the public.

The persistence of the misunderstanding of Reconstruction matters a great deal more than as a historiographical debate, however. Its pertinence to understandings of race and citizenship in the contemporary United States has profound implications. Responding to Clinton's statement, Ta-Nehisi Coates wrote:

> The fact that a presidential candidate would imply that Jim Crow and Reconstruction were equal, that the era of lynching and white supremacist violence would have been prevented had that same violence not killed Lincoln, and that the violence was simply the result of rancor, the absence of a forgiving spirit, and an understandably "discouraged" South is chilling.[19]

For Adam Serwer, the potentially racist implications of Ryan's statement meant that America is "on the precipice of a Second Redemption," one whose "consequences may not be as total, or as dire," as the first but that will nevertheless cause future Americans to "look back at the Obama era much as historians have now come to look at Reconstruction: As a tragic moment of lost promise, a failed opportunity to build a more just and equitable society."[20] Given the course of the

Trump administration, this concern does not seem to have been exaggerated. In 2021, as we begin the Biden administration, our democratic systems appear to need a new Reconstruction from the past four years to ensure that freedoms are protected more permanently.

Sadly, what compels intellectuals like Coates and Serwer and historians like Foner, Downs, and Masur to counter the unique degree of historical misunderstanding of Reconstruction is disappointingly similar to that which compelled W. E. B. Du Bois over eighty years ago to counter a propagandistic version of America's national history that sought to minimize any shame. In Du Bois's opinion it was essential that nations should tell the truth about themselves—something that would require acknowledging that "nations reel and stagger on their way; they make hideous mistakes; they commit frightful wrongs; they do great and beautiful things."[21] As scholars of nationalism and memory have pointed out, nations depend on narratives that draw on both memory and forgetting.[22] Even back in 1935, before historical memory was even a field of study, Du Bois in calling for history to serve as a "measuring rod and guidepost for the future of nations" noted that it is essential to avoid telling a history based on "lies agreed upon" and instead to tell the truth "so far as the truth is ascertainable."[23] With Donald Trump attacking historians in 2020 for not teaching a "patriotic" history that celebrates America as exceptional, it seems the culture wars and battles over historical memory are here to stay.[24] The need for the historian to act as the "remembrancer" of awkward facts that society wishes to forget will not disappear anytime soon.[25]

Indeed, Reconstruction is perhaps the most critical of periods to understand because it can remind Americans that just as a nation can make progress, that same society can backslide as quickly. An accurate description of Reconstruction challenges the notion that America has always been the land of the free and inevitably always will be. The history of the United States is not a linear teleological progression toward increased freedom over time, as some Americans wish to think it. Focusing solely on the serial expansion of freedom obscures the way freedoms have been gained and lost repeatedly in American history— and the complex struggles to maintain them. Admirable moments in American history—American Independence, the abolition of slavery, women's suffrage, the overturning of "separate but equal," and the passage of civil rights legislation— need to be balanced against regressive efforts such as those embodied in the Fugitive Slave Act, the Dred Scott ruling, *Plessy v. Ferguson*, the internment of Japanese-Americans, and the overturning of the preclearance provision in the Voting Rights Act. But a narrative tracing the decreasing and increasing levels of freedom still fails to display the complexity of freedom struggles. In reality, as one group gained a freedom, another segment of the population might lose a different right.[26] Indeed, as some of these essays discuss in detail, at times the gaining of one right might mean abrogating the means of maintaining one's freedom. As Reconstruction makes clear, American history and freedom are chaotic concepts.

The full significance of Reconstruction as a period critical to determining the nature of and limits to freedom in contemporary America remains unacknowledged in public consciousness—yet the need for a public reckoning with our history is sorely needed.

With one exception, all of the essays included here were presented at the "Freedoms Gained and Lost" conference hosted by the CLAW program at the College of Charleston between March 16 and 18, 2018, commemorating the 150th anniversary of the remarkably progressive 1868 South Carolina Constitution.[27] The constitution expanded rights for South Carolinians, including the promise of education for all South Carolinian children and a guarantee of African American men's right to vote. The convention not only included seventy-one Black legislators but also witnessed an impassioned speech calling for women's suffrage by William Whipper.[28] Though not all freedoms were gained in that convention, as it would be another fifty-two years before women would gain that right in South Carolina, it remains a document that drastically expanded freedoms—at least for a time.

The volume opens with an essay by Bruce Baker, based on his keynote lecture at that conference, assessing the state of Reconstruction studies today and explaining why Reconstruction is so important. In his wide-ranging essay, at times philosophical, at times polemical, Baker starts by posing the question of whom Reconstruction was *for*. Answering his own question in broad terms by arguing that it was for "those who hope," Baker challenges historians to consider the *function* of their work when dealing with the period. Confronted with the events of Reconstruction and the ideals driving it, Baker asserts that the historian's responsibility is not just to retell a narrative of the events or offer another academic analysis of the ideals but to approach the period as "a playground for our imagination as we try to reconceive what progress would look like in a damaged world."

Responding to that challenge in their respective ways, the essays that follow Baker's meditation on Reconstruction and its modern meanings are arranged in thematically connected clusters. The first such cluster probes the limits of political change, examining various ways African Americans, whom the Emancipation Proclamation and the Reconstruction Amendments should have established as the beneficiaries of the Union victory, struggled to make political and legal freedoms meaningful in everyday life across the South. Hilary Green challenges us to consider the full range of institutional reform, beyond nominal or even actual voting rights, needed for the real achievement and exercise of freedom. Gaining the right to vote was an essential step in emancipation, but the importance of schooling for maintaining freedom through education cannot be underestimated. Additionally, Green argues that we should expand our study beyond the traditional period of 1863 to 1876 if we are fully to understand the significance of education history and the vital importance of education in maintaining and expanding freedom for African Americans after the Civil War.

While Green examines education in Mobile, Samuel Watts looks at policing in Charleston and New Orleans. Tracking the rise and fall of African American police officers in these two cities represents yet another way of assessing freedom struggles in the urban South. Indeed, Watts argues that the presence of Black officers on the streets of southern cities probably had greater impact on the day-to-day lived experience of urban residents than the political battles in state capitals and in Washington, DC. The right of African Americans not just to benefit from changed laws but to be the agents enforcing those laws represented one of the most fundamental and fought-over changes in the formerly slaveholding states.

Michael Fitzgerald takes the readers from contested urban spaces and legally sanctioned law enforcement to rural western Alabama and extralegal violence. There he finds local successes by African Americans contrasting with statewide trends. While scholars and the public often focus on Klan violence, it is equally important in the last few years of Reconstruction to pay attention to the use of organized armed African Americans as part of the freedom struggle. Fitzgerald challenges an overly simplistic understanding of Reconstruction, one where whites attack Blacks unable or unwilling to defend themselves. As his essay clearly illustrates, African Americans in western Alabama understood that their freedom included the freedom to fight back, and they took advantage of that freedom—sometimes successfully.

The second cluster of essays moves beyond analyses of African Americans' struggles for freedom in the former Confederacy. Expanding out from "the Confederacy," Shannon Smith examines the activity of the Klan in Kentucky. Smith describes a bitterly ironic example of a freedom gained that actually led to a loss of freedom. A border state that provided more troops to the Union than the Confederacy during the war, Kentucky was not covered by the Reconstruction acts because it had not seceded from the Union. Still, the Bluegrass State had its own Ku Klux Klan and racial violence, and the absence of a Republican government at the state level meant that African Americans faced state-sanctioned violence in the guise of the Kentucky militia. When violence erupted in 1871 between armed Black Republicans and white militia members, federal troops were sent to the region to maintain order. Because Kentucky state law forbade Black testimony, white vigilantes who murdered Black community leaders were vulnerable to prosecution in federal court under the Civil Rights Act. When the Democratic-majority Kentucky legislature lifted the ban on Black testimony in state courts, however, the Civil Rights Act ceased to apply. By gaining the freedom to testify, Smith shows, Black Kentuckians ironically lost the promise of federal protection.

Bringing gender analysis to bear, Felicity Turner's essay examines how racial and gendered expectations influenced how infanticide was addressed in courts across the United States. Turner examines how women who committed infanticide sought freedom from both motherhood and prison. The essay demonstrates that contests over freedom were not limited to the South or to Black men. Indeed, women—especially Black women—faced unique challenges when entering the courts. While Black women's legal rights undoubtedly expanded during Reconstruction, prevailing attitudes about race and gender encouraged the view that biology shaped one's abilities, sanity, and morality.

The third cluster of essays continues with an examination of racial disparity in relation to postwar consequences of loyalty or disloyalty to the Union, beginning with a group not typically examined when discussing Reconstruction: northern Blacks. Holly Pinheiro, Jr. looks at the experiences of Black soldiers recruited into the United States Colored Troops in New York and assesses the war's impact on their freedom. Far from finding that their own opportunities had been expanded, African Americans sent South, in part to free other Black Americans, often lost out on the gains their southern brethren gained. Whether through failure to receive their pay on time, war wounds, or court-martials, formerly economically independent African Americans sometimes saw that independence—and hence their freedom—eroded. In one of the bitterest ironies of the postwar arrangements, soldiers in the USCT found that their contribution to the war that ended racial slavery actually diminished their own independence and freedom. Experiencing racial discrimination in a variety of ways, they were often kept in service longer into Reconstruction so that white soldiers could be mustered out first; many lost ground economically as a result of their service, and some even lost their freedom completely, being sent to jail when they sought to return to civilian life before being formally demobilized.

In contrast to the penalties meted out to African Americans loyal to the Union, Brian Fennessy examines efforts for amnesty on behalf of former Confederates. Analysis of these efforts by white Republicans in both the North and the South to include former rebels in the party—often at the expense of African Americans—and of the role of social networks in shaping them is often overlooked in explanations of why Reconstruction was incomplete. Paying critical attention to the social networks that shaped these rehabilitation processes, Fennessy shows that the two mutually incompatible desires of reconstructing the South and quickly reuniting the nation often led to compromises that in the end provided an illusion of national unity at the expense of actual reform locally. In the end, a desire to minimize sectionalism and to legitimate southern governments by attracting white southerners to the Republican Party undermined efforts to create lasting change in the South. Northern Republicans' inability to imagine that Black southerners might provide better leadership than former Confederates undermined Reconstruction. Rather than cementing newly established freedom for African Americans, Republican authorities returned freedoms to former Confederates, allowing them to reassert control locally, disempowering African Americans.

The book then moves to a section that looks at the significance of Reconstruction internationally. If Pinheiro's, Smith's, and Turner's essays illustrate the importance of expanding Reconstruction studies beyond the South, the next three indicate that much can be gained by expanding one's analysis beyond the United States. In the essay that introduces this section, Don Doyle sets out what an international history of Reconstruction might look like. Noting that the historiography of Reconstruction, unlike the historiography of the Civil War, has resisted the turn to transnational approaches, Doyle takes an examination of "foreign relations and the projection of American power" as "one obvious starting point for understanding America in its international context" during the period. Arguing that US foreign policy after 1865 was driven by two chief principles—to promote republican (as opposed to monarchical/imperial) government in the Americas and to bring a definitive end to slavery—Doyle shows how the United States maneuvered to dislodge European empires from the Western Hemisphere and how Reconstruction helped shape the Spanish Caribbean and Brazil.

Bearing that argument out, the essay by Sergio Pinto-Handler, which follows Doyle's broad exploration of what an international turn in Reconstruction historiography might look like, addresses the abolitionist purposes to which the narrative of America's Reconstruction was put by reformist politicians in Brazil in the 1880s. Pinto-Handler contends that abolitionists in Brazil actively deployed positive narratives of emancipation and Reconstruction to seek a Reconstruction in their own nation and in support of their arguments to end slavery in South America.

Memory and renarrativization of Reconstruction was not necessarily subject to such a positive "spin" in the rest of the world, however. Adam Domby's essay, for instance, explores how the rest of the English-speaking world utilized the Lost Cause version of Reconstruction, which recalled the period as a time of corruption and misrule. Domby argues that a slanted memory of Reconstruction served as a form of historical racism that justified not just racial oppression in the South during Jim Crow but colonialism internationally. The supposed failure of African American enfranchisement during Reconstruction became a key talking point not only in the Jim Crow South but among colonial officials and others arguing for undemocratic white rule around the world. At the turn of the twentieth century, tales of the post–Civil War South that laid the blame for racial violence on an "unnatural" forcing of racial equality served as a narrative of the past that justified racialism. This parallel to scientific racism, narratives that contribute to a form of historical racism, continues to shape the world today.

The final cluster of essays also address this topic of historical memory and the often-surprising twists and turns that it can take. Matthew Stanley examines how Reconstruction influenced African American memories of the war. Describing the career of Joseph T. Wilson, the author of *The Black Phalanx* (1882), the first comprehensive history of Black soldiers in the United States, Stanley shows how the failure of Reconstruction to deliver on the promise of emancipation "led Wilson and others to look increasingly inward toward Black community, group reliance, shared decision making, and 'uplift suasion.'" At the same time, Wilson's earlier activism and *The Black Phalanx* preserved a fiercely emancipationist memory of the war.

Ethan Kytle in the final essay gives us an example of wishful thinking that overstated the possibilities for racial reconciliation in the immediate aftermath of the Civil War. Examining how a false memory of a "miscegenation feast" supposedly held by the caterer and former slave Nat Fuller sprang from a few stray remarks, Kytle unpacks the basis for the feast's "reenactment" in Charleston 150 years later in a culinary and cultural event that became one of the hottest tickets in Charleston in April 2015. While the 2015 version was real enough and brought together many of Charleston's leading luminaries—politicians, ministers, intellectuals—the 1865 feast that it ostensibly recreated and celebrated never actually occurred, and accounts that it had happened were in fact based on racist rumors. Kytle's intriguing essay on this curious nonevent serves as a warning for those wishing to find a narrative of Reconstruction that smoothly and comfortably anticipates contemporary efforts at racial reconciliation. The false memory of the dinner that was created implied that Black freedom was accepted by whites far more quickly and that Reconstruction was less contentious than either was in reality. While it may be incumbent on historians to disabuse the general public of the belief that Reconstruction was a failure and of representations of Reconstruction-era politicians as corrupt and incompetent opportunists, it is still vital to maintain scrupulous standards of research and not build counternarratives, however morally and politically satisfying they may be, based on insufficient evidence. Indeed, this narrative of acceptance allows Charlestonians to ignore the very real contemporary legacies of the long history of resisting African American freedom.

As demonstrated throughout these essays, from Green's examination of education to Kytle's study of memory, the fight for freedom—and the counterstruggles to limit freedom—did not end with Reconstruction. And as Baker's clarion call insists, struggles over the meaning of Reconstruction are not merely academic sideshows of interest only to professional historians. On the contrary, those struggles are part of the warp and weft of American history, of America's revolutionary aspirations to liberty and justice for all, and of America's desire to be a global exemplar of freedom. Lincoln's rhetoric of a "rebirth of freedom" took the apparently concrete and permanent legal form of the three key Reconstruction Amendments to the US Constitution, as well as the revised state constitutions. Almost all of the latter had been overturned by the end of the century, and comments by Donald Trump concerning birthright citizenship have made clear that even the former are not necessarily out of jeopardy.[29]

If we learn nothing else from studying Reconstruction, we must surely acknowledge that freedoms gained can be lost again. As Baker ominously comments, "Important parts of the vision of change freedpeople and their allies presented during Reconstruction slipped from their grasp almost immediately, and they are in danger of slipping from ours again just when we are starting to get our public to finally pay attention to Reconstruction." But just as freedoms can be lost, they can be regained. Today, as Black Lives Matter protests have grown, Confederate monuments come down, and calls for a "third Reconstruction" increase, an understanding of the first Reconstruction and its legacies is more important than ever.

**Notes**

1. The 2018 conference opened with the unveiling of a historical marker near the site of the 1868 convention. Speakers at the unveiling included professors Bernard Powers and Bruce Baker, International African American Museum CEO Michael Boulware Moore, and Ehren Foley, of the South Carolina Department of Archives and History. Copies of the remarks made on that occasion can be found at https://claw.cofc.edu/2018/03/15/2747/.

2. Marcus Wood, *The Horrible Gift of Freedom: Atlantic Slavery and the Representation of Emancipation* (Athens: University of Georgia Press, 2010), 2, 29.

3. Nancy Stepan, *The Idea of Race in Science: Great Britain 1800–1960* (London: Macmillan, 1982), 1.

4. Kritika Agarwal, "Monumental Effort: Historians and the Creation of the National Monument to Reconstruction," *Perspectives on History*, January 24, 2017, https://www.historians.org/publications-and-directories/perspectives-on-history/january-2017/monumental-effort-historians-and-the-creation-of-the-national-monument-to-reconstruction.

5. Eric Foner, *The Second Founding: How the Civil War and Reconstruction Remade the Constitution* (New York: Norton, 2019), xxvi, xxix.

6. Foner, *The Second Founding*, 108.

7. For an excellent legal history of Reconstruction, see Laura F. Edwards, *A Legal History of the Civil War and Reconstruction*, 1st ed. (New York: Cambridge University Press, 2015).

8. George M. Fredrickson, *White Supremacy: A Comparative Study of American and South African History* (Oxford: Oxford University Press, 1981), 182–83.

9. "The Suffrage Question," *Brownlow's Knoxville Whig*, July 12, 1865, 2.

10. Joseph Grégoire de Roulhac Hamilton, *Reconstruction in North Carolina* (New York: Columbia University Press, 1914), 156–57.

11. William Edward Burghardt Du Bois, *Black Reconstruction in America*, ed. Henry Louis Gates Jr. (Oxford: Oxford University Press, 2007), 267.

12. For more on discussion of freedoms and the impact of emancipation, see David W. Blight and Jim Downs, eds., *Beyond Freedom: Disrupting the History of Emancipation* (Athens: University of Georgia Press, 2017); Leon F. Litwack, *Been in the Storm So Long: The Aftermath of Slavery* (New York: Vintage, 2010); Mary J. Farmer-Kaiser, *Freedwomen and the Freedmen's Bureau: Race, Gender, and Public Policy in the Age of Emancipation*, 1st ed. (New York: Fordham University Press, 2010); Gregory P. Downs and Kate Masur, eds., *The World the Civil War Made* (Chapel Hill: University of North Carolina Press, 2015); Steven Hahn, *A Nation under Our Feet: Black Political Struggles in the Rural South from Slavery to the Great Migration* (Cambridge, MA: Harvard University Press, 2005); Thavolia Glymph, *Out of the House of Bondage: The Transformation of the Plantation Household* (Cambridge: Cambridge University Press, 2008). Studies of

Reconstruction and freedom have also extended beyond the former Confederacy, just as this volume does. See, for example, Stacey L. Smith, *Freedom's Frontier: California and the Struggle over Unfree Labor, Emancipation, and Reconstruction* (Chapel Hill: University of North Carolina Press, 2013); Kate Masur, *An Example for All the Land: Emancipation and the Struggle over Equality in Washington, DC* (Chapel Hill: University of North Carolina Press, 2010); Mark Wahlgren Summers, *The Ordeal of the Reunion: A New History of Reconstruction* (Chapel Hill: University of North Carolina Press, 2014); Richard White, *The Republic for Which It Stands: The United States during Reconstruction and the Gilded Age, 1865–1896* (New York: Oxford University Press, 2017). New works continue to come out exploring freedom in new ways. See, for example, Nicole Myers Turner, *Soul Liberty: The Evolution of Black Religious Politics in Postemancipation Virginia* (Chapel Hill: University of North Carolina Press, 2020).

13. Gregory P. Downs, *The Second American Revolution: The Civil War–Era Struggle over Cuba and the Rebirth of the American Republic* (Chapel Hill: University of North Carolina Press, 2019), 135.

14. Gregory P. Downs and Kate Masur, introduction to *The World the Civil War Made*, ed. Gregory P. Downs and Kate Masur (Chapel Hill: University of North Carolina Press, 2015), 1.

15. For a comparison of Ghana with the United States, see Rebecca Shumway, "A Shared Legacy: Atlantic Dimensions of Gold Coast (Ghana) History in the Nineteenth Century," *Ghana Studies* 21, no. 1 (2018): 41–62. For a comparison of how emancipation was remembered in Russia and the United States, see Amanda Brickell Bellows, *American Slavery and Russian Serfdom in the Post-Emancipation Imagination* (Chapel Hill: University of North Carolina Press, 2020).

16. Foner, *The Second Founding*, xx–xxi.

17. For more on the neo–Dunning School, see Vernon Burton, "'Reconstructing South Carolina's Reconstruction': Keynote, South Carolina Historical Association, 2017," *Proceedings of the South Carolina Historical Association* (2017), 24; Adam H. Domby, *The False Cause: Fraud, Fabrication, and White Supremacy in Confederate Memory* (Charlottesville: University of Virginia Press, 2020), 11, 177n31.

18. Qtd. in Ta-Nehisi Coates, "Hillary Clinton Goes Back to the Dunning School," *Atlantic*, January 26, 2016, https://www.theatlantic.com/politics/archive/2016/01/hillary-clinton-reconstruction/427095/.

19. Coates, "Hillary Clinton Goes Back to the Dunning School."

20. Adam Serwer, "Is This the Second Redemption?," *Atlantic*, November 10, 2016, http://www.theatlantic.com/politics/archive/2016/11/welcome-to-the-second-redemption/507317/.

21. Du Bois, *Black Reconstruction*, 585.

22. For more on this topic of memory and forgetting, see Marita Sturken, "The Wall, the Screen, and the Image: The Vietnam Veterans Memorial," *Representations* 35 (Summer 1991): 118–42; David W. Blight, *Beyond the Battlefield: Race, Memory, and the American Civil War* (Amherst: University of Massachusetts Press, 2002); Carole Emberton and Bruce E. Baker, *Remembering Reconstruction: Struggles over the Meaning of America's Most Turbulent Era* (Baton Rouge: Louisiana State University Press, 2017);

Bruce E. Baker, *What Reconstruction Meant: Historical Memory in the American South* (Charlottesville: University of Virginia Press, 2007); Ethan J. Kytle and Blain Roberts, *Denmark Vesey's Garden: Slavery and Memory in the Cradle of the Confederacy*, reprint ed. (New York: New Press, 2019). For an explanation of forgetting and remembering, see Domby, *The False Cause*, 3–4, 6, 78.

23. Du Bois, *Black Reconstruction*, 584–85.

24. Donald Trump, "Remarks by President Trump at the White House Conference on American History," September 17, 2020, https://www.whitehouse.gov/briefings-statements/remarks-president-trump-white-house-conference-american-history/.

25. Peter Burke, *Varieties of Cultural History* (Ithaca, NY: Cornell University Press, 1997), 59.

26. For more on this topic of losing freedoms there is a large historiography on the rise of Jim Crow, but good starting points include Heather Cox Richardson, *The Death of Reconstruction: Race, Labor, and Politics in the Post–Civil War North, 1865–1901* (Cambridge, MA: Harvard University Press, 2004); Douglas A. Blackmon, *Slavery by Another Name: The Re-Enslavement of Black Americans from the Civil War to World War Two* (Icon, 2012); Edward J. Blum, *Reforging the White Republic: Race, Religion, and American Nationalism, 1865–1898* (Baton Rouge: Louisiana University Press, 2005); Pippa Holloway, *Living in Infamy: Felon Disfranchisement and the History of American Citizenship* (Oxford: Oxford University Press, 2014). Holloway, for example, points out that the Fourteenth Amendment in some ways actually weakened protections on voting rights even as it protected other rights. Holloway, *Living in Infamy*, 35. These struggles for freedom didn't end with Reconstruction, of course, as seen in Glenda Elizabeth Gilmore, *Gender and Jim Crow: Women and the Politics of White Supremacy in North Carolina, 1896–1920* (Chapel Hill: University of North Carolina Press, 1996).

27. The historical marker commemorating the 1868 South Carolina Constitutional Convention was erected on Meeting Street in downtown Charleston near the "Four Corners of Law" on March 16, 2018. As Professor Bernard Powers commented at the unveiling, "The marker will permanently recognize the era's bold experiment in interracial democracy" and "encourage us to continue the struggle to achieve its highest ideals and that 'new birth of freedom' for which so many lived and died." For a full transcript of the remarks made by all the speakers on that occasion, see https://claw.cofc.edu/2018/03/15/2747/.

28. For more on this event, see Cappy Yarbrough, "'The Mark They Had in Sight': Black Women, Politics, and Suffrage in Reconstruction South Carolina," MA thesis, College of Charleston, May 2020, 21, 23–25.

29. Tennessee's Reconstruction-era constitution, adopted in 1870, was not amended until 1953.

# Whom Is Reconstruction For?

*Bruce E. Baker*

The question this essay addresses is simple: Whom is Reconstruction for? To answer that question, it visits a few historical episodes and, working in an archaeological fashion, excavates layer by layer, working from the present, which may, yet again, be a Third Reconstruction, back to the civil rights movement, the Second Reconstruction. Beneath that is the opening phase of the long civil rights movement, a period I have described as a "Radicals' Reconstruction," and the essay finishes 150 years ago at the South Carolina Constitutional Convention of 1868.[1] My answer is simple: Reconstruction is for those who hope, and invoking its memory in a positive way is a profound and tenacious act of hope.

In 1997, Bryant Simon wrote an excellent essay entitled "Rethinking Why There Are So Few Unions in the South."[2] He turned the usual framing of the regional variant of Werner Sombart's question on its head, arguing that what we should ask is why and how, with such powerful forces arrayed against organized labor and such a history of brutal suppression and disheartening failure, the working class of the South keeps organizing unions at all. Likewise with Reconstruction. Why do Americans, when they want progressive change, keep reaching for the idea of "Reconstruction," despite its disappointments, its grubby compromises, its perpetually unfinished promises of revolution? It is because, for reasons not fully comprehended, for many Americans in the last century and a half, "Reconstruction" represents, as Samuel Johnson said of second marriages, "the triumph of hope over experience."[3]

Whom is Reconstruction for now? That remains to be seen, and it depends on the work of many historians of the period as well as others in universities, schools, museums, parks, government offices, and elsewhere. It is a commonplace in our field to note that the Dunning School, while wrong on both historical and moral grounds, were very engaged with the public. I have argued that this was not entirely a matter of historians influencing the public, since many of the Dunning School historians were shaped less by Dunning and the rigorous, German-influenced scholarship of Columbia University than they were by the white supremacist narrative they breathed in during their upbringing in the South.[4] Partly because of this background, though, their reasoned historical arguments, using evidence and scholarly apparatus, found ready audiences and stamped the popular wisdom and historical memory with an elite seal of approval. When the revisionists came along, writing better history, the reach of their message beyond the academy was diminished, partly because all academic history had become more specialized and had less purchase in the broader public sphere but also specifically because the revisionist interpretation was a direct challenge to entrenched white southern views about race, democracy, and freedom.

Now, some of the infrastructure for bringing sophisticated, academically sound interpretations of history to a broad audience is more developed and has the potential to bring today's historians, and tomorrow's, back to the level of engagement with and influence on public debates seen a century ago.[5] Where today's historians have an advantage over the revisionists is that many of the racist assumptions that underpinned the Dunning School interpretation the revisionists were arguing against have weakened or at least have lost the institutional support of law and education and now generally receive strong popular moral condemnation. Four things have been key to this transformation of public mood: the National Park Service, history curriculum reform since the 1980s, the passage of time, and digital technologies. The first two of these could not have happened in the way they did without the changes brought about by the Second Reconstruction.

One of the last things Barack Obama did as president was to create the Reconstruction Era National Monument in Beaufort, the first National Park Service (NPS) site to take Reconstruction as its primary historical theme.[6] The NPS has focused on themes from American history at its sites since 1936, but as a 2011 study concluded, in recent years history has been less prominent, often under-resourced and administratively separated from interpretation.[7] In the waning days of the Clinton administration, Bruce Babbitt, Secretary of the Interior, and Eric Foner, with the support of many other local and regional historians, began investigating the possibility of creating a multilocation NPS site in and around Beaufort. Senator Ernest Hollings supported the project, and local Congressman Joe Wilson said he would also, but apparently he lied: Wilson's alliance with the Sons of Confederate Veterans stalled the project for over a decade.[8]

We should also see the campaign for the Reconstruction Era National Monument in the larger context of the Second Reconstruction's efforts to make recreational and commemorative spaces in public open to and responsive to all of the nation's population.⁹ Parks were desegregated as part of a broader effort to provide equal access to leisure facilities, but the campaign to desegregate the history presented in public space has proven much more challenging. I will not detour here into a discussion of monuments and their peregrinations—except to say that it was very satisfying to see Nathan Bedford Forrest in the night surrounded by people and dangling at the end of a rope and to see my fellow Tar Heels refusing to be silenced about Silent Sam, the monument of a Confederate soldier that stood proudly at the entrance to the University of North Carolina at Chapel Hill's campus from 1913 until the night of August 20, 2018, when protestors, possibly inspired by the sort of patriotism that motivated the Iron Brigade at the Battle of Gettysburg, dragged it off its pedestal and into a more historically accurate posture for a Confederate soldier from North Carolina: face-down in the dirt.¹⁰ Removing these concrete embodiments of outdated narratives of white supremacy is worth celebrating, but as difficult as it has been, it is the easy part.

The greater challenge is putting in place commemorative spaces based on the real history of Reconstruction.¹¹ Any accurate narrative is tremendously complex and, if historians are involved in writing it, as they should be, hedged about with many qualifiers. Not the easiest thing to fit onto a historical marker. Lapsing into postrevisionist mode for a moment, a lot of the history of Reconstruction is not very uplifting. For these reasons, the National Park Service site at Beaufort is particularly significant because it promises to provide a canvas extensive enough to depict the complexities, including the successes. The Port Royal Experiment, and the peasant proprietor society established on St. Helena Island, is one of Reconstruction's success stories.¹²

Now, can we do the same for the other, less cheerful side of the story and create a national park at Hamburg, South Carolina, or reinterpret Historic Brattonsville in York County, South Carolina, as ground zero of the Ku Klux Klan?¹³ Can we renarrate the story of Reconstruction on the landscape to acknowledge Adam Domby's point that the violence of the period was irreducible and inseparable from the Confederate memorials that remain common across the South? Harder still to imagine in a Martin Luther King Jr.–soaked environment is a recognition in official memory that sometimes, as in central Alabama in 1874, African Americans themselves met violence with violent resistance and that it worked, as Michael W. Fitzgerald explains in this volume. Some of that is conveyed in the Woodrow Wilson Family Home in Columbia, South Carolina, which tells the story of Reconstruction in South Carolina's capital during the period when Wilson was a boy there for four years in the early 1870s. However, were it not for Wilson's later fame as president, it is unlikely the site would have been used just to present the history of Reconstruction.[14] Would similar efforts be made to tell the story of Joseph T. Wilson, the Black veteran, whose story Matthew Stanley tells in this volume, and whose own views evolved over the decades as he continued to respond to the political exigencies of his moment?

What students in schools learn about Reconstruction has also changed dramatically in ways we may only fully appreciate in a few years, after children educated in this new narrative rise to positions of power and influence in national life and older voices die away. It is easy to forget just how bad the textbooks and the teaching of Reconstruction were not so long ago. I'll use myself as an example. I was born in 1971; I studied South Carolina history in the fourth grade in Easley, South Carolina, in 1980, and again in the eighth grade, in 1984. Here is a bit of what the textbook we used in the eighth grade had to say about Reconstruction. The militias were blamed for "murders and burglaries" reminiscent of "the days of Indian warfare" for helpless white families. "Carpetbaggers and scalawags," I was taught, "managed to break up the old feeling of friendship and confidence" between the races. My Black schoolmates were reminded twice in four pages that most of the formerly enslaved people in South Carolina could not read or write. Throughout the text, the term "South Carolinians" refers only to white South Carolinians who supported the Confederacy.[15] That book, first written by Mary C. Simms Oliphant in 1917, was the same one used, with only minor updates, by generations of South Carolina students studying their state's history.[16] Some of those students—Vernon Burton, Charles Joyner, Gaines Foster, Dan Carter, Joel Williamson, George Tindall—kept studying and learned better, but most did not.[17] I am the very last generation to have used the Oliphant textbook. The next year it was replaced by a much better book by Lewis Jones.[18] Some people have marveled at how tenacious the Dunning School story has remained, since revisionists have been in charge of the historiography for over half a century and relics like Oliphant's book have been gone for three decades.[19] But while the most successful of our books do go some distance to shape a fairly elite portion of public opinion, there is a mass of people out there who are my age and older who had the Dunning School version imprinted on their minds at an early age and never really replaced that version with more up-to-date ideas. The changes in textbooks made in the 1980s and early 1990s are only now beginning to have their full effect. We need to be patient just a bit longer.[20]

Perhaps also we need to remember that time passes, but not always as quickly as we might think. When I was writing the end of *What Reconstruction Meant*, I was struck by the fact that Gorrell Pierce, the Grand Dragon of the Federated Knights of the Ku Klux Klan in 1979 when they shot communists in Greensboro, said he had grown up hearing old people talk about their memories of Reconstruction (though now I suspect he might be a bit too young).[21] But let's just do some math. A child is born in 1860, and he has clear memories of Reconstruction and, in some states, could even have been involved in its overthrow. He has a daughter born in 1895, when he is thirty-five. That daughter has a son when she is thirty-five, in 1930. At the age of ten in 1940, that son hears his grandfather, aged eighty, talking about his experiences of Reconstruction. That grandson is ninety years old in 2020. There must yet be thousands of people in the South who heard stories about Reconstruction from those who were there. When that link breaks in the next ten to fifteen years, I think we will see another loosening of the bonds of the white supremacist narrative of Reconstruction.

Something else that makes historical memory in the early twenty-first century significantly different than in the late twentieth century: Digital technology has the capacity to radically democratize access to the best of historical scholarship and also to a lot of the primary sources that professional historians use to construct that scholarship.[22] Even without paying for any subscriptions, anyone with an internet connection can easily access a wealth of nineteenth-century newspapers on "Chronicling America," congressional sources from the "A Century of Lawmaking for a New Nation" collection, digitized copies of manuscript collections from leading archives such as the Southern Historical Collection, published materials gathered on the Internet Archive, bespoke primary-source collections like the one from the "After Slavery" project, and much more.[23] A fairly modest subscription fee brings even more newspapers, manuscript census records, city directories, and military records. While much of the leading scholarship in academic journals remains behind paywalls and not easily accessible to the general public, leading historians are also writing for newspapers and magazines including the *New York Times* and the *Atlantic*, and they are also making cutting-edge scholarship freely available via blogs such as "We're History," "The Conversation," and others. While the high-water mark of revisionism in the historical field happened at a time when the general reading public was increasingly estranged from the work being produced by leading historians, we cannot say the same for the present moment, which is refreshing but also puts a greater responsibility on each of us. Part of this responsibility is, to quote Blain Roberts and Ethan Kytle, "to look the thing in the face," acknowledging the failures and disappointments of Reconstruction along with the neglected triumphs.[24] But we must be careful not to grasp recklessly at shining moments of reconciliation from Reconstruction that do not hold up to scrutiny. When in 1912, in a slightly different context, W. E. B. Du Bois wrote, "This country has had its appetite for facts on the Negro problem spoiled by sweets," he might have been writing about Nat Fuller's feast, the subject of Ethan Kytle's essay in this volume, a too-good-to-be-true interracial dinner in Charleston in 1865.[25] As Jake Barnes said, "Isn't it pretty to think so?"

What does all this amount to, and what would it mean to have a public discourse informed by a historical understanding of Reconstruction that would be closer to what we recognize as correct instead of something Dunning would have approved? At its best, it could be transformative, a Third Reconstruction. Just as C. Vann Woodward popularized the idea of a Second Reconstruction, he seems to have coined the phrase "Third Reconstruction" before the dust had settled on the second.[26] Written in the critical year of 1966, Woodward's essay "What Happened to the Civil Rights Movement?" introduced the idea of a "Third Reconstruction" as a response to the national problems of "slums, housing, unemployment, deteriorating school and family, delinquency, and riots."[27] Since then, the phrase has reappeared every so often, recurring with greater frequency the further we get from the Second Reconstruction. In fact, we might use the rise of the idea of a "Third Reconstruction" as one way to chart the end of the "long civil rights movement."[28] Manning Marable used the phrase "Third Reconstruction" in a 1981 article, and with the election of Bill Clinton, Eric Foner wondered whether it was "time for a Third Reconstruction . . . to address directly the economic inequalities that are the accumulated consequence of 250 years of slavery and a century of discrimination."[29]

Various other political events since then have also been seen as possibly marking the beginning of the Third Reconstruction, including the election of Barack Obama in 2008 and, more recently, the defeat of Roy Moore in the Alabama Senate race.[30] Some distance to the political left of Moore, a New Communist Movement group called the Freedom Road Socialist Organization identifies the "main enemy" of the American people as the "New Confederacy—composed of the most reactionary faction of capital and middle strata, right-wing racists, united in the Republican Party" and calls for "the construction of a broad united front—the Third Reconstruction—as a protracted strategy to defeat the New Confederacy."[31] The phrase has even been applied to the current craze for southern cuisine and to Beyoncé.[32] The emergence of a "Third Reconstruction" can be seen as an abandonment of the hopes of the "Second Reconstruction," but it is equally a hopeful marker of the beginning of something.

The person now most closely associated with the concept of a Third Reconstruction, though, is the Reverend William Barber. Born just after the 1963 March on Washington, Barber became a Christian Church pastor and a key organizer in the Moral Monday movement in North Carolina that became nationally prominent in 2013. His activism has deep roots in his faith but also in his understandings of both the First and Second Reconstructions. Barber's father grew up in Free Union, near Plymouth, North Carolina, an "island of freedom" where "the typical white power structure was not as rigid."[33] In the 1960s, Barber's parents left the comfort and security of Indianapolis to move home to eastern North Carolina to work in the civil rights movement in Washington County.[34] Arguing that "folks who saw a need for change in America had to know this history," Barber realized that in the 2010s "the more we pay attention to the patterns of the First and Second Reconstructions, the more our experience made sense."[35] The movement Barber is involved in seeks to reassert the moral framework around public life and work toward "a reconstruction of the legal and statutory protections that establish justice and ensure the common good," drawing together a variety of related campaigns in "the framework of a Third Reconstruction . . . that creates the opportunity to fundamentally redirect America."[36] Like the Radical Republicans in the 1860s imagining how establishing free labor in the South could transform the entire nation, the Third Reconstruction originates in the South, but its scope is national.

Whom, then, was the Second Reconstruction, the civil rights movement, for? As C. Vann Woodward and others (but particularly Woodward) began to reclaim the notion of a Second Reconstruction from the white supremacists who had first used it, they insisted that the Second Reconstruction must be for African Americans.[37] At the national level, it was to implement and enforce the Reconstruction Amendments, finally allowing them to have the transformative effects on American life they had promised before the Supreme Court and northern worries over politically empowered workers short-circuited them.[38] This is a view of the relationship between power, society, and the state that fit well into the context of Cold War America, when the national state was perhaps as powerful as it has ever been before or since. In our classic understanding of the civil rights movement, protests and activism at a local level—Montgomery, Birmingham, Selma, to pick three from Alabama—leveraged change at the national level in the form of legislation such as the Civil Rights Act of 1964 and the Voting Rights Act of 1965. Then this national legislation was meant to be enforced everywhere, sometimes at the points of paratroopers' bayonets, not just in the places where the original activism had occurred. It assumes the sort of trickle-down nature of power that echoes the famous line from Amos 5:24 that Martin Luther King Jr. used to close his 1963 "I Have a Dream" speech: "Justice rolls down like waters, and righteousness like a mighty stream." This is in fact what happened to a degree, and the lives of African Americans were indeed profoundly changed by the accomplishments of the Second Reconstruction, but only as long as the national state that had created and eventually enforced the Reconstruction Amendments remained powerful and democratically responsive.

As the federal government came under relentless attack in the late twentieth and early twenty-first centuries, the gains of the "finished revolution" of the Thirteenth, Fourteenth, and Fifteenth Amendments began to slip away not just from African Americans but from all Americans. The voting rights enshrined by the Fifteenth Amendment have been slowly chiseled away by gerrymandering and a wave of new and revived restrictions on voting.[39] The Supreme Court hastened this process in *Shelby County v. Holder* (570 US 2 [2013]) by striking down large parts of the Voting Rights Act, including the crucial preclearance statute. But it is not just the Fifteenth Amendment that has been undermined in recent years. The *Citizens United v. Federal Election Commission* (558 US 310 [2010]) decision used a perversion of the due process clause of the Fourteenth Amendment to assert that corporate personhood confers inviolable free speech rights, democratic consequences be damned. And the innocuous phrase in the Thirteenth Amendment—"except as a punishment for crime whereof the party shall have been duly convicted"—has unleashed a carceral state with the modern equivalent of convict leasing and the disfranchisement of a significant fraction of the southern electorate, disproportionately the poor. If the Second Reconstruction was to help African Americans by completing the unfinished business of enshrining rights in the iron-clad guarantees of the federal US Constitution, the last thirty years have been a stark lesson that, as Thomas Wentworth Higginson noted during the First Reconstruction, "revolutions may go backwards."[40]

Another less heralded answer to the question of whom the Second Reconstruction was for is that it was for communities seeking empowerment and the direct expression of the rights and duties of democratic citizenship. In this we can see the direct influence of the first Reconstruction on the second in the form of the Penn Center.[41] When the United States liberated St. Helena Island and the Port Royal area in November 1861, missionaries arrived soon after and set up the Penn School on St. Helena Island.[42] After World War II, the Penn School became the Penn Center and ran training for civil rights leaders. As Vernon Burton explained, rather than being "led by progressive, paternalistic white northerners," Penn Center's work now relied on "white southerners willing to work with African Americans to promote racial justice and equality and to dismantle Jim Crow."[43] The Penn Center supported a local NAACP chapter and worked with St. Helena residents on projects such as a community council and a daycare center.[44] The

Penn Center was one of the models for the War on Poverty's Community Action Programs, since they were to be "developed, conducted, and administered with the maximum feasible participation of residents of the areas and members of the groups served." A key principle of Community Action Programs was "increasing the power of the poor over the institutions which affect their lives," which is a fair description of the First Reconstruction as well. The CAPs had the potential for a radical, bottom-up restructuring of the nation's political economy.[45]

This sort of systemic change in where power lies and how it can be exercised lay at the heart of an earlier revival of Reconstruction that has less of a place in our national story than the famous Second Reconstruction. I have called it "Radicals' Reconstruction," in an obvious nod to Thaddeus Stevens and company in the spring of 1867. We may define "radical" as "a broad term designating those people and organizations working to restructure, in a thorough-going and lasting way, the relations of power—economic, social, and political—between labor and society," and that definition works well for this period in the 1930s and 1940s when a project to reimagine the history of Reconstruction became a crucial part of the intellectual wing of what Jacquelyn Dowd Hall and others in the past fifteen years or so have been calling the Southern Popular Front.[46] This was "an interracial coalition of labor organizers, civil rights advocates, radicals, and left liberals who saw a robust labor movement, the re-enfranchisement of the black and white southern poor, and an activist regulatory and welfare state as the key to reconstructing the South and a reconstructed South as the key to extending the New Deal."[47]

The Radicals' Reconstruction was not primarily for African Americans, as the Second Reconstruction would be. Instead, it was for a biracial working class that would see the South fully integrated into national life for the first time in the nation's history. From the founding of the United States, the South had remained aloof, protecting the economic interests of its elite by protecting the institution of slavery. When that project failed spectacularly in the 1860s, the elite managed to fend off political challenges in the late nineteenth century, but the problem was that the wealth they had gained by remaining distinctive from the rest of the nation was no longer there. By the 1930s, Franklin Roosevelt could announce that "the South presents right now the Nation's No. 1 economic problem."[48] The basis of that problem, as Gavin Wright argued thirty years ago, was that from the Civil War to World War II, the South existed in a separate labor market from the rest of the country, one where unskilled labor earned substantially less and where industrialization had hardened the differences in wages between Blacks and whites within the South.⁴⁹ The Southern Popular Front realized that to change this, strong unions were needed. Activists needed to make whites reconsider why they did not want to ally themselves with African Americans, and changing ideas about Reconstruction were central to that project.⁵⁰

An important episode in the Southern Popular Front happened in Charleston immediately after World War II. Drawing on young organizers brought to the city by the war, the CIO's Food, Tobacco, Agricultural & Allied Workers Union organized the cigar factory in the shadow of the Cooper River Bridge and brought it out on strike in October 1945 in order to end the North-South pay differential. An important part of the campaign was a series of lectures meant to inform the nonsegregated audiences about recent history as a means of galvanizing action.⁵¹ While none of these lectures focused on Reconstruction, the topic was in the air in South Carolina in the mid-1940s. When the South Carolina Progressive Democratic Party was formed by African Americans in 1944, Osceola McKaine framed his keynote address around "evok[ing] the [Reconstruction] past to serve as a background" for "help[ing] history repeat itself." His speech emphasized the political power and offices held by African Americans during Reconstruction; the progressive contributions they made to the state starting with the Constitutional Convention of 1868; and the importance, then and in the 1940s, of cooperation between African Americans and poor whites. "Once more," said McKaine, "our voices will be heard legislating and administering in the cause of freedom and democracy for all classes and all races of our citizens in the State and in the Nation."⁵² To the extent that the contemporary "Fight for Fifteen" movement in Charleston draws on an organizing tradition reaching back to the 1860s, we might agree with the Princeton historian Woodrow Wilson, who wrote in 1901 that "Reconstruction is still revolutionary matter."⁵³

In addition to a national biracial working class, the Radicals' Reconstruction was also about hope for young people and the future, especially toward the end. Like their precursors in the First Reconstruction, participants in the Radicals' Reconstruction were acting in the wake of a massive war that had toppled old structures of power and opened up new possibilities for the future. The clearest example of this was the Southern Negro Youth Congress, which had originated in 1937 as a youth branch of the National Negro Congress.⁵⁴ The experience of war and the acceleration of Southern Popular Front activism brought a new and more experienced generation of young people to the fore by the end of World War II who believed their work for civil rights in the South had to be part of a global movement led by youth to fight racism, end colonialism, and empower the working class. For a variety of reasons, they focused on South Carolina as the location for the next phase of this "vanguard for a postwar movement."⁵⁵ When they met in Columbia's Township Auditorium in October 1946, the meeting was framed explicitly as an effort "to complete the struggle ... begun by our forefathers in the Civil War and Reconstruction period," and they were surrounded by portraits of African Americans who had held federal office during Reconstruction.⁵⁶ As Hilary Green points out in her essay in this volume, the Constitutional Convention in Alabama in 1867 made education a priority as well.

The emphasis on youth that was one characteristic of the Radicals' Reconstruction carries us neatly back to the question: Whom was the original Reconstruction for? One way to approach that question is to look at the work of the Constitutional Convention that met in Charleston in the first weeks of 1868. As part of the conference that led to this book, a state historical marker was finally erected that acknowledges this event: As the marker says, "The 1868 Constitution was a remarkable document for its time" and written by a convention in which "a majority of the delegates ... were African American, some of them former slaves." To understand what they were trying to accomplish, we can examine the proceedings of the convention, nearly a thousand pages long, that detail the hopes and ambitions and frustrations of people, mostly unaccustomed to exercising political power, trying to establish a framework for a more democratic and egalitarian society. Historians have done much of the basic work to study this and other conventions. In the late 1960s and 1970s, Lawrence C. Bryant put together biographical sketches of many of the delegates, work that was expanded in the 1990s by Eric Foner in *Freedom's Lawmakers*.⁵⁷ Ten years ago, Richard L. Hume and Jerry B. Gough published a monumental study of the conventions based on quantitative methods.⁵⁸ Yet the sheer mass of the documentation continues to inhibit thorough and systematic engagement with the substance of the debates and the intricacies of who was arguing what. We need a digital project that would make all of that debate accessible and cross-referenced with the biographical data already available and other information so we can begin to look for patterns and understand the debates that took place in Charleston in the context of the experiences of the delegates from Anderson, from Camden, from Hamburg, from the Independent Republic of Horry County, and elsewhere. Even in the absence of such a resource, some novel and significant themes are already identifiable in the constitutional debates of 1868.

Reconstruction was above all to be for the poor, which marked a tremendous change. Four-fifths of South Carolina's antebellum legislators were slave owners, and as Keri Leigh Merritt asserts, South Carolina "was undoubtedly the most aristocratic or oligarchic state in the United States."⁵⁹ Brian Fennessy's essay here on congressional amnesty depicts an early phase of Reconstruction, where congressional leaders thought they could make the change they wanted by reaching out to any prominent ex-Confederates who had demonstrated that they accepted the Fourteenth Amendment and shared the Republican vision of a South built around free labor. That strategy failed, though, and the 1868 convention found different leadership. The delegates of the Constitutional Convention made it clear that helping South Carolina's laboring poor was a priority. Simeon Corley, a tailor from Lexington, was one of the most outspoken delegates on this point. "I remember in times gone by," Corley stated,

> the State of South Carolina had been ruled by the rich for the rich. . . . I know of no prouder spectacle in the world than to see at the close of the labors of the Convention a Constitution submitted to the people of the State which will let the poor man see for the first time in our history his rights have been respected.[60]

As the convention was ending, Solomon Dill from Kershaw County said, "I have voted in every instance, while here, to the best of my knowledge and ability, for everything that I thought would benefit the poor."[61] It was men like these whom W. W. Ball, editor of the Charleston *News and Courier* in the early twentieth century, blamed for infecting the political system of South Carolina with "the cooties of democracy."[62]

Indeed, few of the delegates could be counted as rich, and many of them, if not from the state's poorest stratum, were certainly of limited means. The study of convention delegates by Richard L. Hume and Jerry B. Gough provides a snapshot. The median wealth of the delegates was only $1,500, just ahead of Florida in last place. Whites from outside the Confederate states who arrived after the war began were the wealthiest of the delegates, with median assets of $7,150, while South Carolina's southern white delegates were the poorest of any of the conventions, with only $1,700 of wealth. Seventy-two of the 121 delegates were Black, with forty-one of these seventy-two having been enslaved.[63]

How did these delegates propose to help the poor? Historians have examined the persistent but futile efforts toward land reform, but they have largely overlooked homestead protection, a means not of giving property to those with none but rather a mechanism to ensure that those who did acquire property could hold on to it.[64] The homestead provision set aside a minimum amount of property that would be "exempt from levy and sale by virtue of any process whatever under the law of the State."[65] A property owner could not borrow against the homestead, but he need not worry about losing it to debt, either. Not all the delegates agreed with the principle of homestead protection, fearing it offered no protection to the truly destitute landless population of the state.[66] Governor James L. Orr argued that the lack of homestead protection "made the American people almost as great wanderers as the Arabs" because "when a farmer planted an orchard or a vineyard, he had no assurance that five years thereafter the result of his care and labor would not pass into the hands of strangers."[67]

This concern for security of tenure as the basis of a widespread proprietary interest that would both build up individual wealth and also anchor stable, landowning biracial communities that would lead to greater social peace and common interest is a classic part of the Republican free-labor ideology that developed in the 1850s, but it is common to other land-reform efforts in this period, such as those in Ireland and Scotland.[68] For poor whites, whose lack of property had been used to keep them out of any meaningful engagement with governance and who had been drifting rootless across the southern landscape for decades, and for freedpeople who had themselves been the most movable form of property and susceptible to being sold away, the prospect of a permanent home (once they had managed to acquire it) must have been welcome, a solid base on which to construct a future.

Delegates in the convention challenged the doctrine of coverture and granted women an independent legal identity, if not an independent political identity. As David Silkenat explains in the context of North Carolina, a woman's "entire legal identity after marriage was subsumed by that of her husband," and her claim for divorce was "not only a claim that she wanted to escape from a failed marriage but also a claim against white male authority."[69] Despite the arguments of some delegates that the convention should not meddle with the sacred marital union, the constitution allowed divorce. Just as importantly, James M. Allen of Greenville introduced a provision to support "the rights of woman, and her ability to possess and control her own property" that also found its way into the final document.[70] William J. Whipper even tried to enfranchise women, arguing, "I believe in universal suffrage. . . . I know the time will come when every man and woman in this country will have the right to vote."[71]

The general thrust of this essay has been a bit old-fashioned, perhaps, a bit against the grain of some of the most recent historical scholarship on Reconstruction. Gregory P. Downs suggests that we need to understand freedpeople's politics "on its own terms, not as a beacon for future generations," and understand the practicalities of the federal government's attempts to get things done, its "efficacy."[72] Downs's excellent argument, which he reiterates in the introduction to *The World the Civil War Made* with Kate Masur, in *After Appomattox*, and even in *Declarations of Dependence*, is that contrary to what historians writing in the era of the Cold War had told us, the national state that came out of the Civil War was not some sort of all-conquering Leviathan but rather, at least in the South, a "stockade state," and it behooved freedpeople and the poor and weak to know, as one African American Red Shirt in South Carolina put it in 1876, "which side de butter was on de bread."[73] While certainly not wrong, many of us feel a bit of a pang at giving up the idea that freedpeople's politics could be "a beacon for future generations." A recent synthesis by Mark Summers moves us further in that direction, insisting that as long as we do not "make the mistake of defining Reconstruction's exclusive end as remaking the South on the basis of equal rights and democracy," we can see Reconstruction as "a lasting and unappreciated success" from a narrow and technocratic perspective.[74] This view brings us back to something that while erudite and sophisticated, looks a lot like David Blight's triumph of reconciliationist and white supremacist visions of the Civil War at the expense of an emancipationist vision. The frameworks of W. E. B. Du Bois, Eric Foner, and Steven Hahn have a teleology, with African Americans moving resolutely toward freedom, and if you can say one thing for teleology, it knows where it is going. Whether they got there or not, freedpeople and their allies during Reconstruction had clear and energetic ideas about the kind of society they were striving toward and about the one they wanted to leave behind.[75]

This sense of motion—progress, even—is there in the sources and not just imposed retrospectively by nostalgic or idealistic historians. To dismiss it raises questions in my mind of, to use the words of Justin Champion, "What are historians for?" Champion, starting from the position that "the activity of being a historian is artistic rather than scientific—historical claims to truth are aesthetic and ethical, rather than empirical and objective," examines the role of historians in public life, something particularly apt for historians of Reconstruction now that the topic is finally getting traction with the public again. Champion suggests,

> Good history is history that is honest—it is also history that is critical, informed, engaged, and committed. It should expose tyranny, celebrate achievement, condemn crimes, explain prejudice, describe sacrifice, honour victims, commemorate the dead, but most importantly, provoke debate. Such history will try to preserve what is slipping from our grasp, and aim to recover what has been lost.[76]

Important parts of the vision of change freedpeople and their allies presented during Reconstruction slipped from their grasp almost immediately, and they are in danger of slipping from ours again just when we are starting to get our public to finally pay attention to Reconstruction.

So, to return to my question: Whom is Reconstruction for? That is up to us, historians and citizens. Reconstruction, and its memory, is good to think with for people trying to bring together a fractured society after a period of trauma. That could come in handy. It is for those trying to reconstruct a better society than the one they have had thus far, so it is useful for new nations—Catalonia and Scotland, for instance. Reconstruction is perhaps the opposite of "restoration," a movement toward something new rather than a return to the old. That is worth remembering. The 1868 Constitutional Convention took place in Charleston, South Carolina, in a city and a state created by and named for a restoration that brought to a decisive end a period of attempted democracy and potentially revolutionary change.[77] Reconstruction is for those who would imagine a future with security based not on walls and separation but on welcoming people from outside the magic circle to our ranks as "citizens and friends."[78]

Of all the uses we make of history and memory, perhaps none is more important than using it as the basis of our political imagination, which Jacquelyn Dowd Hall describes as "the hope for a different future that inspires and is inspired by the study of the past."[79] Americans have tended to use wars as the basis of political imagination: the War for Independence, the Civil War, World War II, the Cold War, and in our dystopian present, the Vietnam War. Perhaps it is time, again, to build our vision of what is possible and what is desirable not on a period of destruction but on a period of reconstruction, to use Reconstruction not as a corpse to be autopsied but as a landscape of possibilities, a playground for our imagination as we try to reconceive what progress would look like in a damaged world. That would be, as Barack Obama said in 2004, a "politics of hope" when "out of this long political darkness a brighter day will come."[80] Maintaining hope is a profound act of courage and resistance in troubled times, but as Hamish Henderson, the great folklorist and poet of postwar Scotland, wrote, "O come all ye at hame wi' Freedom, / Never heed whit the hoodies croak for doom."[81] This is why we must keep working to understand Reconstruction and work to see that others understand it as well. With a clear-eyed and complex understanding of what was, we may leave off grieving what might have been, for revolutions unfinished, and look ahead to what may yet be.

**Notes**

1. Bruce E. Baker, *What Reconstruction Meant: Historical Memory in the American South* (Charlottesville: University of Virginia Press, 2007), 110–45. The lecture on which this essay is based was delivered at the "Freedoms Gained and Lost: Reinterpreting Reconstruction in the Atlantic World" conference in Charleston, SC, on March 16, 2018. Earlier that day, a historical marker commemorating the site of the 1868 South Carolina Constitutional Convention was unveiled in the city. Adam Parker, "New Historic Marker about Reconstruction to Be Unveiled in Charleston," *Post and Courier* (Charleston), March 15, 2018.

2. Bryant Simon, "Rethinking Why There Are So Few Unions in the South," *Georgia Historical Quarterly* 81, no. 2 (Summer 1997): 465–84.

3. Eric Foner, *Reconstruction: America's Unfinished Revolution, 1863–1877* (New York: Harper and Row, 1988); James Boswell, *The Life of Samuel Johnson* (London: Charles Dilly, 1791), 1:487.

4. Baker, *What Reconstruction Meant*, 33–36.

5. See, for instance, Blain Roberts and Ethan J. Kytle, "When the South Was the Most Progressive Region in America," *Atlantic*, January 17, 2018, https://www.theatlantic.com/politics/archive/2018/01/when-the-south-was-the-most-progressive-region-in-america/550442/.

6. Barack Obama, "Presidential Proclamations—Establishment of the Reconstruction Era National Monument," White House, January 12, 2017, https://obamawhitehouse.archives.gov/the-press-office/2017/01/12/presidential-proclamations-establishment-reconstruction-era-national.

7. Anne Mitchell Whisnant, Marla R. Miller, Gary B. Nash, and David Thelen, *Imperiled Promise: The State of History in the National Park Service* (Bloomington, IN: Organization of American Historians, 2011).

8. Jennifer Whitmer Taylor and Page Putnam Miller, "Reconstructing Memory: The Attempt to Designate Beaufort, South Carolina, the National Park Service's First Reconstruction Unit," *Journal of the Civil War Era* 7, no. 1 (March 2017): 39–66.

9. William E. O'Brien, *Landscapes of Exclusion: State Parks and Jim Crow in the American South* (Amherst: University of Massachusetts Press, 2015).

10. Daniel Connolly and Vivian Wang, "Confederate Statues in Memphis Are Removed after City Council Vote," *New York Times*, December 20, 2017, https://www.nytimes.com/2017/12/20/us/statue-memphis-removed.html; Myah Ward and Charlie McGee, "Silent Sam Toppled in Protest the Night before Classes Begin," *Daily Tar Heel* (Chapel Hill), August 20, 2018, https://www.dailytarheel.com/article/2018/08/silent-sam-down.

11. For a thoughtful discussion of some of these challenges, see Nick Sacco, "Public Iconography, Museum Education, and Reconstruction Era History," *Muster: How the Past Informs the Present*, September 29, 2017, https://journalofthecivilwarera.org/2017/09/public-iconography-education-reconstruction-history/.

12. Guion Griffis Johnson, *A Social History of the Sea Islands* (Chapel Hill: University of North Carolina Press, 1930); T. J. Woofter Jr., *Black Yeomanry: Life on St. Helena Island* (New York: H. Holt & Co., 1930).

13. James Folker, "Black Victims of 1876 Hamburg Massacre Get Historical Marker," *Augusta Chronicle*, March 6, 2016, http://chronicle.augusta.com/news-metro/2016-03-06/black-victims-1876-hamburg-massacre-get-historical-marker; Whitney Kimball, "One Man's Fight to Reclaim a Racist South Carolina Monument," *Curbed*, November 4, 2015, https://www.curbed.com/2015/11/4/9904712/south-carolina-racist-monument-reconstruction-augusta-hamburg. The Ku Klux Klan is mentioned briefly and blandly in the section of the Historic Brattonsville website devoted to African American history: http://chmuseums.org/african-american-history-hb/. Of course, the sort of critical (some might say "honest") historical perspective I am suggesting here might not adequately reflect "the nobility of the American character" that Donald Trump believes is the proper subject for historians making statements in the United States; perhaps we should omit discussion of Reconstruction entirely or agree that there were very fine people on both sides. "Remarks by President Trump at the White House Conference on American History," September 17, 2020, https://www.whitehouse.gov/briefings-statements/remarks-president-trump-white-house-conference-american-history/.

14. Jennifer Whitmer Taylor, "Rebirth of the House Museum: Commemorating Reconstruction at the Woodrow Wilson Family Home," PhD diss., University of South Carolina, 2017.

15. Mary C. Simms Oliphant, *The History of South Carolina* (River Forest, IL: Laidlaw, 1970), 282–97, quotations at 291. Thanks to my West End Elementary School classmate Sheila Bagwell Bates for retrieving the quotations for me from this edition of the book.

16. The book was originally written by Oliphant's grandfather, William Gilmore Simms, and then updated by Oliphant as a school textbook in 1917. Mary C. Simms Oliphant, *The History of South Carolina, by William Gilmore Simms, Rev. by Mary C. Simms Oliphant (with Supplementary Chapters)* (Columbia, SC: State Company Printers, 1917).

17. Dan Carter has reflected on how his study of the Simms textbook ill prepared him for the beginning of the Civil Rights Movement: Dan Carter, "Civil Rights and Politics in South Carolina: The Perspective of One Lifetime, 1940–2003," in *Toward the Meeting of the Waters: Currents in the Civil Rights Movement of South Carolina during the Twentieth Century*, ed. Winfred B. Moore Jr. and Orville Vernon Burton (Columbia: University of South Carolina Press, 2008), 404–6. Will Moredock has also reflected on the Oliphant book, including its depiction of Reconstruction: Will Moredock, "Mary C. Simms Oliphant's Troubling History of South Carolina Corruption of the Innocent," *Charleston City Paper*, May 9, 2012, https://www.charlestoncitypaper.com/charleston/mary-c-simms-oliphants-troubling-history-of-south-carolina/Content?oid=4070745.

18. Baker, *What Reconstruction Meant*, 168.

19. Taylor and Miller, "Reconstructing Memory," 56.

20. For the broader context of the shift from Oliphant's book to Jones's, see Gary B. Nash, Charlotte Antoinette Crabtree, and Ross E. Dunn, *History on Trial: Culture Wars and the Teaching of the Past* (New York: Knopf, 1997). Another example of how depictions of Reconstruction in textbooks have changed can be found in Elaine Parsons, "The Cultural Work of the Ku Klux Klan in US History Textbooks, 1883–2015," in *Remembering Reconstruction: Struggles over the Meaning of America's Most Tumultuous Era*, ed.

Carole Emberton and Bruce E. Baker (Baton Rouge: Louisiana State University Press, 2017), 225–61.

21. Baker, *What Reconstruction Meant*, 170.

22. Eric Foner, "Afterword," in *After Slavery: Race, Labor, and Citizenship in the Reconstruction South*, ed. Bruce E. Baker and Brian Kelly (Gainesville: University Press of Florida, 2013), 222.

23. The URLs for these resources are, in order: https://chroniclingamerica.loc.gov/; https://memory.loc.gov/ammem/amlaw/; https://library.unc.edu/wilson/digital-collections/; https://archive.org/; http://www.afterslavery.com/.

24. Blain Roberts and Ethan J. Kytle, "Looking the Thing in the Face: Slavery, Race, and the Commemorative Landscape in Charleston, South Carolina, 1865–2010," *Journal of Southern History* 78, no. 3 (August 2012): 639–84.

25. W. E. B. Du Bois, "The Gall of Bitterness," *The Crisis* 3, no. 4 (February 1912): 153.

26. Baker, *What Reconstruction Meant*, 149–58.

27. C. Vann Woodward, "What Happened to the Civil Rights Movement?," in *The Burden of Southern History*, 3rd ed. (Baton Rouge: Louisiana State University Press, 1993), 177; originally published in *Harper's Magazine*, January 1967, 29–37.

28. Jacquelyn Dowd Hall, "The Long Civil Rights Movement and the Political Uses of the Past," *Journal of American History* 91, no. 4 (March 2005): 1233–63.

29. Manning Marable, "The Third Reconstruction: Black Nationalism and Race in a Revolutionary America," *Social Text* 4 (Autumn 1981): 3–27; Eric Foner, "Time for a Third Reconstruction," *The Nation*, February 1, 1993.

30. Manisha Sinha, "Alabama Makes a Noble Historical Turn, as It Has Many Times throughout Its History," *New York Daily News*, December 14, 2017, http://www.nydailynews.com/opinion/alabama-noble-historical-turn-times-article-1.3698283.

31. Freedom Road Socialist Organization, "2015–16 Main Political Report," http://freedomroad.org/wp-content/uploads/2017/08/MPR-2015-2016.pdf.

32. Julia Bainbridge, "Michael W. Twitty: 'I Want Southern Food to Be the Basis of a New Discussion on Shared Southern Identity,'" *Atlanta Magazine*, September 18, 2017, http://www.atlantamagazine.com/dining-news/michael-w-twitty-want-southern-food-basis-new-discussion-shared-southern-identity/; Daphne A. Brooks, "The Knowles Sisters' Political Hour: Black Feminist Dissent in Sound at the End of the Third Reconstruction," lecture at Stony Brook University, March 22, 2017.

33. William J. Barber II, with Jonathan Wilson-Hartgrove, *The Third Reconstruction: Moral Mondays, Fusion Politics, and the Rise of a New Justice Movement* (Boston: Beacon, 2016), x–xi, quotation at 1. For a discussion of the flexibility of race relations in places like this, see Mark Schultz, *The Rural Face of White Supremacy: Beyond Jim Crow* (Urbana: University of Illinois Press, 2005).

34. Barber II with Wilson-Hartgrove, *The Third Reconstruction*, 2.

35. Barber II with Wilson-Hartgrove, *The Third Reconstruction*, 120. For an analysis of Barber's use of ideas of "Populism," "Fusion," and "Reconstruction" in the context of North Carolina history, see David Silkenat, "From Fusionists to Moral Mondays: The Populist Tradition in North Carolina Politics," *49th Parallel* 27 (2015): 1–13, https://fortyninthparalleljournal.files.wordpress.com/2015/11/silkenat-49thparallel-formatted.pdf.

36. Barber II with Wilson-Hartgrove, *The Third Reconstruction*, 122.

37. Baker, *What Reconstruction Meant*, 156–58.

38. Heather Cox Richardson, *The Death of Reconstruction: Race, Labor, and Politics in the Post–Civil War North, 1865–1901* (Cambridge, MA: Harvard University Press, 2001), 122–55; Foner, *Reconstruction*, 527–31.

39. Sam Fleming, "Battle Lines: The Fight for a Fair Vote in America," *Financial Times*, August 2, 2018, https://www.ft.com/gerrymandering; Brennan Center for Justice, "New Voting Restrictions in America," http://www.brennancenter.org/new-voting-restrictions-america; Pippa Holloway, *Living in Infamy: Felon Disfranchisement and the History of American Citizenship* (New York: Oxford University Press, 2014).

40. Thomas Wentworth Higginson, *Army Life in a Black Regiment* (Boston: Fields, Osgood, & Co., 1870), 47. I am using "First Reconstruction" to refer to the period after the Civil War and emancipation, and not in the sense it is used in Van Gosse, *The First Reconstruction: Black Politics in America from the Revolution to the Civil War* (Chapel Hill: University of North Carolina Press, 2021).

41. Orville Vernon Burton, *Penn Center: A History Preserved* (Athens: University of Georgia Press, 2014), 70–98.

42. Burton, *Penn Center*, 9–14.

43. Burton, *Penn Center*, 70.

44. Burton, *Penn Center*, 71.

45. Stephen M. Rose, *The Betrayal of the Poor: The Transformation of Community Action* (Cambridge, MA: Schenckman, 1972), 91, 116.

46. Chris Green, Rachel Rubin, and James Smethurst, "Radicalism in the South since Reconstruction: An Introduction," in *Radicalism in the South since Reconstruction*, ed. Chris Green, Rachel Rubin, and James Smethurst (New York: Palgrave Macmillan, 2006), 9n3.

47. Jacquelyn Dowd Hall, *Sisters and Rebels: A Struggle for the Soul of America* (New York: Norton, 2020); Jacquelyn Dowd Hall, "Women Writers, the 'Southern Front,' and the Dialectical Imagination," *Journal of Southern History* 64, no. 1 (February 2003): 7.

48. *Confronting Southern Poverty in the Great Depression: The Report on Economic Conditions of the South with Related Documents*, ed. David L. Carlton and Peter A. Coclanis (Boston: Bedford Books of St. Martin's Press, 1996), 42.

49. Gavin Wright, *Old South, New South: Revolutions in the Southern Economy since the Civil War* (New York: Basic Books, 1986), 66–67, 197.

50. Robert Rodgers Korstad, *Civil Rights Unionism: Tobacco Workers and the Struggle for Democracy in the Mid-Twentieth-Century South* (Chapel Hill: University of North Carolina Press, 2003).

51. Robert R. Korstad, "Could History Repeat Itself? The Prospects for a Second Reconstruction in Post–World War II South Carolina," in *Toward the Meeting of the Waters: Currents in the Civil Rights Movement of South Carolina during the Twentieth Century*, ed. Winfred B. Moore Jr. and Orville Vernon Burton (Columbia: University of South Carolina Press, 2008), 252–60; Karl Korstad, "Black and White Together: Organizing in the South with the Food, Tobacco, Agricultural and Allied Workers Union (FTA-CIO),

1946-1952," in *The CIO's Left-Led Unions*, ed. Steve Rosswurm (New Brunswick, NJ: Rutgers University Press, 1992), 69-94.

52. O. E. McKaine, "Keynote Speech," folder "Progressive Democratic Party," Box 8, A. J. Clement Papers, South Caroliniana Library, Columbia, SC.

53. Woodrow Wilson, "The Reconstruction of the Southern States," *Atlantic Monthly* 87 (January 1901): 1. Another example of a very long local tradition of activism is described in M. Langley Biegert, "Legacy of Resistance: Uncovering the History of Collective Action by Black Agricultural Workers in Central East Arkansas from the 1860s to the 1930s," *Journal of Social History* 32, no. 1 (October 1998): 73-99.

54. C. Alvin Hughes, "We Demand Our Rights: The Southern Negro Youth Congress, 1937-1949," *Phylon* 48, no. 1 (1987): 39.

55. Erik S. Gellman, *Death Blow to Jim Crow: The National Negro Congress and the Rise of Militant Civil Rights* (Chapel Hill: University of North Carolina Press, 2012), 228.

56. Gellman, *Death Blow to Jim Crow*, 234-239, quotation at 229.

57. Lawrence C. Bryant, *Negro Legislators in South Carolina, 1865-1894: Preliminary Report* (Orangeburg: School of Graduate Studies, South Carolina State College, 1966); Lawrence C. Bryant, *Negro Lawmakers in the South Carolina Legislature, 1869-1902* (Orangeburg: School of Graduate Studies, South Carolina State College, 1968); Lawrence C. Bryant, *Negro Senators and Representatives in the South Carolina Legislature, 1868-1902* (Orangeburg, SC: [n.p.], 1968); Eric Foner, *Freedom's Lawmakers: A Directory of Black Officeholders during Reconstruction* (New York: Oxford University Press, 1993).

58. Richard L. Hume and Jerry B. Gough, *Blacks, Carpetbaggers, and Scalawags: The Constitutional Conventions of Radical Reconstruction* (Baton Rouge: Louisiana State University Press, 2008).

59. Keri Leigh Merritt, *Masterless Men: Poor Whites and Slavery in the Antebellum South* (Cambridge: Cambridge University Press, 2017), 165, quotation at 170. For a more comprehensive look at the ruling class of South Carolina, see Manisha Sinha, *The Counterrevolution of Slavery: Politics and Ideology in Antebellum South Carolina* (Chapel Hill: University of North Carolina Press, 2000).

60. *Proceedings of the Constitutional Convention of South Carolina* (Charleston: Denny & Perry, 1868), 494-95.

61. *Proceedings of the Constitutional Convention of South Carolina*, 868.

62. W. W. Ball, *The State That Forgot: South Carolina's Surrender to Democracy* (Indianapolis, IN: Bobbs-Merrill, 1932).

63. Hume and Gough, *Blacks, Carpetbaggers, and Scalawags*, 161-63.

64. Paul Goodman, "The Emergence of Homestead Exemption in the United States: Accommodation and Resistance to the Market Revolution, 1840-1880," *Journal of American History* 80, no. 2 (September 1993): 470-98.

65. *Proceedings of the Constitutional Convention of South Carolina*, 44.

66. *Proceedings of the Constitutional Convention of South Carolina*, 485, 494.

67. *Proceedings of the Constitutional Convention of South Carolina*, 50.

68. See, e.g., Fergus Campbell and Tony Varley, eds., *Land Questions in Modern Ireland* (Manchester: Manchester University Press, 2013); Ewen A. Cameron, *Land for the People? The British Government and the Scottish Highlands, c. 1880-1925* (East Linton:

Tuckwell, 1996); Ewen A. Cameron, "Communication or Separation? Reactions to Irish Land Agitation and Legislation in the Highlands of Scotland, c. 1870–1910," *English Historical Review* 120, no. 487 (June 2005): 633–66; Cathal Smith, "Second Slavery, Second Landlordism, and Modernity: A Comparison of Antebellum Mississippi and Nineteenth-Century Ireland," *Journal of the Civil War Era* 5, no. 2 (June 2015): 204–30.

69. David Silkenat, *Moments of Despair: Suicide, Divorce, and Debt in Civil War Era North Carolina* (Chapel Hill: University of North Carolina Press, 2011), 70.

70. *Proceedings of the Constitutional Convention of South Carolina*, quotation at 64, 499, 783–88.

71. *Proceedings of the Constitutional Convention of South Carolina*, 836, quotation at 838.

72. Gregory P. Downs, "Anarchy at the Circumference: Statelessness and the Reconstruction of Authority in Emancipation North Carolina," in Baker and Kelly, eds., *After Slavery*, 99, 100.

73. Gregory P. Downs and Kate Masur, "Introduction: Echoes of War: Rethinking post–Civil War Governance and Politics," in *The World the Civil War Made*, ed. Gregory P. Downs and Kate Masur (Chapel Hill: University of North Carolina Press, 2015); Gregory P. Downs, *After Appomattox: Military Occupation and the Ends of War* (Cambridge, MA: Harvard University Press, 2015); Gregory P. Downs, *Declarations of Dependence: The Long Reconstruction of Popular Politics in the South, 1861–1908* (Chapel Hill: University of North Carolina Press, 2011); Richard Franklin Bensel, *Yankee Leviathan: The Origins of Central State Authority in America, 1859–1877* (New York: Cambridge University Press, 1990); quotation from Edmund L. Drago, *Hurrah for Hampton! Black Red Shirts in South Carolina during Reconstruction* (Fayetteville: University of Arkansas Press, 1998), 103.

74. Mark Wahlgren Summers, *The Ordeal of the Reunion: A New History of Reconstruction* (Chapel Hill: University of North Carolina Press, 2014), 4.

75. Eric Foner, *The Story of American Freedom* (New York: Norton, 1998); Steven Hahn, *A Nation under Our Feet: Black Political Struggles in the Rural South, from Slavery to the Great Migration* (Cambridge, MA: Harvard University Press, 2000).

76. Justin Champion, "What Are Historians For?," *Historical Research* 81, no. 211 (February 2008): 168.

77. Christopher Hill, *The World Turned Upside Down: Radical Ideas during the English Revolution* (London: Temple Smith, 1972). The "world turned upside down" concept was also used as the title of a collection of letters from a South Carolina plantation-owning family covering their financial decline during Reconstruction: Louis P. Towles, ed., *A World Turned Upside Down: The Palmers of South Santee, 1818–1881* (Columbia: University of South Carolina Press, 1996).

78. Virginia Foster Durr, *Outside the Magic Circle: The Autobiography of Virginia Foster Durr*, ed. Hollinger F. Barnard (Tuscaloosa: University of Alabama Press, 1985); Thomas C. Holt, "Slave and Citizen in the Modern World: Rethinking Emancipation in the Twenty-First Century," in Baker and Kelly, eds., *After Slavery*, 32.

79. Jacquelyn Dowd Hall, "'You Must Remember This': Autobiography as Social Critique," *Journal of American History* 85, no. 2 (September 1998): 443.

80. Barack Obama, "Keynote Address at the 2004 Democratic National Convention," July 27, 2004, American Presidency Project, http://www.presidency.ucsb.edu/ws/?pid=76988.

81. Hamish Henderson, *Freedom Come-All-Ye. An 80th Birthday Souvenir for Hamish Henderson. Poems and Songs of Hamish Henderson* (Edinburgh: Chapman Publishing, 1999), 51. For a translation into English and an explanation of the language and imagery, see Dick Gaughan's comments: http://www.dickgaughan.co.uk/songs/texts/freecaye.html.

# Implementing Public Schools

*Competing Visions and Crises in Postemancipation Mobile, Alabama*

Hilary N. Green

In anticipation of implementing the state constitutional convention requirements of the Reconstruction Acts of 1867, Lawrence S. Berry, William V. Turner, and Robert V. Wiggins presented a series of resolutions to the delegates attending the Colored Mass Convention of the State of Alabama. While pledging to "use our power for the good of all," the three men addressed the main obstacle to the creation of a "thorough system of common schools" at the convention—white conservative Alabamians. The men proclaimed in the fourth resolution:

> Calling upon the conservatives to show, by their actions as well as their words, that they are friendly to us, and notifying that we "know our rights and knowing dare maintain them," and that if they execute their threats of making us "vote as they say, or starve," we will call upon the Republican party to deprive them of the property earned by the sweat of our brow, which they have proved themselves so unworthy to possess.[1]

The following day, the *Mobile Daily Advertiser and Register* published a response entitled "Poisonous Doctrines." The article sought to delegitimize African American political power, the state constitutional convention, and any document produced as a consequence. The white author questioned the integrity and intelligence of the African American delegates attending the "so-called 'Colored Mass Convention of the State of Alabama.'" By suggesting the resolutions had sown "the poisoned seeds of a bloody war of castes," the author concluded with a denouncement of the three men and other African American delegates as the "enemies to peace and order, as selfish and heartless conspirators and foes to society."[2] Over the course of two days, the stage was set for the constitutional convention and implementation of the educational mandates created therein. While the African

American and Creole of Color delegates from Mobile led the way in the creation of public schools for Alabamians regardless of race, class, and former servitude, the struggle for the African American public schoolhouse continued in earnest in the newspapers, at the ballot box, and in the courtrooms.

This essay explores the competing visions of white, Black, and Creole of Color Mobilians for a racially inclusive public school system, albeit segregated, created in the 1868 Alabama Constitution and contentiously implemented in the city. The recent scholarship of W. Fitzhugh Brundage, Thomas Holt, Kidada Williams, Ethan Kytle, Blain Roberts, and others has reminded scholars and public audiences that much remains to be learned about the historical period, the African American radical vision for a democratic society, and the constitutions adopted following the Reconstruction Acts of 1867.[3] Indeed, the sesquicentennial anniversary of Reconstruction has revealed the need for deeper understandings of both how national and state politics influenced local politics and how diverse African Americans navigated this terrain to secure the schoolhouse as the vehicle for expressing their vision of freedom and citizenship in the postwar society.[4]

After providing some context of the drafting and ratification of the 1868 Alabama state constitution, the essay delves into how Mobilians competed locally over the implementation of statewide educational mandates. By threatening the entire enterprise, white Mobilians' intense opposition facilitated a shift in African Americans' protest strategies and their relationships with Creoles of Color, the American Missionary Association, and school board members as they sought to ensure quality public schools.[5] Ultimately, the resiliency of African Americans' vision and educational networks prevailed in gaining education opportunities and the freedom literacy and education brought.

The Reconstruction Acts of 1867 transformed African American education into a right of citizenship. This series of federal laws created five military districts encompassing eleven former Confederate states, defined the readmission process, and mandated for Black suffrage.[6] Additionally, it indirectly determined the parameters for a new phase in African American education as a vehicle for defining citizenship at the local, state, and national level and ensured that Black southerners would have a political voice in that process. As a result, Black southerners extended their notions of freedom and citizenship by enshrining the African American public schoolhouse as the embodiment of their emancipation, new political status, and socioeconomic future as a race in the postwar southern landscape transformed by Confederate defeat. Without education, southern African Americans and their white allies felt that their newly gained freedoms could not be sustained. For many, slavery's fiery destruction unleashed widespread educational opportunities in the Freedmen's Bureau schools. No longer a clandestine institution, the African American schoolhouse and the scholastic success achieved by early students made southern African Americans' claims for the franchise, economic independence, and other freedoms clearer and more compelling. The creation of a permanent and inclusive public school system would further cement and expand African American citizenship in the postwar body politic.

Per the new federal mandates within the Reconstruction Acts, Alabama convened a constitutional convention in early November 1867. Contrary to conservative white Alabamians' characterizations, African Americans did not numerically dominate the convention held in Montgomery. Seventy-nine of the ninety-six attending delegates were white. Of the seventeen Black delegates participating in the roughly month-long convention, six were of mixed ancestry, five had free status before the Civil War, several had significant property holdings, and only two "were reported to be illiterate."[7] Attempts by white conservative Alabamians to characterize the delegates as being depraved, ignorant, and social pariahs were just propaganda. Overall, the delegates were largely well educated, literate, US army veterans, business professionals, Freedmen's School educators, and others invested in the Reconstruction project.[8] The five-member delegation from the city of Mobile reflected the convention's racial demographics. John Carraway, a literate former enslaved person, was the assistant editor of the *Nationalist*. Ovide Gregory, a Creole of Color, had previously served as the assistant chief of police during Mayor Gustavus Horton's administration. Carraway and Gregory were joined by the former mayor Horton; Alfred E. Buck, a white Maine transplant to Mobile; and Albert Griffin, the white editor of the *Nationalist*, at the convention.[9] The other delegates were similarly diverse. Together, the assemblage of African American, Creole, and white delegates created a democratic constitution that included the creation of a racially inclusive statewide public educational system as a right of citizenship for all Alabamians.[10]

Not all white Alabamians embraced the 1867 constitutional convention process. The Reconstruction Acts disqualified some white Alabamians who had not yet taken loyalty oaths. Other white conservatives simply refused to participate, which would have unintended consequences for the ratification process outlined in the Second Reconstruction Act. Their inability and/or refusal to participate in the process resulted in a feeling of a lack of representation at the conventions. As a result, white conservatives viewed the political gathering as an imposition on the natural order of society and ridiculed the convention in the press. The *Mobile Daily Register* (formerly the *Mobile Daily Advertiser and Register*) referred to the event as "so-called conventions" or "gorilla conventions" and encapsulated conservative Alabamians' anger over their perceived disenfranchisement and lack of representation. Where convention delegates saw displays of biracial democracy, these holdouts saw illegal, undemocratic, unconstitutional proceedings that yielded too much political power to African Americans. Their attacks set the tone for the convention proceedings, the actions of the delegates, and the complex ratification process and postratification implementation of the state-mandated public school provisions in Mobile.[11]

From the outset, delegates prioritized the creation of a state-funded education system. Most, if not all, Republican delegates had an awareness of the general enthusiasm and success of the Freedmen's Bureau schools in both large urban centers and rural communities. Indeed, John Carraway proposed a resolution providing that the Committee of Public Instruction develop a special ordinance in which African American orphans were included in the new educational article. He also argued for the continuation of African American churches as sites of instruction under the new system. While the convention made the state legislature responsible for resolving these issues, section 6 of article 11 specified that the state establish "schools at which all children of the State, between the ages of five and twenty-one years, may attend free of charge."[12] Other clauses provided the bureaucratic framework for the new state educational system, including the establishment of an agricultural school under the supervision of the University of Alabama regents. The entire system would be paid for through the creation of an education fund seeded by the proceeds of land sales and sustained by a 20 percent of the annual state budget appropriation and a series of new personal and corporate taxes.[13]

Overall, article 11 of the new constitution represented the state's first acknowledgment that it had a responsibility to educate all children regardless of race, class, and previous servitude. Earlier state constitutions and legislation restricted education to white and Creole of Color children, making African American education illegal. The 1868 constitution represented a reversal. Alabama now had an obligation to financially support African American education. R. D. Harper, a state Freedmen's Bureau educational leader, commented that "*in no State* of the Union is there a *more liberal provision* for the cause of Common School Education than in the State of Alabama."[14] The creation of the 1868 Alabama Constitution was quite revolutionary for its educational provisions, display of African American men's political power, and promise of biracial governance. In this regard, the delegates' actions and the final product mirrored the work performed at other conventions creating new state constitutions with similar educational provisions. Indeed, African American public education became a fundamental right of citizenship guaranteed by the post–Reconstruction Acts of 1867 constitutions and supported with state appropriations and new bureaucratic structures across the former Confederate states. This revolutionary reversal embodied the most significant transformation of the southern landscape wrought by emancipation and Confederate defeat.[15]

The revolutionary nature of these constitutions, however, should not minimize the contentiousness of their implementation, especially of the educational provisions. Here, local responses truly matter. To be sure, Alabama received congressional approval for readmission by mid-1868. The Alabama legislature adopted the statewide system in late 1868.[16] Local responses, however, highlight the various competing visions for the new, racially inclusive educational system. While mandating African American public schools as a right of citizenship, partisan debate almost derailed the entire implementation process in Mobile and threatened the entire newly created statewide public school system. In the end, white conservative Mobilians' outright rejection of racially inclusive public schools allowed for the emergence of an expanded African American educational coalition capable of surviving two significant crises before the departure of the Freedmen's Bureau in July 1870. Black Mobilians understood that their postwar vision of freedom, citizenship, and public schools required new partnerships, resilience, and revised protest strategies following the creation of article 11. Otherwise, the newly gained rights of citizenship enshrined in the African American public schoolhouse would become a lost opportunity. The formal adoption of the public school measures in the Reconstruction-era constitutions, therefore, reveals that African Americans' struggle for education as a cornerstone of their vision of citizenship in a racially inclusive society did not end. As suggested by Berry, Turner, and Wiggins, the struggle simply shifted from mere acceptance to the meaningful inclusion of African Americans in the postwar nation no longer defined by chattel slavery.

African Americans' conceptions of freedom, citizenship, and public schooling were not shared by all individuals living in postemancipation Mobile, Alabama. Intraclass and social divisions shaped the Black Mobilian community's responses to the convention, new educational mandates, and transition to public schools. Initially, reservation and mistrust characterized the political debates in the African American and Creole of Color communities. Class divided both communities. Middle-class and elite African Americans and Creoles of Color feared that public education would lower the quality of education for their children. Some individuals advocated for the continuation of a tuition-based system, at the expense of working-class African Americans. Working-class and poor African

Americans feared that educational access for their children would be denied if wealthier community members' visions prevailed. Creoles of Color wanted the continuation of the Creole School in order to maintain their children's separation from poor and working-class African Americans. Reassurances that class differences would not impact access to the public schools, that the Creole School could continue, and that private schools could coexist with public schools permitted some acceptance of the new state educational mandates.[17] An antiratification campaign, however, forced various groups seeking education to overcome internal divisions. Attempts to derail education for nonwhite Alabamians facilitated the development of a unified political strategy that would protect African American and even Creole of Color education. Still, these divergent expectations contributed to a fraught implementation process.

The *Nationalist* proved instrumental in encouraging cooperation between the Creole of Color and African American communities. The *Nationalist*'s editor published a barrage of articles and editorials and actively pursued the Creole of Color and African American communities for their support of the new constitution. For example, Albert Griffin, editor of the *Nationalist*, addressed several of the preconvention charges made by vocal critics in regard to African American education in his October article "The School Question." After affirming the newspaper's support of public schools, Griffin refuted two major charges. First, he argued that the new school boards would be filled with Black and white Republicans, rather than Democrats who would keep students of color from voting and even from reaping the benefits of a free public school education. Second, he argued that parents, rather than the convention, would decide upon whether to have racially separated schools. He felt that parents would vote for the constitution and public schools if the constitution did not make class and racial distinctions.[18]

The *Nationalist* also appealed to white Mobilians. Griffin stressed that the proposed new educational system was a necessity for the state and did not "require both races to attend the same schools." The paper assured readers that neither biracial nor Creole of Color children would attend the same schools as white children. The newspaper's appeal to white Mobilians reflected the concern that African American electoral power alone was not sufficient to achieve the necessary votes for ratification. Even these efforts, however, were not enough.[19]

White conservative Mobilians vehemently opposed the new constitution and the inclusion of African Americans in the state educational system. The new constitution embodied a postwar vision for the region that threatened their social, political, and economic hegemony. The state constitution was considered to be a document created by and for individuals deemed their inferiors and thus did not represent white conservative Mobilians' self-interests. Utilizing local newspapers, they launched a campaign to block ratification. A barrage of articles and editorials in the *Mobile Daily Register* encouraged readers to abstain from voting in the ratification election and thereby force its defeat through failure to obtain the majority of registered voters required for ratification by the Second Reconstruction Act. The Constitutional Committee of Mobile and other organizations representing conservative Mobilians' rage found a willing audience in the *Mobile Daily Register*'s readership. With the support of the *Mobile Daily Register*, many whites opposed ratification.[20]

In addition, the white conservative Mobilians' campaign employed race-baiting tactics within the pages of the *Mobile Daily Register*. Several articles and editorials strongly suggested that economic and social repercussions would be taken against any voter who gave electoral support to the constitution. In "The Election," the *Mobile Daily Register* openly threatened Black and Creole of Color supporters of the constitution. The unknown author proclaimed: "Every colored man who votes in the election for the thing called a constitution makes his record as an enemy of his white fellow citizens." The article then recommended that they "keep out of the election."[21] The *Mobile Daily Register* also attempted to shame and threaten white supporters of the constitution by publishing their names and occupations. Such tactics forced white Republicans, including potential voters who were on the fence, to reaffirm their white Southern manhood or suffer from harassment, loss of employment, social ostracism, and/or night-riding visits.[22] By limiting public discourse, white conservative Mobilians discouraged electoral support throughout the city and entire state.

The antiratification campaign succeeded. At the time of the election, Alabama had approximately 170,000 registered voters. Only 6,700 out of the approximately 75,000 registered white voters participated in the ratification election. The campaign proved incapable of dissuading the majority of African Americans from casting ballots in favor of ratifying the constitution, however. Of the approximately 95,000 registered African American voters, about 63,000 voted. Despite this high turnout, newly enfranchised African American men could not overcome the low turnout among white voters. Results were 70,815 votes cast in favor of ratification and 1,005 against.[23] The conservatives' campaign worked. Although the majority of the votes approved ratification, the election failed to receive the 85,000 votes required by the Second Reconstruction Act. This technicality handed success to the white conservative Alabamians. It also gave Alabama the distinction of being one of two former Confederate states to reject its required constitution for readmission. Mississippi was the other. The *Mobile*

*Daily Register* hailed the victory with articles, editorials, and letters to the editor. Its celebration, however, was short-lived.[24]

White conservative Alabamians' triumph during the initial ratification election forced a change in tactics as well as reception among Black Mobilians. After the failure to ratify, the *Nationalist* devoted its attentions to alleviating the internal divisions within the African American and Creole of Color communities. The strength of the white conservative Alabamians' hegemony provoked a necessity of unity in order to preserve African American education and other postwar gains.[25] With the defeat, African American and Creole of Color Mobilians proved receptive to the vision of an inclusive public school education articulated within the pages of the *Nationalist*. Fear of conservative white Mobilians regaining political ascendancy and power helped minimize the once prevalent intraracial divide.[26] After a congressional intervention, a presidential veto, and a congressional override, state-funded African American public schools became a reality when Congress eliminated the majority-participation requirement for ratification. In June 1868, Congress approved the now-ratified constitution and readmitted Alabama along with five other reconstructed states. By thwarting white conservative Mobilians' vision after Congress intervened, both communities' willingness to put aside class and color differences became a necessary and effective strategy for the next two decades. The antiratification crisis demonstrated the continued need for strong intraracial and biracial coalitions.[27]

African Americans also found encouragement in their Freedmen's Bureau and American Missionary Association allies. During the ratification crisis, other educational partners emerged. Mobile School Commissioners approached the bureau regarding a possible partnership. In an August 1867 letter, C. A. Bradford, secretary of the city's school board, inquired into the feasibility of extending the city's school system to include African Americans, specifically using bureau funds toward school construction and teachers' salaries. The potential alliance would serve both organizations' needs. Access to the bureau's financial networks would greatly improve the board's overall financial situation. Having the full cooperation and support of the Board of School Commissioners would also fulfill the aims of African American education for the Freedmen's Bureau.[28]

Charles W. Buckley, the Alabama superintendent of education for the Freedmen's Bureau, and his successor agreed.[29] Although Buckley initiated negotiations, R. D. Harper completed the process. On January 1, 1869, the bureau relinquished direct control of all its schools, pledged financial support for schoolhouse construction, and continued paying rent on existing schoolhouses until the end of the 1869–1870 academic year. By then, city officials could fully administer the expanded school system of white, Creole, and African American schools. Moreover, the Freedmen's Bureau could officially cease its educational operations, as the newly created state system would be fully implemented. The American Missionary Association agreed to supply the state with qualified teachers while maintaining its ownership of Emerson Institute, a newly opened multistory brick school building. School commissioners agreed to pay the teacher salaries via the newly created state education fund established by the constitution. The bureau-board partnership, the new state constitution, and the failed ratification campaign further pushed the conservatives to the periphery and elevated the vision of white moderates in Mobile. This partnership helped thwart the efforts of anti-ratification proponents and encouraged congressional intervention.[30]

Black Mobilians' expanded educational coalition had achieved relatively satisfactory arrangements for the African American schools by January 1869. While the American Missionary Association retained control over the daily operations of Emerson Institute, the organization had secured one of its agents and other friends on a newly appointed, Republican-dominated city school board. Optimism quickly turned to turmoil as the old and new school boards (each representing different political regimes) competed for power and legitimacy. This struggle threatened the new public school system and had the potential to end the progress made in African American education. The crisis resurrected debates over education first voiced during the state constitutional convention and ratification process in Mobile. The fate of African American public schools rested upon the strength of the partnerships formed by Black Mobilians and their ability to broker a suitable resolution.

The fragility of Black Mobilians' expanded educational coalition revealed itself as the two school boards vied for control over the Mobile schools and their state appropriations. Republican political gains in the city and state resulted in the replacement of the Mayor Gustavus W. Horton's administration–era school commissioners with Republican administration–appointed members. The members of the old board, though, refused to leave office at the end of their scheduled terms and claimed the title as the legitimate board. Acting against state law, former school commissioners still collected taxes and disbursed the funds to Mobile's white schools—while charging tuition in the African American schools. Consisting of former bureau agents and individuals actively involved in the Reconstruction project, the duly appointed new board denounced the actions of the old board. After the recent history of struggle for African American education, a peaceful and timely resolution was not possible.[31] Both the Freedmen's Bureau and the American Missionary Association, two essential African

American educational partners, proved ineffective as both boards jockeyed for control through public relations campaigns and lawsuits.[32]

The school board crisis not only placed the newly created public school system in a vulnerable state, but it raised questions over the Black Mobilians' vision for public schools as a vehicle for citizenship. Many feared that the promise of free schools would be replaced by pay schools. Overall, the African American and Creole communities adopted a "we shall see what we shall see" public front while simultaneously preparing for a new protest strategy of possible boycotts, sustaining independent tuition-free schools, and/or pursuing lawsuits contingent on the final outcome. After a tense year and a half, the new board gained legitimacy from the Alabama State Supreme Court. African American schools had survived this major challenge.[33]

The crisis between the boards had several major consequences. First, the American Missionary Association never relinquished control over Emerson Institute to the new public school system. Their decision prompted another fight between the organization and the school board. Old school board commissioners attempted to undermine the American Missionary Association's authority with the State Superintendent of Public Instruction as well as via legal challenges but failed. These developments, though, justified the Freedmen's Bureau's continued presence in the city until its official closure in mid-1870.[34] Second, the Peabody Education Fund suspended its financial support of the Mobile schools on account of the instability created by the dual school board crisis. The loss of an important financial source created additional uncertainty for the African American public schools.[35] Third, and most significantly, the partial transfer of the Freedmen's Schools and the school board crisis influenced African American protest over the next two decades. Funding concerns remained unresolved. Power struggles over the operation of the new schools between school commissioners, African American parents, and the American Missionary Association continued. Competing visions continued to shape the next phase of African American public schooling in the city.

Nevertheless, African American and Creole of Color communities remained resolute in their fight for education and employed every resource at their disposal. By shifting activism to secure "Quality Public Schools," African Americans and their allies forged ahead and actualized section 6 of article 11, mandating public schools for all Mobilians. Despite suffering real defeats, notably the 1890 defeat of the Blair Education Bill, their vision of African American schools as the vehicle for a racially inclusive democratic society "survived well into the next century. So did their aspirations and faith, and so perhaps did their influence on the generations that followed them."[36] Throughout, they moved toward sustaining a state-funded quality public school system necessary for maintaining a racially inclusive body politic in Alabama and the post–Civil War nation.

The Mobile example is revealing for three reasons. First, it demonstrates that the interplay of local, state, and federal politics matters in understanding the significance of the educational provisions included in the Reconstruction-era state constitutions. The Reconstruction Acts of 1867 and the new state constitutions ushered in major changes in southern education, Black and white. These constitutions provided provisions for a tax-funded educational system for all school-aged children regardless of race and created a more precise link between education and citizenship. As a state right, the reconstructed states now had the obligation to provide a public educational system to all of its citizens, white and Black. Although it took some time to design and implement the official state system, state government officials' embrace of African Americans' postwar notions of education and citizenship had broader consequences on the local level.

Second, the ways that African Americans navigated the postwar terrain in advancing education and how their vision of biracial democracy was articulated require additional research. Acceptance of the postwar notions of African American education and citizenship did not occur immediately in Mobile. Intense white resistance improved African American and Creole of Color relations during the convention and ratification process. The school board crisis threatened the existence of the newly created African American public schools. It tested existing relationships between African Americans, the Freedmen's Bureau, and American Missionary Association. Since these relationships initially proved ineffective, African Americans and their allies shored up their relationship with state officials in order to bring a resolution to the challenge. Although a resolution was eventually reached, white opposition did not cease. Public schools emerged on a shaky foundation but did not collapse. African Americans and their supporters would continue to struggle against critics and reluctant government officials overseeing African American public schools over the next twenty years. Yet African Americans' vision did not waver. Further research on other urban communities using an intersectional approach will yield deeper understandings of the variations produced by similar conditions. Without such studies, a new synthesis for Reconstruction studies is not possible.

Third, and most importantly, a revised periodization, extending beyond the traditional 1877 ending, will make Reconstruction studies relevant in the present and future. Since African American education did not end with the departure of the Freedmen's Bureau or in 1877, our periodization must change. The process of creating and implementing the educational provisions of the 1868 Alabama Constitution influenced not only the transition to public schools but also the initial two decades of those public schools. This phase of African American education saw new social, political, and economic opportunities for Black and Creole of Color Mobilians. State and local boards of education became new partners in African American public schools, while the federal government remained a silent partner if significant problems arose. New challenges became apparent during the implementation process, and old issues remained (for example, a lack of teachers and funding). Again, local possibilities and constraints defined the Black Mobilians' ongoing struggles for educational access and legitimacy but also informed "whether they despaired or reset their sights on other, sometimes more achievable targets."[37] The traditional 1877 ending point, therefore, does not work.

As argued in my previous work, the failed Blair Education Bill of 1890 is a more appropriate terminus ad quem. Setting the endpoint here helps us connect the Reconstruction schools with the Washington–Du Bois debates framing Jim Crow–era schooling. Influenced by postwar educational developments, Senator Henry Blair of New Hampshire embarked on a multiyear fight for "the creation of a permanent, uniform, national, public school system in America supported with federal funds." The federal legislation not only required shifting public school operations from the states to the federal government; it also attempted to complete the postwar vision of Black southerners and their white allies. With the majority of federal funds designated for southern public schools, the federal legislation would have eliminated the financial difficulties endured by Black southerners in their quest for quality public schools. Their respective state and local government partners would have been able to fully fund the educational systems created in the Reconstruction-era constitutions without difficulty and fulfill their obligations to citizens white and Black. Most importantly, federal oversight would have prevented any distribution irregularities and would have ensured a degree of protection similar to the initial Freedmen's Bureau school era.[38] As a result of Blair's comprehensive strategy, his seemingly sensible plan easily passed in the Senate in 1884 and 1886 but passed only narrowly a third time in 1888. It stalled in the House of Representatives each time.[39]

By 1890, Blair, Black Mobilians, and other educational proponents felt that the Fifty-First Congress, better known as the Billion-Dollar Congress, was their last best chance. The political demographics of Washington, DC, changed as a consequence of the 1888 elections. Republicans now controlled the House of Representatives, Senate, and White House. Most significantly, the 1890 congressional agenda centered on questions of race, the status of southern African Americans, and race relations, with debates on the Butler Emigration Bill and Federal Elections Bill. Unlike previous attempts, Blair and his proponents had every reason to believe that the Fifty-First Congress would ensure passage of national educational legislation. The March 20 vote revealed otherwise. In a 31-to-37 vote, African American public schools simply failed to unite Congress and the nation, as the institutions had in 1865 and after the departure of the Freedmen's Bureau.[40]

Maria Waterbury decried the decision in her autobiography, published weeks after the March vote. After teaching in an African American school in the early 1870s, the former American Missionary Association educator was disturbed by the lack of local school funding and northern philanthropy in the wake of the failed federal legislation. To Mobile and Alabama officials, Waterbury demanded: "In view of this state of things in one of the Gulf states, will the South please give the North, a *chance to keep still*, by giving free schools to all its people!" But for her northern audience, she offered a stronger rebuke. Their perceived abandonment of the approximately eight million southern African Americans prompted Waterbury to conclude her autobiography with a pointed question. She asked: "Reader, have you done your duty by them?"[41]

While Waterbury mourned on the written page, Black Mobilians coped with a more immediate concern—the meteoric rise of Booker T. Washington. The Tuskegee president and his industrial education model provided individuals with an alternative model in the wake of the defeated Blair Education Bill. Following the 1895 Atlanta Exposition Address, Washington and his educational model represented the future. Long-standing white partners of African American public schools abandoned their previous Black proponents for Washington. By switching focus, the Peabody Educational Fund and other philanthropists could maintain their commitment to African American education without any guilt. Even Henry Blair openly courted Washington's support for a modified Blair Bill. Nonaligned Black southerners found themselves excluded from the national educational debate. Coupled with defeat of the Blair Bill and the ratification of the Alabama Constitution of 1901, the consequences of this shift ultimately closed the door on the revolutionary moment in African American education.[42]

Black Mobilians responded to these new setbacks by shifting strategies. Since Confederate defeat, they had used education as a means to position themselves as leaders who could uplift not only the race but also the post–Civil War nation. As race relations worsened, individuals educated in the Reconstruction-era schools prepared a new generation for future challenges and access to social mobility. African American normal school–trained educators instilled racial pride and the rhetoric of racial progress through education to their students through their lessons and continued activism within Mobile. As a former Broad Street Academy student recalled, the African American principal "ran the school with discipline and never tolerated any foolishness of any kind on campus. If there was ever any kind of trouble with a pupil it would be dealt with that day with the parents' involvement."[43] Moreover, Black Mobilians refined older strategies, adopted new tactics, and sought new partners. They made full use of the educated professional middle class and educator-activists who had received their training in the public schools, teacher-training institutions, and historically Black colleges and universities (HBCUs). Community activists expected that Emerson Normal, Talladega, Tuskegee, and other HBCUs would continue educating and empowering the next generation. They also maintained an unwavering support for interracial cooperation, the transformative nature of education, racial uplift via education, and their full citizenship status. This twenty-five-year period, therefore, embodies one of the Reconstruction-era successes rather than a failure.

By taking an approach that extends the periodization of the Reconstruction era, contemporary nonacademic audiences, especially African Americans and existing educators, will be able to connect the history of Mobile to their own struggles with resegregation and activism to improve the current public schools. Across the nation, issues of race, class, locality, and policy compromise the provision of a quality public school education to primarily African American, Latinx, and other marginalized school-aged populations. While "state officials bore some responsibility for the quality of education," a 2018 federal court ruling determined that "access to literacy" in the predominantly African American–serving Detroit school district was not a "fundamental right" guaranteed by the US Constitution.[44] The continuing lack of national protections demonstrates the persistent legacy of racism in relation to education and citizenship. As long as these realities exist, the educational experiment forged by African Americans and their allies in postemancipation Mobile remains incomplete.

### Notes

1. "Colored Mass Convention of the State of Alabama," *Mobile Daily Advertiser and Register*, May 4, 1867, 2.

2. "Poisonous Doctrines," *Mobile Daily Advertiser and Register*, May 5, 1867, 2.

3. Luke Harlow, "Introduction to Forum: The Future of Reconstruction Studies," Online Forum: The Future of Reconstruction Studies, *Journal of the Civil War Era*, https://journalofthecivilwarera.org/forum-the-future-of-reconstruction-studies/; W. Fitzhugh Brundage, "Reconstruction in the South," Online Forum: The Future of Reconstruc-

tion Studies, *Journal of the Civil War Era*, https://journalofthecivilwarera.org/forum-the-future-of-reconstruction-studies/reconstruction-in-the-south/; Thomas Holt, "Political History," Online Forum: The Future of Reconstruction Studies, *Journal of the Civil War Era*, https://journalofthecivilwarera.org/forum-the-future-of-reconstruction-studies/political-history/; Kidada E. Williams, "Maintaining a Radical Vision of African Americans in the Age of Freedom," Online Forum: The Future of Reconstruction Studies, *Journal of the Civil War Era*, https://journalofthecivilwarera.org/forum-the-future-of-reconstruction-studies/maintaining-a-radical-vision/; Blain Roberts and Ethan Kytle, "When the South Was the Most Progressive Region in America," *Atlantic*, January 17, 2018, https://www.theatlantic.com/politics/archive/2018/01/when-the-south-was-the-most-progressive-region-in-america/550442/.

4. See Gregory P. Downs and Kate Masur, eds., *The World the Civil War Made* (Chapel Hill: University of North Carolina Press, 2015).

5. Creoles of Color and their descendants claimed an African ancestry mixed with either a French and/or Spanish lineage, often characterized by their light complexion, Catholicism, and pride in their European heritage. Widely known as the "treaty population" in Mobile, stipulations in the Louisiana Purchase and Adams-Onis Treaty of 1819 guaranteed their civil, social, and legal rights and elevated them into a new social status. Hilary Green, *Educational Reconstruction: African American Schools in the Urban South, 1865–1890* (New York: Fordham University Press, 2016), 45–47.

6. Eric Foner, *Reconstruction: America's Unfinished Revolution, 1863–1877* (New York: Harper & Row, 1988), 276–77.

7. Michael W. Fitzgerald, *Reconstruction in Alabama: From Civil War to Redemption in the Cotton South* (Baton Rouge: Louisiana State University Press, 2016), 158.

8. John Hope Franklin, *Reconstruction after the Civil War* (Chicago: University of Chicago Press, 1961), 102; Foner, *Reconstruction*, 316–21; Richard L. Hume, "Carpetbaggers in the Reconstruction South: A Group Portrait of Outside Whites in the 'Black and Tan' Constitutional Conventions," *Journal of American History* 64 (September 1977): 315.

9. Michael V. R. Thomason, ed., *Mobile: The New History of Alabama's First City* (Tuscaloosa: University of Alabama Press, 2001), 123; Alabama Constitutional Convention (1867), *Official Journal of the Constitutional Convention of the State of Alabama, Held in the City of Montgomery, Commencing on Tuesday, November 5th, A.D. 1867* (Montgomery: Barrett and Brown, 1868), 3.

10. Fitzgerald, *Reconstruction in Alabama*, 156–63; Alabama Constitution of 1868, http://www.legislature.state.al.us/aliswww/history/constitutions/1868/1868all.html.

11. "The Convention," *Mobile Daily Advertiser and Register*, November 5, 1867, 2; Fitzgerald, *Reconstruction in Alabama*, 152–54.

12. Foner, *Reconstruction*, 319–33; "Letter from Montgomery," *Mobile Daily Register*, November 10, 1867, 2; Alabama Constitution of 1868, article 11, section 6.

13. Alabama Constitution of 1868, article 11.

14. For a discussion of the antebellum public schools in Mobile, see Sarah L. Hyde, *Schooling in the Antebellum South: The Rise of Public and Private Education in Louisiana, Mississippi, and Alabama* (Baton Rouge: Louisiana State University Press, 2016), 88–102, 146; Fitzgerald, *Reconstruction in Alabama*, 159.

15. James D. Anderson, *The Education of Blacks in the South, 1860–1930* (Chapel Hill: University of North Carolina Press, 1988), 26–27, 32; Heather A. Williams, *Self-Taught: African American Education in Slavery and Freedom* (Chapel Hill: University of North Carolina Press, 2005), 193–94.

16. William L. Barney, *Battleground for the Union: The Era of the Civil War and Reconstruction, 1848–1877* (Englewood Cliffs, NJ: Prentice Hall, 1990), 277; Green, *Educational Reconstruction*, 55.

17. Green, *Educational Reconstruction*, 55–57; Michael W. Fitzgerald, *Urban Emancipation: Popular Politics in Reconstruction Mobile, 1860–1890* (Baton Rouge: Louisiana State University Press, 2002), 112–18.

18. Albert Griffin, "The School Question," *Nationalist* (Mobile), October 3, 1867, 2; Kimberly Bess Cantrell, "A Voice for the Freedmen: The Mobile *Nationalist*, 1865–1869," master's thesis, Auburn University, 1989, 58–60.

19. Cantrell, "A Voice for the Freedmen," 6–7; Albert Griffin, "Address to the White People of Alabama," *Nationalist* (Mobile), January 28, 1868, 3.

20. For articles and editorials encouraging whites to not vote, see "The Crisis," *Mobile Daily Advertiser and Register*, November 13, 1867, 2; "The Proposed Constitution," *Mobile Daily Advertiser and Register*, December 17, 1867, 2; "Do Not Vote," *Mobile Daily Register*, February 4, 1868, 2; and "The Constitutional Executive Committee," *Mobile Daily Register*, January 30, 1868, 1.

21. "The Election," *Mobile Daily Register*, February 4, 1868, 2.

22. "List of White Voters," *Mobile Daily Register*, February 12, 1868, 2; "A Card," *Mobile Daily Register*, February 14, 1868, 2; Fitzgerald, *Reconstruction in Alabama*, 188; Fitzgerald, *Urban Emancipation*, 115; Kidada E. Williams, *They Left Great Marks on Me: African American Testimonies of Racial Violence from Emancipation to World War I* (New York: New York University Press, 2012), 38–39.

23. "Constitution, of 1868 Ratification," http://www.legislature.state.al.us/aliswww/history/constitutions/1868/1868rat.html; Fitzgerald, *Reconstruction in Alabama*, 167–68.

24. Foner, *Reconstruction*, 332–33; Cantrell, "A Voice for the Freedmen," 57, 67–68.

25. Alpha, "What's Next," *Nationalist* (Mobile), February 27, 1868, 2; Cantrell, "A Voice for the Freedmen," 64–68.

26. L. S. Berry, R. D. Wiggins, John Bryant, John Carraway, and James Bragg, "Protest of the Colored People," *Nationalist* (Mobile), September 5, 1868, 2–3; Fitzgerald, *Urban Emancipation*, 128–31.

27. Fitzgerald, *Reconstruction in Alabama*, 166–71.

28. Horace Mann Bond, *Negro Education in Alabama: A Study in Cotton and Steel*, Library of Alabama Classics Series (1939; Tuscaloosa: University of Alabama Press, 1994), 84; C. A. Bradford to C. W. Buckley, August 7, 1867, Unregistered Letters, December 1865–July 1870 (microfilm roll 3), *Records of the Superintendent of Education for the State of Alabama Bureau of Refugees, Freedmen and Abandoned Lands, 1865–1870*, National Archives Microfilm Publication 810, RG105 (Washington: National Archives and Record Service, 1972) (hereafter AL-BRFAL-ED).

29. C. W. Buckley, Entry of Letter to C. S. Bradford, Secretary Mobile County School Board, August 9, 1867, Register of Letters Sent, stamped page 102, Letters Sent, vol. 1, November 30, 1866–January 27, 1868 (microfilm roll 1), AL-BRFAL-ED; C. W. Buckley,

Second Annual Report of the Superintendent of Education, October 1867, pp. 2–3 [handwritten], Reports Sent Annual, 1866–1868 (microfilm roll 1), AL-BRFAL-ED.

30. R. D. Harper to Major General O. O. Howard, October 9, 1868, Letters Sent Ledger, stamped page 98, Press Copies of Letters Sent, September 1868–July 1870 (microfilm roll 1), AL-BRFAL-ED; R. D. Harper to Edwin Beecher, October 19, 1868, Press Copies of Letters Sent, September 1868–July 1870 (microfilm roll 1), AL-BRFAL-ED; R. D. Harper to the American Missionary Association, circular letter, September 1, 1868 (microfilm roll 1), American Missionary Association Archives, 1828–1969, Amistad Research Center, Tulane University, New Orleans, LA (hereafter AMA Papers—Alabama).

31. N. B. Cloud, "Official Report of the Superintendent of Public Instruction on the Troubles in the Mobile Free Public Schools," in Alabama State Board of Education, *Report of the Superintendent of Public Instruction of the State of Alabama to the Governor for the Year 1868–9 Ending 30 September 1869* (Montgomery: John G. Stokes and Company, State Printers, 1869), 35–36.

32. Gustavus W. Horton to E. P. Smith, July 31, 1867, microfilm roll 1, AMA Papers—Alabama; Gustavus W. Horton to the Editors of the *Congregationalist*, September 10, 1870, microfilm roll 1, AMA Papers—Alabama; James Gillette to E. P. Smith, March 16, 1869, microfilm roll 1, AMA Papers—Alabama. For Putnam's responses to attacks, see George L. Putnam to E. P. Smith, May 29, 1869, Putnam to E. P. Smith, September 14, 1869, and Putnam to E. P. Smith, July 14, 1870, microfilm roll 1, AMA Papers—Alabama; A Republican, "The School Question and the Legislature," *Nationalist*, October 11, 1869, 1, columns 1 and 3 in *Transcriptions of the* Nationalist, Mobile Municipal Archives; Mobile *Daily Republican*, October 31, 1870, 2, column 3 in *Transcriptions of the* Mobile Daily Republican, *1870–1872*, Mobile Municipal Archives, Mobile, Alabama.

33. Cloud, "Troubles in Mobile," 36; Earle, "The School Commissioners," *Nationalist*, October 4, 1869, 2, column 2 in *Transcriptions of the* Nationalist, Mobile Municipal Archives; "The School Muddle—The Big Gun Fire," *Nationalist*, October 1, 1869, 2, column 2 in *Transcriptions of the* Nationalist, Mobile Municipal Archives.

34. For promises made, see George Tracey to C. W. Buckley, January 24, 1867, and George Tracey to C. W. Buckley, March 22, 1867, Unregistered Letters, December 1865–July 1870 (microfilm roll 3), AL-BRFAL-ED; Cloud, "Troubles in Mobile," 39–47; George L. Putnam to E. P. Smith, September 14, 1869, October 4, 1869, and July 14, 1870, microfilm roll 1, AMA Papers—Alabama.

35. Peabody Education Fund, *Proceedings of the Trustees Meeting, Held at Philadelphia, 15 February 1871* (Cambridge, MA: Press of John Wilson and Son, 1870), 34, file 2, box 11, Peabody Education Fund Collection, Vanderbilt University, Nashville, TN.

36. Green, *Educational Reconstruction*, 185–99.

37. Williams, "Maintaining a Radical Vision."

38. Thomas Upchurch, *Legislating Racism: The Billion-Dollar Congress and the Birth of Jim Crow* (Lexington: University of Kentucky Press, 2004), 47; Daniel W. Crofts, "The Black Response to the Blair Education Bill," *Journal of Southern History* 37 (February 1971): 42.

39. Gordon B. McKinney, *Henry W. Blair's Campaign to Reform America: From the Civil War to the US Senate* (Lexington: University of Kentucky Press, 2013), 87–88; Green, *Educational Reconstruction*, 187–88; Upchurch, *Legislating Racism*, 47–48.

40. Upchurch, *Legislating Racism*, 2–3, 48, 64–65; McKinney, *Henry W. Blair's Campaign to Reform America*, 129; Crofts, "The Black Response," 59–63; Green, *Educational Reconstruction*, 189–91.

41. Maria L. Waterbury, *Seven Years among the Freedmen* (Chicago: T. B. Arnold, 1893), 198.

42. Green, *Educational Reconstruction*, 193–96; Alabama Constitution of 1901.

43. Paulette Davis-Horton, *The Avenue: The Place, the People, the Memories* (Mobile: Horton, Inc., 1991), 39.

44. Jacey Fortin, "'Access to Literacy' Is Not a Constitutional Right, Judge in Detroit Rules," *New York Times*, July 4, 2018, https://www.nytimes.com/2018/07/04/education/detroit-public-schools-education.html.

# Reconstruction Justice

*African American Police Officers in Charleston and New Orleans*

## Samuel Watts

Writing in June 1865, Henry W. Ravenel deplored the consequences of emancipation and Confederate defeat within his home city of Charleston.[1] Like many of his fellow planters, Ravenel was shocked to see formerly enslaved people swiftly abandoning public deference toward whites as they began to assert themselves on the city streets. "Drest in the most outré style," as Ravenel put it, formerly enslaved men and women rode through the streets in carriages and on horseback, walked in the middle of the sidewalk, and refused to yield to white pedestrians.[2] Such was the political shift in urban life across the South, that children began openly asserting their rights to occupy street space; in Mobile, Kate Cummings asked a group of Black children to move out of her way as she walked alongside the road and was told: "The middle of the road is for you, the sidewalk is for us."[3] Historians have long noted this dramatic social change in southern cities, yet further investigation into the consequences of this shift in urban spatial politics is still needed.[4]

Focusing on Charleston and New Orleans, this chapter examines one aspect of city life that was both materially and symbolically important to the daily lives of African American residents and significantly enflamed white resistance to Reconstruction-era civil rights. For one decade in the nineteenth-century South (between 1867 and 1877), African American men—predominantly formerly enslaved—gained positions of significant local authority through the integration of law enforcement in approximately fourteen cities.[5] With Black policemen patrolling, protecting, and policing white and Black citizens, the integration of the police symbolized the potential absolute reversal in social, racial, and urban power dynamics that Reconstruction promised. This chapter places the narrative of Black police officers in Reconstruction Charleston and New Orleans within the context of the streetscape, linking this often-overlooked episode in southern history to the growing body of literature on Black experiences of space, place, and mobility.[6] Viewed through the lens of urban spatial politics, the significance of the actions and presence of Black police officers not only helps inform historical conceptions of daily life in these cities but furthers our understanding of freedoms both gained and lost in the social revolution of Radical Reconstruction.

As cities, Charleston and New Orleans provide an excellent comparison in this regard. Despite disparate urban cultures, origins, and sizes (geographic and in terms of population), both cities were culturally important to white southern identity. Since 1862, African Americans in New Orleans had previewed the promise and turbulence of Reconstruction under federal occupation.[7] In 1865, formerly enslaved refugees from nearby plantations crossed into both cities seeking protection, work, and freedom, facing the task of rebuilding lives for themselves in an alien environment. Meanwhile, Black veterans from these cities returned home not only better educated (many having learned to read and write in the army) but with a clear sense that they had fought for freedom and won.[8] Both cities had large free Black populations before the war, and, importantly, both cities had racially integrated police forces for almost a decade during Reconstruction. By taking a comparative approach to Reconstruction urban experiences, I am also responding to a lack of urban comparative histories of this era, especially with regard to New Orleans and Charleston, both of which, for entirely different reasons, are occasionally treated by scholars as exceptional or historically separate from the rest of the South.[9]

With extant police department archives and much of the newspaper reporting from this era either wholly whitewashing the history of the police or demonizing the work of Black officers, this analysis requires the historian not only to read against the grain but also to focus on small "moments," episodes, or case studies in the archive that provide insight into the actions of Black police officers and the resonance of their actions within Black urban communities.[10] These case studies will be discussed chronologically, beginning in New Orleans in 1867/1868 and then moving into Charleston in the 1870s, illustrating a history not only of resistance to stubborn racial hierarchies and prejudices but also, importantly, of the construction or projection of new forms of Black identity and masculinity into the new era. Standing on a street corner or walking a beat, these officers were not only important fixtures in the urban landscape and the daily lives of Black and white civilians but also themselves interpreted, performed, and enforced their own visions of radical equality and Reconstruction.

In New Orleans in 1866, Black and white Republicans gathered together at the Mechanics Institute building and attempted to convene a constitutional convention that would ensure equal suffrage to African American men in the state and thus significantly boost the electoral and political strength of the Republican Party.[11] As delegates gathered together, approximately 100 to 150 African Americans marched through the streets in support of the convention.[12] As they arrived at the convention hall, the marchers were met with an organized assault from about 1,000 to 1,500 white protestors, led by the all-white New Orleans police force, two-thirds of whom were former Confederate soldiers (including the police chief).[13] Local police deputized large groups of white civilians for the sole purpose of intimidating and obstructing the convention.[14] After an exchange of gunfire between one deputized white officer and a Black marcher, a large street fight occurred, and the outnumbered marchers fled.[15] The terrified delegates and convention supporters inside the Mechanics Institute bolted the doors as the white mob tried to force their way in; anyone who emerged from the building attempting to surrender was immediately beaten and shot. The siege ended when the police officers leading the mob told delegates inside that they would protect them; then, after gaining entry to the hall, they proceeded to beat, stab, and shoot the unarmed and panicked group. Some Black Republicans waved white flags, some tried to fight back, while others jumped from the windows of the building.[16] Many of the casualties were African Americans who had fled the hall, been caught either by police or the white crowd, and then either bludgeoned to death or restrained and shot in the head, execution-style, with police-issued revolvers.[17] According to official figures tabulated in the ensuing congressional investigation, thirty-eight people were killed and over one hundred wounded.[18]

Under pressure from both General Sheridan to replace at least half of the police with ex-Union soldiers and the *New Orleans Tribune* to hire Black police, Mayor Edward Heath integrated the New Orleans police force on May 30, 1867.[19] With the integration of the force in New Orleans, the South's largest city, African Americans soon gained prominent positions within police forces in smaller cities such as Mobile, Raleigh, Charleston, and beyond.[20] With few exceptions, Black police officers in these cities had no restrictions placed on their arrest powers and were able to perform their duties similarly to their white colleagues.[21] By 1870, there were approximately 350 Black policemen serving in cities across the South, with 182 of them in New Orleans.[22] Out of a citywide force of 647, African American police participation was roughly equivalent to their presence in the city (approximately 26 percent of the population and 28 percent of the police force in 1870 was African American).[23] As in New Orleans, Charleston's police force directly reflected the city's (male) demographics, and so, with African Americans commanding a slim majority of the population, approximately half of all officers were Black in Reconstruction Charleston.[24] It is hard to say how many Black police officers passed through the Metropolitan Police Force in New

Orleans, but John Oldfield has estimated that, in Charleston, at least 150 African Americans served in Charleston from 1868 to 1921.[25] African American police in senior leadership roles in Charleston and New Orleans came largely from a well-educated, conservative (although reliably still Republican), free Black establishment.[26] In New Orleans, these leadership positions would go to prominent African American men like James Lewis, Octave Rey, and C. C. Antoine, while in Charleston, the prominent Black Charlestonian James Fordham (husband of the poet Mary Weston Fordham) would become the nation's highest-ranking police officer, serving as a lieutenant in the city's force for over two decades.[27] The bulk of Black policemen were—like their white counterparts—men from the lower to middle classes who were attracted to the role for its relative stable pay in a period of economic uncertainty.[28]

For many white southerners, who already resented federal occupation, the imposition of Black police officers in southern cities added insult to injury.[29] Indeed, historians of the Dunning School would later include the presence of Black police among their list of historical grievances committed by "scalawags" and "carpetbaggers," justifying the violent restoration of white supremacy and the institution of Jim Crow.[30] Despite the claims of white contemporaries and later historians of the Dunning School, there is no evidence to support the idea that Black police were any more corrupt or abusive with their power than their white colleagues. In fact, in New Orleans, Dennis Rousey has shown how the much-maligned Metropolitan Police were statistically less corrupt, less abusive, and more efficient than any of the city's other law enforcement organizations during the nineteenth century.[31] This was despite the fact that white resistance to the police was a constant threat during Reconstruction, occasionally escalating into armed street battles and an attempted insurrection in 1874 (known as the Battle of Liberty Place).[32] An examination of the available arrest records of Reconstruction-era police in both Charleston and New Orleans shows no evidence of a racial bias on the part of Black arresting officers.[33]

The research of a few key scholars, including W. Marvin Dulaney, Dennis Rousey, and John Oldfield, has established much of what is known about these officers. Fundamentally, this scholarship challenged the idea, put forward by Dunning School historians like Walter Fleming, that Black police in the South (and all other African Americans in government) oppressed white populations through corruption and racially discriminatory law enforcement, with scholars finding that racially integrated police forces were much less likely to discriminate racially and were generally less corrupt during Reconstruction than before or after this period.[34]

More broadly, historians of race relations in the United States have specifically highlighted how urban space was racialized not only in terms of housing but also, importantly, regarding the streetscape. These historians have also noted that public urban spaces were important sites of resistance throughout the nineteenth and twentieth centuries.[35] The determination as to who made way for whom on a busy sidewalk was informed and invested by ideas of race, gender, and deference.[36] The strict regulation of African American bodies, behavior, and mobility within contested public spaces represents one of the pillars of white supremacy throughout the nineteenth, twentieth, and now twenty-first century. Building on research of the streetscape and the power of public symbolism, the following analysis illustrates how African American police officers intervened in the public space, asserted their authority, and performed a new kind of identity, one steeped in the radicalism of the Reconstruction era.

### New Orleans: The Arrest of an "Officier Fédéral"

The French Opera House stood on the corner of Toulouse and Bourbon Streets in New Orleans's French Quarter for sixty years, from its grand opening in 1859 to its destruction in a fire in 1919.[37] Hosting some of Europe's biggest names in opera at the time and being a place for elite Creoles to gather and socialize, the opera house was enjoyed by a broad cross-section of New Orleans society.[38] White, Black, Creole, rich and poor alike, would fill the theater every Tuesday, Thursday, Saturday, and Sunday to hear French lyric opera and socialize at what was a central institution in Creole life and society.[39]

When the audience filed in for an evening's entertainment on Tuesday, December 10, 1867, it is likely they would have sat in the same segregated sections of the theater (segregation in public accommodations not being outlawed until 1868 in Louisiana) as they had before the Civil War.[40] Writing in the *Journal of Negro History* in 1917, Alice Dunbar-Nelson, an African American poet and New Orleans native, described antebellum seating in the French Opera House thus:

> Above the orchestra circle were four tiers, the first filled with the beautiful dames of the city; the second with a second array of beautiful women, attired like those of the first, with no apparent difference; yet these were the octoroons and quadroons.... The third was for the hoi polloi of the White race, and the fourth for the people of color whose color was more evident. It was a veritable sandwich of races.[41]

Creole institutions like the French Opera House favored wealthy Afro-Creoles over the white working class before the Civil War, yet a racial hierarchy based upon the simple Black/white binary (which operated throughout most of the South) was increasingly the norm during Reconstruction.[42] Potentially indicative of the city's high crime rate, the New Orleans police department had designated two officers to watch over each performance.[43] At some point in the evening, an unruly US Army officer began to mock and publicly insult the two police officers on duty before being removed from the theater and spending the night in jail.[44] In a city where crime and violence were daily experiences for many of the city's residents, this relatively minor incident would not have been noted by any of the local newspapers except for the fact that at least one of the officers (we do not know the ethnicity of the second officer) was one of the city's newly appointed African American policemen. The white soldier's attempt to publicly ridicule the men was clearly racially motivated.

The city's most widely read Black newspaper at the time, *La Tribune*, noted that the soldier was handcuffed and delivered to the jail, where "he had all night to reflect on the danger there is in lacking respect for the officers of the law."[45] What these two officers did was to assert very publicly—literally in front of an audience and a diverse cross-section of New Orleans society—that they not only had a moral right to exercise their power (and that this power had to be respected) but that racial abuse and mockery would no longer be tolerated in the public space.

The incident at the French Opera House highlights how from the very beginning Black police in the South felt the need to publicly assert themselves and that they were aware of the power of public symbolism and performance when it came to establishing their authority. While the audience in the French Opera House may have viewed the arrest as an isolated incident, the entire city would soon bear witness to a much broader performance of power, civic duty, and racial equality. Following the introduction of Black police officers in New Orleans in 1867, the city's police force was completely reformed and restructured to meet the task of enforcing law and order in an increasingly violent and uncertain era.[46] In 1868, Louisiana's legislature passed the Metropolitan Police Act, which merged the police of three different parishes (Orleans, St. Bernard, and Jefferson) into one unified police force that would report directly to the state's reliably Republican governor rather than local officials.[47] The creation of this force quickly followed the election of a Democratic mayor in New Orleans and was as much a political power play on the part of Governor Henry Warmoth, a Republican, as it was a genuine attempt to protect the lives and liberties of Republicans and

African Americans from hostile white Democrats.[48] For both white and Black Republicans, as the 1866 New Orleans Massacre had graphically demonstrated, safety from physical violence could not be taken for granted.

The racial integration of the police in New Orleans must also be understood within a broader movement to reform policing in the city and place the police force at the center of rebuilding the city socially and economically. Police commanders and Republican officials embraced a highly progressive set of reforms to the police force; these not only aimed to professionalize the police force but also worked to actively prevent crime in the city via social relief programs.[49] Police were now more rigorously screened for physical or medical issues, and pension plans were introduced for disability, long service, and for families of police killed on duty.[50] Specialist Metropolitan police officers were given the role of working to ensure effective sanitation, inspecting slaughterhouses, public accommodations, tenement buildings, and ferries. These officers would implement wide-ranging public health programs aimed at dealing with the various epidemics of disease that swept through the city during this period.[51]

What are now regarded as progressive police values, such as harm minimization, were embraced by the city's police leadership. They called, for example, for prostitution to be decriminalized and regulated.[52] Similarly, the police performed an important social role in New Orleans, even providing temporary residences for the city's large homeless population, including a shelter for women and soup kitchens that fed indigent men, women, and children twice daily.[53] Alongside all of this reform activity, the police force was simultaneously increased to allow for a much greater police presence in the city streets and for police to patrol designated areas of the city in pairs for the first time.[54] More police walked the streets, and more police were deployed on horseback in order to increase their urban mobility.[55]

Yet the increased presence and activity of the Metropolitan Police in Reconstruction New Orleans was not experienced equally across racial and political divides. White anger at the presence of Black police officers patrolling the city streets translated into both legal challenges to the Metropolitan police's authority and an almost continual stream of violence, intimidation, and organized insurrections against the police and the Republican state government.[56] White Democrats were often as heavily armed as they were hostile; from organizing into "ward clubs" (which were somewhere between social organizations and street gangs) to joining violent white supremacist groups like the White League.[57] White newspapers often publicly derided Black Metropolitans, making them appear at once incompetent, comical, and a threat to white supremacy.[58] Additionally, Democratic-held city councils often withheld taxes in an attempt to starve the Metropolitan Police of its funding.[59] The presence of Black police on the street and their social and economic interventions in the city were clearly experienced and perceived differently according to both racial categorization and political affiliation.

Black police officers constituted not only a visible symbol of racial equality and radical political change on the streetscape but also took an active role in reshaping the southern city in line with progressive reform values. Police reform was thus linked to both urban reform and to racial equality. It was through both a public intervention in urban spaces and increased mobility on the city's streets that the Metropolitan Police made their greatest impact. For many of the city's poor, especially unemployed and formerly enslaved people who received food and housing from the police, the Metropolitans were a visible symbol of both social change and, at once, a vision of public protection and stability. But for many city residents, including the federal officer at the Opera House, Black police represented an unwanted intrusion into the sovereignty of white city space.

### Charleston: The Arrest of William DeSaussure

Like many other Republican-controlled southern cities, Charleston quickly took advantage of the political momentum in the first few years of the Radical Reconstruction era and followed New Orleans's example, introducing Black police officers in July 1868.[60] White conservative Democrats had long feared this. As a racially integrated force was deployed in Raleigh, North Carolina, the *Charleston Daily News* worried that "it would be impossible to endure the tyranny that might be expected from a negro police who, proud of their little brief authority, could use their position for every purpose of insolence, violence and wrong." Hoping that South Carolina "may be spared the painful humiliation which has fallen upon our sister state," the paper warned that a "host of troubles" and a "carnival of crime" would arise if Black police were employed by the state.[61]

In April 1868, South Carolina ratified the new state constitution, which abolished the Black Codes and allowed for interracial marriage, desegregated public education, and universal male suffrage.[62] In horror, one South Carolinian paper wrote: "A like combination of folly, fraud and licentiousness was never before submitted to the judgement of a civilized people. They propose to inaugurate a government on a triangular foundation of ignorance, repudiation and miscegenation." The paper (somewhat accurately) predicted this new state constitution would pave the way for "negro legislators, negro sheriffs, negro constables, negro tax collectors, negro ordinaries, negro judges, negro mayors, negro aldermen, negro police." While Black politicians, the paper reasoned, would be simply an object of ridicule and not a threat to white manhood, "a negro judge to decree away life or property" or "a negro policeman with a club in his hand" would be something else entirely. Again, the specter of "evil" and "anarchy" was raised, together with a veiled threat of violence on behalf of the white men of the state who would not tolerate a Black police presence.[63]

Despite local white anxiety, the city's mayor appointed the first Black policeman in July 1868, and over the next three years approximately fifty African Americans would be appointed to a force that hovered around one hundred officers (therefore matching the city's fairly even white/Black demographics).[64] Some recruits, like James Fordham, Frank Desverney, and George Shrewsbury, came from the formerly free Black middle class and were often literate.[65] Most, however, were formerly enslaved. Most Black policemen were unskilled laborers who, like their Irish counterparts, rushed to join the force, attracted by the prestige, stability, and pay that the role brought.[66] For many prominent white Charlestonians, respecting and deferring to Black police authority was difficult.

On February 21, 1871, an outraged William P. DeSaussure was arrested and brought before Charleston's mayor.[67] Out of all the records of arrests carried out by Black police officers in the city, this incident seems to have stemmed from the most trivial and puzzling action. Whether he needed it as an orthopedic aid or simply as a fashionable marker of his social standing and wealth, the young lawyer walked along Charleston's cobblestone streets with a cane. In this fashion, he was reportedly strolling down Meeting Street when, passing the corner of Meeting and Hassell, he crossed the path of an unnamed Black police officer. The officer's request to DeSaussure was simple, if strange and difficult to obey: not to walk so loudly. The noise of the cane on the pavement apparently bothered the officer; DeSaussure was unsympathetic to the policeman's request and muttered something under his breath, turned away, and walked on. What the white lawyer whispered under his breath at the officer can only be guessed, but it caused the policeman to follow DeSaussure and, when the lawyer failed to stop and continued to talk back, to place his hand on the lawyer's shoulder and ask him to repeat the phrase. DeSaussure then threatened to kill the officer. He was promptly arrested and lodged in the Guardhouse overnight before being taken into the mayor's office the following day to be sentenced (a five-dollar fine). In his account of the event, published in the paper, DeSaussure portrayed the policeman's conduct as totally ridiculous, while not admitting any fault or seeing anything wrong in threatening violence or murder against the Black officer.[68] Indeed, if DeSaussure's testimony is to be believed, the officer almost certainly overstepped his authority—walking loudly hardly classifies as disorderly conduct or any punishable and enforceable crime. The subsequent death threat, however, was, of course, a different matter.

When street battles, riots, and violence plagued Charleston's streets during Reconstruction, this incident seems relatively minor.[69] Although a seemingly small act, this arrest highlights a much broader shift in urban politics and, upon further examination, is layered with deep symbolic meaning and consequence. Perhaps the Black policeman chose to harass DeSaussure in the full knowledge that the white lawyer would both refuse to recognize his authority and put up a fight. The officer could not have picked a better target for this challenge, choosing a wealthy white gentleman, a member of a prominent family, which—along with the Ravenels, Manigaults, Pinckneys, Calhouns, etc.—made up the local aristocracy.[70] The DeSaussure family owned significant amounts of land and several warehouses downtown.[71] Louis DeSaussure had been the city's most successful slave broker, conducted the last known slave auction in Charleston, and in 1860 owned a plantation in St. Helena Parish with seventy-six enslaved laborers.[72] Like many Black policemen, the unnamed officer may well have been born into slavery. That he chose to target a member of one of Charleston's leading families, one strongly associated with both enslaving and enslaved trading, is significant. One could suggest that the officer sought to police the bodily movement of the white pedestrian with the same peremptory manner that formerly characterized white control over African Americans on the street under slavery, enacting a symbolic reversal of the sidewalk etiquette practiced during the antebellum period.

The significance of this power reversal is further understood if one considers the symbolic source of the police officer's authority—his badge—and that object's role in Charleston's Black history. In antebellum Charleston, enslaved people with particular skills were often hired out by their enslavers to work in the city for someone else or to work and live independently of direct supervision.[73] To police and regulate this system, hired-out enslaved people in Charleston were forced to wear small copper badges to identify themselves, preventing potential manipulation of this system by runaways. Several cities in the South, including New Orleans, Savannah, Charleston, Mobile, Wilmington, and Richmond, enacted what were known as slave badge or slave certificate laws during the antebellum period.[74] Despite the prevalence of these regulations and scholarship that suggests that New Orleans also manufactured metal slave badges in the antebellum period, the only known extant examples are from Charleston.[75] Slave badges represent the symbolic complexity and physical materiality of Black experiences of freedom and the city in the nineteenth-century South. They were markers of a kind of freedom, differentiating enslaved people who worked skilled jobs in the city from other enslaved people.[76] Enslaved people who wore these badges often took advantage of both the mobility and profit that could be gained from the hiring-out system. In taverns and on street corners along Charleston's waterfront, hired-out enslaved men and women would drink, socialize, and gamble alongside sailors and migrants, much to the disapproval of the city's respectable whites.[77] Authorities in the South worried that granting badges to urban enslaved people and letting them work as craftsmen resulted in their being "half-freed" and becoming a danger to white society (Nat Turner, for example).[78]

These badges, however, were also symbols of white enslavers' absolute control over the enslaved body and its movement, both granting and limiting urban mobility. Wherever hired-out enslaved people would go in the city, they were forced to wear these badges, serving as a constant reminder of both their inferiority and the fact that they possessed only a guest pass to the space they inhabited.[79] Like themselves, the city belonged to someone else. If hired-out enslaved people interacted with the police, it would most likely be to check that they were wearing their badge.

Many of the enslaved men who wore these badges and bore this physical and symbolic burden would, in the space of a few years, be wearing very similar-looking badges that symbolized not only their control over their own movement and space but also the public space. Formerly enslaved people in New Orleans and Charleston would have experienced the symbolic reversal in fortune and understood the power of the badge as a symbol of freedom. In discarding the slave badge in favor of the police badge, African American officers were appropriating a symbol of past suffering and repression and loading it with a new meaning and purpose.[80] As Wayne Jordan has noted, the "spectacle of former slaves in blue uniforms representing the majesty and authority of the law epitomized the political revolution."[81] The continuity of African Americans wearing badges in Charleston and, at the same time, the powerful reversal of symbolic meaning those objects conferred after the Civil War have yet to be discussed by historians of Reconstruction. Yet, as publicly visible symbols, slave and police badges would have had a marked effect on the lived experiences of both those who wore them and those who bore witness to their meaning on the street.

That this incident occurred because of DeSaussure's use of a cane has even greater significance. In the nineteenth-century South, the cane was often used by white men as both a weapon to intimidate and attack African Americans and also as a symbol of honor and public authority.[82] An 1806 Charleston city ordinance specifically forbade Black city residents to "walk with a cane, club or other stick," adding that every "negro or person of colour" found in contravention of this legislation "shall receive such a number of lashes, as any Warden of the city shall adjudge."[83] When distinguished members of the city's antebellum Black community attempted to assert their right to public respectability through the use of a cane, it triggered extreme reactions among white Charlestonians, and occasionally violence.[84]

The sound of the cane is also an important detail, given it is the cause of the officer's initial admonishment. The physical experience of urban space is as much aural as it is visual, and the aural composition of the nineteenth-century southern city was highly distinct. In cities such as Charleston, New Orleans, and Richmond, the "sonic texture" of the antebellum urban center was primarily shaped by the sounds of African Americans going about their lives in marketplaces, streets, alleys, and public squares.[85] By the middle of the nineteenth century, the "sounds of slavery" saturating urban centers in the South were often a source of racial friction and annoyance for white residents but were also, in the case of both Charleston and New Orleans, regulated by municipal ordinances.[86] Black bodies and Black mobility were objects of regulation from the perspectives of white authorities, as were Black sounds. The aforementioned arrest therefore represents a symbolic reversal of judicial power and social control on multiple connected levels, some particular to Charleston, others to nineteenth-century southern cities broadly.

Ultimately, white resistance to Reconstruction and to the presence of African Americans on police forces, juries, and in government would prevail. Following the election of 1876 and the South's subsequent "Redemption," Black police officers would become a rarity in urban America.[87] In many cities, this transition was quick and dramatic. African American men went from representing half of Montgomery's police force in 1870 to being completely excluded in 1880.[88] In New Orleans, Octave Rey, a Black Union veteran who served as a captain in the police force from 1868, was elected to serve (simultaneously) in the Louisiana State Senate in 1873, and commanded Metropolitan forces during the Battle of Liberty Place, was immediately dismissed following the election of a Democratic state government in 1876.[89] Rey subsequently gained employment in the federal Customs House in New Orleans, under the management of the former Metropolitan Police superintendent Algernon Badger.[90] Working alongside Rey was another former Metropolitan, Rodolphe Desdunes. Desdunes had fought alongside Rey to defend the city in the Battle of Liberty Place and, along with another Customs House employee, Louis Martinet, had cofounded the Comité des Citoyens that would prosecute the case against segregation, bringing *Plessy v. Ferguson* to the Supreme Court in 1896.⁹¹ The US government remained an avenue of employment for African Americans in the Deep South during this period, including very occasionally in federal law enforcement (as collectors in the Bureau of Internal Revenue and as US Marshals).⁹²

Some Black police officers remained in cities like New Orleans and Charleston through the Jim Crow era and into the early twentieth century, yet in far smaller numbers and with far more restrictions on their power than before; if "Redemption" did not end the careers of all Black officers, it heavily constrained them.⁹³ In both Charleston and New Orleans, some Black officers were able to keep their jobs, but recruitment of African Americans virtually ceased. James Fordham, who had served as second lieutenant in Charleston during Reconstruction, would slowly be demoted to third and then fourth lieutenant during the 1880s and 1890s, before eventually being dismissed in 1896 and taking up the far humbler role of security guard in a cotton mill.⁹⁴ Fordham was seemingly held in high esteem by both Black and white Charlestonians, and his praises were regularly sung in local newspapers—yet his long and illustrious career was highly exceptional.⁹⁵

Throughout the South, many African American officers were dismissed well before 1877 or even killed. Peter Crosby, who served as Vicksburg's first Black sheriff, was dramatically run out of town by a drunken white mob in December 1874, reinstalled with federal assistance in January 1875, and then murdered in June.⁹⁶ Only in very exceptional circumstances were African Americans hired in police forces after 1877. In Mobile, for instance, where the Black community retained voting rights and continued to exercise political influence until the beginning of the twentieth century, local Democratic officials appointed some African Americans to the police force in both 1877 and 1885, yet their authority was far more tenuous and limited than it had been in 1867.⁹⁷ In August 1878, Black police officers were appointed in Memphis for the first time—yet it was a yellow fever epidemic and the resulting mass exodus of white Memphians (not racial justice) that motivated local officials to appoint African Americans to this position.⁹⁸ The end of Reconstruction may not have meant the complete dismissal of African Americans from the police, but it represented the first steps in the destruction of a particularly radical vision of American society, of which these officers were a crucial part.

By wearing badges, uniforms, and enforcing not just *the* law but *new* laws, ones protecting African American civil rights, these men were performing an entirely new identity on the urban landscape. Reconstruction changed almost everything in urban society, including who could be a policeman and what a policeman could be. Scholars have most often applied the concept of performance in this particular historical context to the street parade, where the public spectacle of marching through the street could serve a variety of purposes for participants and observers.[99] The end of the war in Charleston was marked by a series of "collective public performances" by the city's Black citizens, marking the death of slavery and the beginning of a new era.[100] Performance and public spectacle were clearly critical forms of mass communication, identity formation, and political expression in the nineteenth-century city, and African Americans in the urban South were highly attuned to the effectiveness of this medium. Until 1867, the role of the Black policeman had gone unwritten; hence it was up to these men to write and perform their own version of the part. Instead of a literal stage, they had the street, the city, the courthouse, and the guard house. For every different location, there were also different intended audiences. Performing the role of the Black Reconstruction police officer required performing an idea of justice, race, and professionalism to Black and white civilians, fellow officers, as well as one's own family and—critically—oneself.

The dramatic rise and fall of Black policemen during Reconstruction encapsulates both the dynamic potential and ultimate disappointment of the era. Far from the halls of state and federal power, Reconstruction was a lived experience that fundamentally affected individuals and communities in cities like Charleston and New Orleans. Black police officers shaped the city space, urban mobility, and the process of Reconstruction, but they were also shaped by it. From guarding over the French Opera House to feeding and housing the poor and homeless, Black police officers in New Orleans worked to protect both the civil rights granted by Reconstruction and those most affected by the sudden changes in southern society and the economy. Like the men and women whom Ravenel observed in 1865, African American police officers were performing a role, using the power of public spectacle and dress to assert individual and collective claims to citizenship and respect. In this way, these small acts stand for a kind of social revolution, one based on a radical reorganizing of southern society around new conceptions of justice and equality. In Charleston and New Orleans, these moments signify a radical renegotiation of the relationship between African Americans, the police, and urban society, a moment that remains relevant to the present despite—or perhaps because of—its brevity.

### Notes

1. Leon F. Litwack, *Been in the Storm So Long: The Aftermath of Slavery* (New York: Vintage, 1980), 259.

2. Litwack, *Been in the Storm*, 259; Wilbert L. Jenkins, *Seizing the New Day: African Americans in Post–Civil War Charleston* (Bloomington: Indiana University Press, 1998), 42.

3. Arthur Remillard, *Southern Civil Religions: Imagining the Good Society in the Post-Reconstruction Era* (Athens: University of Georgia Press, 2011), 48–49.

4. For scholars who described immediate changes in postwar interracial social relations, see Jenkins, *Seizing the New Day*, 30–45; Eric Foner, *Reconstruction: America's Unfinished Revolution, 1863–1877* (New York: Harper & Row, 1988); Bernard E. Powers Jr., *Black Charlestonians: A Social History, 1822–1885* (Fayetteville: University of Arkansas Press, 1994), 78–80; Maurie Dee McInnis, *The Politics of Taste in Antebellum Charleston* (Chapel Hill: University of North Carolina Press, 2005), 329; Jeff Strickland, *Unequal Freedoms: Ethnicity, Race, and White Supremacy in Civil War-Era Charleston* (Gainesville: University Press of Florida, 2015), 168–72. For Dailey's excellent scholarship in this regard, see Jane Dailey, *Before Jim Crow: The Politics of Race in Postemancipation Virginia* (Chapel Hill: University of North Carolina Press, 2000), 103–31.

5. W. Marvin Dulaney, *Black Police in America* (Bloomington: Indiana University Press, 1996), 13, 116–17.

6. For recent scholarship in this field, see Elizabeth Stordeur Pryor, *Colored Travelers: Mobility and the Fight for Citizenship before the Civil War* (Chapel Hill: University of North Carolina Press, 2016); LaKisha Michelle Symons, *Crescent City Girls: The Lives of Young Black Women in Segregated New Orleans* (Chapel Hill: University of North Carolina Press, 2015). For an introduction to the growing body of literature on space and race more broadly, see Brook Neely and Michelle Samura, "Social Geographies of Race: Connecting Race and Space," *Ethnic and Racial Studies* 34, no. 11 (2011): 1933–52.

7. Michael A. Ross, *The Great New Orleans Kidnapping Case: Race, Law, and Justice in the Reconstruction Era* (Oxford: Oxford University Press, 2015), 31–32. For an analysis of New Orleans's early years of federal occupation, see Chester G. Hearn, *When the Devil Came Down to Dixie: Ben Butler in New Orleans* (Baton Rouge: Louisiana State University Press, 2000).

8. John W. Blassingame, *Black New Orleans, 1860–1880* (Chicago: University of Chicago Press, 1973), 1–2, 45–47.

9. There are exceptions to this, with some excellent comparative scholarship being completed by Howard Rabinowitz, Hilary Green, and Lawrence Larsen. See Howard N. Rabinowitz, *Race Relations in the Urban South, 1865–1890* (Urbana: University of Illinois Press, 1980); Hilary Green, *Education Reconstruction: African American Schools in the Urban South, 1865–1890* (New York: Fordham University Press, 2016); Lawrence H. Larsen, *The Rise of the Urban South* (Lexington: University Press of Kentucky, 1985). For the most prominent example of New Orleans exceptionalism in the historical literature, see Louise McKinney, *New Orleans: A Cultural History* (Oxford: Oxford University Press, 2006).

10. The 1925 "Official History" of the Charleston police department, for instance, contains no mention whatsoever of African American participation, pre- or post-1877. See *Official History Police Department of Charleston, S.C.* (1925), Records of the Charleston Police Department, 1855–1991, City of Charleston Records, Charleston County Public Library, Charleston, SC.

11. Foner, *Reconstruction*, 262–63.

12. "The Late New Orleans Riot," *Tri-Weekly Standard* (Raleigh, NC), Tuesday, August 14, 1866, 2. Rousey, *Policing the Southern City*, 117.

13. Dennis C. Rousey, *Policing the Southern City: New Orleans, 1805–1889* (Baton Rouge: Louisiana State University Press, 1996), 115, 117, 140; Ross, *The Great New Orleans Kidnapping Case*, 35.

14. Donald E. Reynolds, "The New Orleans Riot of 1866, Reconsidered," *Louisiana History: The Journal of the Louisiana Historical Association* 5, no. 1 (Winter 1964): 10.

15. Rousey, *Policing the Southern City*, 115.

16. Reynolds, "The New Orleans Riot," 13.

17. James G. Hollandsworth Jr., *An Absolute Massacre: The New Orleans Race Riot of July 30, 1866* (Baton Rouge: Louisiana State University Press, 2001), 122.

18. US Congress, House of Representatives, Select Committee on the New Orleans Riots, *Report of the Select Committee on the New Orleans Riots* (Washington, DC: Gov't Print. Off., 1867), https://lccn.loc.gov/07021382; Stacy K. McGoldrick and Paul Simpson, "Violence, Police, and Riots in New Orleans Political Culture: 1854–1874," *Journal of Historical Sociology* 20, nos. 1/2 (March/June 2007): 90.

19. Dennis C. Rousey, "Black Policemen in New Orleans during Reconstruction," *The Historian* 49, no. 2 (February 1987): 228.

20. Dulaney, *Black Police*, 13.

21. Dulaney, *Black Police*, 13–14.

22. Rousey, "Black Policemen," 225.

23. Rousey, *Policing the Southern City*, 135.

24. Dulaney, *Black Police*, 116; Powers, *Black Charlestonians*, 242.

25. John Oldfield, "On the Beat: Black Policemen in Charleston, 1869–1921," *South Carolina Historical Magazine* 102, no. 2 (April 2001): 153.

26. Rousey, *Policing the Southern City*, 141–43; Oldfield, "On the Beat," 156.

27. Dulaney, *Black Police*, 11, 16; Rousey, "Black Police in New Orleans," 235.

28. Rousey, *Policing the Southern City*, 140; Oldfield, "On the Beat," 156.

29. Dulaney, *Black Police*, 11–13; Oldfield, "On the Beat," 167.

30. For claims of Black police misconduct during Reconstruction, see John S. Reynolds, *Reconstruction in South Carolina, 1865–1877* (Columbia, SC: State Co., 1905), 149, 348; Walter Lynwood Fleming, *Civil War and Reconstruction in Alabama* (New York: Columbia University Press, 1905).

31. Rousey, "Black Policemen," 231.

32. For a study of the violence, paramilitarism, and disorder that constantly threatened New Orleans police, see James K. Hogue, *Uncivil War: Five New Orleans Street Battles and the Rise and Fall of Radical Reconstruction* (Baton Rouge: Louisiana State University Press, 2006). For further reading on the Battle of Liberty Place, see Lawrence N. Powell, "Reinventing Tradition: Liberty Place, Historical Memory, and Silk-Stocking Vigilantism in New Orleans Politics," *Slavery and Abolition* 20, no. 1 (1999): 127–49.

33. I have read and copied all the available original arrest records and morning reports from the Charleston Police Department during Reconstruction and the Metropolitan Police Force in New Orleans. No obvious bias is apparent, although I have yet to undertake a large-scale quantitative examination. The vast majority of arrests in both cities were for public drunkenness, with the guilty parties seemingly representative of all ethnic and social groups in the city. For Charleston, see Arrest Records & Morn-

ing Reports, Lower Wards, 1855–56, 1861–63, 1868–69 (Microfilm POL 2), Records of the Charleston Police Department, 1855–1991, City of Charleston Records, Charleston County Public Library, Charleston, SC; Arrest Records & Morning Reports, Lower Wards, Morning Reports, Main Station, 1869–70, 1883–84 (Microfilm POL 4), Records of the Charleston Police Department, 1855–1991, City of Charleston Records, Charleston County Public Library, Charleston, SC; Reports of Arrests Made in the Second Precinct of the Metropolitan Police District, 1870–1873, v. 1 2/6/1870–2/28/1873 (TPA205 1870–1873), Records of the Metropolitan Police District of New Orleans, 1869–1883, City Archives, Louisiana Division, New Orleans Public Library.

34. For Dunning School interpretations, see Fleming, *Civil War and Reconstruction*, 765; Reynolds, *Reconstruction in South Carolina*, 149, 348. For modern historical findings, see Dulaney, *Black Police*, 13; Rousey, "Black Policemen," 231; Oldfield, "On the Beat," 164; Jordan, "'The New Regime': Race, Politics and Police in Reconstruction Charleston, 1865–1875," *Proceedings of the South Carolina Historical Association* (1994): 50.

35. Robin D. G. Kelley, "'We Are Not What We Seem': Rethinking Black Working-Class Opposition in the Jim Crow South," *Journal of American History* 80 (June 1993): 75–112; Jane Dailey, "Deference and Violence in the Postbellum Urban South: Manners and Massacres in Danville, Virginia," *Journal of Southern History* 63, no. 3 (August 1997): 553–90; Shane White, *Stories of Freedom in Black New York* (Cambridge, MA: Harvard University Press), 2007; Michael J. Klarman, *From Jim Crow to Civil Rights: The Supreme Court and the Struggles for Racial Equality* (Oxford: Oxford University Press, 2004), 50; Tara McPherson, *Reconstructing Dixie: Race, Gender, and Nostalgia in the Imagined South* (Durham, NC: Duke University Press, 2003), 56–57.

36. Klarman, *From Jim Crow to Civil Rights*, 50; McPherson, *Reconstructing Dixie*, 56–57.

37. Michael E. Crutcher Jr., *Tremé: Race and Place in a New Orleans Neighborhood* (Atlanta: University of Georgia Press, 2010), 37.

38. Soprano Adelina Patti is an example of the talent the theater attracted. Jack Belsom, "En Route to Stardom: Adelina Patti at the French Opera House, New Orleans, 1860–1861," *Opera Quarterly* 10, no. 3 (March 1994): 113–30; Crutcher, *Tremé*, 37.

39. Robert C. Clark, "At the Corner of Bourbon and Toulouse Street: The Historical Context of Alice Dunbar-Nelson's 'M'sieu Fortier's Violin,'" *American Literary Realism* 41, no. 2 (Winter 2009): 167–68; Ronald L. Davis, "Classical Music and Opera," in *The New Encyclopedia of Southern Culture*, vol. 12: *Music*, ed. Bill C. Malone and Wilson Charles Reagan (Chapel Hill: University of North Carolina Press, 2008), 44.

40. Caryn Cossé Bell, *Revolution, Romanticism, and the Afro-Creole Protest Tradition in Louisiana, 1718–1868* (Baton Rouge: Louisiana State University Press, 1997), 12.

41. Alice Dunbar-Nelson, "People of Color in Louisiana: Part II," *Journal of Negro History* 2, no. 1 (January 1917): 62.

42. Emily Suzanne Clark, *A Luminous Brotherhood: Afro-Creole Spiritualism in Nineteenth-Century New Orleans* (Chapel Hill: University of North Carolina Press, 2016), 12–13.

43. "Chronique Locale—Crime," *La Tribune de la Nouvelle-Orléans*, December 11, 1867, 1; Ross, *The Great New Orleans Kidnapping Case*, 18.

44. "Chronique Locale—Crime," 1.

45. "Chronique Locale—Crime," 1. This is my translation of the original French, which reads: "ARRESTATION—Un Officier fédéral qui s'était amusé à insulter les officier Picou et Depas tandis qu'ils étaient dans l'exercice de leurs devoirs au Théâtre de l'Opéra, a été coffré et conduit en prison où il a eu toute la nuit à réfléchir sur le danger qu'il y a de manquer de respect aux mandataires de la loi."

46. Rousey, *Policing the Southern City*, 126.

47. *An Act to establish a Metropolitan Police District and to provide for the government thereof*, 1868, no. 74 (LA), in *Acts Passed by the General Assembly of the State of Louisiana at the First Session of the First Legislature Begun and Held in the City of New Orleans, June 29, 1868* (New Orleans: A. L. Lee, State Printer, 1868).

48. Hogue, *Uncivil War*, 66.

49. Rousey, *Policing the Southern City*, 126–59; James K. Hogue, "The Strange Career of Jim Longstreet: History and Contingency in the Civil War Era," in *The Struggle for Equality: Essays on Sectional Conflict, the Civil War, and the Long Reconstruction*, ed. Orville Vernon Burton, Jerald Podair, and Jennifer L. Weber (Charlottesville: University of Virginia Press, 2011), 157.

50. *Annual Report of the Board of Metropolitan Police to the Governor of Louisiana, from October 1, 1873 to December 31, 1874*, Louisiana, Board of Metropolitan Police (New Orleans: Printed at the Republican Office, 94 Camp Street, 1875); Rousey, *Policing the Southern City*, 128.

51. Rousey, *Policing the Southern City*, 130–33.

52. Rousey, *Policing the Southern City*, 134.

53. Rousey, *Policing the Southern City*, 133; George S. Pabis, *Daily Life along the Mississippi* (Westport, CT: Greenwood, 2007), 147.

54. Rousey, *Policing the Southern City*, 131.

55. Rousey, *Policing the Southern City*, 130–31.

56. Justin A. Nystrom, *New Orleans after the Civil War: Race, Politics, and a New Birth of Freedom* (Baltimore, MD: Johns Hopkins University Press, 2010), 76–77. For more detail on the various armed conflicts and insurrections that plagued New Orleans, see Hogue, *Uncivil War*.

57. Pabis, *Daily Life*, 147.

58. "The Condition of the City," "Public Opinion and the State Government," and "Lost," *New Orleans Crescent*, Wednesday, October 28, 1868, 4; "'Colored' Policemen in New Orleans," *Weekly Georgia Telegraph*, November 13, 1868, 1; "They Would Not Go," *People's Vindicator*, Saturday, September 5, 1874, 2.

59. Pabis, *Daily Life*, 147.

60. "The Colored Policemen," *Charleston Daily News*, July 28, 1868, 3.

61. "Loyal Armed Police Force," *Charleston Daily News*, January 11, 1868, 2.

62. *The Constitution of South Carolina, Adopted April 16, 1868, and the Acts and Joint Resolutions of the General Assembly, Passed at the Special Session of 1868, Together with the Military Orders therein Re-Enacted* (Columbia, SC: John W. Denny, Printer to the State, 1868). For a good summary of Reconstruction-era constitutional reform in South Carolina, see James Lowell Underwood, *The Constitution of South Carolina*, vol. 4: *The Struggle for Political Equality* (Columbia: University of South Carolina Press, 1994), 1–57.

The conference that this essay and most of the other essays in this volume were first presented at in 2018 included the unveiling of a new historic marker at the site where this constitution was written.

63. "The Negro Constitution," *Orangeburg News*, April 11, 1868, 4.

64. "The Colored Policemen," *Charleston Daily News*, July 28, 1868, 3; Oldfield, "On the Beat," 155; Powers, *Black Charlestonians*, 242.

65. Oldfield, "On the Beat," 156; Robert N. Rosen, *Confederate Charleston: An Illustrated History of the City and the People during the Civil War* (Columbia: University of South Carolina Press, 1994), 151.

66. Jordan, "The New Regime," 49.

67. "A Hard Case," *Charleston Daily News*, 24 February 1871, page 3.

68. "A Hard Case."

69. For violence and riots in Reconstruction Charleston, see Kate Côté Gillin, *Women, Gender, and Racial Violence in South Carolina, 1865–1900* (Columbia, SC: University of South Carolina Press, 2013); Melinda Meek Hennessy, "Racial Violence during Reconstruction: The 1876 Riots in Charleston and Cainhoy," *South Carolina Historical Magazine* 86, no. 2 (April 1985): 100–12.

70. *Encyclopedia of Virginia Biography*, vol. 4, ed. ed. Lyon Gardiner Tyler (New York: Lewis Historical Publishing Company, 1915), s.v. "William Peronneau de Saussure." See also *DeSaussure family*, DeSaussure family papers, 1716–1938, 1022.00, South Carolina Historical Society. For an overview of the aristocratic culture of antebellum Charleston and its leading families, see McInnis, *The Politics of Taste*.

71. Saul S. Friedman, *Jews and the American Slave Trade* (New Brunswick, NJ: Transaction, 2000), 159.

72. Friedman, *Jews and the American Slave Trade*, 159; L. M. Desaussure, United States Census (Slave Schedule), 1860, South Carolina, St. Helena Parish Beaufort, NARA Microfilm M653 (Washington, DC: National Archives and Records Administration), 40.

73. Richard C. Wade, *Slavery in the Cities: The South, 1820–1860* (New York: Oxford University Press, 1964), 38; Douglas R. Egerton, *He Shall Go Out Free: The Lives of Denmark Vesey*, rev. and updated ed. (Lanham, MD: Rowman & Littlefield, 2004), 64.

74. Harlan Greene, Harry S. Hutchins Jr., and Brian E. Hutchins, *Slave Badges and the Slave-Hire System in Charleston, South Carolina, 1783–1865* (Jefferson, NC: McFarland, 2004), 8.

75. Greene et al., *Slave Badges*, 8; Wade, *Slavery in the Cities*, 40; Juliet E. K. Walker, *The History of Black Business in America: Capitalism, Race, Entrepreneurship*, vol. 1: *To 1865*, 2nd ed. (Chapel Hill: University of North Carolina Press, 2009), 104.

76. Amrita Chakrabarti Myers, *Forging Freedom: Black Women and the Pursuit of Liberty in Antebellum Charleston* (Chapel Hill: University of North Carolina Press, 2011), 206.

77. Egerton, *He Shall Go Out Free*, 69.

78. Walker, *The History of Black Business*, 104.

79. Blassingame, *Black New Orleans*, 8.

80. While no police badges worn by African Americans during Reconstruction remain in any museum collections (as far as I am aware), illustrated newspapers provide

documentary evidence of the appearance of Charleston's Black police officers and that, like officers in New Orleans and other cities, they wore distinct metal badges. Harry Ogden, "South Carolina—Street Characters in Charleston an Afternoon on Main Street," engraving, *Frank Leslie's Illustrated Newspaper*, January 21, 1877, Historic Charleston Foundation, Photography Collection, https://www.historiccharleston.org/research/photograph-collection/detail/street-characters-in-charleston/14321B7D-9288-4558-BE9B-316739296816; Oldfield, "On the Beat," 154. Oldfield notes how Black police in Charleston wore "military frockcoats in winter and blue flannel suits in summer, topped off with Panama hats," which "lent the police an air of special distinction" (162).

81. Jordan, "The New Regime," 49.

82. Michael E. Woods, "Tracing the 'Sacred Relicts': The Strange Career of Preston Brooks's Cane," *Civil War History* 63, no. 2 (June 2017): 117–19; Edmund Lee Drago, "Dr. William Demosthenes Crum's Walking Stick and the Legitimacy of Black Political Power in South Carolina History," unpublished essay in the possession of Professor Simon Lewis, College of Charleston.

83. *Digest of the Ordinances of the City Council of Charleston, from the Year 1783 to July 1818; To Which Are Annexed, Extracts from the Acts of the Legislature Which Relate to the City of Charleston* (Charleston: Archibald E. Miller, Printer, July 15, 1818), 190.

84. Drago, "Dr. William Demosthenes Crum," 8–9.

85. Shane White and Graham White, *The Sounds of Slavery: Discovering African American History through Songs, Sermons, and Speech* (Boston: Beacon, 2005), 175–76.

86. White and White, *The Sounds of Slavery*, 162; McInnis, *The Politics of Taste*, 68; Harold Glymph Talley, "City Council Minutes Reveal Black Life in Charleston and Greenville, South Carolina, 1850–1900," PhD diss., Clark Atlanta University, 1991, 58.

87. Dulaney, *Black Police*, 15.

88. Dennis C. Rousey, "Yellow Fever and Black Policemen in Memphis: A Post-Reconstruction Anomaly," *Journal of Southern History* 51, no. 3 (August 1985): 359.

89. Dulaney, *Black Police*, 17; Nystrom, *New Orleans after the Civil War*, 173.

90. Nystrom, *New Orleans after the Civil War*, 201–3.

91. Nystrom, *New Orleans after the Civil War*, 201–3; Rebecca J. Scott, "The Atlantic World and the Road to *Plessy v. Ferguson*," *Journal of American History* 94, no. 3 (December 2007): 731.

92. Prominent examples include BIR Collector William Henderson Foote, who was murdered in Yazoo City in 1883, and US Deputy Marshall Bass Reeves, who served in Arkansas and Oklahoma. Bettye Gardner, "William H. Foote and Yazoo County Politics, 1866–1883," *Southern Studies* 21, no. 4 (Winter 1982): 398–407; Ash T. Burton, *Black Gun, Silver Star: The Life and Legend of Frontier Marshal Bass Reeves* (Lincoln: University of Nebraska Press, 2008).

93. Dulaney, *Black Police*, 15–17; Howard C. Rabinowitz, "The Conflict between Blacks and the Police in the Urban South, 1865–1900," *The Historian* 39, no. 1 (November 1976): 65.

94. "Charleston Scare—Wild Rumors of a Bloody Riot of Negro Factory Hands," *Watchman and Southron*, September 1, 1897, 8; "Before You South Carolinians," *News and Courier* (Charleston, SC), Tuesday morning, August 8, 1950, 4; Laylon Wayne Jordan,

"Police and Politics: Charleston in the Gilded Age, 1880–1900," *South Carolina Historical Magazine* 81, no. 1 (January 1980): 46.

95. See "Vicious," *Charleston News*, April 15, 1872, 3; "A Bark on Fire," *Charleston News*, December 30, 1872, 4; "Almost a Drowning," *Charleston News*, January 2, 1873, 5; "A Negro on Negro Rights—Plain Talk from Tom Hamilton on the Men of His Race," *Watchman and Southron*, August 14, 1883, 1; "A Riot in Charleston," *Manning Times*, January 31, 1894, 1; "Two Sunday Fires," *Evening Post*, January 6, 1896, 2; "The Doings of a Day," *Evening Post*, February 23, 1895, 4; "The Fordham Case," *Evening Post*, July 6, 1895, 1.

96. "News of the Day," *Alexandria Gazette and Virginia Advertiser*, Saturday, December 6, 1874, 2; "The Negro Sheriff Crosby, of Vicksburg, Shot," *New York Times*, June 8, 1875, 1; George C. Rable, *But There Was No Peace: The Role of Violence in the Politics of Reconstruction* (Athens: University of Georgia Press, 1984), 147–48.

97. Michael W. Fitzgerald, *Urban Emancipation: Popular Politics in Reconstruction Mobile, 1860–1890* (Baton Rouge: Louisiana State University Press, 2002), 230, 263.

98. Rousey, "Yellow Fever and Black Policemen in Memphis."

99. Susan G. Davis, *Parades and Power: Street Theatre in Nineteenth-Century Philadelphia* (Philadelphia: Temple University Press, 1986); Strickland, *Unequal Freedoms*, 190–91.

100. David W. Blight, *Race and Reunion: The Civil War in American Memory* (Cambridge, MA: Belknap, 2001), 67.

# 1874

*Self-Defense and Racial
Empowerment in the Alabama
Black Belt*

## Michael W. Fitzgerald

The picturesque town of Eutaw, in west-central Alabama, is not known today for a great deal. During Reconstruction, though, it tells us much about the possibilities available to people defending their freedom. During the Ku Klux Klan years, Eutaw experienced a spectacular series of terrorist episodes, culminating in October 1870 with a firefight at a Republican electoral rally. There were dozens of Black and a few white casualties. However, four years later, in the depressed year of 1874, well-armed Republicans returned to town. This time they defied the threats of a swelling racist mobilization and held their meeting without interruption. Same location, similar opposition, wholly opposite result: This is the conundrum throughout Alabama's western Black Belt that year. Agricultural depression completely changed the facts on the ground, facilitating freedmen's self-defense. This contrast matters because scholars have largely missed the implications for grassroots Black politics.

Amid our contemporary turmoil over race, conflict over Confederate statues and torch-bearing white supremacists keep historians before the public eye. Inevitably, the Ku Klux Klan becomes a focus of popular discussion. This helpfully draws a wider audience toward Reconstruction scholarship, but there are difficulties with a well-known label being attached to the totality of the era's violence. The Klan's outsize visibility overshadows later movements like the White Leagues, the Red Shirts, and similar groups of the mid-1870s. As George Rable once cautioned, the force employed by these later undisguised terrorists often proved more electorally successful than the Klan. This essay sets out to address that historiographic imbalance by looking at one later episode of "paramilitary politics" and its double-edged relationship to Black political empowerment.[1] We tend to miss that even in the worst areas, changing economic and environmental circumstances might give people surprising opportunities to defend their freedom. In Alabama's western borderlands, freedpeople immobilized by

Map 1

tenantry had proved susceptible to Klan violence early in Radical Reconstruction, but things turned out differently a few years later in the midst of plantation collapse.[2]

The area under examination, in the far western portion of Alabama's central cotton belt, is not altogether typical of the plantation South (see Map 1).[3] It had an unusual history of extreme violence. In this region, Alabama's Black

Belt demographics crossed the Mississippi state line, a situation that encouraged lawlessness. In addition, the Tombigbee and Black Warrior rivers intersect at Demopolis, about thirty miles east of the border, creating a district prone to flooding and consequent disruption. This geographic setting likely contributed to the scale of social conflict, which escalated here in unusual ways. During Alabama's Klan upsurge, roughly from 1868 to 1871, scores of racial killings occurred in half a dozen counties.[4] Bloodletting on this scale was unusual in such overwhelmingly African American areas. According to Steven Hahn, in places where two-thirds of the population was Black, or three-quarters, according to Allen Trelease's older study, a demographic tipping point occurred that discouraged night-riding.[5] The Tombigbee borderland area is one of the few exceptions in the entire South, a Klan hotbed with truly lopsided racial proportions: Sumter County's population in 1870 was 78 percent Black, Greene's 79 percent, nearly the highest numbers in the state. Despite this preponderance, both counties had long and horrifying outbreaks of pervasive Klan violence.[6]

In March 1871, this anomalous situation drew national attention because of a riot just across the state line, in Meridian, Mississippi. Here Klansmen from Alabama massed for a courtroom confrontation, which resulted in a racial pogrom in the streets. The subsequent passage of the Ku Klux Klan Act and ensuing federal prosecutions interrupted organized terror for the time being. The following year, national Democrats' turn toward moderate rhetoric during Horace Greeley's presidential candidacy reinforced that tendency. In this transformed situation, the borderlands thus converged with the less violent pattern further to the east, where "conservative" planters often preferred accommodation to large Black majorities. As this author contended in *Reconstruction in Alabama*, once tenant farming proved lucrative, the threat of resistance, arson, or random retaliation discouraged terrorist activity in the heart of the cotton belt.[7] In this larger context, after the Meridian riot, the western Alabama pattern of cross-border raids became too conspicuous to persist.

Thus for nearly three years in the early 1870s, even this troubled region experienced an interregnum with relatively little organized paramilitary activity. But if Klan-style violence receded, the region's violent legacy influenced the confrontations of the 1874 campaign that finally overthrew Reconstruction. Legions of former Klan participants were still around, some notorious Klan leaders like Steve Renfroe having returned after fleeing arrest, having been implicated in numerous racial murders.[8] But there would be no simple repetition of the earlier Klan rampage four years earlier, because the situation on the plantations had changed. The curious reality is that economic disaster strengthened the freedpeople's capacity for physical resistance, at least in this setting. So as Democrats resorted to intimidation and force in 1874, their prospective victims responded with startling effectiveness.

It took a series of shocks to destabilize the social equilibrium and push the region into renewed conflict. Outside political causes contributed, but western Alabama's paramilitary mobilization owed its full ferocity to plantation collapse. Over the previous several years, wealthy landowners had reestablished profitability due to generally high prices for cotton. One western Alabamian even opined that whites lived "pretty much as they did before the war." Most still held their plantations, he wrote, and they derived "about as large incomes from them as they ever did."[9] The freedpeople may not have seen most of the profits, but given the region's vibrant economy they at least retained some, and the strong job market assured nearly all of food. Labor was in demand, which increased the availability of rental land and shaped how the races interacted. As one unsuccessful planter griped, the freedmen were "patted on the shoulder and *caressed, by many, many, many* whom we once thought, could never be made to stoop so low."[10]

Such complaints underscore the planters' eagerness for laborers and tenants when cotton prices rose above twenty cents a pound. Profits rose in part through large planters' role as middlemen in the flow of credit, a transmission point between northeastern and European bankers and their own tenants. Other landowners settled for rent, depending instead on merchants to provision the hands. In the recent literature on slavery and capitalism, scholars have noted the role of international finance in the system's expansion and functioning.[11] The postwar capital flow resumed on the basis of free labor, but with onetime slaves now feeding themselves, they became vulnerable to periodic interruptions in their access to cash and food. Credit undergirded the social peace, and it proved a fragile recourse. In the spring of 1873, rainfall inundated the region, with flooding injuring the crop and encouraging ruinous insect infestations. The poor prospects inhibited the flow of outside capital to planters and merchants, who, in turn, ceased their provision of credit in mid-crop. The economic mechanisms for feeding hired laborers and tenants failed, with no safety net in place. Some tenants attempted to farm without the means, while others abandoned hopeless crops in the fields. The result was that "such a failure of crops was never known, not averaging over a [cotton] Bale to the Head."[12] These numbers meant economic losses on all sides. Then Wall Street crashed in September 1873, initiating a major depression that worsened for most of the rest of the decade. Labor scarcity turned into redundancy, especially in the formerly productive land along the rivers, creating a situation ripe for conflict. An overseer reported in September, "There are hundreds of Negroes roving about that have been discharged on account of not having made enough to feed them, & many have gone to Mississippi."[13]

Some despondent landowners welcomed an exodus, because their natural tendency was to blame tenant farming and Black behavior for the region's woes. Disappointed planters turned away from cotton for less labor-intensive food crops, in hope of avoiding debt. Evictions followed. Most of the displaced stayed in the region, hoping times would improve, but they needed to eat something. An uprooted, underemployed, and hungry workforce had implications, all of them negative for large landowners. Planters complained of theft, even by current tenants despairing of a payout for their year's work. Given racial animus, one assumes exaggeration, but planters' statements look unequivocal. As one complained, "There is hardly anything left now for them to steal, I learn they are now commencing on the mules to run off with them."[14] And such reports seem possible, if dispirited sharecroppers and other tenants were helping themselves to the crops they themselves had grown and expected to make nothing from. Beyond such issues involving tenants, the economic collapse also engendered a wave of wage demands by hired hands. Strike activity had been nearly unknown for years in the Black Belt, but now such talk spread even in the richest plantation districts. The Sumter County newspaper claimed laborers sought a dollar a day, enraging the paper's editors.[15] From wage demands to fears of wandering brigands, everything pointed toward rising conflict.

These developments served as the backdrop for the final political campaign of Alabama's Reconstruction era, as the elections of 1874 approached. White planters and farmers initially turned toward organizational redress in the form of the Patrons of Husbandry, also known as the Grange, a national protest movement targeting agrarian grievances. While the organization had numerous objectives, in Alabama a central one was inhibiting plantation products from being fenced to unscrupulous merchants, at crossroads "deadfall" stores, as they were termed. One large Hale County planter, Samuel Pickens, pressured merchants to stop buying cotton from freedpeople without permission from landlords or employers. The threat of Granger retaliation forced merchants to comply, at least for some months.[16] The racial overtones of such activities were overt, and this angry agrarian current influenced the Democratic Party; it facilitated a takeover by extreme elements demanding an overt "White Line" policy. The explicit goal was a white monopoly of power, which suggested muscular means. Some resisted the shift toward force, especially landowners in areas where freedmen vastly predominated. In the central cotton belt, many "conservative" planters and editors distrusted their party's turn toward confrontation, but Democratic voters were already roused by the depression and also by Republican proposals for civil rights legislation outlawing segregation in public places. Buoyed by a wave of popular resentment, the Democratic Party officially rejected any appeal to Black voters, in favor of open racism. The Mobile *Register,* for example, called for "a white man's rule, and a white man's government, or ruin and extermination."[17] The state's leading Democratic paper assured readers that armed whites were "equal to ten times their number of a negro rabble."[18]

Alabama's martial sentiment did not congeal into a formal statewide White League, as occurred in Louisiana, so far as can be determined, but analogous bands developed locally.[19] Immediately after the Democratic state convention met, hitherto peaceful areas witnessed white efforts to win governmental sanction for official militias. Failing that, Democratic patrols began riding through plantation districts, which empowered the younger men and more radical elements, as well as men simply disposed toward force. The patrols' aggressiveness varied, and they provoked only scattered violent confrontations across the Black Belt. But in the former Klan strongholds along the Mississippi border, the situation played out explosively. Fearing trouble, Republicans began mobilizing early for the fall campaign, but they mostly avoided public meetings as too dangerous. Surreptitious local groups like the "Friendly Brothers" or "Loving Brothers" began operating. The names were nonthreatening enough, but meetings reportedly discussed plantation grievances along with partisan politics. Rumors spread among jumpy whites, pumped up by apocalyptic rhetoric of imminent race war. And in early August 1874, a Republican lawyer, Walter P. Billings, was gunned down on his return from a party gathering. Eyewitness testimony identified the dozens of gunmen as led by Steve Renfroe, the former Klan leader. Renfroe was not a subtle fellow: He beat a hotelkeeper soon afterward in Livingston for daring to gossip about his participation in the murder.[20] With this first political killing in western Alabama for some years, both sides moved toward armed confrontation.

What followed resembled the basic story of White League–style terrorism elsewhere, but with a distinctive riverine twist. The previous crop failure uprooted much of the plantation population, and in the spring of 1874, disastrous rainfall flooded out still more. Many freedpeople were now in motion, no longer isolated by sharecropping or immobilized by farm work. Even among those renting land, the crop prospects that fall were so wretched that they often had little to lose. Others despaired of a favorable end-of-the-year settlement given the threats of retaliation for voting by landlords. Many Republicans were already sleeping in the woods in fear of the Democratic bands, and their families were often more mobile too, having little property to preserve at home. One federal detective reported that whole tenant families took flight whenever they saw a white face in their vicinity; he said he couldn't gather evidence because he couldn't even talk to the freedpeople.[21] This reality shaped the region's "paramilitary politics." Given the disparity in racial numbers, it was no easy matter for night riders to force a confrontation on favorable ground; at least, they could not do so quickly enough to avoid a political backlash. The Democrats could mobilize hundreds-strong groups from a distance, just as they had during the Klan era, but their prospective victims could simply withdraw into the swamps without leaving any convenient targets. Waiting out the massed horsemen generally secured a tactical impasse, which promised a kind of political victory. Economic disaster, amid widespread flooding, created a mobile guerrilla force of freedmen capable of frustrating the terrorists.

The resulting conflicts across the region defy ready description, save for the evident pattern of falling dominoes. Democrats on a congressional investigating committee observed that "armed bodies of white men" rode in Alabama to "protect the whites against what were feared to be the evil designs of organized clubs of armed negroes."[22] If freedpeople had actually *done* anything, the statement does not indicate what. In western Alabama, it appears the horsemen were often acting on the offensive, threatening potential Black voters, looking for Republican meetings, and harassing participants on their way home. Republicans responded with vigor, taking advantage of the reserves of underemployed men at hand. According to his own statement, the much-threatened Black leader Thomas Ivey assembled "some twenty-five or more men" to guard his house near Coatopa Station. An armed escort accompanied him to his numerous rallies.[23] Whites in the countryside were outraged at the display of force, but the profusion of guns deterred interference at his meetings. Five hundred gathered weekly, sometimes for barbecues. This activity prompted "a good deal of threatening" toward the attendees, but they ignored the violent omens.[24] The terrorists only solved their problem on August 29, by halting a train and murdering Ivey while on the job as a mail agent. With this second Sumter County assassination in a month, things escalated, but the scattered murders did not deter Republican organizing—rather, the opposite. Another freedman, Warren Dew, stepped into Ivey's role. The confrontation only intensified through the first weeks of September. For Dew's allies, the killings demonstrated that Black leaders needed a heavy escort, something grassroots Republican followers hastened to provide. The resulting movements of armed freedmen alarmed whites, and the resulting process of racial polarization further destabilized the countryside.

A hellish hopscotch pattern resulted. Republican activities and self-defense measures prompted insurrection rumors, with disorders jumping from one place to another, fed both by those fleeing trouble and those seeking it. From some out-of-the-way places, only sketchy reports with vague timing exist, but overall there is a good deal of evidence of conflict. In Clarke County, a racial shooting amid Black religious meetings prompted rumors of a rising in early August, leading whites to pour in from adjacent counties. Whatever the threat was, it melted away upon inspection, but neighboring Choctaw County then erupted. Republicans there secretly met to endorse a candidate, and according to the modern study they beat a defector for bearing tales of their activities. A posse summoned Republican Jack Turner and other freedmen to answer charges for this assault, and when they arrived in town bearing arms, jumpy whites intervened, and shooting broke out. Freedpeople fled into the surrounding swamps. It appears no one was killed, but Turner turned up in Montgomery to broadcast exaggerated tales of slaughter across the region and, indeed, before the national public.[25]

Democrats may have "won" most of the individual confrontations in terms of imposing more casualties, but a pattern of ongoing turmoil at harvest time did not achieve the larger end.[26] Nor did it stem the increasing numbers of people hiding in the swamps, now angry, mobile, and ripe for further action. A public confrontation in Greene County opened the prospect of outright warfare. In Eutaw, the scene of Klan-era bloody strife, Republicans determined upon a show of force, a public rally just outside town on September 5. They secreted guns nearby, just in case, with wagonloads brought from the direction of Sumter County. Discovery of the arms by Democrats prompted tense negotiations amid the prospect of a shootout, but cooler heads came to terms: The arms remained just out of Eutaw, along with half the crowd, while a moderate white Republican gave the rest a discreet oration at the courthouse on the virtues of mutual forbearance. The Republican crowd then returned home peaceably, but the inconclusive result unnerved the white population. The local newspaper, the *Whig*, discerned "a crime against law" in Black men entering Eutaw under arms and frightening women. If freedmen used force, the paper pledged, it was "war to the knife and the knife to the hilt."[27]

The escalating rhetoric captures Democrats' frustration, primarily because the episode did not conclude with the accustomed racial lesson. The most confrontation-minded found other opportunities nearby within days. The mechanism seems to have been for well-armed Democratic riders to provoke self-defense measures, which then justified the dispatch of white posses. In Sumter

County, sheriff deputies came to arrest Warren Dew, which provoked a week of turmoil but few casualties. Eutaw's Greene County, on the other hand, descended into chaos. With rumors flying after the rally as freedpeople filtered home, posses began riding into Forkland precinct, an area with a seven-to-one Black majority.[28] Freedmen reportedly were shot; according to the sheriff, his men "imprudently" fired into a gin house filled with armed men apparently sheltering themselves. The posse accidentally killed a boy, while the targets escaped into the woods. Two days later, on September 14, freedmen challenged the passage of white horsemen after a Republican meeting. A parley miscarried, ending in a firefight with one killed, Adrian Robinson, who appears to have been the sole Democrat to die in the entire region-wide disturbances. A posse of twenty-five whites then arrived to make arrests, which prompted another gunfire exchange. The Livingston *Journal* reported three whites and fifteen Blacks killed, though the press often exaggerated the numbers.[29] It appears that at least one freedman and Robinson actually died in these confrontations, with several more men shot, though specifics remain obscure beyond the capture of about ten Black prisoners. For some days, posses searched "the entire county" without result, while some of the Black participants scattered, seeking reinforcements elsewhere.[30]

As whites poured into the Forkland area, encouraged by the Democratic press, nearby Republicans responded to the trouble. At Belmont, across the Tombigbee, State Representative Robert Reed had been organizing Sumter County's Republican clubs since the start of the year. Written death threats curtailed his speaking tours, and he induced forty or fifty allies to guard his home for several nights before a public rally.[31] Then around September 16, there was a confrontation at Durden's ferry, as hundreds of freedmen apparently attempted to cross the river into Greene, to aid their Forkland comrades, though the Republican version is that it was the whites who wanted to cross to the Sumter side, in order to go after the assemblage of freedmen.[32] Reed negotiated for peace, or tried to, while hidden behind willows along his bank of the river. All the while, "we dared them to come over," a white magistrate later testified.[33] Both parties finally desisted in the face of the impasse, as Republicans satisfied themselves with preventing Democratic reinforcements from reaching the area.

After this standoff at the ferry, and with the Greene County freedpeople mostly in hiding or flight, one would have thought things would settle down in the Belmont swamps, but no. One last well-publicized confrontation finally ended the conflict, and on terms that favored the freedpeople. Just after the ferry impasse, an absentee planter on the Sumter side discovered that numerous refugees were hiding on his property; when he protested, they told him they could not return home in safety for a few days. Outraged, the planter sought help from the authorities. Upon his complaint, and amid talk of insurrection, the Sumter County sheriff gathered a large posse, mostly from a Granger gathering in Livingston on September 17, about a day, that is, after the ferry standoff. Scores of armed whites also arrived from across the Mississippi border. This latter feature was not strictly legal; posse members were supposed to be county residents, and in addition no warrants had been issued, both aspects suggestive of a certain laxity toward legality. "All that want to kill Bob Reed, fall in," one participant joked, according to Democratic testimony.[34] The posse mustered an imposing display of force, as Reed counted 215 horsemen searching for him from his hillside vantage point.[35] But the quarry remained hidden in this singularly inaccessible terrain, and the host could not remain indefinitely. Only five arrests resulted, all apparently freedmen fleeing the trouble. Two days' stay accomplished nothing besides stripping Reed's rented farm of possessions—that is, nothing beyond placing themselves in the firing line of national politics, just in the midst of the 1874 congressional election campaign. The army had arrived in Livingston by September 11, in time to witness the ferocious temper of the Granger meeting and the departure of the white posse pursuing Reed. The soldiers soon intervened to stop more dominoes from falling.[36]

By this point, the chaos reverberated widely. Whites reportedly arrived from as far as Louisiana, participants in a subculture of armed tourism.[37] The White League insurrection in New Orleans occurred just then, attempting to overthrow the Reconstruction government of Louisiana, which fed into the sense of a wider confrontation. If Democrats inflicted substantial casualties anywhere in western Alabama, it was at Forkland, and the bloodletting there must have sobered Greene County's freedpeople. After the shootouts, some petitioned for "a dividing line" between the parties because "we caint live together."[38] In Hale County to the east, Forkland escapees were arrested, and a planter there thought his Black neighbors intimidated by the outcome. That reassured him, though his female relations remained uneasy at being left at home alone on Election Day as he attended the nearby polls for the Democrats. Indeed, relatives halfway across the state expressed similar concerns, speculating anxiously on where they would be safest. This underscores the situation's gravity: Numerous parties of freedmen remained at large throughout the western Black Belt borderlands. On favorable terrain most Republican bands weren't ever subdued, and the spreading army presence prevented a further escalation.[39]

Lest the point slip away in confused incident, a comparison to the Klan episode a few years previously in the vicinity is instructive. There were any number of Klan-related raids and confrontations, and the larger ones followed a plotline familiar from the rest of the South. In 1870, in Eutaw, the Republican rally had been broken up by shooting, and a riot ensued, with casualties on the order of twenty to one. The March 1871 riot across the border in Meridian played out much the same way, with whites pursuing fleeing freedpeople through the countryside, some utilizing a train in the process. The Klan mobilization targeted prominent Radicals, and in Sumter County, they killed, exiled, or converted nearly every one by 1870. This tended to be the Klan-era pattern, but it is not at all how the 1874 confrontations played out, literally on the same ground in the case of Eutaw. For all the threats, freedpeople were able to hold their rally in Eutaw's town square without a riot in September 1874. So far as can be determined, only one confirmed death of a freedman occurred in the subsequent conflict at Forkland, with perhaps one more in Clarke County, plus the two August assassinations of the prominent Republicans Billings and Ivey.[40] Elsewhere in the South, scores or hundreds died in lopsided racial slaughters. In eastern Alabama, Barbour County alone experienced *two* major race riots on Election Day, both with disproportionate casualty counts and dozens of Blacks killed or shot.[41] Nothing like that happened in the western Black Belt, despite over a month of conflict and the scale of the racist mobilization. Often as not, agile Republican leaders—all of them Black—slipped away from their pursuers. After Ivey's murder, none of the other prominent leaders died, as supporters devised the means to protect them. When one activist, Bob Thompson, received threats for hosting secret meetings, allies guarded his home. Some reportedly stayed on for months after the election.[42]

This level of popular protection became evident early, from the vicinity of the murdered Ivey. After the two August killings, several white Republican officeholders, intimidated, sanctioned Democrat-dominated posses.[43] If the freedmen meant to oppose white horsemen in arms, they were on their own and on uncertain legal footing. Despite this, in northern Sumter County the legislative candidate Warren Dew rode boldly to public meetings, and his bodyguards exchanged shots with interlopers. His fearlessness encouraged mutual confidence. Dew told his followers, "If there came up any company of disguised men to kill me, we must try to kill one out of that company." Dew wasn't subtle: He bragged about that comment, though he denied rumors he had called for random retaliation. Early in September, a deputy came to arrest him for such talk, and after negotiations for his safety in custody broke down, he fled. While in transit, he heard Mississippi horsemen crossing the border, hundreds of them, vowing his death. After his escape, frustrated riders did considerable damage, reportedly torturing Dew's wife for information and rampaging through the neighborhood.[44] But even with Dew in flight and Ivey dead, supporters rallied. After a posse arrested eighteen or so of Dew's followers, Republicans assembled, many crossing the river from Greene. A white woman, Lucy Jackson, heard of a threatened massacre if Dew was hurt and of a crowd of freedmen marching on Gainesville to release the prisoners. Whites barricaded themselves in the town, and no violence actually ensued—the rumored insurrections *never* materialized in these situations—but Lucy Jackson wrote in palpable alarm. She induced a relative to stay in her home, and when a neighbor borrowed her guns, she kept back her last pistol. As she explained, the neighbor "did not think there would be a fight, but they were getting all the rifles they could, so as to shoot at long range. The Negroes only have shot-guns."[45] This reflection can have provided scarce comfort. It must have been an unsettling world, where elite women performed such calculations of racial firepower. The freedpeople did not need to inflict parity in casualties to prove their point, and the turmoil was certain to attract outside attention as confrontations accumulated. Here as elsewhere during Reconstruction, Black resistance served as a tripwire for national intervention.

By the time of the Forkland fight, the disturbances had gone on for perhaps seven weeks, with the Tombigbee River area in continual turmoil for over three. The conflict there coincided with the White League putsch in New Orleans, and with the November election drawing near, President Grant determined on a show of force. Troops arrived in Livingston and fanned out in the region, preceded by detectives who passed themselves off as former Klansmen. After assassination attempts against the detectives, mass arrests ensued, including some forty members of the posse that had gone after Bob Reed, on the dubious grounds of interfering with mail delivery. Soldiers surrounded a Democratic convention, with Renfroe and his associates marched away in handcuffs for federal trial.[46] The balance of social forces changed instantly in the face of forceful intervention and the prospect of legal consequences. "The swamp was full of white men expecting to be arrested," as Reed happily recalled.[47] It was like pulling a plug. The violence stopped, and, astonishingly, the region passed the rest of the campaign season in relative peace. Republicans held a public rally at the county seat of Livingston, the first in some time. That November, with troops nearby but not at the polling places, few reported disturbances occurred anywhere in the district.

Of course, it did not ultimately matter: The statewide results were not what Grant or the freedmen would have wished. The military arrests likely galvanized racist passions in the rest of the state, which were already raw over the civil rights issue. Democrats gained a whopping 25,000 votes, which brought

Reconstruction to a decisive end in Alabama. Amid the wreckage, however, the local results stand out (see Maps 2 and 3). In this most violent section of the state in 1874, with a fierce history of terrorism, the Republican vote surged. In the six counties under study, the Republican vote went from 8,748 in 1872 to 13,343 in 1874, an increase of over 50 percent. In Marengo County, bordering much of the disorder, the Republican vote increased from 1,608 in 1872 to 3,432 two years later.[48] That is to say, the Republican vote doubled in Marengo County across the rivers from the embattled Belmont and Forkland precincts. Still more strikingly, in Greene County the Democrats lost nearly a third of their vote, while Republicans added hundreds to theirs. Interpreting these results is difficult: It could be

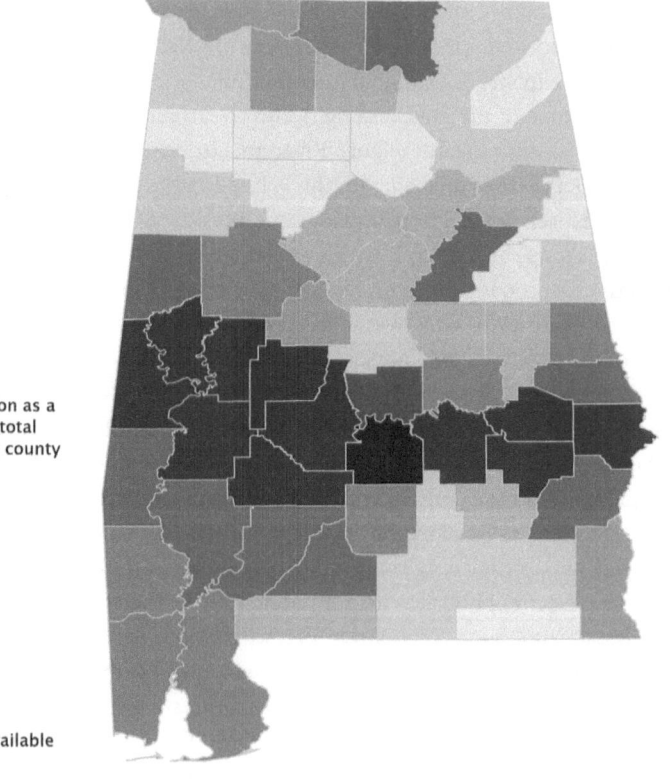

Map 2

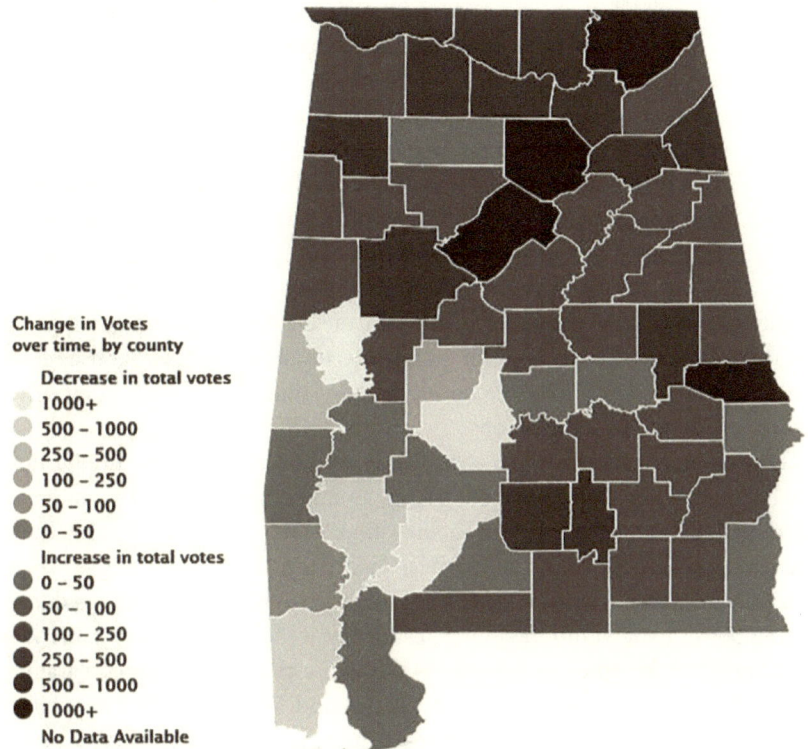

Map 3

that freedmen were voting without coercion, that whites were intimidated from the polls, or that some Mississippians were discouraged from voting illegally. And, of course, the immediate presence of federal troops likely influenced these other factors. What is clear is that White League–style violence backfired where it was most aggressively employed, at least in local electoral terms. And across the state as a whole, even in defeat, Republicans actually gained around four thousand votes.

What, then, do we conclude from this episode? To start with, it is important to give this terrorist mobilization in the western Alabama cotton belt, and others across the South as well, the sort of social analysis that the earlier Klan episode has received. Historians have noticed that the shift to decentralized tenant farming scattered the rural population in ways that enabled Klan operations. The late-1860s terrorism occurred amid agricultural recovery, whereas the mid-1870s version had origins in agricultural dysfunction. The contrast yielded different consequences on the ground. The financial collapse of 1873 uprooted the habits of tentative racial coexistence that had developed on the best cotton lands. As outside credit ceased mid-crop, labor surplus encouraged White Line extremism, and it pointed toward the confrontations to follow. This pattern is true throughout the Black Belt, but the earlier experience of rampant Klan violence in western Alabama exacerbated it. In this rain-sodden terrain, catastrophic crops had another consequence: It made the evicted freedpeople mobile, and it provided them a swampy theater of operations in which they were difficult to defeat. The results proved locally counterproductive for the Democrats, this being the only region in the state where they lost ground electorally in 1874. The consequence here was not its direct influence on Black voting and certainly not its effectiveness in crushing Black aspirations.

One might conclude with an observation on the historiographic implications for Reconstruction politics. Steven Hahn, among others, has noted the proto-Black nationalist overtones of the mobilizations of the mid-1870s, along with the increasing influence of African American leadership. Growing legislative experience certainly encouraged this trend, but there was another dimension to this racial empowerment within the Republican Party. If the Alabama events analyzed here are remotely representative, as politics in the countryside turned paramilitary, different leadership attributes were in demand. When one white Republican ventured into the Forkland disturbances, telling the freedmen to stand down, an angry Black man threatened him, and he fled.[49] The point is that the sort of interracial brokering and legal expertise that white Republican officeholders often provided was less in demand under these circumstances. This was likely one of the factors encouraging the racial-empowerment trends Hahn and numerous others describe. Freedpeople could provide what they needed from leaders for themselves, a point of historiographic significance in terms of the emergence of a politics of Black empowerment in the 1870s.

Black leaders like Bob Reed and Warren Dew took a different approach. They reveled in their effectiveness against their foes, testifying about it later in considerable detail. The whites charged them with provocative rhetoric, especially Ivey and Dew. It may be true, but defiant words served to inspirit their defenders. Their only safety lay in a community roused to protect them, which enabled them to negotiate from a position of some strength. They tried to protect Republican voters through parley and bluster, always backed by the force arrayed behind them. Their leadership profile could not be more different from that of the white Republican officeholders, isolated and fearing for their lives in the county seats.[50] Thus, even knowing the eventual outcome, it is difficult to fault the freedpeople for turning to their own leaders in this final confrontation. One Democratic magistrate, a leader in the Forkland disturbances, discoursed upon the lack of "inward stamina" of African Americans: It was their "natural character . . . to be cowards."[51] He should have known better, and Black leaders had to prove him wrong before their followers to have any hope of preserving their full freedom.

## Notes

1. George C. Rable, *But There Was No Peace: The Role of Violence in the Politics of Reconstruction* (Athens: University of Georgia Press, 1984), 101. The apt phrase is from Steven Hahn, *A Nation under Our Feet: Black Political Struggles in the Rural South from Slavery to the Great Migration* (Cambridge, MA: Harvard University Press, 2005).

2. There is a lively interest in the environmental implications of emancipation, but few have pondered the interaction between the 1870s plantation crisis and political mobilization. See Erin Stewart Mauldin, *Unredeemed Land: An Environmental History of Civil War and Emancipation in the Cotton South* (New York: Oxford University Press, 2019).

3. For the author's broader argument, and for the region in statewide context, see Michael W. Fitzgerald, *Reconstruction in Alabama: From Civil War to Redemption in the Cotton South* (Baton Rouge: Louisiana State University Press, 2017). See also William Warren Rogers, Jr., *Reconstruction Politics in a Deep South State: Alabama, 1865–1874* (Tuscaloosa: University of Alabama Press, 2021).

4. The region is here defined as the contiguous counties of Choctaw, Sumter, and Pickens along the Mississippi border and Clarke, Marengo, and Greene Counties immediately to their east. As for the dead, the index to the three volumes of Alabama Klan testimony totals eleven killed in Greene and twenty-six in Sumter. This represents unusual carnage by contemporary standards, especially where whites were so badly outnumbered. US Congress, *Testimony Taken by the Joint Select Committee to Inquire into the Condition of Affairs in the Late Insurrectionary States* (Washington, DC: GPO, 1872), 8:25, 44–45.

5. Hahn, *A Nation under Our Feet*, 281–82; Allen W. Trelease, *White Terror: The Ku Klux Klan Conspiracy and Southern Reconstruction* (New York: Harper and Row, 1971), 64.

6. *Compendium of the Ninth Census* (Washington, DC: GPO, 1872), 24–25. This proportion understates the reality, in view of the widely reported undercount of African Americans in that census.

7. See Fitzgerald, *Reconstruction in Alabama*, 174–204, 229–36, 257–60.

8. William Warren Rogers Sr. and Ruth Pruitt, *Alabama's Outlaw Sheriff, Stephen S. Renfroe* (1972; Tuscaloosa: University of Alabama Press, 2005), 43–44.

9. See Fitzgerald, *Reconstruction in Alabama*, 257.

10. Fitzgerald, *Reconstruction in Alabama*, 158.

11. Edward E. Baptist, *The Half Has Never Been Told: Slavery and the Making of American Capitalism* (New York: Basic Books, 2014); Sven Beckert, *Empire of Cotton: A Global History* (New York: Knopf, 2014).

12. Fitzgerald, *Reconstruction in Alabama*, 286.

13. See Fitzgerald, *Reconstruction in Alabama*, 288ff., for a more detailed discussion.

14. Fitzgerald, *Reconstruction in Alabama*, 287.

15. *Journal* (Livingston), November 7, 1873.

16. T. A. Hammond to Samuel Pickens, October 8, 1874, Pickens Family Papers, McCall Collection, University of South Alabama.

17. For a discussion of the popular, agrarian overtones of the White Leaguers, see Mitchell Snay, "Democracy and Race in the Late Reconstruction South: The White Leagues of Louisiana," in *Democracy and the American Civil War: Race and African Americans in the Nineteenth Century*, ed. Keven Adams and Leonne M. Hudson (Kent, OH: Kent State University Press, 2016), 83–94.

18. See Fitzgerald, *Reconstruction in Alabama*, 299.

19. See Fitzgerald, *Reconstruction in Alabama*, 299.

20. Fitzgerald, *Reconstruction in Alabama*, 300; US Congress, House, Select Committee on the Condition of Political Affairs in Alabama, 43rd Cong. 2nd Sess., House Report 262 (hereafter cited as "Affairs in Alabama, 1875"), 317, 760, 683; Rogers and Pruitt, *Alabama's Outlaw Sheriff*, 48–49, 66–68; *Beacon* (Greensboro), August 22, October 10, 1874.

21. "Affairs in Alabama, 1875," 1062.

22. See Fitzgerald, *Reconstruction in Alabama*, 303.

23. Thomas Ivey to Gov. Lewis, August 5, 1874, Governor David Lewis Papers, Alabama Department of Archives and History; *Register* (Mobile), September 2, 1874; "Affairs in Alabama, 1875," 658.

24. "Affairs in Alabama, 1875," 17.

25. See William Warren Rogers and Robert David Ward, *August Reckoning: Jack Turner and Racism in Post–Civil War Alabama* (Baton Rouge: Louisiana State University Press, 1973), 24–54; *Register* (Mobile), August 7, 1874; *Beacon* (Greensboro), September 5, 1874; "Affairs in Alabama, 1875," 673. This is the same Jack Turner who would be lynched in a false insurrection scare the following decade.

26. Reconstituting the timing for these complicated episodes is difficult: Here is a timeline drawn primarily from press accounts, especially the Mobile *Register*, which monitored the reports from a distance. The Democratic state convention convened on July 29. Billings was shot on August 1; the Clarke County disturbances began in late July and peaked around August 7, spreading into Choctaw for the Jack Turner shootout on the thirteenth. After some weeks of political activities, Ivey was killed on August 29. The inconclusive Eutaw rally occurred on September 5, with the Dew confrontation several days after that. The Robinson killing at Forkland occurred on the fourteenth, the Durden ferry confrontation about the sixteenth, with the Reed posse arriving on the evening of the eighteenth. As for the army, it arrived in Livingston, the county seat of Sumter County, on September 11, and it spread out in the weeks ahead. This order of events is more precise than the version given in Fitzgerald, *Reconstruction in Alabama*.

27. See Fitzgerald, *Reconstruction in Alabama*, 304.

28. Democrats claimed that a local distribution of federal relief to flood victims had miscarried, prompting the disturbances in Forkland precinct and providing an excuse for white posses. It is difficult to untangle the basis for this convenient version, but one of the Democratic officials suggested he had interfered in the food distribution. If this was the case, it might explain one contributing factor in the unrest. Of course, the previous killings and threats probably had more to do with the freedmen's behavior. See "Affairs in Alabama, 1875," 530, 639, 908; *Beacon* (Greensboro), September 5, 1874.

29. "Affairs in Alabama, 1875," 690.

30. *Register* (Mobile), September 18, 20, 1874; "Affairs in Alabama, 1875," 908–9. There is an excellent description of the initial Robinson firefight in Mary Ellen Curtin, *Black Prisoners and Their World, Alabama, 1865–1900* (Charlottesville: University Press of Virginia, 2000), 12–18. Several of the Black participants in the shootout would serve long prison terms.

31. "Affairs in Alabama, 1875," 18–19.

32. "Affairs in Alabama, 1875," 908, 19, 1180.

33. "Affairs in Alabama, 1875," 909.

34. "Affairs in Alabama, 1875," 920, 1176, 1183.

35. "Affairs in Alabama, 1875," 19; *Journal* (Livingston), September 25, 1874.

36. "Affairs in Alabama, 1875," 1147.

37. "Affairs in Alabama, 1875," 673.

38. Fitzgerald, *Reconstruction in Alabama*, 305; "Affairs in Alabama, 1875," 1022.

39. Affairs in Alabama, 1875," 908; Samuel Pickens to James Pickens, October 22, 1874; [Mary] Pickens to S. Pickens, October 7, 1874; James Pickens to S. Pickens, October 19, 1874, in Pickens Papers, McCall Collection, University of South Alabama.

40. One hesitates to say this is the actual number of deaths because it is probable African Americans were being killed by Democratic bands in out-of-the-way places. The Republican accounts say so, and Democratic newspapers suggest this as well. Still, in terms of open assassinations or firefights sufficiently severe to gather outside notice, this number should be approximately accurate.

41. Fitzgerald, *Reconstruction in Alabama*, 311–12.

42. "Affairs in Alabama, 1875," 17.

43. "Affairs in Alabama, 1875," 1057.

44. "Affairs in Alabama, 1875," 914–17; *Register* (Mobile), September 11, 16, 1874.

45. Lucy Jackson to husband, September 12, 1874, Susalee Smith Papers, University of West Alabama.

46. "Affairs in Alabama, 1875," 1154, 919, 679.

47. "Affairs in Alabama, 1875," 307.

48. The dramatic gains probably owe much to Democratic officials' electoral fraud in the 1872 election, but certainly the results also reflected strong Republican turnout in 1874. Fitzgerald, *Reconstruction in Alabama*, 268–71.

49. "Affairs in Alabama, 1875," 639.

50. "Affairs in Alabama, 1875," 664.

51. "Affairs in Alabama, 1875," 910.

# "They Mustered a Whole Company of Kuklux as Militia"

*State Violence and Black Freedoms in Kentucky's Readjustment*

## Shannon M. Smith

On Election Day, August 7, 1871, six years after the end of the Civil War and just the second year of Black voting rights in Frankfort, Kentucky, several hundred Black and white residents gathered just after the polls closed to hear the election results. When local officials announced that the Republican candidate, former Kentucky attorney general and future US Supreme Court associate justice John Marshall Harlan, had received nearly one hundred votes more than the Democratic incumbent, Preston H. Leslie, the cheering turned to violence. White men chased the assembled Black voters through town until the fleeing Black men turned to stand their ground, throwing bricks, rocks, and other objects at their pursuers. Witnesses asserted that the first shots came from the white crowd, but the Black men quickly returned fire and eventually fled the scene.[1]

Many on each side were wounded, and two white men lay dead. Wounded Black men were removed from the scene by their friends so they would not be arrested. One Black man, Henry Washington, had wounds to his left eye and upper thigh. He was arrested for starting the riot and accused of shooting William Gilmore, a clerk in the state auditor's office. He was lodged in the Frankfort jail with two other Black men, Joseph Roach and William Taylor, who were arrested for disorderly conduct. No white men were arrested for their part in the riot.[2]

That night, crowds of white Democrats patrolled the streets and talked of cleaning out the Black neighborhoods and the "damned white Radicals." Black residents retreated to their homes for the evening. Fearing more violence, Frankfort's mayor, Edmund H. Taylor Jr., called out the local militia, the Valley Rifles, to maintain order on the city streets and to guard the jail. About forty militia members promised to remain at their posts overnight but left around midnight.

Soon at least fifty men on horseback, some in disguise, gathered at the jail and demanded the keys from a frightened and compliant jailer. The prisoner William Taylor reported that one man said, "Let's take 'em out and hang 'em all," but the raiders chose specific targets: Henry Washington, badly wounded from the day's violence, and Harry Johnson, a Black man who had been arrested the prior Wednesday for the alleged rape of a German woman.[3]

The men on horseback took Washington and Johnson to South Frankfort, near the home of Judge George Drane, the county's Republican prosecuting attorney. There the vigilantes hanged Johnson without formality. The mob took more time with Washington. In a grisly example of the "awful ceremonies of the regularly organized bands that prowl around the State committing deeds of violence," reported the Republican *Louisville Commercial*, the men toyed with Washington for several minutes before one man reportedly stated, "May the Lord have mercy on your soul." Washington was jerked from his feet and hanged. Washington's and Johnson's bodies were removed from the tree the next day, placed in coffins, and brought to the courthouse, where their bodies were displayed for a short time with the ropes still around their necks.[4]

In the following days, some Frankfort citizens called for an investigation into the lynching and its effects on the community. Republican newspapers howled with outrage and demanded the prosecution of those responsible. When county judges argued that an investigation might incite further racial violence, the *Louisville Commercial* countered that the investigation was delayed "for fear that some of the sons of our best citizens will be found to be implicated." The *Commercial* continued:

> The mayor and the county judge must have known that the militia could not be relied on. They must know now that the mob that hung the negroes, whom the militia undertook to guard, was composed in pretty large proportion of that militia. They must have known it before the hanging, and must know it now, because pretty much everybody knows it.[5]

Indeed, some of Kentucky's "best sons" and militiamen were implicated in the lynching, which had lasting effects on the rights of African Americans and the role of the federal government in the state.

The election-day rioting and the militia's lynching of Washington and Johnson in August 1871 resulted in a court case that forced the Kentucky legislature to make a decision on an issue that had caused turmoil for several years: Either grant Black people the right to testify in state courts or face ongoing federal intervention in their judicial system. In September, federal marshals arrested several members of the Valley Rifles militia and charged them in a US district court for the deaths of Washington and Johnson. Prompted by their trial, the Democratic-controlled legislature chose to accept Black testimony in hopes of returning the case to a Kentucky state court and ending federal oversight. But that change caused the federal government to withdraw the essential protection of federal courts for Black citizens. Black Kentuckians gained the right to testify in Kentucky courts but lost one of their main avenues to protest the violation of civil rights, while white Democrats rid themselves of unwanted federal supervision. What appeared to be a victory for Black men in the Reconstruction era in fact became a tool for further subjugation.

Black freedoms gained quickly became freedoms lost. Kentucky's social order had long been established through white men's control of particular activities— voting, testifying in court, armed protection of one's home, militia service, and economic independence. As Black men claimed these actions for themselves, they encountered the complexities of establishing Black freedoms following the Civil War. The achievement of some citizenship rights did not mean equality. When they tried to exercise their legal rights by voting, they were driven from the polls. When they defended their interests at elections or in their homes or workplaces, white city and state officials accused them of uncontrolled aggression. Under the guise of maintaining "law and order," the Kentucky state militia wielded tremendous power and flexibility in violently subduing Black citizens who challenged the social or political order. Without the full force of federal military and judicial authority to protect freedpeople, the struggle for freedom and civil rights in border states such as Kentucky was even more tenuous. Pervasive violence dictated the terms of freedom for many freedpeople, even as they sought to use government structures to secure safety and political power. The fight to determine the meaning of emancipation and "practical freedom" occurred at the polls, on the streets, and in the courtrooms of Kentucky.[6]

Kentucky offers important comparisons to former Confederate states during the Reconstruction era. The border state had remained loyal to the Union during the Civil War, sending approximately ninety thousand troops to the Union army while twenty-five to forty thousand chose to fight for the Confederacy. However, by war's end Kentucky appeared more and more Confederate in character. Its southern, pro-Confederate regional identity had grown in response to the expanding reach of the federal government into state affairs and the Union's embrace of emancipation as a war goal. Postwar anger toward the Republican-dominated federal government led to the triumph of the Democratic Party in Kentucky. Because the state had never seceded from the Union, Kentucky did not undergo federal Reconstruction but instead a period of "Readjustment." White men were not disfranchised following the war, and the state was not forced to hold multiracial elections, as other southern states were, until the ratification of the Fifteenth Amendment in 1870. Many white voters—including former Union and Confederate soldiers—found common ground in racial politics, particularly the fear of forced equality with African Americans. The Democratic *Louisville Courier-Journal* argued that Republicans were defeated as a "silent and outstanding protest against years of wrong." As the historian Anne E. Marshall has argued, "voting Democrat was retaliation for the tight reign of martial law during the war, for the perceived injustice of Reconstruction further south, and, most of all, for the violation of racial order in their own state." Even though factions divided the party, Democrats remained in tight control of the state government in Frankfort. The antislavery Republican Party had never been popular in Kentucky, and even the combination of Black and white Republican votes in the 1870s could not unseat Democratic power statewide—although they could influence local elections, as in Frankfort. Unlike most former Confederate states facing Congressional Reconstruction, Kentucky did not elect a Republican governor until 1895. Although vastly outnumbered, Black and white Republicans advocated for their vision of full Black citizenship, free labor, and industry after the end of slavery.[7]

White Democratic voters were infuriated by the ongoing federal presence in their state. Like former Confederate states, the enforcement of federal laws in Kentucky was dependent on the reach of the US Army. In September 1865, over 80 percent of the US Army troops stationed in the Bluegrass region were Black, which caused concern and anger among former enslavers and many white citizens. The army maintained martial law until October 1865, and the Freedmen's Bureau was active until 1868. Although US Army troops were stationed throughout Kentucky in the late 1860s and early 1870s, the state was not under military control. Civil authorities had to request assistance from federal troops before the military could aid local governments, enforce laws, or offer protection. In a state overwhelmingly controlled by Democrats and skeptical of federal intervention, it was unusual for civil authorities to ask for US military assistance. Federal courts remained a prominent icon of federal intervention into the 1870s as they enforced civil rights for freedpeople because Kentucky state courts refused to allow Black witnesses to testify. That was a contentious political issue as white Kentuckians weighed their options—to admit Black testimony or allow ongoing federal intervention in the court system.[8]

The election riot and lynching in Frankfort came at a time of significant demographic change in Kentucky. Slavery had been less vital to Kentucky's economy than it was in the lower South, but nearly 30 percent of white families had enslaved people. Most were small landholders, with more than half enslaving fewer than five people. Yet 95 percent of Black Kentuckians were enslaved before the war, with most residing in the eleven-county Bluegrass region and the corridor between Lexington, Frankfort, and Louisville. Since Kentucky had never seceded from the Union, slavery was legal following the end of the Civil War. Emancipation did not come with the military as it had in Confederate states. About seventy thousand African Americans statewide remained enslaved until passage of the Thirteenth Amendment in December 1865. The wartime defection and enlistment of approximately thirty thousand Black Kentuckians had seemed to white enslavers like an uprising. Nearly 70 percent of enslaved people in Kentucky had ended their bondage by serving in the US Army or through family military affiliations. Many of those enlisted Black soldiers remained stationed in Bluegrass towns into 1866 to guard against Confederate and guerrilla attacks and to maintain civil order, now in a position of power over their former enslavers. With emancipation, some formerly enslaved people purchased their own land and created free Black settlements; others left the state altogether, moving to nearby Cincinnati or other northern Black communities. By 1870, Kentucky's Black population had dropped by 6 percent, with an even greater decrease in the Bluegrass counties. The Black populations of cities like Lexington, Louisville, and Frankfort, however, grew exponentially as formerly enslaved people fled to urban communities seeking employment and safety in numbers. This newfound mobility angered white landowners and white laborers, now competing with Black workers for property and jobs.[9]

The population changes were striking in the capital city of Frankfort on the northwestern edge of Kentucky's fertile Bluegrass region. The population of the county seat of Frankfort grew by nearly 46 percent during the 1860s, with most of that growth coming from the burgeoning Black population, which nearly doubled from 1,282 to 2,335. This boom, combined with the county's moderate overall growth rate, suggests that many African Americans simply shifted their residences from rural areas into the city. As Frankfort's population grew, so did white residents' anxieties. The 1870 census reported that more than 40 percent of the city's population was African American. Many freedpeople settled alongside white neighbors in cheap, working-class areas.[10]

Black migration into the cities—whether to seek better work, to gain safety from violence in the countryside, to get away from former enslavers, or simply because they could—disrupted white men's control of the state's economic and labor systems in the late 1860s and early 1870s. Urban Black residents often had a hard time finding employment. Many Bluegrass towns passed strict vagrancy laws that were enforced only for African Americans, even though many whites also were out of work. Rural Black workers also struggled for power in the changed agricultural economy. Many tried to purchase their own land, yet agricultural wage labor remained more common than ownership, sharecropping, or tenancy.[11]

Black Kentuckians, having demonstrated their loyalty to the Union during the war, turned their focus to demanding the rights and responsibilities of citizenship. In that effort they used many forms of protest and government action: holding large conventions to demand suffrage and the right to testify in court; submitting petitions to local, state, and federal leaders; protesting through the courts; organizing economic boycotts; and pursuing other forms of direct collective action. At an 1867 celebration of the Emancipation Proclamation, the Black political leader William F. Butler argued for the need to fight for one's rights:

> First we have the cartridge box, now we want the ballot box, and soon we will get the jury box. I don't mean with our fists, but by standing up and demanding our rights. We went out and fought the battles of our country, and gained our liberties, but we were left without means of protecting ourselves in the employment of that liberty. We need and must have the ballot box for that purpose.[12]

Black Union veterans asserted the right to protect themselves physically and with the tools of citizenship. Delegates to the 1867 Lexington convention argued that in return for their military service in the Civil War, the government should honor the "well-established principle of just government, that allegiance and protection go together." Black men tried to protect themselves with weapons they brought home from their military service, but local sheriffs seized weapons as veterans disembarked from trains. Black leaders decried the withholding of social and political rights: "We are told to wait. We have already waited til our very manhood cries out if not for protection, for the inalienable right to protect ourselves."[13]

In the face of rampant violence, Black Kentuckians increased their efforts to secure the right to testify in court. African Americans denounced the "unnatural, inhuman and unjust ban" on Black testimony in Kentucky courts, a law that went against the laws of most other states and federal law. One Kentucky case, *Blyew v. United States*, took the question of Black testimony to the Supreme Court in

1871: "To deprive a whole class of the community of this right . . . is to brand them with a badge of slavery," argued the two dissenting justices. "The right for a Black person to testify on his or her own behalf is *his protection against violence and wrong.*" A Black congressional delegation from Frankfort in 1871 argued that while the legislature refused to grant equal rights in the courts, "our people are driven from their homes in great numbers, having no redress [except] in the United States court, which is in many cases unable to reach them." In accordance with the Civil Rights Act of 1866, federal district courts overseen by a US commissioner had taken over cases in which Black people lacked sufficient protection—a move that Kentucky Democrats viewed as a further intrusion of federal power.[14]

Black activism and the threat of federal intervention had an effect. As early as 1867, some white Kentuckians began urging the state legislature to reverse its position on Black testimony just to put an end to such perceived federal interference. But the Kentucky legislature refused to modify its position. "It is the determination of the law-making power to make Kentucky the sole power on the face of the earth . . . where the citizens of the State may be murdered, robbed, or maimed with impunity," wrote the Republican *Frankfort Commonwealth*. "That is why the Legislature will not allow negro testimony in courts of justice."[15]

The state had experienced bouts of anti-Black collective violence since the end of the Civil War, but the Frankfort area had seen an increase in "Kukluxing" in the months leading up to and following passage of the Fifteenth Amendment and Black voting rights in February 1870. Indeed, more lynchings took place in Kentucky in the fifteen years after the Civil War than during any other fifteen-year period. The Bluegrass was the epicenter of the violence in Kentucky, but there was a "virtual yielding of the entire State to this lawless band" as it spread into the more rugged counties surrounding Frankfort. Forced to abandon their homes, their land, and their crops, hundreds of Black people from Franklin and nearby Henry, Owen, and Scott counties fled into Frankfort in the late 1860s and 1870s.[16]

In March 1871, Frankfort's Black citizens submitted an appeal to the US Congress for federal intervention. It listed 116 acts of violence in the previous two years. White raiders were "riding nightly over the country," complained Frankfort residents, "spreading terror wherever they go by robbing, whipping, ravishing and killing our people without provocation." The armed white bands targeted African American men, especially Union veterans, who were politically active or economically successful—taking away weapons, punishing those who pushed for higher wages, intimidating workers into signing labor contracts, or forcing families to abandon their land and crops.[17]

Frankfort's Black residents blamed the violence not only on white regulators but also on Kentucky's Democratic militia—the "organized bands of desperate and lawless men, mainly composed of soldiers of the late rebel armies, armed, disciplined, and disguised." Rather than uphold rights and restore order, Kentucky's militia impeded the effects of emancipation and Black political activism. As the historian Patrick A. Lewis has argued, the State Guard was "the legitimate military organization that complemented Kentucky's paramilitary Ku Klux. . . . Because they were a state sanctioned, funded, and armed body, militia companies had a claim to legal and social legitimacy that no band of night riders could have." The *Frankfort Commonwealth* saw little difference between vigilante white raiders and the state-authorized militia. Instead, when the governor called upon the State Guard, "they muster[ed] a whole company of Kuklux as militia" that committed violence with the sanction of law.[18]

The Kentucky State Guard of the 1870s was a collection of local independent companies, underfunded and disorganized, authorized by the state legislature but without substantial state funding or oversight. The militia's lack of state supervision contributed to struggles between state and local authority because mayors and sheriffs could call out the militia without the governor's approval. Passage of the Fifteenth Amendment in February 1870 prompted the formation of new Bluegrass militia companies, including the Valley Rifles in Frankfort. Such local units were typically composed of middle- to upper-class Democratic white men, often the sons of prominent citizens, who had been too young to serve in the Civil War. Militia companies relied heavily on support from wealthier community members as they were responsible for their own uniforms and equipment, except for weapons, which were distributed from the state arsenal. Young men saw militia service as an opportunity to claim the honor, rights, and privileges that their fathers had enjoyed before the war but that they believed to be threatened by the growing economic and political power of Black men. The *Louisville Commercial* argued, "We have, then, a militia for the State of Kentucky composed of members of one political party, and designed solely to operate against members of another political party. These militia are armed with State guns, are equipped from the State arsenal, and to a man are the enemies of the national government." Because the militia had legitimate social standing, they could enhance their own business and social prospects while claiming the civil authority to preside over elections.[19]

While the militia and regulators tried to maintain control over African Americans through violence, state courts upheld white domination by excluding Black testimony. But the ongoing federal presence through the courts and potential interference of the US Army jeopardized that control. Black political activity, the petitions of white and Black Republicans, and the outcry of white landowners who relied on Black workers placed mounting pressure on Kentucky lawmakers. Republican newspapers blamed the "Kuklux Democracy" in control of the state legislature for their failure to enforce civil order and for refusing to increase local law enforcement funding. The *Louisville Commercial* condemned the "reign of terror" in Franklin County and demanded a federal investigation and federal troops to put an end to the raids, since "*in Kentucky, under Democratic rule, the civil authorities are subordinate to the Kuklux power.*" If the state lacked the power or the will to protect Kentucky citizens, the *Commercial* argued, "the National Government, having both the power and the will, must be appealed to." The paucity of convictions in state courts was a major factor in the federal courts' active stance in Kentucky.[20]

Because the state of Kentucky refused to allow Black testimony in state courts, federal courts intervened. Abraham Lincoln's former attorney general, James F. Speed, believed that the threat of federal enforcement would end the violence. Speed reminded those angry at federal interference in local matters that if "the county authorities do their duty with fidelity, the State will not interfere. Let the State do its duty faithfully, and the General Government will not interfere." This ultimatum prompted growing numbers of white Democratic Kentuckians to rethink their opposition to Black testimony as a means of freeing themselves of federal oversight.[21]

Facing the threat of an increasing militia presence in the region and at the polls, African Americans advocated to protect themselves—in the form of armed self-defense and of legal testimony—to accompany the vote. Black voters faced violent threats at the first elections after the passage of the Fifteenth Amendment in 1870. While the Democratic Party maintained firm control over the state, the votes of Black and white Republicans combined to give the party a majority or near-majority in several Bluegrass counties. White militia groups, trying to intimidate Republican voters through public drilling in the days before the vote, warned that they were prepared to "clean out" Republican voters using weapons from the state arsenal. The militia was an ever-present force at polling places. The August 1870 election saw riots, shootings, and fights between Black and white voters in Lexington, Versailles, and other Bluegrass cities, with several men killed. As a result of this violence, many Republican voters were forced from the polls or left when it was clear that they would not be permitted to vote. A Republican judge in Lexington urged Black voters to persevere: "The Democrats have resorted to the political trick of forming military companies in the hopes of scaring you and keeping you from the polls . . . you have the right to vote, and this right is worth risking something for."[22]

Compared to other parts of the Bluegrass, the Frankfort election was rather calm in August 1870. Black voters turned out to vote but faced many challenges. Democratic election officials reportedly refused to accept the votes of Republicans, claiming that some Black voters were ineligible to vote because they owed back taxes, and used various informal means to disfranchise others. The Frankfort Valley Rifles, armed with weapons from the state arsenal, intimidated voters at the polls. A. G. Hodges, editor of the Republican *Commonwealth*, argued that it would be necessary to find other means of disfranchising Frankfort Republican voters, since the "night marching of the Democratic militia" had failed to scare them away from the polls. Nevertheless, the Kentucky adjutant general issued an order prohibiting militia companies from holding a parade or muster day within five days of the November 1870 general election. That election passed off without violence.[23]

As Frankfort Democrats tried to shore up their power, the hostility of August turned to open violence at a city election in January 1871. A barricade between white and Black voters prevented confrontations for most of the day, but gunfire later erupted between Black and white voters waiting to cast their ballot. An Irish grocer and father of six, William Newman, was killed, and several men were wounded. Democratic papers praised the Valley Rifles for patrolling the election and deterring future Black voters. Such injustice at the polls, argued the *Cincinnati Commercial Tribune*, rendered the growing Republican minority impotent: "When a Republican lobbies he wastes his time, when he talks he wastes his talk, and when he votes he wastes his vote. He is a living, moving, breathing nonentity." City leaders—likely the same men who formed and financially supported the militia company—claimed no knowledge of the militia's presence at the polls, even though witnesses said several "men in high authority" had been aware of the plan.[24]

In response to ongoing election violence and widespread terror campaigns by white regulators throughout the country, Congress passed a series of enforcement acts. Beginning in 1870, US commissioners could request federal troops to protect freedpeople's voting rights and to support the jurisdiction of federal courts, with further authorization in the Ku Klux Klan Act of April 1871. This immediately changed the political and military landscape of Kentucky's Bluegrass region. While there were few federal troops stationed in Kentucky in the summer of 1870, by March 1871 there were 163 troops in Frankfort, 668 in Louisville, and several hundred more in the area. Those numbers rose to 207 in Frankfort in April, and in August 1871, around the time of the election riot, there were 143 troops in Frankfort. While the US Army could make arrests, they had no authority to punish Klansmen. They had to rely on the court system, and especially the reach of federal courts, to enact change.[25]

The Frankfort riot in August 1871 came as no surprise to observers. The response from Kentucky's intensely partisan newspapers, all of it blaming the behavior of the other party's voters, came swiftly. "Of course there were riots," wrote the *Cincinnati Gazette*, "true Kentucky Democrats can hardly hold an election without resorting to bullets." The Republican *Louisville Commercial* complained that "white Democrats have a right to wear arms . . . but for a negro to wear arms to defend his life, or to shoot when attacked, is cause for their indiscriminate massacre." Democratic papers such as the *Frankfort Yeoman* reported on the "bad conduct" of "half-civilized" Black people and applauded Frankfort's white citizens for exercising tolerance at the polls.[26]

A Franklin County circuit court grand jury met at the end of August 1871 to investigate the election riot and lynching. In his charge to the grand jury, Judge William S. Pryor, a Democrat of nearby Henry County, argued that "somebody was responsible" for the "violations of law and order, by Kuklux and mob organizations." Pryor believed that the vigilantes were local men familiar with the city and the jail—a radical statement that placed Pryor in jeopardy of retaliation. Pryor warned the jury of the dire consequences of federal intervention—including the imposition of martial law—if they did not enforce the law. The grand jury examined nearly forty witnesses, Black and white, and placed responsibility for the election riot on the "drunk and defiant" African Americans at the polls. They further concluded that it was impossible to verify who was involved in the lynching, since the parties were disguised. The Republican *Commercial* predictably disagreed with the grand jury's assessment, writing that the group had "been unable, after diligent inquiry, to find out what is known to about every other man in Frankfort concerning the riots there." The jury made no recommendations for arrests. But the case was not closed for good—federal intervention was yet to come.[27]

In August 1871, for the first time since the war, Republicans actually captured some local offices. Although John Marshall Harlan did not win the governor's seat in 1871, Republicans made sufficient gains for the *Frankfort Commonwealth* to proclaim, "The rising tide of Republicanism will swell until it sweeps over the advocate of caste, of lawlessness, and social tyranny. Look at the figures!" Harlan won Lexington and Fayette counties and came within a few hundred votes in other Bluegrass counties. Nearly ninety thousand people statewide voted Republican. The *Cincinnati Gazette* speculated that Kentucky "is not so hopelessly beyond redemption as had been feared."[28]

Democrats retained control of Kentucky's government after the 1871 election, but the newly elected governor Preston Leslie still brought major changes to the state. Determined to rid Kentucky of federal interference, Leslie threw his support behind changing state laws against Black testimony so juries could review all the facts of a case. More importantly, Leslie argued, refusing testimony simply strengthened the federal government's justification for controlling Kentucky courts. Leslie still objected to allowing Black men to sit on juries, however, because he claimed they could not competently make decisions. More and more white Kentuckians agreed with Leslie and pressed the legislature to allow African Americans to testify in court.[29]

The reason for many white Kentuckians' change of heart regarding Black testimony was not just to end federal intrusion in the courts or to begin to change Kentucky's national reputation for lawlessness. The real reason for the agitation hinged on the indictment of members of the Valley Rifles for the lynching of Washington and Johnson. In September 1871, the federal courts still had jurisdiction in civil rights cases. Within a week of the Franklin County court's failure to indict anyone for the murders of Washington and Johnson, federal marshals arrested several prominent young Frankfort men—Richard Crittenden, James Alley, and D. Howard Smith Jr.—on charges of participating in the election-night lynching. The young men were taken to jail in Louisville and charges were filed in the city's US district court. They were accompanied by their fathers "and a number of the prominent citizens of Frankfort, all of whom seemed deeply interested in the grave charge made against the sons of the most prominent and respected citizens of Frankfort." The men were defended by powerful attorneys, including former governor Thomas Bramlette and the recently defeated gubernatorial candidate John Marshall Harlan. With those young men on trial, the *Frankfort Commonwealth* argued that it was impossible for the jury to get all of the facts in the case. There was no way that any Frankfort resident could testify against the accused and then return safely to the city: "He would be hung by a [mob] inside of twenty-four hours, and the dominant sentiment, which is Democratic, would say 'served him right.'"[30]

Newspapers reported that the men were all "respectably connected" in the Frankfort community. And so they were. They were also connected to one another, and several were rising stars in the city. Among those arrested was twenty-six-year-old Howard Smith Jr., the son of the state auditor. He worked as a clerk in his father's office and would have had firsthand knowledge of the close voting results. Alongside Smith was twenty-year-old Richard Crittenden, also a politician's son and the great-nephew of the former governor, senator, and US attorney general John J. Crittenden. Richard's father, John A. Crittenden, was a former deputy sheriff who also served with Smith as a clerk in the state auditor's office. Twenty-one-year-old James Alley, the son of a grocer, had been arrested but released for inciting election violence in January 1871. Marshals issued additional warrants for Howard Walcutt and other sons of prominent families and even a guard at the jail.[31]

The most important association that all these young men shared was their membership in the Valley Rifles. The company had formed in July 1870, with Richard's father, John, serving as one of the judges of the officers' election and possibly as a benefactor. William Gilmore, who was killed in the election riot, was a member of the Valley Rifles and worked with Howard Smith as a clerk in the state auditor's office. He was a recent arrival from Lexington, so the militia company would have offered a way to make friends and create a community in his new city. Such close associations could have prompted his friends to seek revenge against Henry Washington, whom they believed responsible for Gilmore's death. Several other members of the company promptly left town the day after the lynchings.[32]

The lynchings were both political and deeply personal. Henry Washington epitomized the class of Black men whom some powerful white men feared and despised. Washington had escaped life as an enslaved farm laborer to enlist in the US Army and may have patrolled Kentucky until April 1866. That role would have placed him in a position of authority and law enforcement over his former enslaver and the white enslaving class more generally. By 1870, Washington, then thirty years old, had returned to Frankfort and was working as a barber. Henry Washington was certainly more independent and financially secure than the majority of Black men who were employed as day laborers, and he likely ranked in the higher echelons of Frankfort's Black business community. The social position and background of Harry Johnson is less clear, although it was possible that white men saw another opportunity to do away with a Black veteran. Together, the lynchings of Washington and Johnson at the hands of the militia served notice to Black men who dared to challenge the racial order and white men's right to run the city.³³

Commissioner W. A. Meriwether of the US federal court in Louisville began hearing testimony against the Frankfort men on September 23, 1871. The prosecution and Republican newspapers asserted that the Valley Rifles were involved in the deaths of Johnson and Washington with the full knowledge and support of prominent Democrats. The *Louisville Commercial* believed that any Democratic official could quickly name twenty members of the militia who had participated in the lynching. "These militia are sworn to maintain the law," bemoaned the paper's editors, "and yet they refuse to maintain it in the very capital of Kentucky. Was there ever [a] disgrace so overwhelming?" Furthermore, the *Commercial* contended that the members of the Valley Rifles could name the leaders of the lynch mob, but "there isn't power enough in Kentucky to compel them to."³⁴

The prosecution linked the Valley Rifles to the scene of the lynching through the discovery of a needle gun—the weapons issued to the militia from the state arsenal—at the base of the tree from which Washington was hanged. The arsenal superintendent reported that Howard Walcutt had signed for thirteen guns on the day of the riot, but the state arsenal had also issued guns to local citizens during the election brawl. Furthermore, the federal troops stationed in Frankfort also used needle guns, so Valley Rifles officers claimed the weapon had most likely come from them.³⁵

Federal troops had been involved in keeping the peace in Frankfort just before the election. After Harry Johnson was arrested on rape charges, the Valley Rifles had refused to guard the jail on August 2, five nights before the election. Fearing a lynching, Franklin County judge Robert Thompson had requested the assistance of federal troops to protect Johnson, since they could not respond unless called by the governor, mayor, or a county judge. City leaders criticized Thompson for inviting federal assistance in local affairs. He dared not make the same mistake a few nights later by soliciting federal troops to guard Washington, so the mayor requested the Valley Rifles instead.³⁶

Fearing for their safety or their positions in the community, white witnesses were unable or unwilling to positively identify any members of the lynch mob. The *Louisville Commercial* offered a scathing rebuke of witnesses who claimed to know nothing. Even if the Valley Rifles were not involved in the lynching, they had failed spectacularly in their duty to protect prisoners. Fellow militia members offered alibis for the men's whereabouts at the time of the jail raid, and the defense repeatedly asserted that the raiders were not Frankfort men. The real culprits, the defense asserted, were a "body of men [who] came into town *from the country*" and raided the jail.³⁷

The star witnesses for the prosecution were two Black prisoners, Joseph Roach and William Taylor, who had been jailed with Washington and Johnson. Like Washington, Roach was a Union veteran and had gained valuable experience from his military service. He quickly identified Howard Walcutt and Richard Crittenden as the men who had taken Washington and Johnson from the jail. Roach testified that Crittenden, whom he knew well, had been on duty with the militia earlier in the evening talking about a "yellow man who, he said, had pushed him, and he was going to hang him."³⁸

William Taylor had moved into Frankfort after emancipation and had worked for John Walcutt, Howard's grandfather, for three years. He identified several of the jail raiders—Crittenden and Walcutt had entered the jail, James Alley guarded the door, and Howard Smith had been looking in the window. Taylor explained that he had seen the men's faces in the lantern light because they did not disguise themselves until they left with Johnson and Washington. When he heard the men outside stating that they were planning to hang all the Black prisoners, Taylor "was anxious to see who they were; when they came in I looked with all my heart at all of them; because if they were going to hang me I would beg them to let me off." He heard another member of the Valley Rifles bragging the next day that he "had taken two G_d d_n niggers out the night before and broken their d_n necks, and he would take us all out that night." Taylor had been afraid to speak about the incident until the trial, and he and Roach had each feared to testify without the support of the other.³⁹

The defense focused on discrediting Taylor's and Roach's testimony by trying to catch the men in contradictions or by attacking their characters. Conversely, the defense brought in a parade of witnesses to testify to the good characters of the accused. Mayor Taylor, whose son was a member of the Valley Rifles, and several other witnesses asserted that Crittenden, Smith, Alley, and Walcutt were of good character, well behaved, respectful, and peaceable. Alley was discharged by US Commissioner Meriwether, but Crittenden and Walcutt remained in custody.⁴⁰

In October, with Crittenden and Walcutt still under indictment for the lynching of Washington and Johnson, the trial was put on hold. Rumors had circulated in Frankfort that the Ku Klux Klan was planning to travel to Louisville to release the prisoners, but the precaution proved unnecessary. The men were released on bail and returned to Frankfort. Critics believed that the trial was delayed because of the prominent status of the defendants' families and the pressure exerted on the court. Important citizens could typically afford more skillful attorneys to represent them. It was not uncommon in Kentucky for influential local residents to pressure prosecutors and judges—either by bribery or threat—to drop charges against friends and relatives under indictment. But such influence on the federal court was something new: "The Kuklux have already overawed every court of the State in the counties where that organization exists, and now the Federal Court is expected to yield to their demands." US Commissioner Meriwether admitted to feeling such pressure: "When you strike a Crittenden you strike the state." The trial was set to resume in January in the US circuit court, but an overload of cases forced the court to postpone it until the next court session in April.[41]

In addition to defending Frankfort's leading sons, the trial drew increasing attention to the ongoing question of federal authority in state affairs. US district court judge Bland Ballard asserted that the case was only being heard in the US district court because of Kentucky's failure to admit Black testimony, stating jurisdiction "is founded solely upon the denial by the State of Kentucky of the equal protection of the laws to this class of persons." If Kentucky were to change its laws and authorize Black testimony in state courts, the federal jurisdiction would immediately end. In the case against the Frankfort men, wrote the *Louisville Commercial*, "federal authorities stepped in to do what the State could not do"—in essence enacting the role of federal Reconstruction in a state that had never joined the Confederacy. Anger toward the federal government had two causes, the *Commercial* continued: a more strict enforcement of criminal law in federal court than in state courts and "the indignation of a people, not yet accustomed to recognize in their late slaves citizens, with all the rights of citizens, at what they consider and eloquently denounce as the damned impudence of niggers in swearing against White men." The Kentucky legislature realized they could keep cases out of federal court if they just amended the testimony law. Frankfort's representative to Congress vowed publicly that he would "move heaven and earth" to achieve that change.[42]

The white citizens of Frankfort threw their support behind Ku Klux legislation and allowing Black testimony in order to keep their favored sons in Kentucky courts and avoid possible conviction in federal court. Finally, in February 1872, the Democratic legislature made what the Republican *Commonwealth* termed a "vital change in the law of the State." It is likely that Governor Leslie and other politicians acted on pressures from the Frankfort defendants' families, along with the ongoing regulator attacks and concerns about federal interference. Just one day after the bill allowing Black testimony was signed into law, overworked and exhausted Judge Ballard announced that the federal court would no longer hear cases under the Civil Rights Act. By October 1872, the US federal court in Louisville had cleared all Black testimony cases from the docket and returned them to state courts, thus ending the lengthy controversy over federal judicial intervention.[43]

In a bitterly ironic twist, Black Kentuckians, by gaining the right to testify in Kentucky, had lost access to one of their greatest forms of federal protection. With little fanfare or reporting, Crittenden and Walcutt were promptly acquitted on all charges in the Franklin County court. No one was ever convicted for the deaths of Washington and Johnson or fined for participation in the riot.[44]

The lynching of Washington and Johnson after the Frankfort riot was just one episode among the hundreds of acts of violence against African Americans in Reconstruction-era Kentucky. Although election riots were commonplace, the 1871 riot had a lasting impact on the city of Frankfort, Black Kentuckians, and the legal and social order of the state. Black men had long fought for the rights of manhood and citizenship denied them—the rights of military service, the vote, and court testimony; the right to protect their families; the right to choose their workplace and shape their economic future; and freedom of opportunity. The accusations against members of the state militia had forced white Kentuckians to consider the lesser of two evils: Black testimony or federal intervention. Because of the trial, African Americans finally received the right to testify in court, although Black men were not able to sit on a Kentucky jury in a case involving a white man until 1882, and then inconsistently. But as they had discovered with the official attainment of so many other goals, freedoms gained did not mean equality. Indeed, the ability to testify took away the federal courts as a reliable tool to gain other rights. In practice, returning cases involving the violation of Black civil rights to Kentucky courts gave white Democrats even more freedom to act against Black citizens without fear of punishment or federal repercussion.[45]

White militia violence, sanctioned by the Democratic Party, helped restore the white supremacist social order in Frankfort and throughout the state. Both election violence and regulator attacks conveyed the message to the entire Black community that those who challenged the social or political order would face severe consequences. The prominent young men of Frankfort could claim they were upholding law and order through the sanctioned violence of the militia. Richard Crittenden, Howard Walcutt, and the others were too young to have fought in the Civil War, but their fathers had fought and felt keenly their loss of power over the enslaved and to the federal government. The young men could reclaim their heritage of white masculine honor by participating in the militias and reasserting their supremacy over African Americans—especially Black men claiming citizenship rights. By deploying state-sanctioned military violence against African Americans attempting to vote, while also conceding them the right to testify in court, white men in Kentucky remained firmly entrenched at the top of the social hierarchy.[46]

## Notes

1. "Passion and Pistols," *Louisville Courier-Journal*, August 8, 1871; *Louisville Commercial*, August 12, 1871; "The Mob Rule and Reign of Blood at Frankfort," *Louisville Commercial*, August 10, 1871.

2. "Monday Riot," *Frankfort Commonwealth*, August 11, 1871; "Mob Rule and Reign of Blood," *Louisville Commercial*, August 10, 1871; "From Frankfort: Lynch Law Enforced," *Louisville Commercial*, August 9, 1871; "Frankfort Riot," *Louisville Courier-Journal*, August 9, 1871; "The Frankfort Kuklux," *Louisville Courier-Journal*, September 24, 1871.

3. "Mob Rule and Reign of Blood," *Louisville Commercial*, August 10, 1871; "Riots at Frankfort," *Louisville Commercial*, August 9, 1871; "From Frankfort," *Louisville Commercial*, August 9, 1871; "The Louisville Trial," *Frankfort Commonwealth*, September 29, 1871.

4. "The Election Riot," *Louisville Courier-Journal*, August 9, 1871; "The Ceremony of Assassination," *Louisville Commercial*, August 10, 1871; "Lynching at Frankfort," *Louisville Courier-Journal*, August 9, 1871. On George Drane, see Lewis Franklin Johnson, *The History of Franklin County, Ky.* (Frankfort, KY: Roberts Printing, 1912), 168; 1870 United States Federal Census, Frankfort, Franklin, Kentucky; Roll M593-462, Page 148B, Image 301, Family History Library Film 545961, Ancestry.com; "How Our Judges Are Chosen," *Frankfort Commonwealth*, October 13, 1871. On lynching, see Christopher Waldrep, *The Many Faces of Judge Lynch: Extralegal Violence and Punishment in America* (New York: Palgrave Macmillan, 2002), 78–84; W. Fitzhugh Brundage, *Under Sentence of Death: Lynching in the New South* (Chapel Hill: University of North Carolina Press, 1997); Bruce E. Baker, *This Mob Will Surely Take My Life: Lynchings in the Carolinas, 1871–1947* (New York: Continuum, 2008); Amy Louise Wood, *Lynching and Spectacle: Witnessing Racial Violence in America, 1890–1940* (Chapel Hill: University of North Carolina Press, 2009).

5. "The Alarm at Frankfort," *Louisville Courier-Journal*, August 11, 1871; "The Louisville Trial," *Frankfort Commonwealth*, September 29, 1871; Johnson, *The History of Franklin County, Ky.*, 179; "Riots at Frankfort," *Louisville Commercial*, August 9, 1871; "Responsibility," *Louisville Commercial*, August 19, 1871; "Frankfort Mob," *Louisville Commercial*, August 24, 1871. On the importance of family honor to the sons of prominent men, see Lorri Glover, *Southern Sons: Becoming Men in the New Nation* (Baltimore, MD: Johns Hopkins University Press, 2010), 171–84.

6. On white masculine control of the rights of citizenship, see Craig Thompson Friend, *Southern Masculinity: Perspectives on Manhood in the South since Reconstruction* (Athens: University of Georgia Press, 2009), viii–xiii; Linda K. Kerber, *No Constitutional*

*Right to Be Ladies: Women and the Obligations of Citizenship* (New York: Hill and Wang, 1998); Harry S. Laver, *Citizens More Than Soldiers: The Kentucky Militia and Society in the Early Republic* (Lincoln: University of Nebraska Press, 2007). On meanings of "practical freedom," see Gregory P. Downs, *After Appomattox: Military Occupation and the Ends of War* (Cambridge, MA: Harvard University Press, 2015).

7. Aaron Astor, "'I Wanted a Gun': Black Soldiers and White Violence in Civil War and Postwar Kentucky and Missouri," in *The Great Task Remaining before Us: Reconstruction as America's Continuing Civil War* (New York: Fordham University Press, 2010), 212n9; "The Kentucky Election," *Louisville Courier-Journal*, August 9, 1871; Anne E. Marshall, *Creating a Confederate Kentucky: The Lost Cause and Civil War Memory in a Border State* (Chapel Hill: University of North Carolina Press, 2010), 33–54, esp. 33; Hambleton Tapp and James C. Klotter, *Kentucky: Decades of Discord, 1865–1900* (Frankfort: Kentucky Historical Society, 2008), 28–36. On Kentucky's postwar southern identity, see Marshall, *Creating a Confederate Kentucky*, 2–27; Aaron Astor, *Rebels on the Border: Civil War, Emancipation, and the Reconstruction of Kentucky and Missouri* (Baton Rouge: Louisiana State University Press, 2012); Patrick A. Lewis, "'All Men of Decency Ought to Quit the Army': Benjamin F. Buckner, Manhood, and Proslavery Unionism in Kentucky," *Register of the Kentucky Historical Society* 107 (Autumn 2009): 513–49.

8. Mapping Occupation, http://www.mappingoccupation.org; Downs, *After Appomattox*, 236; Victor B. Howard, "The Black Testimony Controversy in Kentucky, 1866–1872," *Journal of Negro History* 58 (April 1973): 157.

9. Marshall, *Creating a Confederate Kentucky*, 11, 12, 34; *Kentucky's Black Heritage: The Role of the Black People in the History of Kentucky from Pioneer Days to the Present* (Frankfort: Kentucky Commission on Human Rights, 1971), 30; Astor, "'I Wanted a Gun,'" 211n50, 37–38, 50–52, 218; Downs, *After Appomattox*, 4–10; Richard Ulack, Karl Raitz, and Gyula Pauer, eds., *Atlas of Kentucky* (Lexington: University Press of Kentucky, 1998), 76–77; Patrick A. Lewis, "The Democratic Partisan Militia and the Black Peril: The Kentucky Militia, Racial Violence, and the Fifteenth Amendment, 1870–1873," *Civil War History* 56, no. 2 (2010): 146, 158. On the freeing of enslaved women and children through a husband or father's military service, see Amy Dru Stanley, "Instead of Waiting for the Thirteenth Amendment: The War Power, Slave Marriage, and Inviolate Human Rights," *American Historical Review* 115 (June 2010): 732–65.

10. Lewis Collins and Richard Henry Collins, *Collins' Historical Sketches of Kentucky: History of Kentucky* (Covington, KY: Collins & Company, 1882), 2:260; Carl Kramer, *Capital on the Kentucky: A Two-Hundred-Year History of Frankfort and Franklin County* (Frankfort: Historic Frankfort, 1986), 113–15, 178–82; "Census of Franklin County," *Frankfort Commonwealth*, October 30, 1870. All population data are taken from the population schedules of the US Census Office, *Eighth Census of the Population of the United States* (Washington, DC: Government Printing Office, 1864); US Census Office, *Ninth Census of Population and Housing* (Washington, DC: Government Printing Office, 1872). On Reconstruction's economic and racial benefits to poor whites, see Keri Leigh Merritt, *Masterless Men: Poor Whites and Slavery in the Antebellum South* (New York: Cambridge University Press, 2017), 326–37.

11. Kramer, *Capital on the Kentucky*, 183; Victor B. Howard, *Black Liberation in Kentucky: Emancipation and Freedom, 1862-1884* (Lexington: University Press of Kentucky, 1983), 94-97, 100; "Communications: Land and Labor," *Christian Recorder*, November 19, 1870; Marion B. Lucas, *A History of Blacks in Kentucky: From Slavery to Segregation, 1760-1891* (Frankfort: Kentucky Historical Society, 1992), 274.

12. "Important to Colored Men," *San Francisco Elevator*, November 29, 1867; Howard, *Black Liberation in Kentucky*, 139-40, 154; *Kentucky's Black Heritage*, 45-46.

13. *Proceedings of the State Convention of Colored Men Held at Lexington, Kentucky, in the A.M.E. Church, November 26th, 27th, and 28th, 1867* (Frankfort, KY: Frankfort Commonwealth Print, 1867), 10; J. Michael Rhyne, "'We Are Mobed & Beat': Regulator Violence against Free Black Households in Kentucky's Bluegrass Region, 1865-1867," *Ohio Valley History* 2 (Spring 2002): 30-34, 38; "Senator Sumner's Bill," *Christian Recorder*, July 6, 1870.

14. John William Wallace, ed., *Cases Argued and Adjudged in the Supreme Court of the United States, December Term, 1871* (Washington, DC: W. H. & O. H. Morrison, 1872), 13:599-600; "Memorial of a Committee Appointed at a Meeting of Colored Citizens of Frankfort, Ky. and Vicinity, Praying the Enactment of Laws for the Better Protection of Life," in *Index to the Miscellaneous Documents of the Senate of the United States for the First Session of the Forty-Second Congress and the Special Session of the Senate, 1871* (April 11, 1871); Howard, "Black Testimony Controversy in Kentucky," 148-65. The Supreme Court justices Joseph P. Bradley and John H. Swayne offered the dissenting opinion in the case of *Blyew et al. v. United States*; see also "The Family of Jack and Sallie Foster," Notable Kentucky African Americans, http://www.uky.edu/Libraries/nkaa/subject.php?sub_id=162. On court testimony as a form of protection, see Pamela Brandwein, *Rethinking the Judicial Settlement of Reconstruction* (New York: Cambridge University Press, 2011), 79.

15. "Negro Testimony," *Louisville Courier-Journal*, September 5, 1871; "Negro Testimony," *Frankfort Commonwealth*, March 10, 1871; Howard, *Black Liberation in Kentucky*, 135, 143-44.

16. George C. Wright, *Racial Violence in Kentucky, 1865-1940: Lynchings, Mob Rule, and "Legal Lynchings"* (Baton Rouge: Louisiana State University Press, 1990), 8-9; "Shelby Kuklux," *Louisville Courier-Journal*, July 21, 1871; "The Kuklux," *Frankfort Commonwealth*, November 17, 1871; "The Kuklux," *New York Times*, April 26, 1872; "Kuklux in Kentucky," *New York Times*, October 5, 1872; Lowell H. Harrison and James C. Klotter, *A New History of Kentucky* (Lexington: University Press of Kentucky, 1997), 238. George C. Wright has determined that at least 117 people were lynched between 1865 and 1874—one-third of the total number of lynchings in Kentucky. On white paramilitary groups in Kentucky, see Lewis, "The Democratic Partisan Militia and the Black Peril"; Tapp and Klotter, *Kentucky: Decades of Discord*, 377-409. On the Ku Klux Klan and similar groups in the South, see Steven Hahn, *A Nation under Our Feet: Black Political Struggles in the Rural South from Slavery to the Great Migration* (Cambridge, MA: Belknap, 2003), 265-313; Allen W. Trelease, *White Terror: The Ku Klux Klan Conspiracy and Southern Reconstruction* (New York: Harper & Row, 1971); Suzanne Marshall,

*Violence in the Black Patch of Kentucky and Tennessee* (Columbia: University of Missouri Press, 1994).

17. "Memorial of Committee of Colored Citizens of Frankfort"; "Stamping Ground Kuklux Outrage," *Frankfort Commonwealth*, January 20, 1871; Mapping Occupation, http://www.mappingoccupation.org. For more on white paramilitary responses to Black labor organization, see Michael W. Fitzgerald, "1874: Self-Defense and Racial Empowerment in the Alabama Black Belt," in this volume.

18. "Memorial of Committee of Colored Citizens of Frankfort"; Patrick A. Lewis, *For Slavery and Union: Benjamin Buckner and Kentucky Loyalties in the Civil War* (Lexington: University Press of Kentucky, 2015), 186; Richard Stone, *A Brittle Sword: The Kentucky Militia, 1776–1912* (Lexington: University Press of Kentucky, 1977), 73–78; "History of Democratic Opposition to Law and Order," *Frankfort Commonwealth*, June 30, 1871. On postwar regulator violence, see Harrison and Klotter, *New History of Kentucky*, 57; Rhyne, "'We Are Mobed & Beat,'" 32; E. Merton Coulter, *The Civil War and Readjustment in Kentucky* (Chapel Hill: University of North Carolina Press, 1926), 83, 358–65. On the withdrawal of federal troops and the use of local militias to maintain order, see Downs, *After Appomattox*, 59–60, 124–27, 216.

19. Stone, *A Brittle Sword*, 73–75; *Acts of the General Assembly of the Commonwealth of Kentucky, Passed at the Adjourned Session Which Was Begun and Held in the City of Frankfort, on Monday the Seventh Day of December, 1864* (Frankfort: State Printing Office, 1865), 97–116; "Report of the Adjutant General of Kentucky to His Excellency Governor Leslie for the Year 1871" (Kentucky Yeoman Office, 1872), 3–9; "Report of the Adjutant General of Kentucky to His Excellency Governor Stevenson for the Year 1870" (Kentucky Yeoman Office, 1871), 9; Lewis, "The Democratic Partisan Militia and the Black Peril," 152–54; *Louisville Commercial*, August 17, 1870. See also Kentucky National Guard History, https://kynghistory.ky.gov/Our-History/History-of-the-Guard/Pages/Reconstruction.aspx. On the role of the militia in enhancing the social standing of young men, see Hahn, *A Nation under Our Feet*, 269–70. On connections between military veterans and white power movements, see Kathleen Belew, *Bring the War Home: The White Power Movement and Paramilitary America* (Cambridge, MA: Harvard University Press, 2018).

20. "March 1871–August 1871," Mapping Occupation, http://www.mappingoccupation.org; "Degeneracy," *Frankfort Commonwealth*, March 17, 1871; *Louisville Commercial*, August 27, 1871; *Louisville Commercial*, May 2, 1872; Howard, "Black Testimony Controversy in Kentucky," 150.

21. "Letter from Hon. James Speed," *Louisville Commercial*, August 2, 1871.

22. Charles L. Davis, "Racial Politics in Central Kentucky during the Post-Reconstruction Era: Bourbon County, 1877–1899," *Register of the Kentucky Historical Society* 108 (Autumn 2010): 348–51; *Kentucky's Black Heritage*, 45–48; "The Democracy Fulfill Predictions," *Louisville Commercial*, August 5, 1870; Lewis, "The Democratic Partisan Militia and the Black Peril," 159–63, esp. 158; "The Harrodsburg Riot—Letter to the District Attorney," *Louisville Commercial*, August 4, 1870; "The Election in Kentucky," *Louisville Commercial*, August 2, 1870.

23. Kramer, *Capital on the Kentucky*, 145; "An Election Farce," *Frankfort Commonwealth*, August 5, 1870; "The Late Farce, Alias the City Election on Monday," *Frankfort Commonwealth*, August 5, 1870; "Annual Report of the Quarter-Master General to the Governor of the State of Kentucky for the Year 1872" (Kentucky Yeoman Office, 1873), 13; "Disfranchisement," *Frankfort Commonwealth*, January 6, 1871; "From Kentucky," *Christian Recorder*, March 16, 1872; "Report of the Adjutant General of Kentucky to His Excellency Governor Stevenson for the Year 1870" (Kentucky Yeoman Office, 1871), 12–13. On informal or alternative methods of Black disfranchisement such as redrawing city boundaries, see Davis, "Racial Politics in Central Kentucky during the Post-Reconstruction Era," 375–78.

24. "The Late City Election," *Frankfort Commonwealth*, January 13, 1871; "Kentucky Affairs: The Murder on Saturday," *Cincinnati Commercial Tribune*, January 13, 1871; Kramer, *Capital on the Kentucky*, 176; "The Kentucky Outrages," *Cincinnati Gazette*, January 18, 1871. Similarly, antebellum violence against abolitionists was conducted with the approval of "gentlemen of property and standing," who blamed it on working-class attackers; Leonard L. Richards, *"Gentlemen of Property and Standing": Anti-Abolition Mobs in Jacksonian America* (New York: Oxford University Press, 1971).

25. "Peacetime Occupation," Mapping Occupation, http://www.mappingoccupation.org.

26. "The Press on the Election," *Cincinnati Gazette*, qtd. in *Frankfort Commonwealth*, August 18, 1871; "Passion and Pistols," *Louisville Courier-Journal*, August 8, 1871; "Riots at Frankfort," *Louisville Commercial*, August 9, 1871; *Louisville Commercial*, August 12, 1871; "Bad Conduct of the Blacks—Two Whites Killed and Several Wounded," *Frankfort Yeoman*, August 8, 1871, reprinted in "Frankfort Riot," *Louisville Courier-Journal*, August 9, 1871.

27. "Judge Pryor's Charge to the Grand Jury," *Frankfort Commonwealth*, September 1, 1871; Robert M. Ireland, "Law and Disorder in Nineteenth-Century Kentucky," *Vanderbilt Law Review* 32 (1979): 282–83; "Report of the Grand Jury—Negro Testimony Admitted—Nothing Developed," *Frankfort Commonwealth*, September 8, 1871; *Louisville Commercial*, September 3, 1871; Howard, *Black Liberation in Kentucky*, 143–44.

28. "The Local State Elections," *Frankfort Commonwealth*, May 12, 1871; Lucas, *History of Blacks in Kentucky*, 307; "Republicanism in Kentucky," *Frankfort Commonwealth*, August 25, 1871; "The Election: A Comparative Vote," *Louisville Commercial*, August 11, 1871; "The Kentucky Election," *Cincinnati Commercial*, and "The Press on the Election," *Cincinnati Gazette*, printed in *Frankfort Commonwealth*, August 18, 1871.

29. "Governor's Message," *Frankfort Commonwealth*, December 8, 1871; John E. Kleber, *The Kentucky Encyclopedia* (Lexington: University Press of Kentucky, 1992), 544–45.

30. Harrison and Klotter, *New History of Kentucky*, 244; "Trial of the Parties Accused of Hanging Henry Washington and Harry Johnson on the Night of the August Election," *Frankfort Commonwealth*, September 29, 1871; "The Frankfort Election Riot," *Louisville Commercial*, September 24, 1871; "Louisville Trial," *Frankfort Commonwealth*, September 29, 1871; Wright, *Racial Violence in Kentucky*, 51. On the debate over civil rights versus justice, see Brandwein, *Rethinking the Judicial Settlement of Reconstruction*.

31. "Trial of the Parties Accused of Hanging Washington and Johnson," *Frankfort Commonwealth*, September 29, 1871. For census information on all the defendants, see 1860 US Federal Census, Frankfort, Franklin, Kentucky, Roll M653-367, Family History Library Film 803367, Ancestry.com; and 1870 US Federal Census, Frankfort, Franklin, Kentucky, Roll M593-462, Family History Library Film 545961, Ancestry.com. On Howard Smith, see "Official Vote for Governor and Lieutenant Governor at the August Election, 1871," *Frankfort Commonwealth*, September 8, 1871. On Richard and John Crittenden, see Francis H. Oxx, *The Kentucky Crittendens: The History of a Family Including the Genealogy of Descendants in Both the Male and Female Lines, Biographical Sketches of Its Members and Their Descent from Other Early Colonial Families* (n.p., 1940), 202; Lowell H. Harrison, *Kentucky's Governors* (Lexington: University Press of Kentucky, 2004), 64–67; Johnson, *History of Franklin County, Ky.*, 182. Thanks to Patrick Lewis for his assistance with Crittenden family history.

32. Special Order no. 3: July 6, 1870, Special & General Orders 1870–79, A.G.O. Ky., Box 29 Adj. General Special Orders, 1862–99, Kentucky National Legion Records (Kentucky Military Records & Research Branch, Frankfort); "Frankfort Riot," *Louisville Courier-Journal*, August 9, 1871; "Kentucky Elections," *New York Times*, August 9, 1871; 1880 US Federal Census, Lexington, Fayette, Kentucky, Roll 413, Page 301A, Image 0043, Enumeration District 065, Family History Library Film 1254413, Ancestry.com. There is no surviving muster roll for the Valley Rifles, but news sources point to the militia involvement of many of the accused men, particularly Richard Crittenden and Howard Smith Jr.; see also Johnson, *History of Franklin County, Ky.*, 179.

33. 1870 US Federal Census, Frankfort, Franklin, Kentucky, Roll M593-462, Page 96B, Image 197, Family History Library Film 545961, Ancestry.com; "Memorial of Committee of Colored Citizens of Frankfort"; "Stamping Ground Kuklux Outrage," *Frankfort Commonwealth*, January 20, 1871. The few details available on Henry Washington are insufficient to identify him definitively in Civil War military records, although he likely served in the 28th or 119th US Colored Infantry; see Compiled Military Service Records of Volunteer Union Soldiers Who Served with the United States Colored Troops: Infantry Organizations, 16th through 30th, Including the 29th Connecticut (Colored), Microfilm Serial M1824, Roll 51, National Archives and Records Administration, Washington, DC, Ancestry.com; Film number M589 roll 91, FamilySearch.org, https://www.nps.gov/civilwar/soldiers-and-sailors-database.htm. There were a number of Black Henrys or Harrisons living in Frankfort in 1871, ranging in age from eighteen to forty-three; see 1870 US Federal Census, Frankfort, Franklin, Kentucky, Roll M593-462, Page 96B, Image 197, Family History Library Film 545961, Ancestry.com; "Judge Pryor's Charge to the Grand Jury," *Frankfort Commonwealth*, September 1, 1871. On the status of barbers in Black communities, see George C. Wright, *Life behind a Veil: Blacks in Louisville, Kentucky, 1865–1930* (Baton Rouge: Louisiana State University Press, 1985), 82–84; Nikki M. Taylor, *Frontiers of Freedom: Cincinnati's Black Community, 1802–1868* (Athens: Ohio University Press, 2005), 104, 133–34.

34. "Responsibility," *Louisville Commercial*, August 19, 1871; "Mob Rule and Reign of Blood," *Louisville Commercial*, August 10, 1871; "The Frankfort Election Riot: Continuation of the Examination," *Louisville Commercial*, September 26, 1871.

35. "The Frankforters," *Louisville Courier-Journal*, September 27, 1871; *Louisville Commercial*, September 30, 1871; "The Frankfort Tragedy: Conclusion of the Examining Trial," *Louisville Commercial*, September 29, 1871; "Louisville Trial," *Frankfort Commonwealth*, September 29, 1871.

36. *Louisville Commercial*, August 12, 1871; "Mob Rule and Reign of Blood," *Louisville Commercial*, August 10, 1871; "Louisville Trial," *Frankfort Commonwealth*, September 29, 1871; *Louisville Commercial*, August 19, 1871. On limiting federal military involvement in local affairs, see Downs, *After Appomattox*, 189–91, 204–6.

37. "Frankfort Election Riot," *Louisville Commercial*, September 24, 1871; "Frankfort Election Riot," *Louisville Commercial*, September 26, 1871; "Trial of the Parties Accused of Hanging Washington and Johnson," *Frankfort Commonwealth*, September 29, 1871; "The Frankforters," *Louisville Courier-Journal*, September 27, 1871; "Frankfort Mob," *Louisville Commercial*, August 24, 1871.

38. "Trial of the Parties Accused of Hanging Washington and Johnson," *Frankfort Commonwealth*, September 29, 1871. On Joseph Roach, see 1870 US Federal Census, Frankfort, Franklin, Kentucky, Roll M593-462, Page 122B, Image 249, Family History Library Film 545961, Ancestry.com.

39. "Trial of the Parties Accused of Hanging Henry Washington and Harry Johnson," *Frankfort Commonwealth*, September 29, 1871; "Frankfort Kuklux," *Louisville Courier-Journal*, September 24, 1871.

40. "Frankfort Election Riot," *Louisville Commercial*, September 26–27, 1871; "Trial of the Parties Accused of Hanging Washington and Johnson," *Frankfort Commonwealth*, September 29, 1871; "The Frankfort Lynching," *Louisville Courier-Journal*, September 26, 1871; "Frankfort Tragedy," *Louisville Commercial*, September 29, 1871; "The Frankfort Tragedy," *Louisville Commercial*, October 1, 1871; "The Frankforters," *Louisville Courier-Journal*, September 27, 1871; "The Frankfort Prisoners," *Louisville Courier-Journal*, October 1, 1871.

41. "The Kuklux Sensation," *Louisville Courier-Journal*, October 6, 1871; Ireland, "Law and Disorder in Nineteenth-Century Kentucky," 283–84; "The Kuklux," *Frankfort Commonwealth*, November 17, 1871; W. A. Meriwether to Benjamin Bristow, November 8, 1871, cited in Howard, *Black Liberation in Kentucky*, 204n84; "The Frankfort Hanging," *Louisville Commercial*, January 25, 1872; "United States Courts—Hons. H. H. Emmons and Bland Ballard, Judges: Circuit Court," *Louisville Commercial*, January 25, 1872.

42. "The Whole Ground Covered," *Louisville Commercial*, October 5, 1871; "Confession and Avoidance," *Louisville Commercial*, September 29, 1871; "The Federal Court," *Louisville Commercial*, November 3, 1871; Meriwether to Bristow, cited in Howard, *Black Liberation in Kentucky*, 204n84.

43. "Negro Testimony," *Frankfort Commonwealth*, February 2, 1872; *Louisville Commercial*, January 27, 1872; "The Law of Evidence in Kentucky," *Louisville Commercial*, January 30, 1872. The federal courts still had jurisdiction over cases tried under the Ku Klux Klan act; "Report of the Military Committee on the Kuklux," *Frankfort Commonwealth*, March 1, 1872; Robert J. Kaczorowski, *The Politics of Judicial Interpretation: The Federal Courts, Department of Justice, and Civil Rights, 1866–1876* (New York: Fordham University Press, 2005), 42; Howard, "Black Testimony Controversy in Kentucky," 165.

44. Wright, *Racial Violence in Kentucky*, 50–51.

45. Harrison and Klotter, *New History of Kentucky*, 247. The first Black jury was assembled in a case involving two Black men in Louisville in 1871; "The First Negro Jury in Kentucky," *New York Times*, June 21, 1872.

46. Stewart E. Tolnay and E. M. Beck, *A Festival of Violence: An Analysis of Southern Lynchings, 1882–1930* (Urbana: University of Illinois Press, 1995), 57–65; Waldrep, *The Many Faces of Judge Lynch*, 67–84; Friend, *Southern Masculinity*, viii–xiii; Glover, *Southern Sons*, 183; Joanne Freeman, *The Field of Blood: Violence in Congress and the Road to Civil War* (New York: Farrar, Straus and Giroux, 2018).

# A Woman of "Weak Mind"

*Gender, Race, and Mental Competency in the Reconstruction Era*

## Felicity Turner

In November 1876, the Court of Oyer and Terminer in Philadelphia tried an African American woman, Evelina Frazier, for infanticide. The state alleged that Frazier had thrown her newborn child into a well. In her defense, Frazier's attorneys claimed that she was of "weak mind." As such, the moral standards that ordinarily applied to all men and women should not apply to Frazier. Buttressing that claim, a local newspaper, the *North American*, observed of Frazier's demeanor in court that she "felt disposed to laugh at anybody that would look at her in the face." Further, she demonstrated a "total unconcern with the proceedings," refusing to engage with either the court or her court-appointed counsel. The defense proved effective, saving Frazier from the scaffold. Instead, the judge sentenced Evelina Frazier to the state penitentiary for two years.[1]

Initially, the court's characterization of Evelina Frazier as a woman of "weak mind" seems a virtue, one that secured Frazier—and women like her—an escape from the death penalty. Only a rational individual—one fully capable of assessing the difference between right and wrong—deserved to face the full force of the law. To be of "weak mind" meant that Frazier was not as rational, that is, as capable of reasoned, intelligent thought, as others. Therefore, the punishment she faced should be reduced accordingly. The sentence reflected the court's view that a person could not be held fully responsible for a crime if not fully aware of the consequences of their actions.

Yet such an interpretation is problematic, obscuring a more complex intersection between ideas about race, gender, and the capacity to reason, all of which converged during Reconstruction. In Evelina Frazier's case, the court extended prevailing gendered assumptions that applied to white women about female culpability for violent crimes to an African American woman. That is, the court assumed women—irrespective of race—less capable of, and therefore less culpable for, violent crime than men. Long-standing views about the innate intellectual capacities of women, assumed inferior to men intellectually, shaped these ideas. As society assumed females less rational than men, logic dictated that women were less capable of planning violent crimes, such as murder, than men. When women did kill, it was often explained as being because they were more passionate than men. As such, they were thought less capable than men of controlling the emotions that inspired them to act. These views had long shaped outcomes in murder cases for all women, both Black and white.[2]

In the case of Black women, however, race complicated the logic that limited the culpability of all women—as compared to men—for violent crimes. As a woman and an African American, society—more broadly—deemed Evelina Frazier as "unfit for freedom," lacking both the intellectual capacity and the moral sensibility to appreciate the gravity of her alleged crime. Characterization as a woman of "weak mind" was not, therefore, as beneficial for Black women as for white; it reinforced prevailing and persistent stereotypes that African Americans were less intelligent than whites. As historians have argued, race—in particular, medical and scientific theories about the intellectual inferiority associated with blackness—served as fundamental to the development of ideas in relation to reason and sanity in the nineteenth-century United States. Building upon ideas established in slavery that freedom would be dangerous to African Americans—an argument supporters of slavery used to justify enslavement—white Americans used claims that African Americans were of "weak mind" during Reconstruction to justify a new form of captivity in the form of incarceration. Within that context, Frazier's alleged lack of intelligence made her less deserving of freedom and, therefore, more deserving of incarceration than a white woman. Indeed, such logic naturalized incarceration for Black women, while denaturalizing it for white women. The logic built upon and contributed to the perpetuation of fears conflating Black freedom with danger.[3]

This essay uses infanticide cases to examine the ways that courts deployed and navigated prevailing beliefs about women's diminished mental capacity in the Reconstruction-era United States. As a crime closely associated with pregnancy and birth, grand juries indicted women far more often than men for infanticide, making the offense a particularly useful lens through which to examine gendered assumptions. Building on recent scholarship that interrogates the problematic ways that gender, race, and class shaped ideas about sanity and the capacity to reason in the nineteenth-century United States, this essay argues that courts used such understandings to restrict the newly found freedom—and rights—of Black women during Reconstruction. In contrast, communities generally deployed similar assumptions—as problematic as they were—in ways that proved more beneficial to wealthy white women attempting to avoid a prison sentence. While this chapter opens with an example from the mid-Atlantic, a closer study of the consequences of these ideas in the South—and their application to Black and white women of different social classes—demonstrates how race intersected with gender and class to shape the outcomes in infanticide cases in ways generally more unfavorable to Black mothers than white. For an African American woman such as Evelina Frazier, the determination that she was of "weak mind" saved her from the death penalty. But she did not escape a custodial sentence altogether, which she might have done had she been a white woman, especially one from the middle or upper classes, charged with the same offense.[4]

By Reconstruction, Americans were clearly not strangers to the idea that women who had recently given birth might harm their children. Indeed, Benjamin Rush, a signer of the US Constitution, was one of the first American doctors to suggest that women's biology—and the functions related to that physiology—predisposed females to insanity in ways that men's biology did not. In his 1811 publication *Diseases of the Mind*—the first American-authored treatise on the subject of mental illness—Rush observed that "menstruation, pregnancy, and parturition" meant that women were "more predisposed to madness than men." In addition, Rush believed solitary life—away from the influence of society and culture—produced madness in females. In other words, absent the reassuring, rational presence of men, women went mad. Rush did acknowledge that in certain cases men were more likely to be gripped by insanity. The examples cited, however, related to external influences, such as "war, bankruptcy, and the habits of drinking." The key factor in Rush's framework was that biology—internal forces that women could not control—dictated women's propensity to madness. For men, in contrast, the travails of life threatened a slow slide into insanity.[5]

By the end of the Civil War, Benjamin Rush's ideas had found a new mouthpiece. In 1864, the leading American gynecologist and obstetrician Horatio Storer—who, in later years, assumed the presidency of the American Medical Association—published a number of treatises in which he discussed the problem of and "management" of "female insanity." In Storer's view, women's minds, like women's bodies, could only be interpreted and understood by well-educated men. Like Rush, Horatio Storer firmly identified physiology—internal or "reflex" factors—as the cause of female insanity. In an April 1864 medical treatise, Storer detailed a case in which a woman—approaching her monthly menses—gradually became insane, eventually committing suicide. As menstruation approached, the woman—who was white and married—became depressed. After her menses arrived, she "practised self pollution"—masturbation—compounding her feelings of depression, "disgust and regret." That night, she killed herself via a series of "eleven incisions" to the throat and an additional injury to the arm. Menstruation, argued Storer, created a "disturbance" in the liver. That "disturbance," in turn, prompted "mental derangement," evidenced initially by actions such as "self pollution" and eventually by suicide. As Storer observed, the patient's "suicidal impulse" peaked at the moment of her "period." Menstruation, argued Storer, made the patient more tolerant of pain, which, in Storer's view, explained the large number of wounds. The subject could have achieved her goal, he noted clinically, with far fewer injuries.[6]

The gendered implications of Horatio Storer's argument had far-reaching implications, at least one of which was counterintuitively beneficial for some women in the post–Civil War United States. Storer's case study of the suicidal menstruating woman might have been extreme. She was, after all, only one woman. In contrast, a large portion of the adult female population throughout the globe menstruated regularly without killing anyone. But, in tying a woman's mental faculties—indeed, her capacity to reason—so closely to her physiology, Storer suggested that females could not help how they acted. Women, as he defined them, were born with ovaries and a uterus. Those biological organs dictated how women thought and how they behaved. Accordingly, Storer's argument implied, women should not be held to the same legal standards as men, because they naturally possessed a diminished capacity to reason. Women could not, so Storer's logic went, help themselves.[7]

The assertion that women should not be held responsible for crimes committed while menstruating extended arguments made by physicians in Europe. British doctors, in particular, had primarily focused on criminal acts, such as murder, perpetrated by pregnant women, or those who had recently given birth. Using logic akin to that adopted by Horatio Storer, these British and European gynecologists rooted justifications for women's criminal behavior in biology. Storer, however, clearly linked body and mind, explaining how—in his view—physiology influenced mental faculties, which then potentially generated insanity. The madness then prompted a criminal act. Across the Atlantic, some doctors flattened such logic even further. The medical practitioner William Sedgwick, for example, suggested that "pregnancy itself, independent of legal proof of insanity, can justly be urged as an excuse for crime." If a woman were pregnant, madness could be assumed. Her state of mind—a determination if she were sane or not—need not be independently verified or demonstrated.[8]

Over time, the medical profession in the United States extended the biologically essentialist arguments developed by obstetricians in relation to menstruation and its impact on women's mental faculties to other specifically female physiological functions. Within that context, childbearing was an obvious source of women's diminished capacity for reason. US physicians used the term "puerperal insanity" to refer to a wide range of symptoms and behaviors specific to females of childbearing age. The varied symptoms included fever, delusions, homicidal behavior, and suicidal impulses. Medical advice suggested practitioners attempting to diagnose a woman with the disease mark any unusual changes in religious beliefs, appetite, sleep patterns, and bowel movements. A marked increase in profanity, obscenity, promiscuity, and use of violence signaled the potential onset of puerperal mania. An inability to lactate also suggested puerperal insanity. Finally, physicians identified a woman's marked lack of interest in the world around her and in caring for her family as symptomatic of the illness. In short, only the ability to endure pregnancy without any complaint might safely assure a medical practitioner that puerperal insanity had not afflicted a particular patient.

Typically, physicians suggested that the symptoms of puerperal insanity occurred in association with childbirth: just before or just after, although symptoms could and did persist well beyond labor. Broadly speaking, puerperal insanity could include a range of moods or effects, including mania, melancholy (also referred to as depression), and dementia. Short bursts of hyperactive and excitable activity characterized the manic state. In contrast, physicians considered dementia—another form of puerperal insanity—as a chronic state, one that might require institutionalization for a period of years. Treatments varied depending upon the nature of the illness. For melancholia and mania, doctors recommended sleep and isolation, although for different reasons. A depressed woman might kill someone, while company might agitate the mind of a woman already in an excited and manic state. Physicians also recommended ice packs as a means of soothing the nerves. Although some physicians favored enemas and bloodletting, those treatments generally fell out of favor in the later decades of the nineteenth century. Some cases, such as mania, could be treated at home, provided a doctor attended regularly to monitor the patient. These cases tended to resolve rapidly, ending, as one physician optimistically explained, in either "recovery or death." Cases of depression and insanity, in contrast, usually required long-term hospitalization. In the second half of the nineteenth century, that meant institutionalization in an asylum.[9]

In all cases of puerperal insanity, medical doctors recommended that women avoid overstimulation. The medical profession considered puerperal insanity, like hysteria, "nervousness," and neurasthenia, a disease of civilization. Firmly established ideas about the expected behaviors of white women, the anticipated social and cultural roles of white women, and the connection between white women's biology and destiny formed the foundation of these beliefs. Civilized women—white middle- and upper-class women—were meant to be mothers who cared for and nurtured families. White men, in contrast, provided for families both financially and functionally. Adult males corralled and controlled the emotions of wives and children. Men exercised discipline and self-control over themselves and the family members of whom they had charge.[10]

Within an atmosphere of tightly regulated and controlled passions, the stimuli of civilization presented a challenge to men and women alike. Rapid urbanization, the growth in industrialization, increasing opportunities for education: All of these changes potentially overexcited the nervous system. Society assumed that men, as leaders, as fathers, and as providers, were more firmly buttressed against the rigors of life, although overcivilization did tax the nerves of some men. Assumed to have more fragile nervous systems and mental states than men, women were more likely to literally lose their minds. The slope from sanity to insanity—from reason to loss of reason—appeared much shorter and steeper for women than for men. Essentially, courts—reflecting prevailing cultural views—assumed that a woman's grip on reason was always tenuous. Females, therefore, could descend more easily and more rapidly from sanity into chaos. Such logic had implications for men too, implications that reinforced the link between women and irrationality. Biologically essentialist arguments feminized madness. If females were naturally more irrational than men, then men who lost their grip on sanity assumed the disabilities of women. Men who lacked full control over their mental faculties were emasculated, "unmanned," as it were. Men who lost their reason were no longer men. Essentially, they became—if not literally, then metaphorically—women.[11]

Prevailing ideas about race and the intellectual capacities of African Americans further complicated the powerful and persistent assumptions about gender and reason. In the early republic and the antebellum periods, both those who supported slavery and those who did not had developed biologically essentialist narratives to explain the allegedly inferior intellectual and mental capacities of African Americans. Rush, for example, had argued in the late eighteenth and early nineteenth centuries that slavery explained the lack of intelligence demonstrated by Africans in the United States. Absent slavery, Rush proposed, a Black American constituted the equal of a white citizen. Slavery, observed Rush, condemned Africans to a "feeble" state, both in body and mind. Thus, while he reinforced prevailing stereotypes that African Americans were less intelligent than whites, Rush identified slavery as the reason. Unfortunately, however, even as Rush argued against slavery, he reinforced a powerful discourse that linked blackness to intellectual inferiority.[12]

At the same time as Benjamin Rush endeavored to mount an argument against slavery on the basis that the institution enfeebled Blacks in relation to whites, those who supported slavery—owners of the enslaved and medical doctors alike—developed a powerful narrative in the first half of the nineteenth century in which they pathologized blackness. As the historian Rana Hogarth has persuasively demonstrated, the "medicalization" of blackness—while it proved convenient for owners of the enslaved—provided a language through which white, male physicians in particular demonstrated mastery over Black bodies. By defining, diagnosing, and identifying illnesses and characteristics specific to Black bodies, white southern medical professionals asserted their authority to make claims in relation to all bodies. Like their northern colleagues, southern physicians related ailments of the mind to physical attributes. The New Orleans-based physician Samuel Cartwright, for example, linked the color of one's skin to the color of all of an individual's organs. The "shade of pervading darkness," Cartwright claimed, manifested in "the membranes, the muscles, the tendons and in all the fluids and secretions." Darkness even tainted the brain. As such, a Black man's brain was smaller than that of a white man, argued Cartwright. Indeed, he wrote that African Americans possessed "a nature not unlike that of a new-born infant of the white race." He argued Black Americans required enslavement, therefore, as their underdeveloped minds meant they were naturally unsuited for the responsibilities of freedom. Cartwright identified a number of illnesses specific to African Americans, including "drapetomania"—running away—and "rascality," defined as a "stupidness of the mind and insensibility of the nerves." Both diseases, argued Cartwright, demonstrated the inherent mental weakness of the African American mind as compared to that of whites. Similarly, the early anthropologists Josiah Nott and George Glidden argued in 1854 that interaction with whites produced some "improvement" among Africans "imported into, or born in, the United States." Nonetheless, Nott and Glidden claimed, such improvement was akin to taming horses. While some benefits might accrue to Black Americans as a result of interacting with whites—an ongoing justification for the alleged benefits of slavery to Blacks—"improvement" ultimately remained limited. The "natural" condition for Blacks was, therefore, slavery. Thus both antislavery and proslavery narratives of race and medicine contributed to racist beliefs about African Americans.[13]

Extending Samuel Cartwright's logic, some proslavery supporters identified freedom—not blackness alone—as the primary cause of madness. Many southern physicians, for example, argued that insanity prevailed far more widely among free Blacks in the northeast than enslaved Blacks in the southeast. To support that claim, they turned to the 1840 US Census, which recorded statistics of the "insane and idiots" for the first time, including among the enslaved. Supporters of slavery from across the nation lauded the figures, which allegedly demonstrated the disparately high ratios of insanity among free Blacks as compared to enslaved people. According to the census, rates of mental illness and intellectual impairment—"idiocy"—were about ten times higher among free Blacks in the northeastern states than among the enslaved in the southeastern states. The ardent supporter of slavery and senator from South Carolina John Calhoun, for instance, waxed lyrical about the figures on the floor of Congress. The census demonstrated, argued Calhoun, that freedom directly correlated with high rates of insanity in the African American population. Given that outcome, slavery was a natural and necessary state for Blacks in the United States. Although a prominent northeastern physician of insanity famously discredited the statistics in 1845, supporters of slavery continued to reinforce the view that slavery served to "protect" Blacks from the dangers of freedom. Almost a decade after Dr. Edward Jarvis ridiculed the census's conclusions through diligent and careful research, the southern medical doctor John Galt echoed Calhoun's claims, observing insanity was much lower among the enslaved than it was among free people because the enslaved were "removed from much of the mental excitement, to which the free population of the union is necessarily exposed in the daily routine of life." Throughout the antebellum era, proslavery physicians and politicians united in the belief that insanity was unknown in the enslaved population, a view later widely repeated and reinforced after the Civil War.[14]

The competing narratives in relation to race, intelligence, and sanity advanced by abolitionists and proslavery supporters converged during Reconstruction. For antislavery activists in the early republic such as Benjamin Rush, African Americans were as susceptible to insanity as white Americans. In all respects, free Blacks were equal to whites, suggesting all individuals possessed mental faculties subject to potential overstimulation by the vices of civilization. Proslavery supporters, in some ways, had adopted similar logic, identifying the responsibilities of the civilized world as potentially dangerous. Yet supporters of slavery diverged in an important way from the arguments of abolitionists by refusing to recognize that African Americans could achieve equality to whites. By constructing African American mental capabilities as naturally lesser than those of white

Americans, those who supported slavery justified their "peculiar institution" and characterized freedom as inherently dangerous to African Americans. While most Blacks in the United States remained enslaved, the construction of freedom as the danger—rather than blackness—served the purposes of white southerners. But after the Civil War, the varying narratives converged, lumping blackness, intellectual impairment, and freedom into one basket. Freedom and blackness became conflated, and so blackness, not freedom, became the problem.

Compounding the problems faced by Evelina Frazier and those like her, the parallel narratives converged at a moment—Reconstruction—in which states across the nation, not just in the former Confederacy, redoubled efforts to incarcerate African Americans. As one medical professional from Maryland observed in relation to the newly emancipated, "Unrestrained freedom . . . has had the effect of multiplying their desires and wants, but together with them it has also multiplied greatly their disappointments, and in very many instances the price of liberty to them has been the prison, the almshouse and the insane asylum." The statement was certainly accurate in relation to the case of Evelina Frazier. Upon her arrest, the police removed Frazier from her residence to the Philadelphia Hospital and Almshouse. Police then removed Frazier to the local jail, where she remained until sentencing at the conclusion of her trial. Frazier allegedly killed her son in July, with the court finally sentencing her to prison for two years in November. In total, Frazier remained incarcerated for almost thirty months, cycling through the various sites of state surveillance: the almshouse, the jail, and finally the state prison. Although Frazier escaped the scaffold, she did not escape the growing power and reach of the carceral state.[15]

In 1876, the Philadelphia Court of Oyer and Terminer tried Evelina Frazier within the context of three entangled narratives in which the dangers of unrestrained blackness, femininity out of control, and unfettered freedom combined. To combat the frightening specter these narratives produced, white Americans turned to the penal system as a way of limiting the freedom and power of all African Americans, women and men. Although the racial composition of the jury that decided Frazier's fate remains unknown, racial and gendered stereotypes shaped the outcome of her case. As Frazier was a woman, the court elected not to put Frazier to death, a determination consistent with decisions in infanticide cases involving both Black and white women across the nation during Reconstruction. The court did not, however, spare Frazier entirely. After all, she was Black. The court's use of the phrase "weak mind" suggested something different from madness or insanity. Indeed, the term reinforced, rather than challenged, prevailing racialized conceptions about the low intelligence of African Americans and their unsuitability for freedom. Within this context, courts justified custodial sentences for Black women as a form of mercy. Prison was better than the alternative, namely, death.[16]

The case of Evelina Frazier was not an isolated example. Certainly, juries did not find every African American woman accused of infanticide during Reconstruction guilty. Nor did they let every white woman walk away. But, for African American women in particular, certain options generally remained closed. The use of insanity as a defense was one such option of which they could rarely avail themselves with any success. Consider, for instance, the 1871 case of a Black woman, Leah Scarborough, in Baltimore, Maryland. Scarborough reportedly confessed to murdering her newborn infant, claiming she did so as she was unable to support the child. Tried for infanticide in July 1871, the court found Scarborough guilty as charged and the judge sentenced Scarborough to death. Reporting on the case, newspapers focused on Scarborough's "lack of intelligence" and her alleged inability to mentally and intellectually comprehend "the nature of consequences of her crime." Yet accounts also evinced significant sympathy for Scarborough, characterizing her—like many white women—as a victim of seduction. In particular, newspapers singled out Scarborough's seducer, a "well-known white citizen." An invisible line had been crossed, so it seemed. Interracial relationships were known of and about, but in this case, the judge's very public action—sentencing Scarborough to death—had moved this particular interracial relationship from out of the shadows. The crime, after all, attracted little attention. The sentence, however, generated public outcry in both white- and Black-owned newspapers.[17]

Calls for clemency came from various quarters. The *New National Era*, a prominent African American newspaper headquartered in Washington, DC, ran a number of articles and editorials pleading the cause of Scarborough. One of those who sought clemency on Scarborough's behalf was a white male doctor originally from North Carolina, Edward Warren. A former surgeon general of North Carolina and a former professor of medicine at the University of Maryland, Warren had served the Confederacy with distinction in the Civil War. When the war ended, he returned from his native North Carolina to Maryland, where his medical expertise was sometimes called upon in legal cases. In Scarborough's case, Warren reviewed the evidence at length, preparing—as he explained in his memoirs—"an argument in support of the proposition that the child had never breathed." The governor of Maryland granted Scarborough clemency, but not based on the repeated assertion that Scarborough was "insane." Rather, the governor exercised clemency on the basis that uncertainty existed about the baby's status at birth. If the infant was not born alive, then Scarborough could hardly be convicted of murder. She should certainly not be sent to death for that crime.[18]

The governor of Maryland commuted Leah Scarborough's death sentence to a prison term of five years. Newspapers acknowledged that Leah Scarborough was a victim of the well-established and well-worn seduction narrative. In Scarborough's case, that narrative was further complicated by the fact that her seducer was white. As a Black woman, however, Scarborough's story had a different ending than that of a white woman in the same position. Rather than escaping punishment entirely—as often happened with white women—Scarborough faced a prison term. The *National Era* applauded the commutation of the death sentence but challenged the logic that dictated Scarborough should serve any prison sentence at all. If the medical evidence proved the infant had not been born alive, then—argued the *National Era*—Scarborough should not find herself languishing in prison. Scarborough was both victim of the white man who seduced her and victim of "prejudice and negro hate." Scarborough's crime: being Black. The *National Era* called for an outright pardon.[19]

Seven years later, in Washington, DC, yet another "colored" woman, Louisa Wallace, faced the death penalty. In April 1878, local officials placed Louisa Wallace under arrest as she was suspected of murdering her newborn infant. The coroner summoned a physician. The doctor performed a postmortem examination on the corpse, concluding the child had been born alive, in spite of Wallace's protestations to the contrary. Doctor King also conducted an examination on the body of Louisa Wallace in order to confirm that she had recently given birth.[20] By 1878, such close, physical examinations of a woman's body—by a man—had become increasingly common, if not yet commonplace. In December 1878, the court sentenced Wallace to death for her crime, although the jury recommended a request for clemency be made to the president.[21] After a successful request for a retrial, Wallace was found guilty a second time in April 1879. When initially polled, the jury found 9 to 3 in favor of finding Wallace guilty. There were nine white men on the jury, and three Black men. The jury later returned with an 11 to 1 verdict.[22]

In their interpretation of Louisa Wallace's conduct and behavior, newspaper reports drew on racial stereotypes that constructed Black women as less intelligent. One report noted that Wallace laughed frequently—and inappropriately—throughout her trial, with her counsel, Belva Lockwood, often requesting that Wallace curtail her outbursts. Another account concurred with the view that Wallace lacked intelligence, characterizing Wallace as the "lightest hearted person in the court-room."[23] Newspapers commented on her facial features, drawing on the "science" of craniology that predicted a person's intelligence based on the size of his or her head. Indeed, the president justified her commutation of sentence on the basis that Wallace was an "ignorant, colored woman." These accounts echoed those printed in the *North American*, the Philadelphia newspaper that had reported on Evelina Frazier's case just three years earlier. What Evelina Frazier and Louisa Wallace shared was an apparent failure to conform to accepted and expected standards of respectable womanhood. Although each had allegedly killed her child, the court—and the public—still expected a performance of shame and regret, a request for forgiveness that might inspire mercy.[24]

Conforming to a well-established pattern with such cases involving Black women, President Rutherford B. Hayes commuted Louisa Wallace's death sentence to a three-year term in the penitentiary.[25] The "severe" punishment for her crime was interpreted as a means of placing limits on the alleged growth of the crime of infanticide, particularly among "colored" women in the nation's capital.[26] Although Wallace escaped the scaffold, Washington, DC, did not have a women's prison. Accordingly, Wallace was sent to Albany Penitentiary in New York.[27] Incarcerated since her arrest in April 1878, Wallace served almost four years in two different penal institutions. While the president commuted Wallace's death sentence, as a Black woman—and a former enslaved woman—she did not receive the mercy of a full pardon.[28] Instead, she was metaphorically, if not literally, reenslaved, forced to serve a prison term out of state, far away from family and friends.

Wallace's case did not end with her commutation. Several friends who testified in Wallace's defense were tried and convicted for perjury. One of these friends was described by the newspaper as a "yellow girl" and/or a Native American.[29] Like Wallace, Fanny Smith was sentenced to the Albany penitentiary. She was required to serve a term of two years.[30] Letha Matthews, a Black woman sixty-two years of age, was sentenced to five years in the Albany State Penitentiary for alleged perjury in Louisa Wallace's trial. Sentenced in February 1880, Matthews died in Albany five months later.[31]

Louisa Wallace's trial demonstrated how race affected not only the accused but those related to the individual convicted of the crime. The power of the carceral state rippled outward in the case of Louisa Wallace, capturing both Fanny Smith and Letha Matthews in its wake, costing Matthews her life. Fanny Smith—known colloquially as "Indian Smith"—testified, in her defense, that she had been paid to lie. The person who approached her was Louisa Wallace's lawyer, a white man. His reputation was impugned in open court by Smith, and he vigorously defended himself against the claims, characterizing Smith as a liar. The characterization was a difficult charge for Smith to refute, given she was on trial for perjury. Further, she was a woman and not white. Smith found few people willing to accept her narrative of events.

As the example of Evelina Frazier indicates, during Reconstruction public perceptions of African American women as less intelligent than white women—even white women who committed heinous crimes—were not limited to the former slave-owning states. In Rockport, Indiana, in February 1877, the local sheriff committed Eliza Henderson—described as a "young negress"—to jail. Henderson faced a charge of infanticide, allegedly having strangled her newborn infant. The local newspaper called for a fitting punishment for the crime, although it noted that Henderson was unlikely to be fully responsible for the murder. She was, after all, a woman with "a very low degree of intelligence." Indeed, she was an "imbecile." The same racialized prejudices that made Henderson susceptible to being assumed less intelligent meant that she was less likely to be fully responsible for the crime but also that she bore some culpability. Indeed, the *Rockport Democrat* attributed partial blame for the murder to the white man who had allegedly fathered the child, the "son of a well to do farmer" in a nearby town. No Black woman was capable of committing such a crime, alleged the newspaper, unless urged to do so by a white male who possessed the faculties of reason that enabled him to plan the murder. Yet, even as the Indiana newspaper, the *Jasper Weekly Courier*, condemned the actions of the seducer and extended concern for the suffering of Henderson, it called for swift justice. Even those not intelligent as others, so it seemed, should be punished for their crimes. That the newspaper could claim Henderson was less intelligent, rather than insane, seemed extraordinary given her reported mental state. The *Jasper Weekly Courier* characterized Henderson as distraught, almost suicidal. Only the care of a local doctor—white and male—ensured she had not acted on her impulses. To the contemporary reader, such a state of mind might seem more consistent with a disturbed mind, that is, insanity, than purported idiocy. But in Reconstruction America, Henderson's suicidal tendencies only reinforced prevailing beliefs that she was unfit for the responsibilities of freedom. As such, the community demanded incarceration, rather than care.[32]

The fate of African American women charged with infanticide is thrown into sharp relief when compared with cases involving white women, particularly those able to draw on the insanity defense. Assumed naturally more "civilized" than Black women, white women—particularly middle- and upper-class women—appealed to the defense of insanity as a means of mitigating culpability for the crime of infanticide. Importantly, the successful deployment of the defense did not mean that those who used it required incarceration in an asylum or facility for the insane. Rather, the defense relied upon the premise that childbirth resulted in a temporary loss of sanity for the afflicted woman. As such, even if a court deemed an accused woman insane at the moment of the crime, such a defense did not mandate long-term incarceration. In contrast, courts characterized a "weak mind"—lack of intelligence—as a permanent state, one related to race rather than gender. As such, a "weak mind"—as opposed to insanity—justified a prison sentence. Temporary insanity, in contrast, did not.

The case of Hannah Cox from Greensboro, North Carolina, illuminates the possibilities of a successfully deployed insanity defense. In September 1874, local police arrested a well-dressed, softly spoken young white woman at an Indianapolis train station. Although the police placed Cox in the state prison as she awaited her transfer back to North Carolina for trial, the *Greensboro Patriot* characterized the incarceration as necessary for "safekeeping and treatment," not as punishment. That Cox committed the crime with which she was charged was not in dispute. Several days earlier, Cox had given birth to a son in secret. She had then slit the child's throat and stuffed the bloody corpse in a carpet sack before making her escape. Indeed, Cox's cognizance of her wrongdoing was demonstrably evident, given that she fled the state after committing the offense. When she finally faced the Guilford County Superior Court in December 1874 on trial for infanticide, Hannah Cox had few options if she wished to escape a prison sentence.[33]

Given these circumstances, Hannah Cox leveraged what she could, appealing to prevailing ideas about insanity as a means to explain her actions. Three physicians testified in Cox's defense, attesting to the history of insanity in her family. Of those physicians, the most persuasive was Dr. Eugene Grissom, the superintendent of the North Carolina Insane Asylum. Grissom argued that it was definitely more likely for a woman to lose her sanity at the moment of birth, particularly when there was a history of insanity in the family. In that regard, the court heard from a number of witnesses, testifying about the "eccentric" nature of Cox's aunt. In addition, Hannah's father—Neri Cox—acknowledged to the court that he suffered from "falling down" disease. Grissom argued that Neri Cox's daughter, Hannah, had likely inherited the illness, resulting in "epileptic insanity" at the moment of birth. The jury acquitted Hannah Cox of the crime on the basis she was insane when she committed the act.[34]

Although Hannah Cox successfully employed the defense of insanity, in rare cases, the fate of African American women extended to white women. In those cases, courts assumed poor white women so ignorant that insanity—a defense of the civilized, ergo the educated—could not be employed. Historians know little about Sarah D. Johnson of Iredell County, North Carolina: not the name denoted by the initial "D" or even if the "D" was accurate. Reports of Johnson's age, for instance, varied widely. At least one report estimated she was as young as fifteen; other accounts suggested seventeen or eighteen. No one could say for sure. In contrast, newspaper accounts recorded in unerring detail the names of the judge, the Hon. David Schenck; the prisoner's court-appointed counsel; the prosecuting attorneys; the witnesses, for both the prosecution and the defense; and the members of the jury. What surviving records do indicate about Johnson is that she faced the Superior Court in mid-1877 charged with infanticide. That she killed her newborn infant was not in dispute, as the corpse "was found buried in a potato field with its throat cut." Nonetheless, the court appointed four white men, one of whom was a US congressman, to provide legal counsel for the accused woman. Those men recommended a plea of insanity.

The testimony, however, was inconsistent with such a plea. Witnesses testified that Johnson was "half witted" and "without common sense." She was "strange." David Schenck, the judge, characterized Johnson as an "imbecile" in his diary, observing that "she weeps bitterly and then laughs heartily." One physician, Dr. Hugh Kelly, testified as an "expert" witness on behalf of the defense. Drawing on his forty years' experience as a physician, Dr. Kelly argued that childbirth sometimes produced insanity. The "sympathy between the uterine system and the brain" explained why women were more apt to lose reason at the moment of giving birth, Kelly explained to the court. Unfortunately, in the eyes of the jury, all the evidence proved in Johnson's case was that she was not very intelligent. They concluded that she was not insane or at least not so at the time she committed the crime. The jury pronounced Sarah Johnson guilty of infanticide. The judge, in turn, sentenced Johnson to death. The governor commuted the sentence to ten years in the state penitentiary, but Johnson was dead within a year.[35]

Whoever Sarah Johnson was, the community that decided her fate considered her as deserving of the same fate as a Black woman. The terms used to categorize and describe her were those usually reserved for African American women accused of infanticide—and for African Americans, more generally—particularly in the late-nineteenth-century South. Johnson was not insane, a privilege usually reserved for white women. Rather, she was not very intelligent. She was "different" from the norm. Nowhere was this more clearly indicated than in one final newspaper account that noted Johnson's passing in prison. Even in death, Johnson was unique. She was the only white female incarcerated at the North Carolina State Penitentiary at the time.[36]

The fate of Johnson is thrown into stark relief when juxtaposed with that of the white male indicted with her, Frank Houston, the alleged father of the child. Sarah Johnson, the principal witness in Houston's case, alleged that Houston coerced her into murdering the infant. She did so under threat of death. But Johnson was doubly damned by the community's assessment of her intellectual capacity and sanity. The court tried the two offenders separately, determining Sarah Johnson's fate before Frank Houston's trial began. Although the court concluded Johnson was not insane, the community questioned Johnson's competence as a reliable witness, particularly in relation to the word of a white man, Frank Houston, whose sanity was not questionable. Community sentiment turned strongly against Frank Houston, the man who seduced the innocent and "virginal" Sarah Johnson. But condemnation of that behavior did not translate to a guilty verdict. Frank Houston walked away free from both jail and the burden of an unwanted child. In contrast, although Sarah Johnson escaped the noose, she died in prison.

For many Americans during Reconstruction, the act of infanticide signified insanity. No rational mother would kill her child. Therefore, only a loss of reason could explain such an irrational act. The problem with the causal link between insanity and infanticide is that it was a circular narrative without a circuit breaker. What came first? If infanticide, then the logic followed that the mother must be insane. If mania, then that explained why the mother committed infanticide. The beauty of the narrative was that it minimized culpability for the crime, enabling some mothers—especially white middle- and upper-class women—to escape the public theater of a trial for the crime, a guilty verdict if tried, or a harsh sentence if found guilty. Even as women made claims to the franchise and equal rights to men in civil courts and civic arenas on the basis of sameness, a focus on the difference of females from men—a difference allegedly rooted in biology—provided an escape route for some women in the context of criminal proceedings.

The problem with the narrative is that it trapped all women—of whatever race or ethnicity—within a framework in which biology dictated destiny. If essentially different from men, women could never be equal. Middle- and upper-class white women may have gained, or retained, the freedom to maneuver within the local legal system by conforming to gendered stereotypes that constructed women as more passionate and less capable of restraining emotions than men. Yet that freedom came at a cost, reinforcing prevailing ideas that women—of whatever race—did not deserve the same rights of citizenship as men. The freedom to walk away from serious criminal charges such as infanticide demanded that all women give up claims to an expanded range of political and civil rights: that is, the rights that white men possessed.

For African American women, the logic proved even more problematic. Excluded from exercising the full rights of citizenship by virtue of both race and gender, the narratives deployed by white women in infanticide cases could not be used in the same ways by African American women. Black females remained circumscribed by narratives that denied their intelligence. As such, they could not deploy insanity—a defense only available to the "civilized"—in the same ways that white women were able to do. Courts acknowledged that Black women accused of killing their newborn infants deserved mercy, but those women still remained condemned to pay for the crime of transgressing the invisible "color line" in such a visible manner. While prison sentences could be reduced and women spared from the death penalty, African American women—unlike white women—were less likely to escape punishment for their crimes entirely.

The Fourteenth Amendment to the Constitution expanded a broad range of civil rights to all of the newly emancipated, including women. But in local courts across the country—not just the former states of the Confederacy—the extension of these civil rights at the federal level often made a limited difference to the daily lives of Black women enmeshed in the tangle of the criminal justice system. Although African American women accused of infanticide appealed to the same gendered stereotypes as white women, those ideas about feminine behavior assumed different meanings when refracted through the lens of race. For African American women, unrestrained and passionate acts of violence served primarily as indicative of racist, not gendered, beliefs that characterized all African Americans—male and female—as "unfit" for citizenship.

Infanticide cases from Reconstruction-era courts and newspapers demonstrate that the freedom that accompanied the end of slavery and expanded civil rights proved messy and complicated for Black women across the nation. Although accused African American women sought to exercise the same freedoms as white women—to appeal to particular gendered ideas of and about female emotions and (lack of) intelligence as a means to limit culpability for the crime—Black women did not achieve the same outcomes or results. The stereotypes pertaining to gender always intersected with those related to race. Those ideas and beliefs about the capacities of African American women, therefore, produced particular outcomes, but they remained outcomes that ultimately limited the range of options available to—and the freedom of—Black women accused of infanticide, particularly in comparison to white women charged with committing the same crime.

## Notes

1. "A Mother's Terrible Crime," *The Times* (Philadelphia), July 26, 1876, 4; "A Batch of Homicides" *The Times* (PA), October 12, 1876, 1; and "An Infanticide Sentenced," *North American* (Philadelphia), November 3, 1876, 1.

2. For a discussion of the ways that juries struggled to convict women for these reasons during Reconstruction, see Wendy Gamber, *The Notorious Mrs. Clem: Murder and Money in the Gilded Age* (Baltimore, MD: Johns Hopkins University Press, 2016). The assumption about women's inability to plan a violent crime was so powerful that in rare cases the assumption even extended to African American women, including enslaved women before the Civil War. The best-known example of a community's disbelief in the face of evidence that an enslaved woman committed a violent crime is that of Celia, an enslaved woman from Missouri, who allegedly murdered her owner, cut him into pieces, and then burned the pieces in the fireplace. In this instance—as in many others—local communities struggled with the idea that women, regardless of race, possessed the physical strength to overpower a man and dispose of his body. In addition, the community grappled with the calculated and planned method in which Celia allegedly disposed of the body. For analyses of Celia's case, see Wilma King, "'Mad' Enough to Kill: Enslaved Women, Murder, and Southern Courts," *Journal of African American History* 92, no. 1 (Winter 2007): 37–56; and Melton A. McLaurin, *Celia, a Slave: A True Story* (New York: Avon, 1991).

3. As Susanna Blumenthal, *Law and the Modern Mind: Consciousness and Responsibility in American Legal Culture* (Cambridge, MA: Harvard University Press, 2016), has persuasively demonstrated, the law constructed the ideal citizen in the nineteenth-century United States as an able-bodied, rational white male, the person whom Supreme Court Justice Oliver Holmes described in 1881 as the "reasonable man." For recent studies that examine the socially constructed nature of the relationship between race and mental illness in the nineteenth-century United States, see Wendy Gonaver, *The Peculiar Institution and the Making of Modern Psychiatry, 1840–1880* (Chapel Hill: University of North Carolina Press, 2018); Yvonne Pitts, "Civic Capacity and Participatory Citizenship in Nineteenth-Century United States," in *The Routledge Research Companion to Law and Humanities in Nineteenth-Century America*, ed. Nan Goodman and Simon Stern (New York: Routledge, 2017), 311–22; Mab Segrest, *Administrations of Lunacy: Racism and the Haunting of American Psychiatry at the Milledgeville Asylum* (New York: New Press, 2020); Martin Summers, *Madness in the City of Magnificent Intentions: A History of Race and Mental Illness in the Nation's Capital* (New York: Oxford University Press, 2019). For an incisive analysis of the development of the scientific and medical basis for the argument perpetuated during slavery that freedom was dangerous to African Americans, see Christopher Willoughby, "Running away from Drapetomania: Samuel A. Cartwright, Medicine, and Race in the Antebellum South," *Journal of Southern History* 84, no. 3 (August 2018): 579–614.

4. For the scholarship that examines the intersection of ideas about race and reason in the nineteenth century, see the literature cited in note 3. For the intersection of ideas about gender, sanity, and reason, see Lauren McIvor Thompson, "'The Reasonable (Wo)man': Physicians, Freedom of Contract, and Women's Rights, 1870–1930," *Law and History Review* 36, no. 4 (November 2018): 771–809; Kim Nielsen, *Money, Marriage, and Madness: The Life of Anna Ott* (Urbana: University of Illinois Press, 2020); Yvonne Pitts, "Disability, Scientific Authority, and Women's Political Participation at the Turn-of-the-Twentieth Century United States," *Journal of Women's History* 24, no. 2 (Summer 2012): 37–61.

5. Benjamin Rush, *Medical Inquiries and Observations upon the Diseases of the Mind*, 5th ed. (Philadelphia: Grigg and Elliot, 1835): 57–58.

6. See Horatio Robinson Storer, "The Medical Management of Insane Women," *Boston Medical and Surgical Journal* 71, no. 11 (October 13, 1864): 209–18; Horatio Robinson Storer, "Cases Illustrative of Obstetric Disease—Deductions Concerning Insanity in Women," *Boston Medical and Surgical Journal* 70, no. 10 (April 7, 1864): 189–200.

7. Storer, "Cases Illustrative of Obstetric Disease," 194.

8. William Sedgwick, "Article IX—On the Legal Responsibility of Pregnant Women," *Medical Critic and Psychological Journal* 3, no. 12 (October 1863): 700. For further discussion of the negative implications of the "pregnancy as illness" framework for women in Great Britain, see Anne Digby, "Women's Biological Straitjacket," in *Sexuality and Subordination: Interdisciplinary Studies of Gender in the Nineteenth Century*, ed. Susan Mendus and Jane Rendall (London: Routledge, 1989), 192–220.

9. For case studies and summaries of the symptoms typical of puerperal insanity during this period, see T. W. Fisher MD, "Two Cases of Puerperal Insanity," *Boston Medical and Surgical Journal* 79, no. 2 (1869): 233–34; James MacDonald MD, "Puerperal Insanity," *American Journal of Insanity* 4 (October 1847): 113–63; William W. Morland MD, "Extracts from the Records of the Boston Society for Medical Improvement," in *American Journal of the Medical Sciences* 26, ed. Isaac Hays (1853): 345–46; "Summary: Puerperal Insanity," *American Journal of Insanity* 22 (July 1865): 137–39; R. M. Wigginton MD, "Puerperal Insanity," *Transactions of the Wisconsin State Medical Society* (Milwaukee: Cramer, Aikens & Cramer: 1875): 40–47. See also Nancy Theriot, "Diagnosing Unnatural Motherhood: Nineteenth-Century Physicians and 'Puerperal Insanity,'" *American Studies* 30, no. 2 (Fall 1989): 69–88. For the origins and development of "puerperal insanity" as a defense for infanticide in a British context, see Hilary Marland, *Dangerous Motherhood: Insanity and Childbirth in Victorian England* (New York: Palgrave Macmillan, 2004).

10. For the classic formulation of the argument that hysteria and related illnesses were diseases associated with civilization, see Gail Bederman, *Manliness and Civilization: A Cultural History of Gender and Race in the United States, 1880–1917* (Chicago: University of Chicago Press, 1995); Laura Briggs, "The Race of Hysteria: 'Overcivilization' and the 'Savage' Woman in Late-Nineteenth-Century Obstetrics and Gynecology," *American Quarterly* 52, no. 2 (June 2000): 246–73.

11. See Yvonne Pitts, *Family, Law, and Inheritance in America: A Social and Legal History of Nineteenth-Century Kentucky* (New York: Cambridge University Press, 2013), 114–40.

12. For Benjamin Rush's use of science and medicine to justify the abolition of slavery, see Eric Herschthal, "Antislavery Science in the Early Republic: The Case of Dr. Benjamin Rush," *Early American Studies* 15, no. 3 (Spring 2017): 274–307.

13. See Samuel Cartwright, "Report on the Diseases and Physical Peculiarities of the Negro Race," *New Orleans Medical and Surgical Journal* 7 (1850–1851): 691–715; John Duffy, "A Note on Ante-Bellum Southern Nationalism and Medical Practice," *Journal of Southern History* 34, no. 2 (May 1968): 269; Rana Hogarth, *Medicalizing Blackness: Making Racial Difference in the Atlantic World, 1780–1840* (Chapel Hill: University of North Carolina Press, 2017), 1–4; Gretchen Long, *Doctoring Freedom: The Politics of African American Medical Care in Slavery and Freedom* (Chapel Hill: University of North Carolina Press, 2012), 37; Peter McCandless, *Moonlight, Magnolias, and Madness: Insanity in South Carolina from the Colonial Period to the Progressive Era* (Chapel Hill: University of North Carolina Press, 1996), 155; Willoughby, "Running away from Drapetomania"; Josiah C. Nott and George R. Glidden, *Types of Mankind* (Philadelphia: Lippincott, Grambo & Co., 1854), 259–60.

14. Albert Deutsch, "The First U.S. Census of the Insane (1840) and Its Use as Pro-Slavery Propaganda," *Bulletin of the History of Medicine* 15 (May 1944): 469–482; John M. Galt, "Asylums for Colored Persons," *American Psychological Journal* (1853): 78–88; Gerald N. Grob, *Edward Jarvis and the Medical World of Nineteenth-Century America* (Knoxville: University of Tennessee Press, 1978), 70–75; Edward Jarvis, "Insanity Among the Colored Population of the Free States," *American Journal of the Medical Sciences* 7 (1844): 71–83; John S. Hughes, "Labeling and Treating Black Mental Illness in Alabama, 1861–1910," *Journal of Southern History* 58, no. 3 (August 1992): 436–39; Paul Schor, *Counting Americans: How the US Census Classified the Nation*, trans. Lys Ann Weiss (New York: Oxford University Press, 2017), 30–41.

15. *Report on the Public Charities, Reformatories, Prisons and Almhouses, of the State of Maryland, by C. W. Chancellor, M.D., Secretary of the State Board of Health, Made to His Excellency, John Lee Carroll, Governor, July, 1877* (Frederick, MD, 1877), 14–15, qtd. in Gerald N. Grob, "Class, Ethnicity, and Race in American Mental Hospitals, 1830–75," *Journal of the History of Medicine* 28, no. 3 (July 1973): 227. For the growth of the gendered carceral state, particularly in the South, during Reconstruction and beyond, see Kali N. Gross and Cheryl D. Hicks, "Introduction—Gendering the Carceral State: African American Women, History, and the Criminal Justice System," *Journal of African American History* 100, no. 3 (Spring 2015): 357–65; Sarah Haley, *No Mercy Here: Gender, Punishment, and the Making of Jim Crow Modernity* (Chapel Hill: University of North Carolina Press, 2016), 17–57; Talitha LeFlouria, *Chained in Silence: Black Women and Convict Labor in the New South* (Chapel Hill: University of North Carolina Press, 2015), 21–60.

16. For an assessment of how courts treated women in infanticide cases during Reconstruction, see Felicity Turner, "Rights and the Ambiguities of the Law: Infanticide in the Nineteenth-Century U.S. South," *Journal of the Civil War Era* 4, no. 3 (September 2014): 350–72.

17. See "News of the Day—Criminal Court," *Alexandria Gazette*, July 3, 1871, 3; "Sentenced to Death," *New York Times*, July 4, 1871; Sarah A. Shimm, "Women to the Rescue!

A Life at Stake!," *New National Era* (Washington, DC), July 27, 1871; "Personal, Political, and General," *New York Times*, August 14, 1871; "Reading of the Death-Warrant to a Woman," *New York Times*, August 16, 1871.

18. Edward Warren, *A Doctor's Experience in Three Continents* (Baltimore, MD: Cushings & Bailey, 1885), 368–69; "Leah Scarborough," *New National Era*, September 21, 1871, 2; "News of the Day," *Alexandria Gazette* (Alexandria, MD), September 22, 1871, 2.

19. "Sentence of Leah Scarborough Commuted," *New National Era*, September 28, 1871, 2.

20. "A Woman Arrested on Suspicion of Child Murder," *Evening Star*, April 27, 1878, 4. See also Jill Norgren, *Rebels at the Bar: The Fascinating, Forgotten Stories of America's First Women Lawyers* (New York: New York University Press, 2013), 95.

21. "Under the Scaffold," *National Republican* (Washington, DC), December 21, 1878, 4; "A Woman Convicted of Murder," *New York Herald*, December 21, 1878, 3.

22. "The Child-Murder Case," *Evening Star* (Washington, DC), April 5, 1879, 4; "The Conviction of Louisa Wallace," *Evening Star*, April 7, 1879, 4; "Guilty of Infanticide," *National Republican*, April 7, 1879, 4.

23. "Convicted of Murdering Her Infant," *Evening Star*, January 24, 1879, 5.

24. In her close study of the Black woman Hannah Mary Tabbs—accused of murder in Philadelphia in 1887—the historian Kali Gross examines the ways that Black women who challenged accepted norms of femininity fared within the late-nineteenth-century criminal justice system. Kali Nicole Gross, *Hannah Mary Tabbs and the Disembodied Torso: A Tale of Race, Sex, and Violence in America* (New York: Oxford University Press, 2016).

25. "Reprieve," *Alexandria Gazette*, June 16, 1879, 2; "Saved from the Gallows," *National Republican*, June 17, 1879, 4; "Saved from the Gallows," *Evening Star*, June 18, 1879, 1. Only the president possessed authority to grant pardons or commute sentences in the District of Columbia.

26. "The verdict . . .," *Evening Star*, April 12, 1879, 2, 4; "The Death Penalty," *National Republican*, April 14, 1879, 1.

27. "Prisoners Sent to Albany Penitentiary," *Evening Star*, June 24, 1879, 4; "Gone to Albany," *National Republican*, June 24, 1879, 4.

28. "Charge of Child Murder," *Evening Star*, April 3, 1879, 4.

29. "Charge of Perjury on a Murder Trial," *Evening Star*, April 8, 1879, 4; "Trial for Perjury," *Evening Star*, May 16, 1879, 4; "The Perjury Case," *Evening Star*, May 17, 1879, 8; "The Case of Letha Matthews," *Evening Star*, May 19, 1879, 4.

30. "Sentenced for Perjury," *Evening Star*, June 13, 1879, 4; "Convicted of Perjury," *National Republican*, February 9, 1880, 4.

31. "Sudden Death of a Woman in Jail," *Evening Star*, June 28, 1880, 4.

32. "Child Murder," *Jasper Weekly Courier* (Jasper, IN), February 23, 1877, 4, reprinted from the *Rockport Democrat* (Rockport, IN); "The State," *Indiana State Sentinel* (Indianapolis), February 28, 1877, 7.

33. "Infanticide," *Greensboro Patriot* (Greensboro, NC), September 9, 1874, 3; "A Quakeress Criminal," *Inter Ocean* (Chicago), September 20, 1874, 2. Indicted in Randolph County—as that is where the offense occurred—that case was removed to Guilford County. "State News," *Charlotte Observer*, December 20, 1874, 2.

34. "State vs. Hannah Cox," *Greensboro North State* (Greensboro, NC), December 18, 1874, 3; "Hannah Cox," *Carolina Watchman* (Salisbury, NC), December 24, 1874, 3.

35. For David Schenck's recollections of the trial, see Diary of David Schenck, January 1, 1877–December 31, 1822, 41, Southern Historical Collection, University of North Carolina, Chapel Hill. For newspaper accounts, see "Iredell Superior Court," *Observer* (Raleigh, NC), July 24, 1877, 3; "Sentenced to Death," *Carolina Watchman* (Salisbury, NC), July 26, 1877, 2; "State News," *Danbury Reporter* (Danbury, NC), June 13, 1878, 3. Of the four men appointed as counsel for Sarah D. Johnson, one was Major William McKendree Robbins. At that time, Robbins was a member of the US House of Representatives. He lost his bid for reelection in 1878.

36. "Sarah D. Johnson," *Farmer & Mechanic* (Raleigh, NC), June 20, 1878, 80.

# Idealism versus Material Realities

*Economic Woes for Northern African American Soldiers and Their Families*

## Holly A. Pinheiro, Jr.

On October 23, 1863, Sergeant Henry S. Harmon of the Third United States Colored Infantry (USCI) penned a letter to the *Christian Recorder*, an African American newspaper publishing in Philadelphia, Pennsylvania. Since the press had a broad audience in multiple northeastern states, it is plausible that he intended his musings to spread beyond the Keystone State.[1] Harmon's self-reflective piece touched on several topics, including his belief that serving as a United States Colored Troops (USCT) soldier affirmed his relationship to the Union and allowed him to become an armed liberator to his enslaved brethren. He explained to readers that he was not alone, writing, "Now a great many of us have sworn to go forth to battle for our country's rights, our rights, [and] our people's rights."[2] For Harmon, military service was about more than national reunification. It was also about restructuring American society to recognize the humanity of enslaved people, ensuring political and civil rights were awarded to African Americans, and providing new freedoms to all African Americans.

Before enlisting, Harmon (a Philadelphia native) was a sailor.[3] Harmon's ability to work a civilian occupation that most northern African Americans could not was in itself astounding.[4] However, even more impressive was how Harmon (the son of formerly enslaved parents) became a prominent political figure in Florida after the Civil War.[5] Throughout the late nineteenth century, he was extremely accomplished, having served in Florida's House of Representatives, becoming the first African American to pass the state's bar and later a practicing attorney.[6] Harmon's life provides a remarkable example of a northern freeborn USCT veteran who directly benefited from soldiering, in terms of dramatic improvement to his economic, social, and political status. As such, Harmon has attracted the attention of a number of scholars, who have examined both his wartime experiences and, more frequently, his postservice life.[7] What these historians have failed to indicate, however, is that Harmon's experience was in fact exceptional—maybe unique, even. As a result of focusing on success stories like Harmon's, a narrative of African American male heroism and uplift has misleadingly come to dominate the historiography of African American soldiers' wartime and postwar experience. For many African Americans who fought in the USCT, the selfless commitment to the cause of freedom for their enslaved brethren in the Confederacy did not in fact enhance their own freedom and, in many cases, resulted not only in physical injury and psychological damage but also in economic constraint and loss of social status.

Few scholars detail the postwar lives of less accomplished northern freeborn USCT veterans, and even fewer pay attention to these soldiers' families. The majority of Civil War scholarship privileges the lived experiences of white veterans and their kin, north and south, often relegating African Americans, especially freeborn, to peripheral figures who receive limited analysis, usually in a study's later section.[8] Studies of African American veterans focus on men such as Harmon because of their impressive postwar success. However, Harmon's experience is only one small part of the story of USCT veterans and not exactly representative. Many northern freeborn USCT veterans had very different, often even negative, experiences that affected their subsequent careers. In many cases, freeborn African Americans actually lost some of their freedom and economic mobility. An examination of these men, men whose military service won freedom for others but caused their own freedom to be constrained, is long overdue. Furthermore, while their stories may not be the only ones, their lived experiences are critical when thinking about USCT service and its legacies. By focusing on how freedoms, broadly defined, were gained and lost by soldiers in the USCT during the Civil War and Reconstruction, we can begin to think about what else freeborn African American soldiers and their families lost as a result of their military service.

By investigating the lives of USCT veterans and their kin in the immediate postwar period, one discovers that many suffered significantly even as their emancipated brethren saw an expansion to their rights and opportunities. Through an exploration of court-martials, the extended lengths of service USCT troops experienced after Robert E. Lee's surrender, and veterans' subsequent inability to establish financial independence as civilians given their wartime disabilities (psychological, physical, and emotional), this essay provides a new understanding of how participating in reconstructing American society did not always improve the lives of northern freeborn African Americans. In fact, many actually lost physical and economic freedom during and sometimes long after the war ended.

This essay focuses on a small but select group of northern freeborn USCT soldiers who experienced significant hardships throughout the mid- and late nineteenth century. Given the limited documentation of the lives of these historically marginalized people, it is not possible to extrapolate definitively from these soldiers' life stories, but examining the federal census, compiled military service records, military court-martial records, African American newspapers, and Civil War pension records reveals a considerable amount about the lived experiences of African Americans who struggled to become liberators. The people examined here are neither entirely singular nor fully representative cases. They do, however, provide counternarratives to the triumphal stories of men like Henry S. Harmon.

All Civil War enlistees regardless of race quickly discovered that becoming a soldier meant that each man had to relinquish some fundamental aspects of his freedom and identity.[9] Regardless of a soldier's race or station in life before the war, the US Army demanded conformity (by force if necessary) to the rigid structure and training of military life. Immediately on encountering the harsh reality of military service, soldiers found themselves confronted by strict limitations on all aspects of their lives: when and where they moved, what they ate, what they wore.[10] The difficulty of conforming to these constrictions was compounded by the enlistees' gender ideology, which hinged on self-reliance as a key component of masculinity. Organizing an assortment of individual men, from all walks of life, into soldiers was a grueling process but essential for the US Army to accomplish its objectives.[11] Unsurprisingly, many men came into conflict with military regimen after discovering that the ideal and reality of soldiering could not coexist.[12]

Race was, sadly, a determining factor in how US Army soldiers experienced the Civil War. In the first two years of the war, northern African American men were not even allowed to enlist.[13] Only following federal legislation, including the Militia Act of 1862 and the Emancipation Proclamation, did the creation of the various USCT regiments occur. Once USCT enlistment began, many northern African American communities, because of economic inequality, were incapable of providing local bounties (payments raised by local people and organizations) to provide immediate monetary aid to the men or their cash-strapped families. Conversely, various northern white communities privately funded local bounties, sometimes monthly, for soldiers and their nuclear dependents.[14]

In the absence of private support, USCT soldiers were dependent on federal bounties, but that payment was often deferred. Federal bounties were financial enticements that the US Army used in the hopes of getting men to enroll by promising payments varying from one hundred to three hundred dollars. For instance, a random sample of 185 Philadelphia-born soldiers in Pennsylvanian USCT regiments reveals that the majority of the men received federal bounties only after the war was over. Until mid-1864, the US Army had mandated that these soldiers would have to wait until their regiments demobilized before they could receive their promised bounties.[15] Resentment continuously festered among many USCT soldiers, sometimes even boiling over, since the US Army enforced numerous racially discriminatory policies. Some USCT soldiers wrote letters of complaint, penned op-eds, defied orders, and even went on strike to demonstrate their dissatisfaction with their soldiering, especially when they experienced threats or slights (real or imagined) to their manhood.[16]

USCT soldiers learned, as many white soldiers did too, that pay disbursement was a problem that affected them and their families. Given the frequent movements of army regiments and a limited number of paymasters, many soldiers suffered without regular payments; the paymasters tended to arrive only sporadically, which meant that all too often they were distributing money months in arrears.[17] When the paymaster appeared, some soldiers cheered at the realization that they would finally get their back pay. John C. Brock, a Forty-Third USCI quartermaster, informed the *Christian Recorder* of a delayed payment while at camp in Petersburg, Virginia. "We had been expecting him for some time," Brock said, referring to the paymaster, "and at last he came, with greenbacks in abundance."[18] However, the irregularity of monthly pay angered other northern USCT soldiers. Twenty-Second USCI soldier William L. Miller vented that his regiment had not received money since December 1863, when the regiment mustered in. Miller complained, "Our pocket-books are getting very flat."[19] Unfortunately, Miller did not get paid until February 1865.[20]

Even though pay infrequency was a universal issue for all enlisted men, the lower pay, mandated by military policy, made the situation for USCT soldiers even worse. When USCT soldiers were paid, it was barely half of what a white soldier expected. Until 1864, all USCT soldiers received seven dollars monthly, while their white counterparts earned thirteen dollars. The salary disparity created financial insecurity on the home front—and thus endangered the economic independence of USCT soldiers' families.[21] One disgruntled USCT soldier, writing under the pseudonym "Bought and Sold," criticized the federal government and the US Army in a letter to the *Christian Recorder*, writing, "Seven dollars will not pay the rent, let alone keeping a family of three and in most cases six and nine."[22] Countless other northern USCT soldiers felt similarly. Some chose to express their anger in print to inform the home front of the ways that some USCT soldiers felt disrespected by a racist military policy that established pay inequality for men of the same rank. Another soldier complained to the *Christian Recorder* that "they have the insolence to offer us seven dollars a month, expecting that the men would take it; but we had more sense than that, for we did not enlist for that amount of money."[23] Realizing that race determined their rate of pay, USCT soldiers rapidly became aware of the bitter irony that their actions as emancipators actually jeopardized their own immediate families' finances and undermined their claims to equality.

Racist practices in the US Army did not end when the Civil War did. Immediately following the war, numerous US Army officials, all white men, reasoned that white soldiers' lengthy tenure warranted their earlier release.[24] By contrast, USCT soldiers, many of whom had served just as long, were required to remain in service and were sent to work to accomplish national objectives, such as occupying former Confederate states, subduing Native American tribes, protecting freedpeople, and defending the Mexican-American border from a possible French invasion. For Thirty-First USCI enlisted men, such as Albert A. Peckham, military service, like many other USCT soldiers, continued long after pursuing Robert E. Lee's forces to Appomattox Court House, Virginia, where he surrendered.[25] Thus, the US Army and federal government expected more of USCT troops for less, but rarely were the regiments given credit for the significant work that they performed.

Issues over money sometimes led to various forms of military disobedience among USCT soldiers, which occasionally resulted in court-martials. In August 1865, while stationed in Texas, Peckham was charged with forgery and prejudice to good order and military discipline after his regiment discovered that he had fraudulently signed a paycheck as both Private David Hall and Lieutenant Albert Latham. In doing so, Peckham effectively stole ten dollars from Private Hall (another USCT soldier). Peckham eventually pled guilty to the charges. As a result of his actions, Peckham was sentenced to a period of six months of hard labor, which lasted until after the Thirty-First USCI mustered out on November 7, 1865. While in prison, Peckham received no pay.[26] Having first enlisted to bring freedom to others and subsequently been deployed to protect his nation against foreign invasion, this soldier's military career resulted in him literally losing his freedom, costing him six months of military pay and hindering his chances of receiving a pension after the war.

Military records do not explain the motive for Peckham's brazen actions. It is still possible, however, to speculate what motivated his activities by contextualizing his military service. Peckham, an eighteen-year-old Connecticut native, chose to enlist in the Thirty-First USCI. He later incurred a wound after a shelling on May 10, 1864, that placed him in and out of multiple hospitals until November.[27] Months after he had returned to the regiment, the Thirty-First USCI was deployed to the Southwest. Perhaps during this time Peckham was slighted by Hall and Latham in some undisclosed way. It is also feasible that he no longer wanted to be in the US Army and used his defiant actions to demonstrate his opposition to the rigid structures of military life. Whatever his motivation(s), he had his freedom and wage-earning ability taken away at exactly the same time many formerly enslaved people were beginning to exercise new freedoms.

For many northern freeborn USCT soldiers, the immediate postwar period was an exhilarating time but also potentially dangerous, as they were on the front lines of restructuring American society. For some African American men, remaining in the US Army was vital: They understood the role they had to play in protecting the newly acquired rights of freedpeople from ex-Confederates, by force if necessary.[28] Others felt that USCT service needed to continue until northern racism abated and African American men gained voting rights.[29] While national policies after the war saw national reunification as the primary objective, many USCT soldiers viewed themselves more specifically as freedom purveyors and protectors of African Americans.[30]

For others, the idealism motivating their military service did not supersede African American soldiers' legitimate material concerns over the risks to their own lives or their families' survival caused by remaining in service after Lee's surrender. During his time in Texas, Henry Carpenter Hoyle, a Forty-Third USCI soldier and Philadelphia native, wrote back east to tell other northern African Americans that he and some members of his regiment, because of familial and financial concerns, desired to return to civilian life. Hoyle noted, "There are many down here worrying themselves about home and money. I am well aware what it is to be without money and away from home."[31] Undoubtedly northern freeborn USCT soldiers sincerely cared about having the humanity and rights of all African Americans recognized and protected nationwide. However, the realities of home, especially in the immediate postwar period, were ever-present in the minds and lives of African American men on the front lines.

After the Confederate Army surrendered, some USCT soldiers turned their attention homeward. Asking to leave the military was not always looked upon positively within USCT regiments. For instance, Garland H. White, a chaplain in the Twenty-Eighth USCI, mocked members of his regiment for openly pining to reunite with their kin, scolding that "some silly-minded men talk sometimes about home, and I have to quiet them by assuring them that all will come right in the end."[32] White's dismissive and condescending tone illustrates that he was deaf to the soldiers' pleas to return home, and he failed to understand the combination of social, financial, and emotional pressures caused by the soldiers' continued separation from their families.[33]

By August 20, 1865, Charles W. Cole, another Philadelphia native, detailed that he and numerous Twenty-Ninth USCI soldiers wanted to end their soldiering. "The home fever," Cole vented, "is raging here among all the soldiers, and all seem eager to start north at once. I am sick and tired of camp life and long for the hour to come when I can return to the City of Brotherly Love, and join the friends and loved ones at home."[34] Alexander Heritage Newton, a fellow Twenty-Ninth USCI soldier, later confirmed his comrade's assertion in a 1910 regimental history, recalling, "It is needless to say, that the home-fever spread more rapidly than any fever that had ever prevailed in our ranks. We looked for and patiently awaited the day when we would be mustered out."[35] These USCT soldiers, and many others, chafed at the fact that the war was over but their service was not. The Twenty-Ninth USCI did not muster out until November 6, 1865.[36]

By the summer of 1865, many USCT regiments remained in operation. In numerous cases, being forced to remain in service after the Civil War officially ended cost the men more than money. They paid with the loss of their physical and mental health. Multiple USCT regiments became accustomed to illness. The Philadelphia native and Third USCI soldier William B. Johnson lamented that his comrades' deteriorating health rendered them ineffective in Jacksonville, Florida. "While there," he wrote, "the men suffered, fevers raged throughout the camp, and out of 800 men, there were not 300 fit for active service."[37] While some men returned to the ranks, others did not.

The US Army's decision to place numerous USCT regiments in Texas was cataclysmic for some enlisted men. The further that the regiments moved from established supply routes, the more deadly military service became. The US Army's inability to provide healthy nutrition and clean drinking water was a recipe for disaster. In July 1865, nearly half of the ten thousand soldiers stationed in Brazos fell ill from contaminated water. Many USCT soldiers purchased clean water from the Rio Grande River that some entrepreneurial bottlers sold at ten cents each.[38] In this instance, African American men had to decide whether to tap into their finances or risk drinking bad water that could lead to death from typhoid fever, chronic diarrhea, dysentery, or cholera.[39] The aforementioned Charles W. Cole noted that men were not merely homesick but physically sick as well. He informed the *Christian Recorder* that disease was now routine, noting, "Our hospitals are filled with the sick, but the boys are getting used to it."[40]

Cole, luckily, survived to write about the conditions of his regiment on the Mexican-American border. Not all of his comrades were so fortunate. In fact, despite having come through the deadly conflict to free enslaved people, many USCT soldiers now found themselves risking death by disease in supposedly "free" Texas. As Garland H. White wrote: "No set of men in any country ever suffered more severely than we in Texas. Death has made fearful gaps in every regiment. Going to the grave with the dead is as common to me as going to bed."[41] White's dire tone illustrates that the reality of dying, at least while stationed in Texas, caused him and others to come to terms with their mortality. When enlisting, USCT soldiers had no doubt confronted the risk of their possible demise in armed combat against Confederates. They had probably not foreseen what was to happen to many in reality, that death would come slowly and painfully in regimental camps and hospitals from viruses and microbial bacteria.[42]

When demobilization of USCT regiments finally came, between late 1865 and 1867, honorably discharged USCT soldiers finally received their enlistment bounties. For USCT veterans and their kin, these sizable lump-sum payments were welcomed, though long overdue. Some African American men used their cash on themselves, as they reclaimed their individuality in civilian life.[43] Others, especially those with children, took their money and returned home, to provide a much-needed substantial financial injection into their households. When Nathaniel Logan mustered out of the Sixth USCI, for instance, he finally received his one hundred dollars bounty.[44] Since Logan had a wife and young child, and multiple fictive kin residing with them, it is plausible that he used his enlistment to keep their complex household economically stable immediately upon returning.[45] Even the receipt of their bounties, though, did not ensure economic stability, regardless of the amount, for USCT veterans or their kin.

After surviving the war, some USCT veterans discovered that their war wounds—both seen and unseen—made moving on from the war extremely difficult. Even worse, some of these men could not find employment because of their various disabilities. Thomas Moore, for instance, suffered from rheumatic pain that kept him from working.[46] Other USCT veterans with severe physical deformities, like George Roland, found it nearly impossible to work.[47] Perhaps some of these USCT veterans viewed their unemployment as a failure to fulfill their supposed masculine obligations as wage earners.[48]

Meanwhile, some northern African American civilians began to recognize and emphasize that USCT soldiers needed civilian jobs after the war. For instance, the *Weekly Anglo-African*, an African American newspaper published in New York City, informed its readers that they had a responsibility to help the men find work, as "above all let us not forget to have doors open for them to enter into any employment or business they may desire."[49] Hiring soon-to-be USCT veterans would allow them to resume their economic independence, which some men considered an essential masculine trait.[50] The *Weekly Anglo-African*'s editorial, while idealistic, illustrates the persistent commitment that some northern African Americans maintained to honor the sacrifices that USCT soldiers made as freedom purveyors and national heroes.

Despite the *Weekly Anglo-African*'s best efforts, many USCT veterans, for different reasons, struggled to find regular employment. Aside from their individual disabilities, social conditions also militated against them; reconstructing the nation did not lead to an end to northern racism, even for the men responsible for restoring the Union.[51] Numerous able-bodied USCT veterans, sadly, came to realize what many civilian African Americans already knew, that racist social expectations would continue to limit most African American men in the postwar period to unskilled occupations.[52] The USCT veterans George Ross, Jacob Pernell, Henry Johnson, and James Richmond could find work only as laborers in 1870, during a period when whites—civilian and veteran—were quicker to find employment in northern cities like Boston in a variety of semiskilled, skilled, and professional occupations.[53]

Not all northern USCT soldiers had difficulty finding regular paid work, however, and some even became financially successful working various semiskilled and skilled occupations. For instance, some Philadelphia-born USCT veterans impressively navigated occupational racial discrimination as barbers, fishermen, waiters, drivers, and farm laborers.[54] Unfortunately, their experiences were not universal, as other northern USCT veterans worked as laborers or found only temporary work.

The unemployability of many USCT veterans meant that they needed to find new ways to earn money.[55] Civil War pensions, beginning in 1862, became a potential avenue for some African American invalid veterans—and possibly dependents, both nuclear and sometimes extended kin—to receive economic restitution for their wartime sacrifices and postwar problems.[56] Applying for a pension was not easy, however, and approval of one's application was never guaranteed. In many cases, records of illnesses and wounds did not exist because the soldiers had not received formal medical treatment, and frequently USCT soldiers distrusted the white medical profession because of its institutional racism.[57] In some cases, even with evidence, some USCT veterans still did not have their pensions approved.[58] For instance, Charles Brant included testimony from the former lieutenant colonel Loren Burritt confirming that Brant had received an injury during the Battle of Olustee. Unfortunately, the Bureau of Pensions rejected Brant's case, since it noted that there was no record of him getting treatment in a regimental hospital.[59] Similarly, even though Charles Jervis was pension eligible, he did not apply for an invalid pension until the US Congress passed the revised 1890 pension law, which permitted veterans with disabilities not directly connected to an invalid applicant's military service to apply.[60] Before 1890, Jervis, for unknown reasons, did not submit a pension application. Maybe Jervis felt that the Bureau of Pensions might claim he had developed his physical pain outside of service. Whatever their individual circumstances, these veterans and many others like them continued to struggle after the war without any financial recompense from the government that had called on them to risk their lives in the pursuit of freedom for their formerly enslaved brothers and sisters.

While pensions were meant to help those the Bureau of Pensions deemed "worthy," the rigorous and invasive application process usually privileged white applicants over African Americans. A combination of financial issues, racism, and a complicated bureaucratic system often kept African American veterans and dependents from applying for a pension in the first place. Some USCT veterans could not afford the lawyers, for instance, or find witnesses, or provide suitable documentation to substantiate their claims, which deterred many potential applicants.[61] Additionally, the rigorously bureaucratic process, including an invasive scrutinization of both the bodies and the personal lives of veterans, their kin, and even community members, might have deterred African American veterans from applying for a pension.[62] Historians also note that pension agents, all of whom were white men, usually believed that most African American claimants were trying to defraud the federal government out of money.[63] Thus even after the war ended, racist assumptions and practices continued to restrict African Americans. While white soldiers had enjoyed higher pay during the war, swifter demobilization at its end, and more generous treatment in relation to pensions after the war, USCT veterans continued to struggle economically with little to no acknowledgment of material recompense for the physical, emotional, and psychological toll that their military service had taken on them.[64]

By enlisting, and in exchange for their efforts to garner freedom for formerly enslaved people, many northern freeborn USCT soldiers effectively lost their own freedom and had their long-term economic independence and ability to earn wages jeopardized. While a few notable individuals like Henry S. Harmon launched themselves to higher social status through military service, for many, serving temporarily in USCT regiments caused immediate and sometimes lasting economic hardship for their families, exacerbating preexisting poverty in the face of persistent racial discrimination. Ironically, therefore, military service had the potential to damage many African American families' economic situations in ways overlooked by historians who emphasize a triumphant narrative of racial progress. The military service of northern freeborn USCT soldiers may have been critical in emancipating their formerly enslaved brothers and sisters in the South (and protecting them once they had been freed). However, at the same time, those very contributions caused significant and, in many cases, lasting economic adversities that thwarted their own ability to establish financial independence.

Racism was inescapable for all African Americans. USCT military service may have changed the lives of formerly enslaved people, but it also demonstrated to freeborn northern USCT soldiers and their families that soldiering would not end racial discrimination. While abolitionists celebrated the changes that freedpeople experienced, enlisted men continued to have to deal with racism both during and after the war in ways that negatively affected themselves as well as their families. Discriminatory practices while in service, the result of policies established by the War Department, put the minds and bodies of African American soldiers at greater psychological and physical risk than their white counterparts. As the war raged on, these problems also extended to the home front in ways that no one had foreseen.

For African Americans, while the Civil War brought nominal freedom for formerly enslaved people, it also created great losses for USCT soldiers and their families after the war. In having brought about feelings both of jubilation and of agony, it is clear that there was no monolithic experience among African Americans: Soldiers, their kin, and formerly enslaved people all experienced the war and its long-term effects differently. Examining the experience of African American soldiers and their families during and after the war indicates how complicated the war's outcomes were for African Americans. Yes, the war brought formal freedom and certain constitutionally enshrined political rights, but it also failed to set the conditions that could secure that freedom or render it economically meaningful. The struggles to achieve those conditions continue to this day.

### Notes

1. Eric Gardner, *Black Print Unbound: The* Christian Recorder, *African American Literature, and Periodical Culture* (Oxford: Oxford University Press, 2015), 4–6, 10, 36–40, 84–91; Andrew J. Rusk, "Letter from a Soldier," *Christian Recorder*, April 16, 1864.

2. Henry S. Harmon, "For the *Christian Recorder*. Camp of 3d. United States," *Christian Recorder*, November 7, 1863.

3. *Compiled Military Service Records of Volunteer Union Soldiers Who Served with the United States Colored Troops, 2nd through 7th Colored Infantry including 3d Tennessee Volunteers (African Descent), 6th Louisiana Infantry (African Descent), and 7th Louisiana Infantry (African Descent)*, Microfilm Serial: M1820, Microfilm Roll: 20, Film Reel: 1638. Hereafter, "Compiled Military Service Records."

4. "Free Blacks," *Frederick Douglass' Paper*, October 19, 1855; Jane E. Dabel, *A Respectable Woman: The Public Roles of African American Women in Nineteenth-Century New York* (New York: New York University Press, 2008), 66–73.

5. US Census Bureau, Seventh Census of the United States, 1850, M432 (Washington, D.C.: National Archives and Records Administration, 1850).

6. Darius J. Young, "Henry S. Harmon: Pioneer African American Attorney in Reconstruction-Era Florida," *Florida Historical Quarterly* 85, no. 2 (Fall 2006): 183–88.

7. See John F. Fannin, "The Jacksonville Mutiny of 1865," *Florida Historical Quarterly* 88, no. 3 (Winter 2010); Murray D. Laurie, "The Union Academy: A Freedmen's Bureau School in Gainesville, Florida," *Florida Historical Quarterly* 65, no. 2 (October 1986); Andrew T. Tremel, "The Union League, Black Leaders, and the Recruitment of Philadelphia's African American Civil War Regiments," *Pennsylvania History: A Journal of Mid-Atlantic Studies* 80, no. 1 (2013); Jerrell H. Shofner, "Militant Negro Laborers in Reconstruction Florida," *Journal of Southern History* 39, no. 3 (August 1973); Larry Eugene Rivers and Canter Brown Jr., "'A Monument to the Progress of the Race': The Intellectual and Political Origins of the Florida Agricultural and Mechanical University, 1865–1887," *Florida Historical Quarterly* 85, no. 1 (Summer 2006); Young, "Henry S. Harmon."

8. See Edmund J. Raus Jr., *Banners South: A Northern Community at War* (Kent, OH: Kent State University Press, 2005); Jonathan M. Steplyk, *Fighting Means Killing: Civil War Soldiers and the Nature of Combat* (Lawrence: University of Kansas Press, 2018); Paul Taylor, *"The Most Complete Political Machine Ever Known": The North's Union Leagues in the American Civil War* (Kent, OH: Kent State University Press, 2018); Gerald Linderman, *Embattled Courage: The Experience of Combat in the American Civil War* (New York: Free Press, 1987).

9. Lorien Foote, *The Gentlemen and the Roughs: Violence, Honor, and Manhood in the Union Army* (New York: New York University Press, 2010), 119, 128, 146, 152, 158; Reid Mitchell, *The Vacant Chair: The Northern Soldier Leaves Home* (Oxford: Oxford University Press, 1993), 45–46, 56–61.

10. James J. Broomall, "Wartime Masculinities," in *The Cambridge History of the American Civil War*, vol. 3: *Affairs of the People*, ed. Aaron Sheehan-Dean (Cambridge: Cambridge University Press, 2019), 4–11.

11. Lesley J. Gordon, "Armies and Discipline," in *The Cambridge History of the American Civil War*, vol. 2: *Affairs of the State*, ed. Aaron Sheehan-Dean (Cambridge: Cambridge University Press, 2019), 160–62; Dora L. Costa and Matthew E. Kahn, *Heroes and Cowards: The Social Face of War* (Princeton, NJ: Princeton University Press, 2008), 73; Joseph M. Beilein Jr., "Householder and General: Lee's War as a Household War," in *Household War: How Americans Lived and Fought the Civil War*, ed. Lisa Tendrich Frank and Leeann Whites (Athens: University of Georgia Press, 2020), 39.

12. Raus Jr., *Banners South*, 21–22; Harmon, "For the Christian Recorder"; Cecilia Elizabeth O'Leary, *To Die For: The Paradox of American Patriotism* (Princeton, NJ: Princeton University Press, 1999), 25–26.

13. James M. McPherson, *The Negro's Civil War: How American Blacks Felt and Acted during the War for the Union* (New York: Vintage, 1991), 32; William Seraile, *New York's Black Regiments during the Civil War* (New York: Routledge, 2001), 17.

14. Ryan W. Keating, *Shades and Green: Irish Regiments, American Soldiers, and Local Communities in the Civil War Era* (New York: Fordham University Press, 2017), 57–58, 80, 87, 98, 139, 161–62; Nina Silber and Mary Beth Sievens, eds., *Yankee Correspondence: Civil Letters between New England Soldiers and the Home Front* (Charlottesville: University Press of Virginia, 1996), 133, 135.

15. James G. Mendez, *A Great Sacrifice: Northern Black Soldiers, Their Families, and the Experience of the Civil War* (New York: Fordham University Press, 2019), 66–67.

16. Foote, *The Gentlemen and the Roughs*, 119, 128, 146, 152, 158.

17. William Marvel, *Lincoln's Mercenaries: Economic Motivation among Union Soldiers during the Civil War* (Baton Rouge: Louisiana State University Press, 2018), 167–68; Military Pay," Civil War Trust, http://www.civilwar.org/education/history/warfare-and-logistics/logistics/pay.html.

18. John C. Brock, "Good News at Last," *Christian Recorder*, August 20, 1864.

19. William L. Miller, "Letter from the Front," *Christian Recorder*, September 17, 1864.

20. Compiled Military Service Records, Microfilm Serial: M1823, Microfilm Roll: 44, Film reel: 1296.

21. Ira Berlin, Joseph P. Reidy, and Leslie Rowland, eds., *Freedom: A Documentary History of Emancipation, 1861–1867*, series 2: *The Black Military Experience* (Cambridge: Cambridge University Press, 1982), 668–80.

22. "For the Christian Recorder. Yorktown, Va., February 6, 1864, Mr.," *Christian Recorder*, February 20, 1864.

23. "D.I.I.," "For the Christian Recorder," *Christian Recorder*, August 6, 1864.

24. Joseph T. Glatthaar, *Forged in Battle: The Civil War Alliance of Black Soldiers and White Officers* (Baton Rouge: Louisiana State University Press, 1990), 209–10; Noah A. Trudeau, *Like Men of War: Black Troops in the Civil War* (Boston: Little, Brown, 1998), 461–62; Andrew F. Lang, *In the Wake of War: Military Occupation, Emancipation, and Civil War America* (Baton Rouge: Louisiana State University, 2017), 17–18, 130, 161, 188–89.

25. "United States Colored Troops. 31st Regiment, United States Colored Infantry," https://www.nps.gov/civilwar/search-battle-units-detail.htm?battleUnitCode=UUS0031RI00C; "Black Soldiers on the Appomattox Campaign," https://www.nps.gov/apco/black-soldiers.htm.

26. Compiled Military Service Records, Microfilm Serial: M1992, Microfilm Roll: 11, Film Reel: 1177, 1186–1887.

27. Compiled Military Service Records, Microfilm Serial: M1992, Microfilm Roll: 11, Film Reel: 1150, 1164–1170, 1184.

28. Edwin Redkey, ed., *A Grand Army of Black Men: Letters from African-American Soldiers in the Union Army, 1861–1865* (Cambridge: Cambridge University Press, 1992), 179; Berlin et al., eds., *Freedom*, 738–39; Lang, *In the Wake of War*, 198–199.

29. Garland H. White, "An Interesting Letter from the 28th U.S.C.T.," *Christian Recorder*, October, 21, 1865.

30. David W. Blight, *Beyond the Battlefield: Race, Memory, and the American Civil War* (Amherst: University of Massachusetts Press, 2002), 81–82.

31. Henry Carpenter Hoyle, "Letter from Brownsville, Texas. Benefit of Colored Soldiers," *Christian Recorder*, September 23, 1865.

32. White, "An Interesting Letter from the 28th U.S.C.T.," *Christian Recorder*.

33. Berlin et al., eds., *Freedom*, 664–669.

34. Charles W. Cole, "Letter from Texas," *Christian Recorder*, August 25, 1865.

35. Alexander Heritage Newton, *Out of the Briars: An Autobiography and Sketch of the Twenty-Ninth Regiment Connecticut Volunteers* (Philadelphia: AME Book Concern, 1910), 83.

36. "United States Colored Troops. 29th Regiment, United States Colored Infantry," https://www.nps.gov/civilwar/search-battle-units-detail.htm?battleUnitCode=UUS0029RI00C.

37. William B. Johnson, "Letter from 3d U.S.C.T.," *Christian Recorder*, August 12, 1865.

38. Isaac J. Hill, *A Sketch of the 29th Regiment Connecticut Colored Troops* (Baltimore: Daughtery, Maguire, & Co., 1867), 34.

39. Compiled Military Service Records, Microfilm Serial: M1820, Microfilm Roll: 17, Film Reel: 115; Microfilm Roll: 21, Film Reel: 941; Microfilm Roll 23, Film Reel: 252; Microfilm Roll: 27, Film Reel: 1107; Microfilm Roll: 25, Film Reel: 1464; Microfilm Roll: 77, Film Reel: 269; Microfilm Roll; 74, Film Reel: 660; Microfilm Roll: 78, Film Reel: 1502.

40. Cole, "Letter from Texas."

41. White, "An Interesting Letter from the 28th U.S.C.T.," *Christian Recorder*.

42. Jim Downs, *Sick from Freedom: African-American Illness and Suffering during the Civil War and Reconstruction* (Oxford: Oxford University Press, 2012), 24, 28; Gretchen Long, *Doctoring Freedom: The Politics of African American Medical Care in Slavery and Emancipation* (Chapel Hill: University of North Carolina Press, 2012), 70–72.

43. Deposition of Charles Howard, August 16, 1916, in Charles Howard, Twenty-Sixth USCI pension file, NARA, Washington, DC.

44. Compiled Military Service Records, Microfilm Serial: M1820, Microfilm Roll: 76, Film reel: 358.

45. US Census Bureau, Eighth Census of the United States, 1860, M653 (Washington, DC: National Archives and Records Administration, 1860).

46. Deposition of Herman Boedicken, June 19, 1890; Deposition of Thomas Moore, March 27, 1888, in Thomas Moore, Twentieth USCI pension file, NARA, Washington, DC.

47. 1875 Medical Examination; 1879 Medical Examination, in George Roland, Sixth USCI pension file, NARA, Washington, DC.

48. Seth Rockman, *Scraping By: Wage Labor, Slavery, and Survival in Early Baltimore* (Baltimore, MD: John Hopkins University Press, 2009), 54–56, 69, 72, 75, 77, 84–87, 92, 141–42, 160–62, 168–72.

49. "Our Colored Soldiers," *Weekly Anglo-African*, May 27, 1865.

50. Michael Les Benedict, *Preserving the Constitution: Essays on Politics and the Constitution in the Reconstruction Era* (New York: Fordham University Press, 2006), 103.

51. Paul A. Cimbala, *Veterans North and South: The Transition from Soldier to Civilian after the American Civil War* (Santa Barbara, CA: Praeger, 2015), 68, 85–86.

52. W. E. B. Du Bois, *The Philadelphia Negro*, reprint ed. (Philadelphia: University of Pennsylvania Press, 1996), 345; Thomas H. O'Connor, *Civil War Boston: Home Front and Battlefield* (Boston: Northeastern University Press, 1997), 238–40.

53. US Census Bureau, Ninth Census of the United States, 1870, M593 (Washington, DC: National Archives and Records Administration, 1870) (hereafter "US Census, 1870"); O'Connor, *Civil War Boston*, 238.

54. US Census, 1870, M593.

55. Russell L. Johnson, "'Great Injustice': Social Status and the Distribution of Military Pensions after the Civil War," *Journal of the Gilded Age and Progressive Era* 10, no. 2 (April 2011): 148; Theda Skocpol, *Protecting Soldiers and Mothers: The Political Origins of Social Policy in the United States* (Cambridge, MA: Belknap, 1992), 127.

56. Skocpol, *Protecting Soldiers and Mothers*, 106.

57. Margaret Humphreys, *Intensely Human: The Health of Black Soldiers in the American Civil War* (Baltimore, MD: John Hopkins University Press, 2008), 20–21, 57–77; Jane E. Schultz, *Women at the Front: Hospital Workers in Civil War America* (Chapel Hill: University of North Carolina Press, 2004), 136; Mezurek, *For Their Own Cause*, 183.

58. See Donald R. Shaffer, *After the Glory: The Struggles of Black Civil War Veterans* (Lawrence: University of Kansas Press, 2004); Brandi Clay Brimmer, "All Her Rights and Privileges: Women and the Politics of Civil War Widows' Pensions," PhD diss., University of California–Los Angeles, 2006; Megan J. McClintock, "Impact of the Civil War on Nineteenth-Century Marriages," in *Union Soldiers and the Northern Home Front: Wartime Experiences, Postwar Adjustments*, ed. Paul A. Cimbala and Randall Miller (New York: Fordham University Press, 2002).

59. Charles Brant's pension file offers no conclusive reason why his case never led to a decision, even though he provided evidence. Letter from Loren Burritt, composed on June 12, 1867, in Charles Brant, Eighth USCI pension file, NARA, Washington, DC.

60. Richard Reid, "USCT Veterans in Post–Civil War North Carolina," in *The Civil War Veteran: A Historical Reader*, ed. Larry M. Logue and Michael Barton (New York: New York University Press, 2007), 165.

61. Shaffer, *After the Glory*, 123–32; Larry M. Logue and Peter Blanck, *Race, Ethnicity, and Disability: Veterans and Benefits in Post–Civil War America* (Cambridge: Cambridge University Press, 2010), 113–14.

62. Shaffer, *After the Glory*, 123–25; Russell L. Johnson, *Workers into Warriors: The Civil War and the Formation of the Urban-Industrial Society in a Northern City* (New York: Fordham University Press, 2003), 239–41.

63. Shaffer, *After the Glory*, 126–34; Sven E. Wilson, "Prejudice and Policy: Racial Discrimination in the Union Army Disability Pension System, 1865–1906," *American Journal of Public Health* 100, suppl. 1 (2010): 56–58, 60.

64. Donald R. Shaffer, "'I Do Not Suppose That Uncle Sam Looks at the Skin,'" in *The Civil War Veteran*, ed. Logue and Barton, 202.

# "Works Meet for Repentance"

*Congressional Amnesty and Reconstructed Rebels*

Brian K. Fennessy

Less than three years after Confederate defeat, Massachusetts congressman Henry Dawes urged his colleagues that "such men as Gantt, of Arkansas, and Governor Holden, of North Carolina, and Governor Patton, of Alabama must be drawn by the strongest possible cords into support of this Government." Gantt was a former Confederate colonel. Holden had signed his state's secession ordinance. Patton was a plantation owner who served in Alabama's wartime legislature. "Longstreet!" Dawes continued. "Who would not rather today trust General Longstreet than any man who sneaked through four years and saved his neck by acting neither for the rebellion nor for the Union." The men that Dawes named were disqualified from holding office by either the Fourteenth Amendment's officeholding ban or the federal loyalty oath. And yet, unlike the majority of former Confederates, they had joined the Republican Party. In the parlance of the time, they were "reconstructed rebels," and Dawes wanted to lift their "political disabilities."[1]

Many historians have sought to explain the North's "retreat from Reconstruction," but in the process they risk obscuring how reconstructionist and reconciliationist imperatives sometimes merged. Such was the case when Congress offered amnesty to reconstructed rebels. From the very beginning of Congressional Reconstruction, Republican policy combined intervention in southern politics with North-South reconciliation and a gradual restoration of prewar elites to power. To their credit, Congress did not merely take former rebels at their word, as President Andrew Johnson did in his own amnesty policy. Rather, as several Republicans in Congress put it, they only wanted to help ex-Confederates who had performed "works meet for repentance." By this phrase, they meant former rebels who spoke in support of Congressional Reconstruction, defended the political rights of Blacks, and voted for Republican candidates. Congress was careful—they had endorsements from local Republican leaders to prove these men's new allegiances. Even so, white Unionists and Black southerners were more reliable allies and arguably more deserving of support. National leaders sought to empower these previously marginalized groups, but as Dawes's words indicate, they simultaneously imagined a leadership role for reconstructed rebels.[2]

For their part, reconstructed rebels saw congressional amnesty as a way to build the Republican Party's capacity to govern in their own communities. Historians often characterize white southern Republicans as advocates of general amnesty.[3] However, southern Republicans' use of the Fourteenth Amendment's officeholding ban to temporarily restrict white officeholding for partisan advantage has escaped scholarly attention. Southern Republicans did urge a more general, or even universal, amnesty bill to conciliate and win greater white support, but in the short term they used the officeholding ban to preserve state and local offices for Republicans, including reconstructed rebels who benefited from individual relief from political disabilities.[4]

This essay joins the growing scholarship on the limitations and meaning of citizenship in the late nineteenth century. More particularly, historians have begun to explore the role that allegiance played in southern claims to citizenship during this period, as well as how officials evaluated those claims and decided categories of belonging.[5] Political disabilities were a key part within the postwar redefinition of citizenship. The Fourteenth Amendment's first section extended citizenship to include African Americans by basing it on native birth, while the third section both limited officeholding rights for former Confederates and enabled Congress to remove the same restriction by a two-thirds vote. Before the General Amnesty Act of 1872, Congress removed political disabilities on an individual basis, in the process equating party loyalty with national loyalty. Public support for the Republican definition of national citizenship became the standard for measuring whether white southerners were "reconstructed." Ironically, that same principle of uniform national citizenship later undermined the rationale for maintaining officeholding restrictions, leading to the separation of reconstructed citizenship policy from partisan identity as both parties moved toward general amnesty.

The Fourteenth Amendment was the centerpiece of Republican nation building. Passed by Congress in 1866 and ratified in 1868, its first section defined citizenship as belonging to "all persons born or naturalized in the United States" and guaranteed the "privileges or immunities of citizens" and "equal protection of the laws." Additional sections tinkered with the South's congressional representation, banned former Confederates from holding office, and guaranteed the national debt.

The historian Eric Foner has argued that the officeholding ban detailed in the third section "aimed to promote a sweeping transformation of Southern public life" by making "virtually the entire political leadership in the South ineligible for office." Not all ex-Confederates were excluded; since the ban was limited to prewar officeholders only, it restricted an estimated twenty thousand former Confederates. These men would not be able to hold future office at any level. And though the amendment did not go into effect until its ratification in 1868, the Reconstruction Acts of 1867 included provisions disqualifying and disfranchising the same group while the southern states wrote new constitutions. A federal test oath from 1862 also prevented a larger section of white southern society—anyone who had aided the Confederacy, regardless of whether they held prewar office—from holding a federal job, from congressman down to postmaster.[6]

However, the Fourteenth Amendment also stated that Congress could remove the officeholding disability by a two-thirds majority. From June 1868 until the Amnesty Act of 1872, Congress bestowed amnesty individually on 4,616 former Confederates who had been subject to exclusions based on the Fourteenth Amendment, Reconstruction Acts, or federal test oath. These recipients of congressional amnesty were listed by name in statute books.

It is important to note how this policy differed from President Johnson's earlier program of presidential amnesty. Johnson had been far more lenient, promising to restore the civil rights and political privileges of ex-Confederates so long as they renewed their allegiance to the United States. The Fourteenth Amendment overrode this presidential amnesty: Congressional Republicans decided to create their own policy, one that would help only Confederates who had proven their support for Congressional Reconstruction. The officeholding ban was both more and less radical than Foner suggested—it transformed public life not only by taking old political leaders out of it but also by encouraging a segment of them to support the Republican Party. Yet, in doing so, it returned a subset of the prewar elite to positions of power.

Of the total number of reconstructed rebels, the recipients of congressional amnesty were only a subset. Historians have estimated that some 20 percent of white southerners voted with the Republican Party during Reconstruction. Of these southern white Republicans—"scalawags" was the epithet of the time—some had been active Unionists, while others were former Confederates. In the Upper South, white Republican voters ranged between as much as 25 to 30 percent of total registered white voters, given the high number of former Unionists. In the Lower South, the white Republican vote was less than 10 percent of white voters, and a greater proportion of it would have been Confederate veterans. James Baggett's study of roughly seven hundred white southern Republican leaders identified Confederate civilian and military service among 26 percent in Upper South states east of the Mississippi River, 56 percent in southeastern states, and 32 percent in states west of the Mississippi.[7]

Despite the small number of reconstructed rebels compared to overall population, congressional Republicans saw cultivating them as a necessity. Only in South Carolina, Mississippi, and Louisiana could Republicans afford to ignore the white vote. Elsewhere, southern whites were necessary to secure statewide majorities. Moreover, despite their interest in creating a new kind of nation, congressional Republicans feared that a failure to win some degree of southern white consent would make Reconstruction illegitimate by Republicans' own sense of democratic norms. Ohio senator John Sherman, for example, argued that the Military Reconstruction Acts should protect African Americans in their life and property and that they should benefit from universal suffrage, but he said he would not deprive former rebels of the ability to vote on the new constitutions. To do so, he worried, would "violate the republican doctrine that all governments be founded on the consent of the governed" and "supersede one form of oligarchy in which the blacks were slaves by another in which the whites are disenfranchised outcasts." Confederate leaders could be banned temporarily from holding office, but only as a means of giving Reconstruction a head start and buying time to cultivate white support.[8]

While the southern states were rewriting their constitutions in the spring of 1868, congressional Republicans were confronted with the possibility that their most experienced allies in the South might not be able to hold office in the new governments. Nevada senator William Stewart tested the waters by offering a bill for the relief of Alabama governor Robert Patton's political disabilities. Immediately, questions were raised about Patton's wartime loyalty. Stewart evaded, claiming, "I did know the particulars of that, but they have escaped my memory." Actually, Stewart considered wartime loyalty unimportant. "I have rather been investigating what he did since the rebellion," Stewart continued. Another senator agreed, "It does not make so much difference what a man did in the past; if he is willing now to come forward and unite with us upon our plan and method of reconstruction, act cordially with our friends in the conventions, and agree to reconstruct upon the basis we have laid down, why should we not relieve disabilities?"[9]

Support among Senate Republicans was assured when Jacob Howard offered a formula for proceeding. Howard announced, "I understand that Mr. Patton has shown his faith by his works." He would support Patton's relief and act similarly on any "case of this kind," while also insisting on "proof to the Senate that the party has really shown his faith by his works; in short, that he has done works meet for repentance." Howard's choice of language was biblical, evoking the Second Letter of James: "What doth it profit, my brethren, though a man say he hath faith, and have not works? Can faith save him?" Any duplicitous rebel might claim to love the Union, as many had done while petitioning for presidential amnesty. The only ones who could be trusted with office, Howard maintained, were those whose postwar behavior gave proof to their confessions of faith.[10]

Though Thaddeus Stevens buried the bill for Patton's relief in committee, Republican congressman John Bingham brought up his own bill to relieve James Longstreet and seventeen others. Representative John Logan of Illinois voiced the objections of the radical faction of House Republicans. "I know that Mr. Longstreet, called General Longstreet, wrote a letter accepting the situation," he admitted, but Logan considered the letter insufficient. He argued that if that were enough, "every rebel general would write one to be relieved from disability under the law." Logan made his case even more plainly by criticizing the inclusion of Georgia's Confederate governor Joseph E. Brown in the bill. "Governor Brown is a politician," Logan said. "He saw the handwriting on the wall, and the war having ceased he has taken advantage of it." Building to a more general position, Logan asserted, "No people ever lived on earth who loved political power as these leaders at the South do, and, in my judgment, there are no people who will change their opinions faster and oftener than will these people for the purpose of obtaining power." Logan was skeptical of rebel motivations, especially after so many of them had taken advantage of President Johnson's lenient amnesty only to turn around and use their public power to oppress Black and white Unionists.[11]

William Kelley of Pennsylvania was one of the first to respond to Logan. Kelley had corresponded with half of the men in Bingham's bill, including Joe Brown, whom he had also met in person. Kelley insisted that Brown had done more than any man to convince white Georgians to accept Congressional Reconstruction. He also vouched for the group as a whole and said that they had done "works meet for repentance." James Garfield took up Kelley's argument. "It belongs not to us but to the Searcher of all hearts," Garfield avowed, "to decide whether a man sincerely loves the Union. All we can fairly ask is that he will do what is required, and as soon as we are assured of that we should be willing to remove the disabilities now imposed upon him by our laws." Even John Farnsworth, who had lost a son in an ill-fated cavalry charge against Longstreet's corps at Gettysburg, defended the former general. Farnsworth told the House that "without probing very deeply into the recesses of Longstreet's heart, I would only inquire, is he acting heartily with the loyal people of the country?" In response to another representative who objected that Longstreet only accepted the situation "under duress," Farnsworth replied, "I do not care whether it is under duress or not. One man like Longstreet can do the loyal cause in the South more good than a thousand ordinary men." Southern elites were particularly valuable to Republicans.[12]

Farnsworth revealed another layer of concern. The Reconstruction Acts, by combining Black suffrage with temporary white disfranchisement and disqualification for office, might lead to "a white man's party and a black man's party." Though sympathetic to the rights of freedpeople, Farnsworth feared that if parties in the South divided on racial lines, "the black man's party will go to the dust." Since the Reconstruction Acts had allowed Black southerners and white Unionists to create revolutionary state constitutions, former Confederates excluded from participation could argue that they had no stake in the product. Without white southern consent, Farnsworth reasoned, it would take military force to prevent the constitutions from being overturned. Farnsworth believed that rewarding loyalty and allowing rebels back into some positions of power would prevent the racialization of party politics.[13]

Congressional Republicans also alluded to the need for experienced leadership in the new South. Henry Dawes, who would later gain notoriety as the architect of racist assimilationist Indian policies, was focused in 1868 on assimilating rebels. Listing off the most prominent prewar leaders in the bill, Dawes argued that "the mind and character and the influence which those men must necessarily exert in those States are absolutely essential and necessary to a healthy reconstruction of those States." The implication was that white southerners, once reconstructed, would provide better leadership than Black southerners. While northern Republicans believed former slaves were worthy of citizenship, they also associated political virtue with education and wealth, which often fell along racial lines.[14]

Some of the supporters of congressional amnesty, such as Dawes in the House and Sherman in the Senate, were moderates on Black civil rights. It may be unsurprising that they would advocate a policy that empowered white men. However, Garfield and Farnsworth were early supporters of Black suffrage and still supported congressional amnesty for whites. William Kelley and Henry Wilson consistently advocated for both Black civil rights *and* reconstructed rebels. Even

Thaddeus Stevens frequently consulted the leader of North Carolina's Republican apparatus, William W. Holden, and later asked him for a list of reliable names for relief. Radical and moderate proponents of African American rights alike agreed that they should reward white southerners for joining the party, give them a stake in the success of Reconstruction, and even allow them to hold power.[15]

In June 1868, both houses of Congress agreed to a bill with over a thousand names. Before it passed, however, Democrats seized the opportunity to object to its partisan nature. James Brooks, a Democratic representative from New York, complained that the bill "selects men of one particular school of politics for pardon and omits all others." Farnsworth retorted that his party could not help it if all southern Democrats were die-hard rebels. Asked whether loyalty meant support of the Reconstruction Acts, which Democrats also saw as partisan, Farnsworth explained that it was "necessary that a man who acted with the rebels during the war shall give some evidence of repentance" and that it was "very good evidence of repentance when he gives the reconstruction measures of Congress his cordial support. If he cooperates with the loyal people of his State, black and white, and helps in good faith and heartily to reconstruct and restore this State upon the basis of liberty and equality, he gives evidence of returning loyalty and repentance." Another Democrat asked whether opposition to Black suffrage therefore made a man a rebel. Farnsworth denied this formula as an absolute rule but admitted that he considered it evidence against a man's reconstruction: "If we find that all rebels oppose negro suffrage, it casts a little suspicion upon men who oppose it, whether you call them rebels or not." Party loyalty proved national loyalty, and works that furthered Reconstruction proved both.[16]

Only a few of the names in this first bill were avowed Democrats, and a conference between the two houses struck them out. Nearly all of the names came from lists provided by state constitutional conventions, which were dominated by southern Republicans. The House Select Committee on Reconstruction and the Senate Judiciary Committee also used their own contacts to vet the names. Patton's name was left out, possibly because he objected to the Alabama Constitution, which included additional disfranchisement measures. Though the June amnesty bill slighted Patton, it included both Brown and Longstreet. Neither man had run for office, but southern Republicans had run other men who were disqualified. For example, Holden was the Republican candidate for governor in North Carolina, and it was only because of the amnesty bill that he and numerous other reconstructed rebels were able to take their seats. Ultimately, the Fortieth Congress provided relief to 1,431 former rebels. The Forty-First Congress acted on another 3,185, including some moderate Democrats who accepted the legality of Reconstruction and Black suffrage.

In 1860, southern secessionists had feared the extension of Republican patronage networks into the South.[17] In 1868, those fears were validated. Once relieved of their disqualifications, the initial recipients of amnesty recommended others, who in turn wrote applications for relief. Freed from their political disabilities, many then served in federal, state, and local offices. Nowhere was the careful use of amnesty and patronage networks by reconstructed rebels to multiply their power clearer than in North Carolina.

North Carolina had an exceptionally high number of reconstructed rebels in its Republican Party. According to James Baggett, 73 percent of white Republican leaders served or held office in the Confederacy. Governor William W. Holden conducted an extensive review of applications for amnesty—twice. The first time, in 1865 while he was provisional governor, he had forwarded pardons to President Johnson. At that time, Holden's understanding of loyalty focused on the wartime past. Only the "straitest sect" of Union men, he declared, would rule. By 1868, he again found himself vetting amnesty applications. This time, however, he was a Republican governor, and his definition of loyalty had shifted. "Well, we all experienced in 1865 a kind of penticostal [sic] repentance among rebels," he recalled. Rebels had given "lip service" to Union loyalty back then. In 1868, however, "*bona fide* repentance and *good works*" would be necessary. To receive amnesty, Holden announced, former rebels "must vote, talk, write, travel, labor, and spend their money for the Republican party, the nation, and government, as other loyal men do."[18]

Leading Republicans sought to tap into local networks and used amnesty to do so. A North Carolina congressman recommended two men because "they will make us friends in their *neighborhoods*." Local contests for power also made amnesty necessary and pushed applications for relief from the bottom up. In late July 1868, a Republican leader in Fayetteville called Holden's attention to the unfortunate circumstance that two of the town's commissioners could not qualify for office under the Fourteenth Amendment. This was a major problem because the other local officers who *could* qualify *would not* be qualified, since it was the job of town commissioners to certify them. The writer emphasized the urgency of the matter by mentioning that the district court circuit would begin in two weeks. The new legal order of Reconstruction, which now protected the rights of both Blacks and whites, required that Holden quickly appoint interim commissioners free from the officeholding ban.[19]

Disqualification from local office also meant that someone else would get the job, perhaps even a die-hard rebel, since the Fourteenth Amendment had only banned rebels who held prewar office. If reconstructed rebels who held prewar office remained under the ban, unreconstructed rebels who did not hold prewar office had a greater chance of taking power. For example, Starkey S. Harrell was a Republican superior court clerk in Hertford County. In addition to his petition for amnesty, he wrote a pointed letter to his congressman. "I do not crave the office I hold, but am unwilling to yield an inch until subjection of Rebel sympathizers is plain," Harrell fulminated. "If I am unable to hold the office," he warned, "the whole county will be in possession of secessionists." A couple of months earlier, Governor Holden asked the chairman of the House Select Committee on Reconstruction to stop a general amnesty bill—one without regard to partisan loyalty or works—because "we have not yet held our township elections. It is important that no general relief should be granted until these offices are filled." Likely it was cases like Harrell's that Holden had in mind. Reconstructed rebels needed amnesty to get in, but unreconstructed rebels needed to be kept out.[20]

Multiple levels of Republican officials handled pleas for relief before they reached the House Select Committee on Reconstruction. When North Carolina's constitutional convention met in the spring of 1868, delegates produced the names of men from their counties whom they wanted relieved. Sometimes the delegates relied on information from even more local sources to determine who needed and deserved amnesty. A delegate from Robeson County closed a lengthy petition on behalf of another Republican, "All the *loyal* men of my county unite with me in this petition." The constitutional convention added the man's name to the list they sent to Congress, and the House Select Committee on Reconstruction included him in the first amnesty bill. After this initial list by the constitutional convention, applications generally moved from individual towns to the Republican State Committee, then to the state's congressional representation, and finally to the House Select Committee on Reconstruction, all the while picking up endorsements at each level.[21]

The contents of the petitions suggest what it meant on a personal level to be "*thoroughly reconstructed*," as one North Carolinian put it. Applicants typically began their letters by describing the reason for their disqualification: any offices they held before the war, whether they were affected by the Fourteenth Amendment or the federal test oath, and their subsequent involvement with the Confederacy. Applicants sometimes sought to excuse their involvement in the rebellion. In North Carolina, many petitioners argued that in their hearts they had never been rebels at all. However, being "reconstructed" meant something different than claiming wartime Unionism. Successful petitioners universally expressed their support for the Fourteenth Amendment and the Reconstruction Acts. A typical petition stated that the author was "in favor of supporting the Reconstruction measures of Congress & the state governments established thereunder."[22]

Some petitioners were more specific. A soon-to-be internal revenue assessor wrote that "he has been active & persistent in supporting the reconstruction measures of Congress & in public speeches & newspapers of his state, he has advocated, on all occasions, the principles of the Radical Republican party." A future Republican mayor of Charlotte mentioned voting for Grant in the 1868 presidential election, editing a newspaper "in favor of universal suffrage," and supporting all party nominees, even "to his great pecuniary loss and the alienation of his friends and business." Another petitioner described himself as "a pioneer in the land of equal rights and manhood suffrage." By contrast, a petitioner who wrote that he would comply with the acts of Congress "until they may be legally altered or amended" was not relieved. Together the petitions suggest that reconstructed rebels and Congress adopted an understanding of loyalty based on postwar works, such as voting, canvassing, writing, speaking, advocating for the freedpeople, and bringing additional converts into the party.[23]

The public nature of these works made it difficult for applicants to get away with lying. Multiple levels of gatekeepers stood between the applicants and amnesty. Holden told the chairman of the House committee that North Carolina's "rule in regard to relief from disabilities in this state is, that the Republican State Committee investigate each case in which relief is asked, and that none but those recommended by the Committee be proper cases to be relieved." The secretary of the state committee wrote to his counterpart at the congressional level, "We desire to prevent any man from being relieved from political disabilities unless sanctioned by the members of Congress from this state or recommended by the Republican State Executive Committee." North Carolina's congressional delegation also asked that no more names be added to relief bills until it could review them first.[24]

The petitions that ended up in the hands of the House Select Committee on Reconstruction reflected this vetting process. Almost all of the North Carolinians who applied and successfully got their names onto a relief bill were endorsed by the secretary of the state committee or by a Republican congressman. Petitions that lacked endorsements were not acted upon, and neither were those that included the signatures of numerous citizens yet failed to go through the party officials. Lieutenant Governor Tod Caldwell successfully blocked a petition by writing, "There is not a more stiff necked rebel in this county, Burke.... He is the rebel candidate for Superior Court Clerk in this County."[25]

Amnesty was a key party-building and nation-building tool that allowed southern Republicans to create networks linking individuals to centers of state power. Moreover, it gave a powerful cohort of reconstructed rebels a stake in maintaining biracial democracy. Yet, in doing so, it also channeled greater power to a subset of the prewar elite.

Congressional amnesty, both in effect and by intention, empowered a specific group of southerners. One of Holden's advisors wrote, "It is to the interest of the Republican party to conciliate and win over the white men of the country. Indeed I think the very existence of the party at the South will depend on our success in such an effort." Amnesty was part of that effort, as it offered leadership roles to white southerners who were otherwise excluded. Moreover, amnesty had a strong class dimension, as one North Carolinian indicated when recommending an application: "We need such Republicans as he is to fill offices where business capacity is required." Even though the Reconstruction Acts gave poor whites and former slaves unprecedented access to government power, Reconstruction's northern architects wanted the state governments to be managed at the top by prewar elites who embraced the new order.[26]

Black southerners had mixed feelings about empowering members of the prewar elite. The New Orleans *Tribune*, for example, was skeptical of James Longstreet's conversion in 1867. A bilingual newspaper dedicated to serving the city's Black and Creole communities, the *Tribune* argued, "Our only advisors should be ourselves. None of these so called wise men . . . has our interest or welfare at heart. They speak for their people, not us." However, when Grant appointed Longstreet surveyor for the Port of New Orleans in 1869, the attitude of the *Tribune* changed dramatically. Its editorials called him "an enlightened man, a true patriot," and used him as a foil to criticize unreconstructed rebels: "After having shown bravery on the battlefield, he demonstrated in political life a great moral courage and, if his example were followed by our fellow citizens of the South, all our dissensions would soon be appeased."[27]

African American leaders sometimes opposed restricting the rights of ex-Confederates because they feared that it would undermine their own claim to citizenship. As the New Orleans *Tribune* put it, "If we refuse the franchise to any class, it can as well be withheld from us." However, few supported universal amnesty from the officeholding ban. More often, they paired individual amnesty with support for Reconstruction, as the authors of the Fourteenth Amendment had done. Black leaders like James Rapier of Alabama and Hiram Revels of Mississippi offered resolutions to help reconstructed white southerners regain the right to hold office. Twenty-eight members of the Alabama legislature signed a petition to grant amnesty to Samuel Rice, the former chief justice of the state supreme court, who had joined the Republican Party after Grant's election. As evidence of Justice Rice's trustworthiness, the signers testified that he had consistently advocated equal rights during the eighteen months after his conversion and that "he has ever shown his faith by his works."[28]

African American support for their political friends, however, did not mean that their interests always aligned. The issues most important to reconstructed rebels were getting their states readmitted to Congress quickly, funding railroad projects that would raise land values and produce tax revenue, and achieving social stability by stopping Klan violence and conciliating whites. Most of all, as shown by their petitions for amnesty, they hoped to regain their prewar political and social status. African Americans, for their part, wanted Reconstruction to mean not only basic bodily autonomy and political participation but also other kinds of equality, freedom, and self-determination. Reconstructed rebels often pushed against African American demands for equal access to public services and opportunities to purchase land from insolvent whites. John Alfred of Wilmington wrote a letter to Holden on behalf of "the Colard [sic] people of north carolina," who "are very much dissatisfied with the laws we are working under." Alfred accused Holden of "doing Every thing" for the benefit of whites—who "did not put you in the office"—instead of helping the African Americans who elected him. Districts with a Black majority sometimes elected native whites, but compared to white-majority districts, they were more likely to choose representatives of their own color. In the 1870s, African Americans began to push even more vigorously for greater political representation to promote their rights where native whites were not.[29]

Southern Unionists and northern settlers were sometimes quicker than African Americans to challenge reconstructed rebels' leadership. One Georgia Unionist protested against a petition for amnesty, writing, "If the Fourteenth Amendment means anything . . . if the test oath means anything, they mean to exclude just such men." In Arkansas, a northern emigrant told Congress that "there is no disposition on the part of the Union men in Arkansas to confer office on those who have been in rebel service; we are willing to have them come into our church as converts, but are disposed to let them occupy back seats for some years to come." However, the objections of white Unionists did more to weed out unreconstructed rebels who sought amnesty deceptively than to stop Congress from rewarding verified converts to the party.[30]

Congressional amnesty was partially based on the assumption that Reconstruction needed the support of native southerners to give it legitimacy. At the same time though, African Americans and unconditional Unionists were native southerners too. To them, their consent was enough to mean that Reconstruction was not being imposed from outside. Northern Republicans saw these groups as vital partners in reconstructing the South, yet they were insufficient in northern eyes. They saw that white southerners were necessary to secure Republican majorities in all but a few states. They also knew that conservative southerners would see any government by African Americans and lower-class whites as illegitimate. Perhaps most importantly, white northerners shared with southerners the basic assumption that elite white men were more civic minded, even though for Republicans it came with the caveat that they must respect the rights of African Americans.

The Enforcement Act of May 1870 authorized the federal government to prosecute individual violations of voting rights. It also required the Justice Department to prosecute southerners who held office in violation of the Fourteenth Amendment's officeholding ban. Attorney General Amos Akerman, himself a recipient of amnesty, instructed US attorneys to vigorously enforce the law not only against the Klan but also against ineligible officeholders. However, Akerman's men did not get far with these cases before the Amnesty Act of 1872. Most of the enforcement came directly from the Republican state governments themselves.[31]

Enforcing the ban against unreconstructed rebels depended on Republicans holding the state legislature. In North Carolina, the presiding officers of the general assembly notified Holden of vacancies caused by ineligible candidates being elected. Holden then ordered new elections for the vacant seats. In one case, a vacancy caused by ineligibility led to the election of a Republican Confederate veteran, John W. Stephens, who was later murdered by the Klan. In contrast to North Carolina's vigorous application of the officeholding ban, Georgia Republicans were either unable or unwilling to eject ineligible whites because of an even partisan split in the legislature. The ultimate result was that a bloc of conservative Republicans combined forces with Democratic legislators, several of them ineligible for their seats, to instead expel thirty-two Black legislators.[32]

The Georgia imbroglio not only demonstrated the haphazard enforcement of the ban; it also highlighted the ambiguous and contested nature of postwar citizenship. Black Georgians could vote under the Reconstruction Acts and the new state constitution. Anti-Reconstruction conservatives, though, argued that officeholding was not one of the "privileges or immunities of citizenship" protected by the Fourteenth Amendment and that the state constitution said nothing about officeholding. African Americans and their allies disagreed. A meeting of African Americans in Savannah petitioned Congress, saying the expulsion of the Black legislators was "an unjust deprivation of our most sacred rights as citizens." Joseph Brown, who received amnesty and became Chief Justice of Georgia's Supreme Court, ruled in a test case that since prewar statutes had recognized all citizens as eligible to hold office, African Americans now had that right under the new constitution as well. Even more decisively, Congress remanded Georgia to military oversight, reinstated the Black legislators, and removed the ineligible whites from the legislature.[33]

If officeholding was a right of citizenship, though, what did this say about the citizenship of ex-Confederates who were prevented from holding office? Reconstructed rebels who petitioned for congressional amnesty saw officeholding as a right of citizenship, just as African Americans did. The language of one suppliant can be found in almost every petition: He asked "that he may be relieved of his disabilities, and be permitted to spend the remnant of his days in the full enjoyment of all the rights and privileges of an American citizen." Reconstructed rebels admitted that they had lost full citizenship rights by constitutional authority but also believed that they merited an exception because of their support for Reconstruction. Petitioners from Georgia also included their opposition to the expulsion of the Black legislators as evidence that they were fully reconstructed.[34]

Reconstructed rebels used the combination of exclusion and amnesty to their advantage, but after gaining control in their states, they began to move toward general or universal amnesty. Such magnanimity, they hoped, might pacify discontented whites or at least undercut the argument that Republicans were giving Blacks more rights than whites. Holden used his message to the legislature at the end of 1869 to suggest the time for general amnesty had arrived. James Lusk Alcorn of Mississippi, campaigning for governor in late 1869, paired universal amnesty and universal suffrage as his platform. A Virginia Republican who only a few months earlier had opposed general amnesty because "these people are not and *cannot* now be loyal" wrote to an ally in Congress following the state's first election arguing that the masses only needed "nursing." He believed generosity would win their gratitude and "turn their hate into friendship."[35]

Meanwhile, Democrats and "liberal" Republicans who favored reconciliation with former Confederates condemned selective amnesty as an example of political corruption. The frequent accusation was that Republicans were "peddling out pardons." One petition, though satirical, reflected this view of amnesty as a corrupt business. The front of the application read "James B. Kennedy of Emanuel NC, recommended by Eggs, chicken, fish, and venison" and, inside, "Dear Jake, Do please remove my disabilities & eggs chicken & fish as well as venison . . . will be yours etc, James B. Kennedy." Even the Republican *New York Times* assailed the "bitterly proscriptive" policy of "retailing pardon as a recompense for partisanship." Piecemeal amnesty, it said, "suggests a system of bargain and sale, of subserviency on one side and patronage on the other, of rewards doled out to partisan adherents and punishment inflicted on all who dare to be opponents." The *Times* instead called for "a measure removing all disabilities as a means of promoting reconciliation, local and national."[36]

By the 1870s, white northerners increasingly came to see white southerners as having been sufficiently reconstructed. Ironically, even as the Ku Klux Klan and other paramilitary groups were terrorizing African Americans, southern Democrats like Lucius Quintus Cincinnatus Lamar promised to respect the Reconstruction Amendments and protect African Americans. Lamar and other "Redeemers" accused the southern Republican governments of corruption, while giving nominal assent to the Republican vision of uniform citizenship. Redeemers also made peace with middle-class proponents of an industrial "New South." The latter even included former Republicans like Joseph Brown, who defected back to the Democratic Party.[37] If being "reconstructed" meant acceptance of the Fourteenth Amendment, free-labor institutions, and middle-class norms, it began to seem to some northerners that identity as a Republican was no longer a prerequisite for loyalty as it once was.

When the Forty-Second Congress met in the spring of 1871, Republicans no longer had a supermajority, and it appeared politically expedient to undercut Democrats with a general amnesty bill. The congressional debate over the bill is a window onto the shifting conversation about reconstructing individuals. First, Republicans argued that the ban was not stopping the perpetrators of Klan violence and that it might even be fueling it. Second, they adopted the Democrats' view that the ban robbed the South of its most capable leaders. These arguments dovetailed with the Democratic refrain that Reconstruction was discriminatory against whites and that equality before the law required lifting the restriction on officeholding. The Amnesty Act of 1872 removed disabilities from all but a few hundred ex-Confederates who held high political office or military commissions before the war. Passed with bipartisan support, it reflected not only a concession to expediency but a consensus that the reconstruction of individuals was largely complete.

In the debates about the general amnesty bill, Democrats criticized Congressional Reconstruction and argued that equality before the law was a lie without amnesty. In the congressional hearings on Klan violence, Representative Frank Blair of Missouri aimed to show that the disturbances were caused by the officeholding ban and not racism. Later, speaking in favor of the general amnesty bill, he accused Black southerners of seeking "to degrade and humiliate the white people of this country." James Beck of Kentucky revived the charge that Republicans were "peddling out" amnesty and argued, "We ought to put all men, white as well as black, upon terms of equality before the law." If some adult white men could not hold office, he reasoned, they were not equal to African Americans. Implicitly reminding his colleagues that Reconstruction had been about both reforming whites and transforming institutions, he promised, "If this bill passes, then the work of reconstruction of individuals as well as States is at an end."[38]

Congressional Republicans lamented that their policy had become unworkable. Nevada senator William Stewart admitted that such "special legislation" had led to "embarrassment." Stewart considered it "impossible for Congress to investigate and pass upon the cases of individuals with any degree of fairness and impartiality." John Logan of Illinois criticized southern Republicans for advocating universal amnesty but then delaying the bill when it looked like North Carolina's wartime ex-Confederate governor Zebulon Vance would be elevated to the Senate. Logan pointed out that some of the Senate's current members—such as Alcorn of Mississippi—had done no less than Vance to support the Confederacy and that President Grant had brought an ex-Confederate, Amos Akerman, into his cabinet. Ironically, in a previous Congress, Logan had opposed even minimal amnesty because he did not believe rebel converts were sincere; now he suggested that if such men were relieved, amnesty should not be withheld from ex-Confederates who remained with the Democrats.[39]

Republicans argued that general amnesty would pacify former rebels, even if they did not deserve such magnanimity. John Farnsworth, an architect of the earlier amnesty policy, argued that disqualification from office had not prevented terrorist violence in the South. The Klan was the problem, he said, and the officeholding ban did not target night riders. Instead, he agreed with Frank Blair that it created more strife. Farnsworth pointed out that those who had only reluctantly gone into the Confederacy could not hold office, while their former slaves could. Luke Poland of Vermont struck the same chord, claiming that proscription made the banned whites into martyrs.[40]

Robert Elliott, an African American congressman from South Carolina, responded to Farnsworth's claim that the ban targeted the wrong people. Elites encouraged and financed night-riding, Elliot said, even if they did not participate themselves. Other Republicans insisted that former rebels needed to prove they were reconstructed. According to Massachusetts senator George Hoar's reading of the Fourteenth Amendment, banned individuals could not hold political office until it was clear that they had changed their minds. The Tennessee Unionist Horace Maynard agreed that the Republican Party's embrace of universal amnesty in its platform was conditional on white southerners first showing that they were law-abiding. James Nye of Nevada joined Charles Sumner in arguing that the general amnesty bill should be tied to a supplemental bill for Black civil rights. Only by accepting the latter, he argued, could rebels show they were "in earnest about this thing." This was the old formula, that faith must be accompanied by works. Now, however, more Republicans were implying that amnesty should be freely distributed as an act of grace.[41]

In addition to believing that amnesty would be effective as a peace offering, Republicans came to see white proscription as illegitimate. As Pennsylvania senator John Scott put it, local and state governments in the South lacked both "character" and "capacity." Scott alleged that disorder in the South was attributable to the disqualification of good men and the election of bad ones. "I am satisfied," he concluded, "that the character of many of the local administrations in the South can be very much improved by removing these disabilities." Scott's southern colleagues agreed. Frederick Sawyer of South Carolina claimed that it was because a "large number of men in the southern States were shut out from the possibility of holding State and Federal offices that we have had so many abuses in the local government of those States." Lack of proper leadership had made his state's government "a disgrace to civilization." William Kellogg, who had come to Louisiana after the war, thought that amnesty would undercut the argument of hostile whites that they were taxed unjustly by "adventurers," a label typically applied to men like himself.[42]

Ironically, these arguments helped create a perception of misrule and illegitimacy in the South. By repudiating the officeholding ban, Republicans implied that native white elites were the South's natural leaders and that their own hold on power—even if they too were native southerners—was based on the rigging of institutions.

The Fourteenth Amendment repudiated the Supreme Court's *Dred Scott* decision and wrote birthright citizenship into the Constitution. The amendment's authors hoped that a uniform standard of citizenship would result in homogeneous institutions across the land, in contrast to the prewar South's "peculiar institution." By the end of the nineteenth century, however, uniform citizenship was eroded by judicial interpretation, Jim Crow's badges of inferiority, and other discriminatory legislation, such as the Chinese Exclusion Act.[43] Even in the 1860s, congressional Republicans often fell back on ideas of heterogeneity and second-class citizenship when asked about the Fourteenth Amendment's implications for women and Native Americans.[44]

The exclusion of ex-Confederates from officeholding was written into the amendment itself. Though the ban was always meant to be temporary, the exclusion and congressional amnesty should inform how we understand the postwar redefinition of citizenship. Congress intended the ban to exclude Confederates first, then transform them and return them to power through selective amnesty. Reconstructed rebels, for their part, did perform works supporting Black freedom, verifying their faith in nonracial citizenship. At the same time, their active use of the amnesty process reflected a desire to reestablish the authority of white elites. Their efforts to regain not only citizenship but also control foreshadowed their enemies' arguments for "home rule" in the mid-1870s.

The partisan and racial implications of the officeholding ban were its undoing. Selective amnesty favored Republicans over Democrats. African Americans could hold office, but unreconstructed rebels who held prewar office could not. Congressional Republicans came to perceive this situation as a contradiction of their political faith in equal rights and homogeneous citizenship. The movement toward general amnesty also reflected the growing dissociation between partisanship and loyal citizenship, fed by growing confidence among white northerners as time passed that white elites were reconstructed citizens. A process that had been set up to transform white southerners through exclusion and amnesty ultimately restored them to power and gave them a role in restricting Black freedom later in the century.

### Notes

1. *Congressional Globe*, 40th Cong., 2nd Sess., 1710.
2. *Congressional Globe*, 40th Cong., 2nd Sess., 766, 1931. On the "retreat from Reconstruction," see William Gillette, *Retreat from Reconstruction, 1869–1879* (Baton Rouge: Louisiana State University Press, 1979); Richard H. Abbott, *The Republican Party and the South, 1855–1877* (Chapel Hill: University of North Carolina Press, 1986); Heather Cox Richardson, *The Death of Reconstruction: Race, Labor, and Politics in the Post–Civil War North, 1865–1901* (Cambridge, MA: Harvard University Press, 2001); David W. Blight,

*Race and Reunion: The Civil War in American Memory* (Cambridge, MA: Harvard University Press, 2001); Edward J. Blum, *Reforging the White Republic* (Baton Rouge: Louisiana State University Press, 2005); Charles W. Calhoun, *Conceiving a New Republic: The Republican Party and the Southern Question, 1869–1900* (Lawrence: University of Kansas Press, 2006).

3. For southern Republican support for the Amnesty Act of 1872, see Terry L. Seip, *The South Returns to Congress: Men, Economic Measures, and Intersectional Relationships, 1868–1879* (Baton Rouge: Louisiana State University Press, 1983), 131; Abbott, *The Republican Party and the South*, 216. Relatedly, for opposition to additional state-based restrictions on white political rights, see Michael Perman, *The Road to Redemption: Southern Politics, 1869–1879* (Chapel Hill: University of North Carolina Press, 1984), 13, 26. Others have noted, however, that wartime Unionists typically opposed amnesty measures and pushed for disfranchisement of ex-Confederates. For example, see Michael W. Fitzgerald, *Splendid Failure: Postwar Reconstruction in the American South* (Chicago: Ivan R. Dee, 2007), 82.

4. The most comprehensive study of congressional amnesty is William Adam Russ Jr., "Congressional Disfranchisement, 1866–1898," PhD diss., University of Chicago, 1933. Jonathan Truman Dorris, *Pardon and Amnesty under Lincoln and Johnson: The Restoration of Confederates to Their Rights and Privileges, 1861–1898* (Westport, CT: Greenwood, 1953), has a chapter on congressional amnesty, but it is derivative from Russ's dissertation. Also see Abbott, *The Republican Party and the South*, which is one of the few monographs to even mention congressional amnesty before the Amnesty Act of 1872. However, none of these works examine the individual petitions for amnesty that are collected in the records of the House Select Committee on Reconstruction.

5. Susanna Michele Lee, *Claiming the Union* (New York: Cambridge University Press, 2014); William A. Blair, *With Malice toward Some: Treason and Loyalty in the Civil War Era* (Chapel Hill: University of North Carolina Press, 2014); Carol Emerton, *Beyond Redemption: Race, Violence, and the American South after the Civil War* (Chicago: University of Chicago Press, 2015); Erik Mathisen, *The Loyal Republic: Traitors, Slaves, and the Remaking of Citizenship in Civil War America* (Chapel Hill: University of North Carolina Press, 2018); Jonathan White, "'I Do Not Understand What the Term 'Loyalty' Means': The Debate in Pennsylvania over Compensating Victims of Rebel Raids," in *Contested Loyalty: Debates over Patriotism in the Civil War North*, ed. Robert M. Sandow (New York: Fordham University Press, 2018).

6. Eric Foner, *Reconstruction: America's Unfinished Revolution, 1863–1877* (New York: Harper & Row, 1988), 259–60; Russ, "Congressional Disfranchisement," 36.

7. James Alex Baggett, *The Scalawags: Southern Dissenters in the Civil War and Reconstruction* (Baton Rouge: Louisiana State University Press, 2002), 274–79. For estimates of the white Republican vote during Reconstruction, see Allen W. Trelease, "Who Were the Scalawags?," *Journal of Southern History* 29, no. 4 (1963): 458; William C. Harris, "A Reconsideration of the Mississippi Scalawag," *Journal of Mississippi History* 32 (February 1970): 38; Carl Degler, *The Other South: Southern Dissenters in the Nineteenth Century* (New York: Harper & Row, 1974), 193; Abbott, *The Republican Party and the South*, 137,

159; Hyman Rubin III, *South Carolina Scalawags* (Columbia: University of South Carolina Press, 2006), xxi.

8. *Congressional Globe*, 39th Cong., 2nd Sess., 154.
9. *Congressional Globe*, 40th Cong., 2nd Sess., 766.
10. *Congressional Globe*, 40th Cong., 2nd Sess., 766.
11. *Congressional Globe*, 40th Cong., 2nd Sess., 1930–31.
12. *Congressional Globe*, 40th Cong., 2nd Sess., 1931, 1933.
13. *Congressional Globe*, 40th Cong., 2nd Sess., 1933.
14. *Congressional Globe*, 40th Cong., 2nd Sess., 1710. On white northerners' disillusionment with African American citizenship, see Richardson, *The Death of Reconstruction*.
15. Michael Benedict, *A Compromise of Principle: Congressional Republicans and Reconstruction* (New York: Norton, 1975), 339–77; William W. Holden to Thaddeus Stevens, February 17, 1868, Papers of the House Select Committee on Reconstruction (HSCR), National Archives and Records Administration, Washington, DC.
16. *Congressional Globe*, 40th Cong., 2nd Sess., 2414–15, 3301.
17. Steven A. Channing, *Crisis of Fear: Secession in South Carolina* (New York: Simon and Schuster, 1970), 235.
18. Baggett, *The Scalawags*, 275; William C. Harris, *William Woods Holden: Firebrand of North Carolina Politics* (Baton Rouge: Louisiana State University Press, 1987), 164, 180–85; *Weekly Standard* (Raleigh), June 24, 1868.
19. John T. Deweese to Benjamin F. Butler, March 16, 1869, Application #11047 S. W. Smith and B. V. Smith, HSCR; Ralph Buxton to William W. Holden, July 31, 1868, Governor's Papers, State Archives of North Carolina, Raleigh.
20. S. S. Harrell to C. L. Cobb, March 25, 1869, Application #11023 S. S. Harrell, HSCR; W. W. Holden to George Boutwell, January 28, 1869, HSCR.
21. O. S. Hayes, Petition on Behalf of James Sinclair, Correspondence of the State Constitutional Convention of 1868, State Archives of North Carolina.
22. John A. Richardson to Oliver Dockery, December 8, 1868, Application #11004 J. A. Richardson, HSCR. For examples of suppliants seeking to excuse their support of the Confederacy, see S. S. Harrell to Congress, March 25, 1869, Application #11023 S. S. Harrell; and H. M. Pritchard to Congress, [April? 1868], Unnumbered Application H. M. Prichard, HSCR. The last quotation is from Samuel Reeves to Congress, n.d., and Samuel Reeves to N. Boyden, Application #11038 Samuel Reeves, HSCR.
23. W. F. Henderson to Congress, undated, Application #11017 W. F. Henderson; H. M. Pritchard to Congress, [April? 1868], Unnumbered Application, H. M. Prichard; James Sinclair to William D. Kelley, Unnumbered Application James Sinclair; Neil S. Stewart to Congress, November 25, 1868, Application #11022 Neil S. Stewart, all in HSCR.
24. Thomas L. Tullock to the House Select Committee on Reconstruction, December 9, 1868, HSCR; North Carolina Congressional Delegation to Thaddeus Stevens, n.d. 1869, HSCR.
25. Tod R. Caldwell to T. L. Tullock, April 23, 1868, Application #11005 J. B. and J. R. Kincaid, HSCR.

26. William B. Rodman to Holden, May 5, 1868, William Woods Holden Papers (private collection), State Archives of North Carolina; Robert E. McDonald to N. B. Judd, July 14, 1868, Application #11048 R. C. Cook, HSCR.

27. *Tribune* (New Orleans), April 11, 1867; *Tribune*, February 24, 1869. The latter is in French; my translation.

28. *Tribune* (New Orleans), September 25, 1866; L. S. Speed et al. to the Senate, Application of Samuel F. Rice, Papers of the Senate Select Committee on Removal of Political Disabilities, National Archives and Records Administration, Washington, DC. For examples of African American leaders supporting selective amnesty, see Loren Schweninger, *James T. Rapier and Reconstruction* (Chicago: University of Chicago Press, 1978), 57; Edmund L. Drago, *Black Politicians and Reconstruction in Georgia* (Baton Rouge: Louisiana State University Press, 1982), 45; Michael W. Fitzgerald, *Reconstruction in Alabama: From Civil War to Redemption in the Cotton South* (Baton Rouge: Louisiana State University Press, 2017), 159.

29. John Alfred to W. W. Holden, April 24, 1868, Governor's Correspondence, State Archives of North Carolina; Perman, *The Road to Redemption*, 137–39. There is a large literature on factionalism and racism within the southern Republican parties, but for a few examples involving reconstructed rebels, see *Proceedings of the Constitutional Convention of South Carolina* (Charleston: Denny & Perry, 1868), 1:17; Amos Akerman to William Walker, August 1, 1871, Akerman Letterbooks, University of Virginia Special Collections; William B. Rodman to Camilla Rodman, February 16, 1868, Rodman Papers, East Carolina University, Greenville, NC.

30. Fitzgerald, *Reconstruction in Alabama*, 145; Howell C. Flournoy to Henry L. Dawes, December 29, 1868, Application #6029 John H. Christy, HSCR; *Report of the Joint Committee on Reconstruction* (Washington, DC: Government Printing Office, 1866), 124. Adam Domby examines Unionist efforts to keep ex-Confederates disenfranchised, though the targets of their protests were usually not Republican coverts, in Adam Domby, "War within the States: Loyalty, Dissent, and Conflict in Southern Piedmont Communities, 1860–1876," PhD diss., University of North Carolina at Chapel Hill, 2015, 343–50.

31. *US Statutes at Large*, 41st Cong., 2nd Sess., Ch. 114, Sec. 14 and 15, 142–43; Amos Akerman to R. McPhail Smith, October 21, 1870; and Akerman to Darius Starbuck, October 17, 1871, Letters Sent by the Department of Justice: Instructions to US Attorneys and Marshals, 1867–1904, National Archives and Records Administration, College Park, MD.

32. Tod Caldwell to Holden, September 9, 1868, Governor's Papers; and Governor Holden Letterbook, October 2, 1868, both in the State Archives of North Carolina; *The Eagle* (Fayetteville), November 12, 1868; Elizabeth Studley Nathans, *Losing the Peace: Georgia Republicans and Reconstruction, 1865–1871* (Baton Rouge: Louisiana State University Press, 1968), 105–13, 120–23.

33. *Atlanta Constitution*, September 4, 1868; *Condition of Affairs in Georgia*, 40th Cong., 3rd Sess., House Mis. Doc. no. 52, p. 89; *White v. Clements*, 39 Georgia Reports 232 (1869).

34. Application #6042 Dickenson H. Walker, HSCR. For an example of a petitioner mentioning his support for the Black legislators, see Application #6059 T. J. Speer, HSCR.

35. Holden Letterbooks, November 16, 1869, State Archives of North Carolina; James Lusk Alcorn to Bassett G. Lawrence, *The Friar's Point Delta*, September 1, 1869, clipping in the Rainwater Collection, Mississippi Department of Archives and History, Jackson; G. K. Gilmer to unknown recipient [House Select Committee on Reconstruction], January 27, 1869; and G. K. Gilmer to Halbert E. Paine, December 11, 1869, HSCR.

36. *Congressional Globe*, 41st Cong., 2nd Sess., 1462; Application #1914 James B. Kennedy, HSCR; *New York Times*, June 23, 1868. On the "Liberal" movement, see Andrew L. Slap, *The Doom of Reconstruction: The Liberal Republicans in the Civil War Era* (New York: Fordham University Press, 2010), 90–95; Mark Wahlgren Summers, *The Ordeal of the Reunion* (Chapel Hill: University of North Carolina Press, 2014), 154–55.

37. Edward Mayes, *Lucius Q. C. Lamar: His Life, Times, and Speeches, 1825–1893* (Nashville: Pub. House of the Methodist Episcopal Church, South, 1895), 184–92, 662–65; Parks, *Joseph E. Brown*, 475–77; C. Vann Woodward, *Origins of the New South, 1877–1913* (Baton Rouge: Louisiana State University Press, 1951), 20.

38. *Congressional Globe*, 42nd Cong., 1st Sess., 103, 62.

39. *Congressional Globe*, 42nd Cong., 2nd Sess., 240, 281.

40. *Congressional Globe*, 42nd Cong., 1st Sess., 62-63, 104-105.

41. *Congressional Globe*, 42nd Cong., 1st Sess., 103; 42nd Cong., 2nd Sess., 105; 42nd Cong., 1st Sess., 103; 42nd Cong., 2nd Sess., 495.

42. *Congressional Globe*, 42nd Cong., 2nd Sess., 247, 273, 279.

43. Richard White, *The Republic for Which It Stands: The United States during Reconstruction and the Gilded Age, 1865–1896* (New York: Oxford University Press, 2017), 1–3.

44. See Laura Free, *Suffrage Reconstructed: Gender, Race, and Voting Rights in the Civil War Era* (Ithaca, NY: Cornell University Press, 2015); Stephen Kantrowitz, "'Not Quite Constitutionalized': The Meanings of 'Civilization' and the Limits of Native American Citizenship," in *The World the Civil War Made*, ed. Gregory P. Downs and Kate Masur (Chapel Hill: University of North Carolina Press, 2015); Catherine A. Jones, "Women, Gender, and the Boundaries of Reconstruction," *Journal of the Civil War Era* 8, no. 1 (2018), 111–31.

# Toward an International History of Reconstruction

## Don H. Doyle

The premise of this volume of essays is to open new approaches to the Reconstruction era as part of its sesquicentennial commemoration and particularly to reconsider the freedoms gained and lost during this troubled chapter in our history. Historians of late have been busy expanding the geographic boundaries of Reconstruction, moving out of the familiar southern habitat to the North and West. This essay aims at showing the possibilities for viewing Reconstruction from outside the nation by considering the gains and losses for freedom abroad in the years immediately following the American Civil War.

One obvious starting point for understanding Reconstruction in its international context is US foreign relations and the projection of American power and influence in the world. Underlying both domestic and foreign policies during this period were parallel and complementary objectives. Domestic Reconstruction grew out of the Radical Republican analysis of what caused the rebellion. Slavery, as Radicals saw it, had perverted republican institutions, creating a servile class and powerful aristocracy, each based on inherited status. The Constitution mandated Congress to "guarantee" a republican form of government in every state. To establish the rebel states on a republican foundation, the Radicals argued, the federal government must destroy slavery, enfranchise the freedpeople, and curb the power of the former slaveocracy. We need not deny any punitive, humanitarian, or other motivations of domestic Reconstruction to understand that the overriding objective was the practical one of eliminating the cause of the past rebellion to diminish the chances of another.[1]

Reconstruction-era foreign policy had similar and complementary objectives. During the Civil War, the Union was surrounded by adversarial, sometimes hostile, antirepublican, and proslavery regimes. To the south, of course, was the rebellious proslavery Confederacy. In Mexico, France toppled the republican government and installed Maximilian as monarch of the Empire of Mexico. At the end of the United States war, Maximilian offered asylum to Confederate refugees and their slaves, which General Ulysses Grant predicted would become the base for an endless revanchist war against the United States.

Also to the south, the Spanish Caribbean offered its ports to Confederate blockade runners and raiders. Spain also took cruel advantage of the United States war to invade and recolonize the Dominican Republic and then bully Peru and Chile into war, all part of Spain's vainglorious effort to reassert influence over Spanish America. To the north, the British had menaced the Union with threats of war during the *Trent* Affair and gave refuge to Confederate terrorists and assassins. From Canada, Confederate agents conducted a raid on a defenseless Vermont town and an arson attack on New York City, and British authorities would not extradite the culprits. Other Confederate agents, notably those involved in the John Wilkes Booth conspiracy, used Montreal as a site to hatch their plot to kidnap or assassinate President Lincoln.[2]

After the war, Secretary of State William Seward, together with several other key actors, set out to mitigate these threats using a combination of diplomatic pressure and threats of military or other coercive forces to encourage the withdrawal of European empires and put an end to slavery. What Seward envisioned was a zone of republican or republican-friendly governments surrounding and supporting the United States.

Concurrent with this effort to expel European empires, a new version of the Monroe Doctrine emerged, primarily in response to Maximilian's empire in Mexico. The French insisted the Mexican people had freely chosen a monarchical government and approved Maximilian as their emperor. Therefore, they posited, the goal of France's intervention was not to subjugate or colonize Mexico but to help restore monarchical order and Catholic moral authority, which the new Mexican republic had upended. President Monroe in 1823 had warned Europe against any further colonization of the Americas. The new Monroe Doctrine held that the Americas were the refuge of republican institutions. Any European empire seeking to impose a monarchy on the ruins of an American republic posed a danger not just to the United States but to all American republics. There was also the implication that existing European colonies, such as British North America, Russian America, and the Spanish Caribbean, threatened the peace of American republics. These novel readings of the Monroe Doctrine, by the way, were not Seward's invention. They emerged from an aggressive American public and Congress, which left Seward catching up with the new anti-imperialist mood.

The familiar narrative of post–Civil War foreign policy portrays William Seward as the architect of what Walter LaFeber and others call America's "New Empire" and the lead up to the imperialist turn of 1898. Seward was genuinely interested in building an infrastructure for the expansion of US commerce. His plans included ports and coaling stations in the Caribbean and Pacific, a canal across Central America, and a submarine telegraph cable across the Pacific. Still, he eschewed anything like military conquest and the subjugation of foreign territory and people. Historians sometimes refer to commercial expansion as imperialism, but there was a distinction with a real difference between that and territorial conquest and governance of distant acquisitions.³

The only territory acquired under Seward's watch was the purchase of Alaska from Russia and an uninhabited atoll in the Pacific, later known as Midway Island. Nor did the United States acquire any territory under Seward's successor, Hamilton Fish, during the Grant administration. Not that there was no public enthusiasm or opportunity for such aggrandizement. Indeed, one of the striking features of the immediate postwar period was the remarkable number of empires, colonies, and countries that invited the United States to consider purchase and annexation, including Cuba, offered by both Spanish and Cuban revolutionaries; the Dominican Republic; and Danish colonies in the West Indies and Greenland.⁴

The real achievement of US foreign policy during Reconstruction was not imperialist expansion, commercial or territorial. It was the expulsion of European imperialism from the Americas. Two years after the Civil War, no fewer than four European empires effectively withdrew from the American hemisphere. The withdrawals happened within days in March and April 1867. France pulled out of Mexico; Russian America became part of the United States; and British North America formed the Dominion of Canada, a self-governing, mostly autonomous federal state. Spain evacuated the Dominican Republic in the summer of 1865. In April 1867, it effectively ended its aggression in South America by agreeing to have the United States mediate peace.

The imperial march out of the American hemisphere in 1867 was due only in part to recent proof of America's hard-power military threat. Before America's Civil War, the idea that any popularly elected government could carry out a protracted war, especially a civil war, was thought to be nearly impossible. Governments that had to answer to a fickle voting public would find it difficult to press military-age men into service and extract revenues from civilians. Under the strain of war, republics were doomed to descend into anarchy or despotism, so the thinking went.⁵

European observers of the American Civil War were impressed with the capacity of both sides to field massive citizen armies and sustain four years of war at extraordinary cost in blood and treasure. The Union's presidential election was an equally impressive test of republican mettle. Lincoln's reelection in the face of significant popular opposition to the war and emancipation of the slaves was no less impressive a demonstration of democratic will. Until that election, European political leaders and investors in Confederate cotton bonds continued to believe the Confederacy would outlast the Union's will to fight.[6]

In April 1865, the United States had the largest armed force in the world. It was a nation at arms, with more than one million men still enlisted and a navy of more than seven hundred ships. European observers feared that, before putting its mighty army away, America would strike against Canada, Mexico, Cuba, or perhaps other targets, partly as retribution against those European powers that had aided the Confederacy but also out of what most saw as the natural instinct of well-armed nations for self-aggrandizement. These concerns proved groundless. Exhausted by war and straining under enormous public debt, the United States quickly demilitarized after 1865. For all the bluster about the nation's Manifest Destiny and the triumph of republican government, except for some saber-rattling on the Mexican border and some loose talk in Congress about annexing Canada, the United States engaged in no military aggression abroad during Reconstruction. But European powers did not know that in 1865, and the fear of America's military prowess and will undoubtedly hastened the withdrawal of European empires.[7]

On America's southern border, the Republic of Mexico, led by President Benito Juárez, had two empires to expel: the Empire of Mexico ruled by Maximilian and the occupation forces of the French Empire that protected his throne. In forcing the French to withdraw, Seward's adroit diplomatic pressure together with Grant's effective use of the US military compelled Napoleon III to get out of Mexico. No less important, nongovernment arms suppliers, recruiters, and volunteers played an important but unsung role in saving Mexico's republic.

The French argued that its intervention in Mexico was not in violation of the Monroe Doctrine because the Mexican people had elected to have a monarchical government and invited Maximilian to its throne. This seemed specious to most Americans, but there was some truth to this argument. Mexican conservatives, led by Catholic clergy and Creole landed elites, were active collaborators in the overthrow of the Mexican republic. They objected to the secularization of the republican state, particularly the "Juárez laws" that stripped the church of its property and its monopoly on education. Conservatives first rose in armed rebellion in 1857 in what became the War of the Reform, a four-year civil war that ended about the time the United States war began. After failing to defeat the republicans at arms, the Mexican conservatives turned to the monarchs of Europe and Pope

Pius IX, seeking allies to do what they could not accomplish at the ballot box or on the field of battle.

France's Emperor Napoleon III became an eager ally of Mexico's "Church Party," as it was often called. For years Napoleon III had nurtured a "Grand Design" for regenerating the "Latin race" in the Americas; thwarting the baleful influence of Anglo-Saxon republicanism, Protestantism, and individualism on both continents; and restoring the glory that his uncle, Napoleon I, had achieved for France. Mexico was the key to Napoleon's design for Latin America, notably his plan for a canal through Central America that would make France a dominant global power spanning the Pacific and Atlantic oceans.

The Grand Design was not only for France's geopolitical aggrandizement. The idea of a Latin race bound by similar languages and the Catholic religion was a transnational concept that encompassed Spanish, Portuguese, Italian, and French peoples in both hemispheres. Republican institutions were unsuited to the Latin temperament, the theory went. Evidence of political instability was apparent throughout the Spanish-American republics. The Empire of Brazil was the exception proving the rule that republicanism and Latin culture did not mix well. The Latin race required the firm hand of monarchy and the moral authority of the Catholic Church. Mexico, under European tutelage, would present a model of order to other troubled Spanish-American republics. They would seek alliances with Mexico, forming a Pan-American Latin-Catholic hegemonic force opposed to the invasive spread of Teutonic republicanism southward from the United States.[8]

Once it became clear after First Bull Run that the United States was descending into a protracted civil war, Napoleon III immediately seized the opportunity to launch his Grand Design. It began in October 1861 when France, Britain, and Spain met in London to form the Tripartite Alliance. Their purpose was supposedly to recover debts owed by Mexico to their citizens. The Spanish and British withdrew not long after the invasion began. In May 1862, the French continued their march toward Puebla, the gateway to the capital. The heroic stand by Mexican republicans at Puebla (celebrated now as Cinco de Mayo) delayed their entry into Mexico City for more than a year. Another year would pass before Maximilian arrived in Mexico and took the throne in May 1864.[9]

Throughout the war, Seward continued to warn European powers that the Union would "wrap the world in flames" if any dared lend aid to the rebellion. But he was afraid even to mention the Monroe Doctrine, let alone defend it, out of his logical fear that any aggression against the French would throw them into the welcoming arms of the Confederacy. For their part, Confederate envoys in

France, following their Latin strategy, assured Napoleon III their government did not subscribe to the Monroe Doctrine, and it welcomed the French effort to establish an orderly monarchy in place of anarchy in Mexico. Napoleon, in turn, recognized that the southern rebellion was essential to his Grand Design, at least as a temporary distraction preventing US intervention, perhaps as a permanent buffer state between the United States and the Empire of Mexico.[10]

As Seward continued his timid policy of neutrality and in the face of the French incursion in Mexico, Republicans in Congress began staking out a bold position in defense of the Monroe Doctrine. They also had the support of Matías Romero, Mexico's ambassador to Washington. Romero worked endlessly to arouse the American public and the Lincoln administration to defend the Monroe Doctrine against Maximilian and the French.[11] His efforts began to pay off toward the end of the war. In April 1864, as Maximilian was making his way from Trieste to Mexico, the Republican congressman Henry Winter Davis rose before the House of Representatives to present a joint resolution denouncing the "deplorable events now transpiring in the Republic of Mexico." The Congress of the United States, the resolution read, declares that "it does not accord with the policy of the United States to acknowledge any monarchical government erected on the ruins of any republican government in America under the auspices of any European power." The resolution passed without dissent in both houses. The only debate came from a conservative Democrat, Congressman Samuel Cox, who wanted "more emphatic" language against what he called the "*Arch Dupe* of Louis Napoleon." Seward reassured the French that Congress did not make foreign policy, but it was clear to all that American politicians of both parties and much of the public were closing ranks behind the new Monroe Doctrine.[12]

The Republican Party platform in 1864 underscored the growing importance of the Monroe Doctrine in a plank that denounced the forceful "overthrow of Republican Government on the Western Continent" and European efforts to "obtain new footholds for Monarchical Government . . . in near proximity to the United States." These efforts, the Republican platform asserted, were "menacing" to the "peace and independence" of the United States. In November, in addition to reelecting Lincoln, Republicans gained massive majorities in the House and Senate. France and all of Europe took notice.[13]

Interest in the Monroe Doctrine, in its new aggressive tone, surged in early 1865 when rumors came out of the Hampton Roads peace talks that the North and

South might reunite in a joint military operation in Mexico. They would drive out the French, topple Maximilian, and restore Juárez and the republic to power or, as Jefferson Davis thought, colonize it with ex-Confederates.[14] Lincoln and Seward never took the scheme seriously. Still, murmurs of US retaliation against those European powers that supported the rebellion or took advantage of it by invading Latin American countries continued to resound in the press at home and abroad.

In France, the liberal opposition felt emboldened by the Union's impending victory. They exploited public discontent over the expense and stupidity of the Mexican venture. On April 10, 1865, opposition leader Jules Favre rose before the Corps Législatif to denounce the whole scheme. "We deplore more than ever the blood flowing in Mexico for the benefit of a foreign prince, the disregard of popular sovereignty, and our policy committed to an erroneous course." Recall the troops, Favre demanded.[15]

Five days later, news of Appomattox arrived in Paris, and the liberal leader Eugène Pelletan proposed that the Corps Législatif issue a note of congratulations to the United States. "The slaveholding rebellion is stricken to the earth, and the American republic is reinstated in its majestic unity." When Bonapartist deputies scoffed at this, Pelletan shot back, "Do not laugh, gentlemen, you may be heard on the other side of the Atlantic."[16]

Indeed, Americans and Mexican republicans were listening to the French debate the future of Mexico, and the French opposition was joining hands with the United States in favor of republicanism on both sides of the ocean. In France and America, they were warning Napoleon III that the cost of his Grand Design might be a disastrous war with the powerful army and navy of the United States.

Though Seward and his minister in Paris, John Bigelow, welcomed these signs of discontent in France, they had quietly devised an understanding with France that the United States would remain neutral toward Maximilian so long as the French agreed to withdraw its troops. Seward worried that, if challenged by the United States, the volatile French emperor would lead France to war in defense of France's national honor and try to drown the opposition in a burst of patriotic élan. Neither France nor the United States could afford such a war, and Seward, therefore, counseled patience and diplomacy.

Then, in early April, Seward suffered a terrible carriage accident that left him with a broken jaw and arm. He was recuperating at home on the night of April 14 when an assassin sent by John Wilkes Booth broke into his room and, after his gun jammed, slashed Seward's face and throat with a knife. Seward survived only by falling off the bed, but together with his previous injuries, the attack left him barely able to speak and in no condition to carry on his duties for weeks.[17]

Meanwhile, General Ulysses S. Grant, the commanding general of a massive army of more than one million battle-tested soldiers, felt there was no time for patient diplomacy. France would never voluntarily pull out until Maximilian's regime was ready to stand on its own. Juárez's beleaguered republican army was in no position to force the French out or oust Maximilian. To delay, Grant feared, would allow die-hard Confederates to cross into Mexico, join Maximilian in arms, and continue the war against the Union from across the border. The French would withdraw, Grant felt certain, only when they understood the alternative was war with the United States. Besides, after the way France had treated the Union during the Civil War, it was time to settle scores. "I regard the act of attempting to establish a Monarchical Government on this continent, in Mexico, by foreign bayonets as an act of hostility against the Government of the United States," he wrote to President Johnson. "If allowed to go on until such a government is established I see nothing before us but a long, expensive and bloody war; one in which the enemies of this country will be joined by tens of thousands of disciplined soldiers embittered against their government by the experience of the last four years."[18]

Grant had been conferring with Matías Romero since April 1865, and the two became fast friends and trusted collaborators. Grant agreed with Romero's premise that the two rebellions, one instigated by the Church Party in Mexico and the other by slaveholders in the United States, were integrally linked. Both were in rebellion against a popularly elected republican government. The success of the Mexican rebellion depended on that of the southern rebellion. Neither republic would be safe so long as either rebellion lived. Confirming the latter point, Maximilian was encouraging Confederate veterans to colonize northern Mexico. He wanted them to serve as a buffer against US intervention. Though Mexico had long ago abolished slavery, Maximilian had crafted a decree permitting Confederate immigrants to continue slave labor in all but name. It was a way of inducing white southerners to settle in Mexico, and it took little imagination for Grant or anyone else to imagine it would mean slavery would live on in Mexico.[19]

Both Romero and Grant were impatient with Seward's timid policy toward the French intervention in Mexico. While Seward lay incapacitated at home, Grant decided to carry out his own brand of foreign policy. In April 1865, he ordered General Phil Sheridan to the Texas border to take command of 52,000 soldiers. Sheridan was to crush any remaining Confederate resistance, stop the flow of

Confederate migrants crossing into Mexico, and then quietly supply arms and supplies to Juarez's army. Grant further instructed him to do all he could to strike fear in the French that the United States might invade Mexico and join arms with Juárez's republicans.[20]

Juárez's republican army, weakened by desertion and demoralization, had retreated to Paso del Norte (present-day Ciudad Juárez), on the US border. The Mexican army needed men, arms, and uniforms. Grant and Sheridan quickly, and perhaps unfairly, concluded Mexico's republican military leaders were not up to the task. The Mexicans, Grant wrote Sheridan in October 1865, "have no great leader capable of using even the resources at their disposal. It will take some man from the United States to fill the place."[21]

What Grant had in mind was a fantastic scheme he had worked out in collaboration with Romero. Union veterans would muster out of service but be allowed to keep their weapons. Those willing to volunteer would cross into Mexico and enlist with Mexico's republican army. The Mexican government would pay their salary, but with money borrowed from the United States. Once in Mexico, they would serve under the command of General John Schofield, whom the Mexican military would commission. Grant regarded Schofield as one of his most able generals and someone who could lead the American volunteers to victory for Mexico.[22]

Grant arranged for Schofield to have a year's leave of absence from the army. On July 25, 1865, he informed Sheridan that Schofield was coming to the Rio Grande on an "inspection tour." Meanwhile, Grant instructed Sheridan not to send back any stores of arms and ammunition from Texas and instead to "place them convenient to be permitted to go into Mexico if they can be got into the hands of the only government we recognize in that country." "We want," giving a perfunctory bow to Seward's concerns, "to aid the Mexicans without giving cause to a War between the United States and France." Then he added with an elegant dash of sarcasm, that "between the would-be Empire of Maximilian and the United States all difficulty can easily be settled by observing the same sort of neutrality that has been observed towards us for the last four years."[23]

Meanwhile, the American public was weighing in on the Monroe Doctrine and its obligation to rescue Mexico from the tyranny of European monarchs. Beginning in May 1865, a wave of newspaper ads and articles publicized a bellicose popular movement surging among Union veterans to "Go with Grant Again" and march "on to Mexico." Popular songs popped up, some mocking Maximilian, others boasting of America's readiness to march on Mexico.[24] To avoid flagrant violation of US neutrality, agents of the Mexican government, several of them former Union officers, led the recruitment drive for volunteers to liberate Mexico. It was disguised as an organization promoting "Mexican Emigration." One agent, William H. Allen, an Ohio veteran, claimed no fewer than 103,000 volunteers ready to serve as what the *New York Times* dubbed the "Crusaders for Saint Monroe."[25]

In San Francisco, Mexican and American agents recruited and armed several hundred officers and men, some of them forming what Juárez would call the American Legion of Honor, who made their way to Mexico to join the struggle against Maximilian. The actual number who came into Mexico to raise their swords against Maximilian is impossible to determine with any precision. Estimates ranged from two to three thousand and up to ten thousand American volunteers. Both sides had reason to underplay the degree and importance of American involvement: the United States because it violated neutrality laws and Mexico because of pardonable national pride and internal political rivalry. The French and Maximilian's imperial officers, in turn, complained of substantial American involvement. Some honest exaggeration may have been attributable to the many surplus Union uniforms worn by Mexican soldiers. Whatever their actual numbers, the prospect of disciplined American soldiers coming into Mexico caused tremors in Mexico City and Paris.[26]

All this time Seward, suffering profound pain and unable to speak clearly because of the knife wounds on his face and an iron brace fastened to his broken jaw, learned about Grant and Romero's schemes from his sickbed at home. He was determined to put a stop to General Grant's self-appointed mission to invade Mexico. On June 16, he made his way with assistance from his home on Lafayette Square to the White House, to attend the weekly cabinet meeting. He was there to warn the president and cabinet of the dangers Grant was inviting in Mexico.

Grant went first, laying out his plan for immediate military intervention to uphold the Monroe Doctrine, pay France back for its transgressions, and prevent a costly and endless war with the nest of Confederate slaveholders assembling across the border. Then Seward rose, his feeble voice barely audible but his force of mind undeniable. Napoleon III would pull out of Mexico, Seward assured the cabinet, once it was made clear that the United States was never going to recognize Maximilian's regime and would never tolerate a European monarch imposed upon a neighboring country. Earlier, Seward had dangled the possibility of granting recognition to Maximilian, but this was only to keep the French from taking sides with the Confederacy. He now recognized the political winds blowing strongly in favor of intervention in Mexico but saw that Grant and Sheridan, together with Romero, were stampeding into a costly and wholly unnecessary war.[27]

Seward gave another reason to avoid US military intervention in Mexico, one that bears close attention among those who remember Seward as the prophet of America's Manifest Destiny. The "on to Mexico" chorus of 1865 was all too reminiscent of the spirit of southern filibusterism in the 1840s and 1850s, replete with promises of fabulous riches for the taking and loose talk of annexing northern Mexico's silver-mining district. Once American troops invaded Mexico to drive out the French, Seward warned, "We could not get out ourselves." An army of republican liberation would become an army of imperialist conquest. At the end of the cabinet meeting, it looked as though Seward had at least won the ear of President Johnson and bought some time. "Seward acts from intelligence, Grant from impulse," cabinet member Gideon Welles recorded in his diary.[28]

Seward came out of the cabinet meeting still furious with Grant and Romero for going around him to the president. He was determined to derail Grant's outlandish plan for a thinly disguised US intervention in Mexico. In a masterful ploy, Seward invited General Schofield to meet with him over a long meal in Cape May, New Jersey. Seward suggested to the impressionable general that his talents would better serve his country if he went to Paris as Seward's special agent. "I want you to get your legs under Napoleon's mahogany, and tell him he must get out of Mexico." Schofield, duly flattered, accepted the mission in early August. Then Seward stalled, perhaps to let the pressure build in Paris and Mexico, or possibly because he had already disrupted Grant's scheme simply by enlisting Schofield.[29]

Schofield finally left for France in early November 1865. His arrival in Paris aroused great attention in the Parisian press. Soon after he arrived, at a widely publicized Thanksgiving Day dinner at the Grand Hotel, he delivered a toast that caught everyone's attention. He began with warm salutes to the historic friendship between France and America. Then he made what the French might take as ominous comments about how America's Civil War had revealed such a remarkable capacity for making war, this in a democratic nation where government rarely intruded into daily life. Emperor Napoleon seemed wary of meeting with Schofield, but Bigelow arranged meetings between Schofield and several of Napoleon's most trusted advisers. None could have missed Schofield's urgent message that the United States would not tolerate the French in Mexico much longer. The Parisian press speculated on Schofield's mysterious mission, causing rumors about the prospects of war with America to fly and creating a "big scare" among holders of Mexican imperial bonds, whose hopes rested with Maximilian's survival.[30]

Schofield never got his legs beneath Napoleon's mahogany, but thanks to the Parisian press, his public diplomacy campaign left a mark. Bigelow reported to Seward that relations with the United States had preoccupied all the journals in France. Feelings were "intense," and "it alarms the government" that "something must be done," he added. Bigelow also suggested to Seward that stirring up some "specimen of congressional eloquence" on the Mexico Question might motivate French investors and politicians to reconsider matters. He advised against any "rash play" that might lead to war and leave the United States taking on Mexico as a client. Nothing would please the emperor more, Bigelow warned, than finding a way of "taking Mexico off the end of their spear, with our own." This was precisely Seward's warning to the cabinet.[31]

Bigelow continued to apply quiet pressure on France's foreign minister, Drouyn de Lhuys. He expressed alarm over Maximilian's Black Decree in October 1865, which ordered summary executions for all those bearing arms against the imperial government. He also made it clear that by encouraging ex-Confederates to colonize northern Mexico, Maximilian had effectively reopened the door to slavery. "It is settled," Seward instructed Bigelow to tell de Lhuys, "that African Slavery in any form ought henceforth to cease throughout the world."[32]

Together, Grant and Sheridan's hard-power threats and Seward and Schofield's soft-power public diplomacy proved successful. In his annual address to the Corps Législatif in January 1866, Emperor Napoleon III announced the departure of French troops from Mexico, to be done in staged withdrawals ending in November 1867. Later, Napoleon moved the final departure up to March 1867, this in light of Germany's fearsome display of military prowess in the lightning war between Austria and Prussia in the summer of 1866. French troops did evacuate as planned, leaving Maximilian to face defeat and execution before a Mexican firing squad that June. Later that month, President Benito Juárez entered Mexico City to reclaim the capital for the Republic of Mexico.

The French evacuation from Mexico coincided with the creation of the Canadian Confederation, an amalgamation of several of Britain's North American colonies: Upper and Lower Canada (Quebec and Ontario), along with Nova Scotia and New Brunswick. The Dominion of Canada continued as part of the British Empire and though it was closer to republican than monarchical in its structure of government, as the name suggested, Canada's leadership was staunchly monarchical in sympathy. The making of Canada was a complicated story of many parts. Behind the impulse to form a confederation was the long-held dream in the United States, and fear in parts of British North America, that it would naturally become annexed into the giant republic to the South. Both sentiments heightened in the 1860s. The irritation with Britain over its aid to the Confederacy led some Americans to expect that the *Alabama* Claims might be settled by Britain ceding all or some of its North American colonies to the United States. The Russian sale of what became Alaska added an unexpected element by placing British Columbia between two jaws of the United States, which made that colony a likely target for annexation.

Meanwhile, Irish-American Fenians were conducting raids into Canada and Nova Scotia, trying to inflame Britain. Though the Fenian raids never posed much of a threat, they highlighted the worrisome task of having to defend distant colonies from the well-armed and irascible American republic. In the end, the Dominion of Canada was born with ease, its border with the United States became a famous example of peaceful coexistence, and Canada took its place as an exemplary model of modern democracy, one many Americans would come to envy. On the North American continent, the Monroe Doctrine and Seward had realized his vision of a zone of friendly neighbors.[33]

For a time, it looked like the Spanish Caribbean might move in the same direction. Unlike Russia, Britain, or France, Spain clung with unusual tenacity to the remains of its American empire. In the face of growing political unrest in Madrid and fierce resistance from Dominican and allied Haitian guerrilla fighters, Spain withdrew in humiliation from Santo Domingo in the summer of 1865.[34] At the same time, Spain provoked war with Peru and seized its guano-rich Chincha Islands. When Chile refused coaling rights to the Spanish fleet, the fleet bombarded Chile's virtually defenseless port of Valparaiso. Peru and Chile formed an alliance that soon included Ecuador and Bolivia. The so-called Chincha Islands War became the Spanish–South American War, one of the more disgraceful of imperial Spain's exploits.[35]

Spain had a well-deserved reputation as an ossified relic of Europe's Old Regime, clinging to lost empires and captive to powerful ultramontane Jesuits and the Catholic Church. The Bourbon dynasty had ruled the country since 1700, and its incumbent, Isabella II, had ascended to the throne when she was a toddler in 1830. The reactionary Carlist faction of the Bourbon dynasty was outraged that a woman held the throne and waged a series of futile wars trying to depose her. The Carlists suspected that her son and heir, Alfonso, had been fathered by a captain of the guard, one of a series of romantic affairs she carried on while married to her hapless cousin, the Infante Francis, whom Isabella loudly complained was effeminate. Anxious to shore up her eroding support, Isabella II dabbled in politics, favoring reactionary generals and ultramontane Jesuit clergy and indulging their vainglorious fantasies of reclaiming Spain's imperial glory by cheap victories in Africa and Latin America.[36]

Spain was also the last European nation to permit slavery. Cuba's dependence on slave labor, the continued profitability of its sugar plantations, and exaggerated fears of racial violence and economic disarray accompanying emancipation had kept the "Ever Faithful Isle" loyal to Spain even as other colonies declared independence and abolished slavery. The racial fears that united whites in support of slavery in the South were in full play in Cuba during much of the nineteenth century. "When Cuba ceased to be Spanish she would be African," was the time-honored threat used to fasten Cuban whites to Spain. Their loyalty, and the fear underlying it, was disrupted by the republican revolution that shook Cuba for ten years beginning in 1868 and no less by events in the United States.[37]

Strangely, historians have either ignored or outright denied the role played by American events and foreign policy in bringing slavery to an end in the Spanish Caribbean, but Cubans and Spaniards at the time understood it clearly. Seward's treaty with Britain in 1862 to suppress the slave trade constituted a severe blow to the future of Cuban slavery. Then Lincoln's Emancipation Proclamation and the Thirteenth Amendment freed two-thirds of all slaves in the American hemisphere, leaving Spain alone with Brazil holding on to an institution the European-American world had abandoned. Whatever failings Reconstruction may have had in the United States, its impact on slavery in the Spanish Caribbean and Brazil is undeniable.[38]

The eyes of Cubans, slave and free, had been fixed on the war raging to their north. Cuban slaveholders and Spanish government officials in Cuba were generally sympathetic to the Confederacy, whose victory would secure slavery in the Caribbean. General Francisco Serrano, the captain-general at the head of the Spanish government in Havana, confided to a Confederate agent, "my heart and soul are with your struggle for independence." Serrano and his successor, Domingo Dulce, had opened the ports of Cuba to blockade runners sustaining the Confederacy, and Havana became an important gateway in the Atlantic passage between the South and Europe.[39]

Though Cuba's sugar economy remained profitable, the slave labor system depended on the continued importation of slaves from Africa, and actions by the United States effectively ended that nefarious commerce. Until the Civil War, the United States, given the dominant political leverage of Southern slaveholders, had refused to allow British patrols to search American ships suspected of slave trading, and the flow of African slaves to Cuba continued under the protection of the American flag.

That changed in the spring of 1862 when William Seward and British ambassador Richard Lyons concluded the Lyons-Seward Treaty for the Suppression of the Slave Trade. By this treaty, the United States and Britain agreed to the mutual right to search ships suspected of slave trading. The agreement was part of Seward's wartime diplomatic strategy to win British support to the Union side and align the Union cause with the cause of human liberty in the public mind abroad. The Lyons-Seward Treaty, however, had implications far beyond wartime diplomacy. It was clear to all that, if the Union won, slavery in Cuba was doomed.[40]

Cubans, white and Black, enslaved and free, were divided into Confederate sympathizers and supporters of Lincoln. Among the latter, the Cuban historian Emilio Santovenia wrote, "were Cubans who wanted to renew their homeland politically, socially, and economically, from white men burning with deep concerns to free blacks waiting at the port of Havana for . . . the latest news . . . and to show their joy for the victories of the one who rightly had become the redeemer of the African race in America."[41] For progressive-minded Cubans, Lincoln came to personify the Union but also their hopes for reform, beginning with abolition. "In the decree of liberty for its Negroes," one Cuban later wrote, "the United States defined also the future of the Creole slaveowners."[42]

That future would be abolition, whether Cuba's slaveholders wanted it or not. "The time in which Cuba and Puerto Rico trembled before the thought of becoming African is over," a group of Cubans wrote to Queen Isabella II in mid-1865. Spanish reformers agreed: "The war in the United States is finished," one announced before the Spanish Cortes, "and being finished, slavery in the whole American continent can be taken as finished."[43]

Signs of growing support for Lincoln and the Union were evident earlier. "The Cubans even the slaveholders can scarcely refrain from manifesting their sympathy" for the Union cause, the US consul in Havana reported in October 1862.[44] He noted that Cuba's slaves "mingle with their songs the significant refrain 'Avanza Lincoln, Avanza, tu eres nuestra esperanza' [Onward Lincoln, onward, you are our hope]." The chant took on greater meaning after news of Lincoln's Emancipation Proclamation arrived in Cuba. The "colored population are certainly somewhat agitated," another consul reported in October 1863; "the words 'Lincoln advances' are often heard in their songs and conversations among themselves."[45]

News of Lincoln's assassination caused "an unparalleled demonstration of grief" among Cubans, "especially among the Negroes," one observer noted in April 1865. Men and women of all races wore black armbands with an image of Lincoln and "a device representing the American eagle." They wore these emblems in defiance of Spanish authorities who feared racial unrest and censored the press to ensure the many eulogies to Lincoln made no allusion to him as *El Gran Emancipador*.[46] Young José Martí, the future hero of Cuban independence, a boy of twelve at the time, remembered openly weeping for Lincoln, who became his lifelong hero.[47] Images of Lincoln could be seen hanging on the walls of Cuban homes. "In small modest rooms as well as in mansions which sheltered the high minded progressive leaders," the image of Lincoln "became an expression of the high Cuban aspiration."[48]

It was telling that the Spanish Abolitionist Society, led by Puerto Ricans along with a few Cubans, was formed in Madrid soon after Lincoln's reelection and commenced activities in that propitious moment, April 1865, when the Spanish world was singing the praises of Lincoln, *El Gran Emancipador*.[49] Among the society's first victories was an act promulgated by the Spanish Cortes in July 1866 to end the slave trade to the Spanish Caribbean in July 1866.[50]

In the face of the new realities created by the American Civil War, growing international pressure to end the slave trade, and revolutionary stirrings in Spain, the Spanish government in October 1866 delegated a reform commission to address the future of the Spanish Caribbean. At first, the commission devoted most of its efforts to such "reforms" as encouraging slave reproduction, supplementing the labor supply with Asian coolies, and coercing free Blacks to work. Conservative delegates tried to shut down any discussion of ending slavery until the Cuban delegation eventually presented a plan for gradual emancipation. The solution was to free children born to slave mothers and cut off the importation of slaves by enforcing a strict ban on the international slave trade.[51]

Underlying the hopes for Spain's program of Cuban reform in 1866–1867 was the terrifying thought that, if it failed and if some orderly plan for emancipation were not put in place, Cuba would descend into revolution, race warfare, and economic collapse. Conservatives pointed to Lincoln and the United States as an example of what Cuba must avoid. Reformers, however, began to see the United States as a model for emancipation and progress of a kind they wanted to emulate. When Spain failed to implement the reform measures of 1867, that set the stage for revolutionary thunderbolts to strike on both sides of the Atlantic.

In Spain, a coalition of liberal opponents to the Bourbon dynasty, led by generals Juan Prim and Francisco Serrano, seized power on September 18, 1868. It was a mostly peaceful operation, later dubbed the Glorious Revolution. Still, the revolution drove Queen Isabella II into exile in France and declared a liberal government that would be organized as a peculiar amalgam of constitutional monarchy and democratic election of the Cortes by universal manhood suffrage. The monarch, to be selected later, would have to come from outside the Bourbon dynasty.[52]

Less than one month following Spain's September revolution, on October 10, 1868, Carlos Manuel de Céspedes, a Cuban planter and lawyer, raised the flag of rebellion near his home in Yara, in the eastern portion of the island. Céspedes knew Prim from their days as students in Barcelona, and though there is no evidence of coordination, Cuban rebels knew about the revolution in Spain. The *Grito de Yara* proclaimed "Independencia y Cuba libre," meaning independence of Cuba from Spain and freedom for the enslaved, at least for those willing to join the Liberation Army.[53]

William Tinker, an American living in Cuba, provided a fascinating description of enslaved Cubans flocking to the revolutionary banner:

> They understood that they were free, and that their freedom had been given to them by the republic of Cuba, and their former masters, and they understood that their freedom had resulted in some way from the emancipation of slaves in the United States. They had pictures of Abraham Lincoln, and spoke of him familiarly as the *emancipador*, or emancipator.[54]

The success of the Cuban insurrection depended heavily on those slaves and free colored who joined the rebel Creoles. By some estimates, slaves and free colored constituted over half the rebel Liberation Army, or the "Mambi" army, as it came to be known. It was a multiracial force that included Black and white officers. The familiar fears of "Africanization" no doubt distorted the estimates of the racial mix in both directions, but all agreed that slaves and free colored played a crucial role in the rebel army.[55]

No less critical than the needs of the army for soldiers was the revolution's need for foreign aid, and that meant the United States, the only nation in proximity with the resources and ideological sympathy to support the Cuban republican revolution. Having waged war against a slaveholders' rebellion to perpetuate slavery, the United States was never going to side with the Cuban rebels unless they emphatically renounced slavery. If the Confederacy's experience offered any lessons, Cuba's rebels were unlikely to find Britain, France, or any European power willing to aid a rebellion to perpetuate slavery. During the first months of the revolution, Céspedes had equivocated on emancipation. At first, he decreed only slaves who fought for the republic would be free. Then he added that freedom would come only if and when the rebellion succeeded.[56]

Spain's colonial officials in Havana supplemented its small regular army with a group known as the Spanish Volunteers. It was a Cuban citizen militia, originally organized in the 1850s to resist the filibustering expeditions led by Narciso López and launched from the United States with the support of southern slaveholders. By January 1869, the Spanish Volunteers had mobilized a force of over twenty thousand infantry and 13,500 cavalry; their numbers rose to over eighty thousand before the war ended. Men were also coming over from Spain determined to keep Cuba in the empire and keep slavery in Cuba. Spanish forces were well armed with Remington rifles purchased in the United States. The Mambi army relied on older rifles and muskets, and their most effective assaults involved full-out charges swinging machetes.[57]

The Spanish Volunteers soon gained effective control of the Cuban government, deposing moderate government officials and dictating an all-out war of extermination against what they viewed as a slave revolt aided by white traitors. They massacred rebel soldiers on the spot, slaughtered civilians, pillaged food, and razed homes and entire villages at will. In Spain, the liberal government tried to appease the Cuban rebels with promises of reform, including freedom of speech and Cuban representation in the Cortes. The conservatives and Volunteers instead appealed to Spain's stubborn national pride and cowed the liberal appeasers. The vicious war in Cuba dragged on for a decade with no resolution.[58]

In April 1869, a group of young, educated revolutionaries, among whom were the sons of the most eminent families of Cuba, called an assembly in Guáimaro to establish the revolution on a firm foundation of republicanism and abolition. The new corps of revolutionary leaders gathered at Guáimaro saw Céspedes acting like a dictatorial warlord. If they were to win aid and recognition from the United States, the Cuban rebels would have to begin by creating a constitutional republic with a representative legislature. Within a single day, the Guáimaro Assembly drafted a liberal constitution that provided for a representative unicameral republic. The assembly agreed to elect Céspedes as president only because under the new constitution, the president served at the pleasure of the legislature.

The other crucial prerequisite to US aid and recognition, the Guáimaro Assembly understood, was an unequivocal declaration of total and immediate abolition. Article 24 of the new constitution thus declared, "All inhabitants of the Republic are entirely free."⁵⁹

The Guáimaro constitution and its provision for total abolition were sure to win support in the United States. A large and influential segment of Americans had taken great interest in the Cuban rebellion, which they came to see as consonant with their country's opposition to monarchy and slavery. The Cuban rebels desperately needed material support from the United States if they were to carry on the revolution. Less well known is that the new rebel leaders gathered at Guáimaro also wanted nothing less than Cuba's annexation by the United States. During the assembly at Guáimaro, a passionate debate erupted over a proposal to petition the newly inaugurated president, Ulysses S. Grant, to annex Cuba. One lone delegate, Eduardo Machado, "protested what he called patriotic suicide." He could not "resign himself to Cuba having risen to break the chains of slavery only to lose its personality in the bosom of the great American republic."⁶⁰

Antonio Zambrana, a Havana lawyer and politician, answered Machado's concerns in what some described as a "brilliant speech" favoring "the incorporation of Cuba into the great American federation." "The war has been undertaken to carry out the freedom of Cuba, not to ruin the country," Zambrana began, referring to the recent devastation wrought by the Spanish general Valmaseda. "If we can achieve this object, without ravaging the land, making Cuba become part of the splendid American constellation, we must not continue fighting for an independence that, if realized, would leave the country reduced to rubble, and to the most frightful desolation." Should the United States reject our plea, Zambrana concluded, "before returning to the Spanish yoke, we will request the protectorate of Great Britain."⁶¹ Zambrana's speech hushed the assembly, and it immediately approved the motion to petition the United States, with only Machado dissenting. Zambrana drafted the "exposición" to President Grant, which, as one Cuban observer later noted, was "virtually confessing to the impotence of the nascent Republic of Cuba."⁶²

It was telling that in one of its last items of business the Guáimaro Assembly voted to adopt as the national flag the banner under which Narciso López led his raid into Cuba in 1851, apparently to honor what the delegates saw as the first symbol of rebellion against Spanish rule. None of the delegates seemed bothered by its association with American filibustering and annexation, to say nothing of its proslavery associations. Instead, Zambrana hailed "the flag of '51" as "a glorious testimony that Cubans had long been fighting tyranny." Not incidentally, the

López flag of 1851 would become the national flag of Cuba in 1902 and continued as such after the revolution of 1959.[63]

American public opinion of all political persuasions seemed to rally in favor of the Cuban revolution. Massive public meetings took place in New York to advocate US aid to the revolution. At one of them, Democratic mayor Oakley Hall linked the Cuban cause to that of the Union: "In vain do we rejoice over the abolition of slavery in this country, if we do not at the same time rejoice at the striking off of the chains of slavery, in order that they may become soldiers of the revolution." The meeting resolved that "we as citizens of the Republic of North America and near neighbors of the island, recognize a special obligation toward the patriots who are toiling and fighting for its emancipation from European tyranny." By emancipating their slaves, the Cuban patriots had demonstrated that "they share the most substantial ideas of modern democracy." Therefore, the meeting urged the US government to recognize the belligerent rights of the rebels immediately.[64]

A similar but grander meeting at New York's Cooper Union came shortly after the promulgation of the Guáimaro constitution. The organizers decorated the hall with American and Cuban flags and filled the air with patriotic music from a "very loud" brass band. The resolutions called for the immediate recognition of the Republic of Cuba as a belligerent nation. Their purpose was "to give heart to a brave people who are struggling for republican institutions" that will "make Cuba a worthy sister Republic of the United States."[65]

A pamphlet authored by the famed American abolitionist Wendell Phillips included useful information on the Cuban revolution, complete with an English translation of the Guáimiro constitution. Phillips insisted it was the United States' responsibility to "republicanize and Americanize this continent and the islands that belong to it" and to "increase the power, influence, and commerce" of the United States. "Never was there a case in the history of America," he proclaimed, "which appealed more earnestly for the application of the Monroe Doctrine than that of Cuba."[66]

The US House of Representatives also passed a resolution expressing sympathy and urging recognition of belligerent rights for the Cuban insurgents. Cuban rebels greeted these tidings with great joy and took them as sure signs of eventual American aid. Meanwhile, clandestine shipments of men and arms were making their way to Cuba despite declarations of neutrality from Washington.[67]

Whatever Congress or the American public wanted for Cuba, Hamilton Fish, Secretary of State under President Grant, would not recognize the Cuban rebels as legitimate belligerents, let alone as a sovereign government. It was far from clear to Fish that the rebellion could succeed in defeating the Spanish loyalists, especially without aid from the United States. There was also a grave risk in violating the fundamental principle of Union diplomacy during the Civil War, specifically that any foreign interference on behalf of a domestic insurrection was an act of war. It seemed especially unseemly to turn against Spain's new liberal government, which the United States had only recently welcomed into the family of nations. Spain, for a moment at least, was in the vanguard of European democracy, and the United States had every reason to think it might serve as a model for other European countries. Furthermore, the United States was preparing its case against Britain for aiding the southern rebellion in the *Alabama* Claims. To assist the Cuban rebels would discredit the entire case by putting the United States in much the same abominable role it was accusing Britain of taking.[68]

Besides the legal and diplomatic conundrum the Cuban question presented, Fish and others in the cabinet were skeptical of rebel claims that they had constituted a viable government with an army sufficient to defend itself, one of the prerequisites international law imposed for recognizing belligerent rights. Fish and many others also harbored doubts about the cultural and racial qualifications of the Cuban population for self-government, to say nothing of annexation into the United States. The "Latin race" in the Americas, many in the United States thought at the time, was inexperienced in self-government and had demonstrated little success in its practice. As to annexation, Fish regarded the Cubans as an alien people whose language, religion, and mixed racial character made them ill-suited to membership in the United States. In his view, continued "evolution under Spanish tutelage" might serve the Cuban people better than independence. Furthermore, Fish reasoned that the United States, still very much in the throes of Reconstruction, was hardly in a position to take on another war-torn slave society. In Cuba, as with Santo Domingo and other Caribbean islands, cultural prejudice, anti-Catholicism, and racial partiality all worked against US imperialist expansion.[69]

Given all these concerns and with due attention to diplomatic protocol, Fish insisted that the United States negotiate exclusively with Spain, not the rebels. The Cuban civil war was heating up just as the Grant administration took office in March 1869. It was not until the summer of 1869 that Grant sent over Daniel Sickles, a larger-than-life man with a checkered career that combined some controversial diplomatic experience with a notable lack of diplomatic discretion, especially when it came to women. He was notorious for having shot and killed his young wife's lover on Lafayette Square before the Civil War, a crime to which he successfully pleaded temporary insanity. He had lost a leg at Gettysburg and moved about on crutches "as though they were medals," one admiring Spanish woman remarked. Rumors had him and the deposed Queen Isabella II caught up in a romantic affair, which seemed to surprise no one.[70]

Fish sent Sickles to Spain with instructions to offer the good offices of the United States in mediating peace in Spain's civil war in Cuba. He also set clear terms on which peace would be settled: Cuba to be independent, slavery to be abolished, Cuba to pay Spain no more than 100 million dollars, the United States to guarantee payment, and complete armistice during negotiations. The terms Fish outlined would advance the overriding objectives of postwar US foreign policy that Seward had pursued. It would rid the hemisphere of European monarchies, put an end to slavery, and foster a zone of friendly, independent, and ideally republican nations surrounding the United States. Fish's instructions also proposed an offer of US aid in financing the purchase of Cuba's independence from Spain.[71]

Had peace mediation succeeded, it would have been a brilliant diplomatic victory all around. It would have meant peace and independence for Cubans, one more imperial European flag disappearing from the American hemisphere, and Spain enriched and still friendly toward the United States. The payments were to have come out of revenues from Cuba's export trade in sugar. All parties understood that the US loan was like a mortgage and that, should Cuba default on payments, as the banker, the United States could take possession of Cuba. America was making a generous offer, Fish thought, and he made it clear that if Spain did not accept it, he would feel justified in recognizing the belligerent rights of the rebels.[72]

As the war in Cuba raged on, however, Prim faced enormous pressure from nationalist elements who insisted on making Cuba a point of national honor. Spain could consequently not negotiate peace with the Cuban rebels unless and until they laid down their arms; to do otherwise would mean national humiliation. Meanwhile, the price of national honor seemed to be rising by the day. Having been presented with Fish's proposal of up to 100 million dollars, Prim countered with 150 million, throwing Puerto Rico into the bargain. Before it was over, Prim raised the proposed sum to 200 million. He was trying to extract more money for Spain's barren treasury, but he miscalculated America's interest in buying Cuba at any price. By the end of September 1869, the United States withdrew its offer to mediate peace.[73]

While the peace mediation stalled, Fish put pressure on Spain to declare some plan of emancipation. The Guáimaro declaration of abolition and the evidence of rising support for the rebels in the American press and public only added to the pressure. One month after the Guáimaro Assembly, Spain's colonial minister, Segismundo Moret y Pendergrast, presented an emancipation bill to the Spanish Cortes. As Moret explained it to the skeptical deputies, the rebel Cubans, being "familiar with North American customs and language . . . have been able from the first moment to give to the insurrection a special character, presenting it as the flag of liberty against the flag of tyranny." This act, Moret, argued, would give to the world "definite proof . . . slavery is dead, and is finished forever in Spanish dominions." The Moret Law provided for gradual emancipation by declaring that all children born to slave mothers in Cuba and Puerto Rico after September 17, 1868 (the day before the Glorious Revolution), shall be free. The law also granted freedom to slaves of sixty or more years of age, a provision arguably more cruel than it was humane. Finally, Moret's bill countered the rebel promise of emancipation by offering freedom to all slaves who fought for Spain.[74]

Emilio Castelar, a historian, author, ardent republican, zealous abolitionist, and huge admirer of Lincoln (he kept a statue of him breaking the chains of the slave on his mantel), rose in the Cortes to oppose Moret's morally uninspiring legislation. He proposed full and immediate abolition on the American model. For Castelar and liberal Spain, Abraham Lincoln embodied republican virtue, and his example of immediate, uncompensated emancipation for all slaves was one Spain—the last bastion of slavery in Europe—must emulate. Lincoln, "a man of wisdom and political prudence," realized that "all waiting was impossible" and that "gradual steps are impracticable in reforms demanded by justice and humanity."[75]

Castelar turned to American Reconstruction, which he viewed as the successful enfranchisement of a once-downtrodden race.

> Since then [1865] the United States, having converted its slaves into men, have devoted themselves to turning those men into citizens. . . . And today, gentlemen, those beings who were formerly not even men, are freer than the first of the sons of Europe. Those men who could not learn to read, because the southern gentlemen murdered anyone who would dare to give them a book, have today innumerable schools. Those men who were like beasts of burden, wretched as the reptiles that crawled among the cotton and the cane, are free men, are American citizens; they sit in the Congress and the Senate of Washington.

Castelar's speech went on for hours that day; however, his arguments did not persuade his more conservative colleagues. It was, nonetheless, extraordinary evidence of the international inspiration taken by America's experiment in emancipation. The Cortes passed the Moret Law on July 4, 1870, as though to dare the United States to defy this plodding, conservative gesture toward emancipation.[76]

The practical effect of the Moret Law was mitigated by Spanish authorities in Cuba who refused even to publish, let alone enforce, the law. Fish was disgusted with Spain's supposedly liberal government and its reluctance to abolish slavery. The Moret Law, he wrote to Sickles, "may rather be called a project for relieving the slave owners from the necessity of supporting infants and aged slaves, who can only be a burden, and of prolonging the institution as to able-bodied slaves." Under Spain's plan for abolition, "the children of slave mothers born after the decree are to be free, but no provision is made for their support. . . . All slaves who reach the age of sixty-five years [later amended to sixty], when the powers of labor are going, and when they may be supposed to have earned some right to a support in their few remaining years, are to be turned adrift and are given a freedom that may have ceased to be desirable." Spain had failed to live up to what the United States "had a reasonable right to expect." It had betrayed its tacit agreement "to cordially co-operate with us in the extirpation of this blot on the civilization of America." In resignation, Fish wrote to Sickles, "We shall nevertheless regard this as the entering wedge for the eventual destruction of a pernicious system of labor, and shall hope that Spain will soon see that it is for her interest to go further and faster in the direction of emancipation."[77]

The Cuban insurrection ended after ten years, but the revolution that began in 1868 remained unfinished. José Martí, the iconic hero of Cuban independence, had spent his youth under arrest in Cuba for revealing his sympathies with the revolution before authorities deported him to Spain. He later made his way to the community of revolutionary Cuban exiles gathered in New York City. In an 1889 letter to the *Evening Post* (New York), Martí blasted a recent article filled with bigotry toward Cubans. He took the occasion to explain why the dream of becoming part of the United States had faded for him and many other Cuban revolutionaries. "No self-respecting Cuban would like to see his country annexed to a nation where the leaders of opinion share towards him the prejudices excusable only to vulgar jingoism or rampant ignorance. . . . They admire this nation, the greatest ever built by liberty, but they dislike the evil conditions that, like worms in the heart, have begun in this mighty republic their work of destruction.... We love the country of Lincoln as much as we fear the country of Cutting," referring to a similar example of bigotry recently reported in Texas.[78]

Martí grieved that the United States had fallen into the hands of powerful business interests and racist nationalists. They had little affinity with the ideals of universal republicanism and emancipation that he remembered animating the United States. The "country of Lincoln" that Martí lamented disappearing had struggled with imperfect but not empty results to reconstruct a war-torn nation, pacify the rebel South, emancipate the enslaved, and elevate freedpeople to full and equal citizenship.

If domestic Reconstruction closed on a record of mixed success and missed opportunities, international Reconstruction met with several lasting achievements. Seward and Fish's adroit statecraft played a decisive role in several successful phases of US foreign policy in the immediate postwar years. So, too, did the potential threat of US military hard power, which had proved formidable in the late war.

No less critical to the projection of American power and influence in the postwar world was America's vast store of ideological soft power coming out of the Union's hard-won victory. The almost magical appeal Lincoln had among the common people abroad and the enthusiasm liberals abroad had for America's surprisingly resilient republican experiment were phenomena no European government could afford to ignore. Together, these elements played an essential role in the decision of France and Russia to withdraw from North America. Though the British did not abandon its North American colonies, the creation of Canada as a self-governing, mostly independent country brought to an end both the American dream of eventual annexation and Britain's anxiety over the problem of defending its distant American possessions. Spain pulled out of Santo Domingo and ceased its outrageous assaults on helpless Latin American republics. But it held fast to its remaining colonies in the Spanish Caribbean. If the United States failed to aid the Cuban rebels' struggle for independence, the rebels' hopes for US aid and recognition induced them to declare abolition. The United States also pressured Spain to put slavery on the slow road to extinction, a road Brazil followed, not incidentally. Together, the projection of American power and influence in the world during Reconstruction deserves credit for freedoms gained in the world beyond America's borders.

## Notes

1. Forrest A. Nabors, *From Oligarchy to Republicanism: The Great Task of Reconstruction* (Columbia: University of Missouri Press, 2017).

2. Adam Mayers, *Dixie and the Dominion: Canada, the Confederacy, and the War for the Union* (Toronto: Dundurn, 2003), 105; William A Tidwell, *April '65: Confederate Covert Action in the American Civil War* (Kent, OH: Kent State University Press, 1995), 107, 119, 145.

3. Walter LaFeber, *The New Empire: An Interpretation of American Expansion, 1860-1898* (Ithaca, NY: Cornell University Press, 1963), 1–60; Ernest N. Paolino, *The Foundations of the American Empire: William Henry Seward and US Foreign Policy* (Ithaca, NY: Cornell University Press, 1973).

4. Donald Marquand Dozer, "Anti-Expansionism during the Johnson Administration," *Pacific Historical Review* 12, no. 3 (1943): 253–75; on the Dominican Republic, see Nicholas Guyatt, "America's Conservatory: Race, Reconstruction, and the Santo Domingo Debate," *Journal of American History* 97, no. 4 (2011): 974–1000; Christopher Wilkins, "'They Had Heard of Emancipation and the Enfranchisement of Their Race': The African American Colonists of Samaná, Reconstruction, and the State of Santo Domingo," in *The Civil War as Global Conflict: Transnational Meanings of the American Civil War*, ed. David T. Gleeson and Simon Lewis, (Columbia: University of South Carolina Press, 2014), 211–34. References to the mostly secret offers from Spain's revolutionaries to sell Cuba are found in John Bigelow, *Retrospections of an Active Life: 1865–1866* (New York: Baker and Taylor, 1909), 3:496–97; John Bigelow, *France and the Confederate Navy, 1862–1868* (New York: Harper and Brothers, 1888), 191–92; James Morton Callahan, *Cuba and International Relations: A Historical Study in American Diplomacy* (Baltimore, MD: Johns Hopkins University Press, 1899), 376–77; Allan Nevins, *Hamilton Fish: The Inner History of the Grant Administration* (New York: Ungar, 1936), 189–90; Edgecumb Pinchon, *Dan Sickles, Hero of Gettysburg and "Yankee King of Spain,"* (Garden City, NY: Doubleday, Doran, 1945), 226–28.

5. Don H. Doyle, *The Cause of All Nations: An International History of the American Civil War* (New York: Basic Books, 2015), chap. 4.

6. On cotton bond prices as an indicator of confidence in CSA victory, see Doyle, *The Cause of All Nations*, 258–59, 271.

7. Clayton R. Newell and Charles R. Shrader, *Of Duty Well and Faithfully Done: A History of the Regular Army in the Civil War* (Lincoln: University of Nebraska Press, 2011), 304; Nathan Miller, *The US Navy: A History* (Annapolis, MD: Naval Inst. Press, 1997), 144; "US Military Manpower—1789 to 1997," http://www.alternatewars.com/BBOW/Stats/US_Mil_Manpower_1789-1997.htm.

8. Alfred J. Hanna and Kathryn A. Hanna, *Napoleon III and Mexico: American Triumph over Monarchy* (Chapel Hill: University of North Carolina Press, 1971); Stève Sainlaude, "France's Grand Design and the Confederacy," in *American Civil Wars: The United States, Latin America, Europe, and the Crisis of the 1860s*, ed. Don H. Doyle (Chapel Hill: University of North Carolina Press, 2017), 107–24; Stève Sainlaude, *France and the American Civil War: A Diplomatic History* (Chapel Hill: University of North Carolina Press, 2020).

9. Hanna and Hanna, *Napoleon III and Mexico*; Thomas D. Schoonover, *Dollars over Dominion: The Triumph of Liberalism in Mexican-United States Relations, 1861–1867* (Baton Rouge: Louisiana State University Press, 1978); Brian R. Hamnett, *Juárez* (London: Longman, 1994).

10. Doyle, *The Cause of All Nations*, chaps. 5, 8.

11. Matías Romero, *Mexican Lobby: Matías Romero in Washington, 1861–67*, ed. Thomas D. Schoonover (Lexington: University Press of Kentucky, 1986); Matías Romero, *A Mexican View of America in the 1860s: A Foreign Diplomat Describes the Civil War and Reconstruction*, ed. Thomas David Schoonover (Teaneck, NJ: Fairleigh Dickinson University Press, 1991); Schoonover, *Dollars over Dominion*; Robert W. Frazer, "Latin-American Projects to Aid Mexico during the French Intervention," *Hispanic American Historical Review* 28, no. 3 (1948): 377–88.

12. Dexter Perkins, *The Monroe Doctrine, 1826–1867* (Baltimore, MD: Johns Hopkins University Press, 1933), 2:451; *Congressional Globe*, House of Representatives, 38th Cong., 1st Sess., 1408.

13. Frazer, "Latin-American Projects"; "Republican Party Platforms: Republican Party Platform of 1864," http://www.presidency.ucsb.edu/ws/index.php?pid=29621.

14. Francis P. Blair Sr. to Jefferson Davis, Friday, December 30, 1864; Blair, "Suggestions Submitted to Jefferson Davis, President," January 12, 1865; Blair, Memorandum of Conversation with Jefferson Davis, January 12, 1865; Blair to Lincoln, February 8, 1865, all in the Abraham Lincoln Papers, Library of Congress, https://www.loc.gov/collections/abraham-lincoln-papers; William C. Harris, "The Hampton Roads Peace Conference: A Final Test of Lincoln's Presidential Leadership," *Journal of the Abraham Lincoln Association* 21, no. 1 (Winter 2000): 30–61.

15. *Corps Législatif*, April 10, 1865, qtd. in Foreign Relations of the United States (FRUS), 1865, part II, 258, HeinOnline, https://heinonline.org.

16. *Corps Législatif*, April 15, 1865, qtd. in FRUS, 280.

17. Glyndon G. Van Deusen, *William Henry Seward* (New York: Oxford University Press, 1967), 411–16; Walter Stahr, *Seward: Lincoln's Indispensable Man* (New York: Simon and Schuster, 2012), 431–32, 435–40.

18. Grant to Johnson, Washington, June 19, 1865, in Ulysses S. Grant, *The Papers of Ulysses S. Grant*, ed. John Y. Simon (Carbondale: Southern Illinois University Press, 1988), 15:156.

19. Romero's meticulous dispatches detail his dealings with Grant. See Matías Romero, *Correspondencia de la legacion mexicana en Washington durante la intervencion extranjera, 1860–1868*, vol. 5, *1865* (Mexico City: Imprenta del Gobierno, 1871). English translations of select dispatches are found in Romero, *A Mexican View of America in the 1860s*; Romero, *Mexican Lobby*.

20. Philip Henry Sheridan, *Personal Memoirs of P. H. Sheridan* (New York: Charles E. Webster, 1888), 2:205–29.

21. Grant to Sheridan, Washington, October 22, 1865, in Grant, *Papers*, 15:362–63.

22. Grant, *Papers*, 15:265; John McAllister Schofield, *Forty-Six Years in the Army* (New York: Century, 1897), 379–80. The proposed loan from the United States opened the door to claims on Mexican territory as indemnity should Mexico default.

23. Romero, *Mexican Lobby*. On Schofield and arms to Mexico, see entries for May 30, June 5, 27, 28, 1865; Grant to Sheridan, July 25, 1865, in Grant, *Papers*, 15:285–86; Schofield, *Forty-Six Years*, 336–39; John M. Schofield, "The Withdrawal of the French from Mexico: A Chapter of Secret History," *Century Illustrated Monthly Magazine* 54, no. 1 (May 1897): 128–37.

24. Ricardo Resendiz, "¡Fuera de México! La doctrina Monroe en las representaciones estadounidenses sobre el Segundo Imperio Mexicano," MA thesis, Universidad de Guanajuato, 2019; "Revival of Filibustering: From the *Courrier des États-Unis*, May 8," *New York Times*, May 9, 1865; "The Mexican Emigration Scheme," *New York Times*, November 4, 1865.

25. Robert B. Brown, "Guns over the Border: American Aid to the Juarez Government during the French Intervention," PhD diss., Ann Arbor, University of Michigan, 1951, 65–70; Robert Ryal Miller, "Arms across the Border: United States Aid to Juárez during the French Intervention in Mexico," *Transactions of the American Philosophical Society* 63, no. 6 (January 1, 1973): 34.

26. Estimates of American volunteers, Union and Confederate, for Mexico are summarized in Lawrence Douglas Taylor Hansen, "Voluntarios extranjeros en los ejércitos liberales mexicanos, 1854–1867," *Historia Mexicana* 37, no. 2 (1987): 205–37; Robert Ryal Miller, "Californians against the Emperor," *California Historical Society Quarterly* 37, no. 3 (1958): 193–214; Robert Ryal Miller, "Lew Wallace and the French Intervention in Mexico," *Indiana Magazine of History* 59, no. 1 (March 1963): 31–50; Robert Ryal Miller, "The American Legion of Honor in Mexico," *Pacific Historical Review* 30, no. 3 (1961): 229; Robert Ryal Miller, "Plácido Vega: A Mexican Secret Agent in the United States, 1864–1866," *The Americas* 19, no. 2 (1962): 137–48.

27. Schofield, "The Withdrawal of the French from Mexico."

28. Gideon Welles, *Diary of Gideon Welles* (Boston: Houghton Mifflin, 1911), 2:317; Stahr, *Seward*, 440–46, quotation at 444.

29. Schofield, *Forty-Six Years*, 336–39; Schofield, "The Withdrawal of the French from Mexico," 129; Albert Joseph Griffin, "Intelligence versus Impulse: William H. Seward and the Threat of War with France over Mexico, 1861–1867," PhD diss., University of New Hampshire, 2003, 116. Some thought Seward had tricked Schofield into going to Paris to get him away from Grant and Mexico; see Henry M. Wriston, *Executive Agents in American Foreign Relations* (Baltimore, MD: Johns Hopkins University Press, 1929), 780–81.

30. Schofield, *Forty-Six Years*, 341; Bigelow to Seward, Paris, December 8, 1865, in John Bigelow, *Retrospections of an Active Life: 1865–1866* (New York: Baker and Taylor, 1909), 3:265–66; Malakoff, "The Mystery of Gen. Schofield's Visit," *New York Times*, December 31, 1865.

31. Bigelow to Seward, Paris, December 21, November 30, 1865, in Bigelow, *Retrospections*, 3:287, 255.

32. Bigelow to Drouyn de Lhuys, Paris, November 22, 1865, in Bigelow, *Retrospections*, 3:235.

33. Brian Jenkins, *Fenians and Anglo-American Relations during Reconstruction* (Ithaca, NY: Cornell University Press, 1969); Phillip Buckner, "'British North America

and a Continent in Dissolution'": The American Civil War in the Making of Canadian Confederation," *Journal of the Civil War Era* 7, no. 4 (2017).

34. Anne Eller, *We Dream Together: Dominican Independence, Haiti, and the Fight for Caribbean Freedom* (Durham, NC: Duke University Press, 2016); Anne Eller, "Dominican Civil War, Slavery, and Spanish Annexation, 1844–1865," in *American Civil Wars: The United States, Latin America, Europe, and the Crisis of the 1860s*, ed. Don H. Doyle (Chapel Hill: University of North Carolina Press, 2017), 147–66.

35. James W. Cortada, "Spain and the American Civil War: Relations at Mid-Century, 1855–1868," *Transactions of the American Philosophical Society* 70, no. 4 (January 1, 1980): 93–102; William Columbus Davis, *The Last Conquistadores: The Spanish Intervention in Peru and Chile, 1863–1866* (Athens: University of Georgia Press, 1950).

36. John Kiste, *Divided Kingdom: The Spanish Monarchy from Isabel to Juan Carlos* (History Press, 2011), 22, 23, 34–36, 37–38, 73.

37. Sickles to Fish, Madrid, June 26, 1870, in *Correspondence of the Department of State in Relation to the Emancipation of Slaves in Cuba, and Accompanying Papers: Transmitted to the Senate in Obedience to a Resolution* (Washington, DC: GPO, 1870), 16.

38. Steven Hahn cites the lack of notice by Cuban scholars, including Ada Ferrer and Rebecca Scott, among others, to suggest the American Civil War had no significant effect on abolition, or much else, in Latin America. Steven Hahn, "What Sort of World Did the Civil War Make?," in *The World the Civil War Made*, ed. Gregory P. Downs and Kate Masur (Chapel Hill: University of North Carolina Press, 2015), 338–39, 353n11, 353n12. Two good summaries of the interconnected history of the United States and Cuba are Luis Martínez-Fernández, "Political Change in the Spanish Caribbean during the United States Civil War and Its Aftermath, 1861–1878," *Caribbean Studies* 27, nos. 1/2 (1994): 37–64; Matt D. Childs, "Cuba, the Atlantic Crisis of the 1860s, and the Road to Abolition," in *American Civil Wars: The United States, Latin America, Europe, and the Crisis of the 1860s*, ed. Don H. Doyle (Chapel Hill: University of North Carolina Press, 2017), 204–18. Arthur Corwin's classic study of Spanish and Cuban abolition makes a strong case for US influence on slavery in Cuba; see Arthur F. Corwin, *Spain and the Abolition of Slavery in Cuba, 1817–1886* (Austin: University of Texas Press, 1967), 43, 63, 84, 143–44, 147, 176, 203, 209, 241–43, 245, 256, 276–77, 284. See also Gregory P. Downs, *The Second American Revolution: The Civil War–Era Struggle over Cuba and the Rebirth of the American Republic* (Chapel Hill: University of North Carolina Press, 2019), 116–18.

39. Martínez-Fernández, "Political Change," 38–39.

40. Childs, "Cuba, the Atlantic Crisis of the 1860s, and the Road to Abolition"; Corwin, *Spain and the Abolition of Slavery in Cuba*, 147, chap. 11; Christopher Schmidt-Nowara, *Empire and Antislavery Spain, Cuba, and Puerto Rico, 1833–1874* (Pittsburgh: University of Pittsburgh Press, 1999), chap. 5; Christopher Schmidt-Nowara, "From Aggression to Crisis: The Spanish Empire in the 1860s," in *American Civil Wars: The United States, Latin America, Europe, and the Crisis of the 1860s*, ed. Don H. Doyle (Chapel Hill: University of North Carolina Press, 2017), 133; Seymour Drescher, *Abolition: A History of Slavery and Antislavery* (New York: Cambridge University Press, 2009), 328–29.

41. Ramiro Guerra y Sánchez et al., *Historia de la nación cubana* (Havana: Editorial Historía de la Nación Cubana, 1952), 4:31.

42. Philip S. Foner, *A History of Cuba and Its Relations with the United States* (New York: International Publishers, 1962), 2:131–35; Corwin, *Spain and the Abolition of Slavery in Cuba*, 140.

43. Corwin, *Spain and the Abolition of Slavery in Cuba*, 162–63.

44. Robert Schufeldt to Seward, October 12, 1862, qtd. in Martínez-Fernández, "Political Change," 39–40.

45. Schufeldt to Seward, Havana, January 14, 1862; Savage to Seward, Havana, October 3, 1863, qtd. in Dale T. Graden, *Disease, Resistance, and Lies: The Demise of the Transatlantic Slave Trade to Brazil and Cuba* (Baton Rouge: Louisiana State University Press, 2014).

46. Foner, *History of Cuba*, 2:133–34; Emeterio S. Santovenia, *Lincoln* (Buenos Aires: Editorial Americalee, 1948); Emeterio S. Santovenia, "Pasión cubana por Lincoln," *Revista de la Biblioteca Nacional José Martí*, no. 1 (1953): 59–72; Emeterio S. Santovenia, *Lincoln in Martí: A Cuban View of Abraham Lincoln* (Chapel Hill: University of North Carolina Press, 1953).

47. Foner, *History of Cuba*, 2:133–35; Santovenia, *Lincoln in Martí*, 62–63; Santovenia, "Pasión cubana por Lincoln."

48. Guerra y Sánchez et al., *Historia de la nación cubana*, 4:31; Emeterio S. Santovenia, "Reaffirmation of the Colonial Regime," in *A History of the Cuban Nation*, vol. 4, *Break with the Mother Country, 1837–1868*, ed. Ramiro Guerra y Sanchez et al. (Havana: Editorial Historía de la Nación Cubana, 1958), 33.

49. Corwin, *Spain and the Abolition of Slavery in Cuba*, 154–61; Schmidt-Nowara, *Empire and Antislavery Spain, Cuba, and Puerto Rico*, 6–7, 87, 98, 129–30; Schmidt-Nowara, "From Aggression to Crisis," 135–38.

50. Corwin, *Spain and the Abolition of Slavery in Cuba*, 154–61, 177–78, 181–82.

51. Corwin, *Spain and the Abolition of Slavery in Cuba*, chap. 11.

52. Corwin, *Spain and the Abolition of Slavery in Cuba*, 218.

53. Ada Ferrer, *Insurgent Cuba: Race, Nation, and Revolution, 1868–1898* (Chapel Hill: University of North Carolina Press, 1999), 22–31; Corwin, *Spain and the Abolition of Slavery in Cuba*, 222–26.

54. Affidavit of William C. Tinker, *Struggle for Independence in the Island of Cuba*, 41st Cong., 2nd Sess., HED 160 (Washington, DC: GPO, 1870), 175.

55. Ferrer, *Insurgent Cuba*, 47–54. For a wonderful account of life with the Mambi army, see James J. O'Kelly, *The Mambi-Land* (New York: J. B. Lippincott, 1874).

56. Childs, "Cuba, the Atlantic Crisis of the 1860s, and the Road to Abolition"; Corwin, *Spain and the Abolition of Slavery in Cuba*, 230–34; Ferrer, *Insurgent Cuba*, 22–29.

57. José M. Hernández, *Cuba and the United States: Intervention and Militarism, 1868–1933* (Austin: University of Texas Press, 2013), 25.

58. For accounts of the Ten Years War, see Ferrer, *Insurgent Cuba*; Guerra y Sánchez, eds., *History of the Cuban Nation*, vol. 4, *Break with the Mother Country*; Ramiro Guerra y Sánchez, *A History of the Cuban Nation: The Ten Years War and Other Revolutionary Activities*, trans. James J. O'Mailia, vol. 5 (Havana: Editorial Historía de la Nación Cubana, 1958); Ramiro Guerra y Sánchez, *Guerra de los diez años, 1868–1878*, 2 vols. (Havana: Editorial de Ciencias Sociales, 1972).

59. Constitución de Guáimaro, article 24, https://archivos.juridicas.unam.mx/www/bjv/libros/6/2525/7.pdf; Guerra y Sánchez, *Guerra de los diez años*, chap. 15; Ferrer, *Insurgent Cuba*, 26–27.

60. The fullest account of annexationist sentiment at Guáimaro is found in Antonio Pirala, *Anales de la Guerra de Cuba* (Madrid: Felipe González Rojas, 1895), 1:581–82. In contrast, Ada Ferrer, *Insurgent Cuba*, makes only passing mention of annexationist sentiment; Downs, *Second American Revolution*, also slights rebel Cuban annexationists.

61. Pirala, *Anales*, 1:581–82; see also Antonio Zambrana, *La república de Cuba* (New York: N. Ponce de Leon, 1873), 45.

62. Pirala, *Anales*, 1:581.

63. Pirala, *Anales*, 1:673.

64. "Cuban Independence: Immense Mass Meeting at Steinway Hall," *New York Times*, March 26, 1869.

65. "Cuban Independence: Large Meeting at Cooper Institute Last Evening," *New York Times*, May 5, 1869.

66. Wendell Phillips and Plutarco González y Torres, *The Cuban Question and American Policy, in the Light of Common Sense* (New York: L. H. Biglow, 1869), 12.

67. Foner, *History of Cuba*, 2:200.

68. Phillip E. Myers, *Dissolving Tensions: Rapprochement and Resolution in British-American-Canadian Relations in the Treaty of Washington Era, 1865–1914* (Kent, OH: Kent State University Press, 2015).

69. Nevins, *Hamilton Fish*, 180, 194; Eric T. Love, *Race over Empire: Racism and US Imperialism, 1865–1900* (Chapel Hill: University of North Carolina Press, 2004).

70. Pinchon, *Dan Sickles*, 234, 236–37, 242–48, 257–58, quotation at 237.

71. James Morton Callahan, *Cuba and International Relations: A Historical Study in American Diplomacy* (Baltimore, MD: The Johns Hopkins University Press, 1899), 376–77; Nevins, *Hamilton Fish*, 189–90; Pinchon, *Dan Sickles*, 226–28.

72. Nevins, *Hamilton Fish*, 196–97.

73. Nevins, *Hamilton Fish*, 191–200, 231–48, 617; Lester Langley, *The Cuban Policy of the United States: A Brief History* (New York: Wiley, 1968), 65.

74. Corwin, *Spain and the Abolition of Slavery in Cuba*, 245–57.

75. *Correspondence on Emancipation of Slaves in Cuba*, 16–17; for a full text of the speech in Spanish, see Emilio Castelar, *Abolición de la esclavitud* (Madrid: J. A. García, 1870); Callahan, *Cuba and International Relations*, 405–6. See also Corwin, *Spain and the Abolition of Slavery in Cuba*, 249–51; Carolyn P. Boyd, "A Man for All Seasons: Lincoln in Spain," in *The Global Lincoln*, ed. Richard Carwardine and Jay Sexton (New York: Oxford University Press, 2011), 103–4.

76. *Correspondence on Emancipation of Slaves in Cuba*, 16–17; Castelar, *Abolición de la esclavitud.*

77. Fish to Sickles, June 20, 1870, in *Presidential Message on Emancipation of Slaves in Cuba*, 41st Cong., 2nd Sess., SED 113 (Washington, DC: GPO, 1870), 16–17, 12–14; Corwin, *Spain and the Abolition of Slavery in Cuba*, chap. 13; Foner, *History of Cuba*, 2:221–23.

78. Foner, *History of Cuba*, 2:336–37; see full text of letter at "José Martí: Letter to the Editor March 25, 1889," http://www.christusrex.org/www2/fcf/martilettertoeditor.html.

# The Dream of a Rural Democracy

*US Reconstruction and Abolitionist Propaganda in Rio de Janeiro, 1880–1890*

*Sergio Pinto-Handler*

Brazil's abolitionists were avid students and propagandists of Atlantic history. In the final decade of Brazilian slavery, a popular abolitionist movement in Rio de Janeiro made a romantic narrative of emancipation and Reconstruction in the United States part of its antislavery argument. On February 2, 1881, Rio's *Gazeta da Tarde* published a series of articles on the consequences of North American abolition. The *Gazeta* was a popular, affordable daily paper run by abolitionists from Rio's Black community.[1] Using statistics to encapsulate the freedoms won after North American emancipation, the paper's editors informed their readers that over the course of the 1870s, the Black population of South Carolina grew at a rate of 45.3 percent, outpacing the 35 percent growth rate of the white population. In Brazil, where plantation mortality rates had been destructively high for centuries, this was a remarkable fact. "To anybody familiar with economic or social science," the *Gazeta* opined, "this victory of the African race over the *yankee* race is of inestimable value! To advance in population and in agriculture," the paper continued, "is to increase in power, in wealth and in morality. For when individuals multiply it is because Family, Science and Morality are in progress."[2] Readers read that across the United States "the African race [was] increasing in numbers and in wealth, harvesting and multiplying ... laying the foundations for a Rural Democracy across the Mississippi Valley, in South Carolina, in Georgia, Alabama, Arkansas and Texas." Two days later, the *Gazeta* published a similar synopsis from the *Galveston News*. The editors trusted that the facts of abolition would dispel "the sophistry of slavocrats" who insisted that emancipation would lead to economic ruin and social disorder.[3]

This view of the Reconstruction-era United States was critical to the political argument of abolitionism in Rio de Janeiro, and the articulation of a specific and propagandistic history of US abolition in Brazilian politics over the course of the

1880s was a unique moment in the broader history of transnational connections between Brazil and the United States. For much of the nineteenth century, Brazilian intellectuals looked to the other massive slave society of the Americas and painted race relations in the United States as harsh and inhumane, arguing that the sharp forms of racial hierarchy and exclusion in that country were a direct product of North American slavery's seemingly exceptional cruelty.[4] Slave owners, politicians, and intellectuals depicted Brazilian slavery as relatively benign by comparison and the country's race relations as more fluid than those of the United States. At the turn of the twentieth century, after the abolition of slavery across the hemisphere, Brazilian intellectuals from across the racial spectrum used the horrors of the postemancipation US South to bolster an emerging sense of Brazilian racial exceptionalism.[5] But in the 1880s, after the abandonment of Reconstruction in the United States and as new forms of popular antislavery and republican mobilization challenged the old monarchical boundaries of Brazilian politics, Rio's abolitionists turned this comparison on its head. Like many Latin American liberals—and like many enslaved and free people of color across the Americas—activists in Rio held up emancipation in the United States as the crown jewel of an Atlantic-wide success story of the transition to free labor.[6] The newspapermen, intellectuals, and organizers of the abolitionist movement popularized a carefully constructed image of harmonious progress in North America and held that up as the reverse image of Brazil's supposed economic backwardness, social dysfunction, and political instability.

Abolitionists formed this argument in response to a specific planter narrative, one that developed in tandem with a broader current of conservative and racial thought in the late nineteenth century. In this volume, Adam Domby shows how the mythology of the Lost Cause and a particular narrative of the racial "lessons" of Reconstruction served as an important ideological foundation for the articulation of white supremacy and the global expansion of colonial rule. On account of Brazil's multiracial demographics—as well as the elite's idealization of the "prodigious progress" of the late-nineteenth-century United States—Brazilian planters tended not to entirely reject the idea that abolition could be a positive good.[7] But they were nevertheless eager to highlight the economic challenges, social disruptions, and political upheavals that accompanied slavery's end. They invoked countless horror stories, from the Haitian Revolution at the dawn of the century, to socioeconomic disruptions after abolition in the French and British Caribbean, and to the contemporary example of Cuban rebellion and slave resistance. They looked to history and saw that abolition created a crisis of labor. They therefore demanded indemnification, vagrancy laws, and a subsidized (white) immigrant replacement labor force. Abolitionists correctly pointed out that these were stalling tactics aimed at preserving slavery for as long as possible. Planters used history to deflect the abolitionist challenge as well as to argue for a set of policies that would have prevented emancipation from being the first step toward the project of broader reform that animated Brazilian popular abolitionism.[8] These were not just battles over the future but over how the past should be understood.

To dismiss these planters' demands (or the "sophistries" that the *Gazeta* sought to dispel with numbers), Rio's abolitionists built a different narrative of history. They argued that abolition in the United States was an exemplary success. Anybody who read Rio's abolitionist press would have read that in the United States ex-slaves were moving westward, working productively and in social harmony on plots of land they owned. Across the North American republic, they argued, technological improvement spurred prosperous and equitable market relationships, while political participation was open to men of all races. Rio's abolitionists used this history to build a three-pronged program for Brazil's national future. They promised that abolition, land reform, and technological advancement would drive a Brazilian "renaissance," an age of national renewal modeled on the "prodigious progress" of the United States. Faced with slavocrats' charges that abolition would lead to anarchy, this promise to replicate North American successes and build a Brazilian "rural democracy" was an important weapon in the abolitionists' rhetorical arsenal. The creative reading of history on which these arguments for emancipation rested is the subject of this essay.

As abolitionism gained political traction, this propagandistic view of history and an ambitious image of Brazil's future were spread by an increasingly active abolitionist movement. On the streets of the capital, an energetic group of abolitionists laid the groundwork for Brazil's first mass movement. At the forefront of popular abolitionism in the city was José do Patrocínio, the son of a freed slave and a pharmacist who took over the editorship of the *Gazeta da Tarde* in June 1881. Helping craft abolitionism's political strategy and propaganda was André Rebouças, the most prominent Black intellectual in the abolitionist movement and the architect of their plan for a "rural democracy." Both figures were ideologically complex. Patrocínio's political thought was a blend of late-nineteenth-century radicalisms—he famously used the pen name Proudhon in homage to the French anarchist Pierre Proudhon—with classical republicanism. He emerged over the course of the abolitionists' campaigns as one of the most prominent voices in the radical street politics of nineteenth-century Rio. Rebouças was a genteel monarchist and a physiocrat who placed Brazil's hope in the dream of very slowly creating a yeoman republic. His plan for rural democracy relied on the idea that the emperor—who was himself an admirer of republican government—could use the political relationships of the monarchy to guide the processes of emancipation and land reform that would eventually lay the foundation for a modern, republican, and democratic society. The most prominent historical example of this twin process of social modernization and political reform that abolitionists pointed to was Reconstruction in the United States. Along with a cadre of elite intellectuals, Rebouças crafted a vision of global modernization and a parallel image of Brazil's potential future. Patrocínio then carried this propaganda out into the street, making demands for rural democracy into a ubiquitous and effective abolitionist slogan.

A key figure in building the abolitionist narrative of history was one of Rio's most prominent academics, Dr. Nicoláu Joaquim Moreira, a close friend of José do Patrocínio and an officer in the Associação Geral Emancipadora, the popular abolitionist club.[9] Born in Rio in 1824, Moreira earned his doctorate at the Faculdade de Medicína do Rio de Janeiro and by 1880 was an advisor to the emperor, a board member of the Museu Nacional, the vice president of the Sociedade Auxiliadora da Indústria Nacional, and editor of the journal for Brazil's Instituto Agricola.[10] Throughout his career, Moreira published works on an array of subjects, including suicide, scarlet fever, agronomy, and economics. Over the course of the 1870s, he lectured frequently on agronomy at the Museu Nacional and established a reputation as a thoughtful scholar of postemancipation history, global immigration, and agricultural modernization.

On September 28, 1880, just weeks after a new abolitionist law failed in parliament and on the ninth anniversary of the passage of the 1871 law that technically freed all children born to enslaved mothers, the *Gazeta da Tarde* published a supplement to its daily edition that consisted of two parts: "Heroes and Martyrs of Abolition" and "The Speech and Manifesto of Dr. Nicoláu Joaquim Moreira to the Associação Geral Emancipadora."[11] "Heroes and Martyrs" was a biographical homage to a pantheon of abolitionist heroes. Over the course of the 1880s, Rio's abolitionists glorified the achievements of the "genius" Wilberforce, the "saintly" and "martyred" Lincoln, and the "brave" General Grant. The supplement in the *Gazeta* blessed Pedro Claver, the Catalan priest and the patron saint of slaves. The *Gazeta* thanked the French thinker Montesquieu and the entire Quaker sect for laying the intellectual and spiritual foundations of antislavery. The paper narrated a full biography of Abraham Lincoln, whom the editors erroneously described as born into a Quaker family. Lincoln was a key figure in this pantheon, often taking on Christ-like characteristics. On the eighteenth anniversary of the Emancipation Proclamation, the *Gazeta* commemorated the anniversary of Lincoln "freeing the slaves," noted that he had been "repaid" with assassination, but assured its readers that "the United States [was] strong and glorious." "*Santo Lincoln*," the paper plaintively concluded.[12] In his speech and manifesto, Nicoláu Moreira would show how and why the United States was "strong and glorious."

This local professor pointed out that humanitarian sympathy held little sway in debates over emancipation. "I am not here to pierce your hearts or awaken your sentimentalism," Moreira explained, "for this I lack the ability; moreover, our adversaries refuse to debate [the issue] on this terrain."[13] Planters were concerned with profits and stability. It was precisely on these two concerns that Moreira set his analysis. He cited some dramatic economic statistics from the Caribbean, cherry-picking evidence to argue that a supposed economic rebound after abolition in the export economies of the French and British Caribbean had been quick and painless. As abolitionists would continually do when telling the history of the postemancipation US South, he neglected to mention innovations in brutal forms of social control and economic coercion on the sugar islands of the nineteenth-century Caribbean. Responding to the assertion that abolition would bring economic ruin, Moreira made the classic antislavery argument that free labor was more profitable and productive than slave labor. This was an old abolitionist argument, and many planters now disputed such assertions. Therefore, Moreira did what abolitionists would do for the rest of the decade: He broadened that analysis out to explain the clear relationship he saw between slavery and general economic backwardness. The "salutary" experience of the postwar US South, he argued, foretold the "transition" Brazil would go through once slavery was totally abolished.

To prove the negative impact slavery once had on the US South, Moreira compared the economic performance of the antebellum South to that of the northern states in terms of capital and labor productivity. To make the economic lesson (or propaganda) straightforward, although not necessarily accurate, he divided gross regional economic production by population and acres of land. According to his findings, in 1860, an acre of land in the free North yielded an average of $8 of economic value, while a worker produced $312.[14] In the slave South, productivity was roughly half that of the North, with an acre of land yielding only $3.50 of economic output and a worker producing a mere $171.[15] Looking at these rough and broad economic data led him not only to make the standard abolitionist critique of slavery's supposed inefficiency but to expand that observation out into a broader explanation for Brazil's seeming underdevelopment.

Moreira began by criticizing the supposedly gross inefficiency with which antebellum slaveholders—and their contemporary Brazilian counterparts—combined labor and capital. In doing so, he made many dubious assumptions and used a repertoire of abolitionist tropes about plantation agriculture. He argued that in the United States, antebellum planters were supposedly averse to any sort of technological improvement and claimed that their "refusal" to diversify their exports or alter their patterns of land use had brought dire ecological consequences to the landscape of the South. He argued that Brazil's planters were no different. Faced with poor productivity and perennially exhausted land, all slaveholders supposedly suffered from constant debt and were held hostage to the whims of global financial or commodity markets. The defeat of the Confederacy and the crisis of slavery in Brazil seemed to prove not only that slavery impeded the productivity of all factors within the world of the plantation but that it was a cancer on any economy, polity, and society in which it existed.[16]

Moreira sought to make this point empirical by critiquing the way that large-scale, slave-based plantation agriculture allocated investment capital, a particularly important question for people concerned with the fortunes of Brazil's capital-scarce, postcolonial economy. He calculated that the slave population of the antebellum South was worth twenty-four million dollars more than the plantations enslaved people worked on, even if one included the supposedly meager capital improvements and fluctuating value of planters' assets. Moreira asserted that US planters found themselves—and the antebellum South as a region—in a particular bind on the eve of the Civil War: Productivity allegedly faltered to the point where the capital invested in planters' labor force exceeded planters' total worth, thus trapping the capital needed to make the improvements critical to the modernization of plantation agriculture. This inefficiency led to "the disgraceful state of the US South, which," Moreira suggested, could perhaps "serve as a mirror through which to examine the problems of our own agricultural sector."[17] Abolitionists made the idea that the dysfunctional *latifundia* had the economy in a stranglehold the root of their political argument. This claim would shape abolitionist propaganda and debates for the rest of the decade.

Mocking planters' insistence that immediate abolition would ruin them, Moreira sarcastically invited his audience of elites and working people "to see what the agricultural disasters were that [the former Confederacy] survived through after emancipation."[18] When it came to the production of plantation staples, Moreira reported increases across all sectors of the plantation economy: Tobacco exports rose 48 percent between 1866 and 1877; cotton production increased by 17 percent between 1860 and 1880; in Louisiana, between 1869 and

1876, sugar production rose 92 percent and molasses production by 120 percent. Concurrently, the US economy saw a dramatic increase in broader agricultural production between 1860 and 1880: Wheat production increased 154 percent; corn production increased a staggering 4,300 percent; butter exports increased by 4,000 percent, and cheese exports by 812 percent.[19] Abolitionists brought their audiences "proof" that the United States had increased in wealth and productivity precisely thanks both to abolition and to a seeming revolution in patterns of land ownership. Mimicking this progress by replacing the slavery of the *latifundia* with a free-labor rural democracy was the keystone of their promise of national renewal.

There were a number of logical holes and empirical flaws in the abolitionists' analysis of events abroad. And even closer to home, the economic success of Brazil's own slave plantation economies—particularly in the state of São Paulo—challenged the dubious notion that free labor was more efficient or profitable than slave labor. But the larger flaw was one that abolitionists were keenly aware of. The end of slavery might bring economic revitalization, but what about the larger implications of emancipation? How could a slave society survive abolition without disintegrating into social disorganization and political chaos?

Abolitionists were only partially able to answer this question. In his speech to the AGE, Moreira delved into the postemancipation history of the Atlantic world, with a focus on "public tranquility and the morality and stability of families."[20] Citing data from the French and British Caribbean, he illustrated how marriage increased and crime fell in the aftermath of abolition. But the truly momentous social and political transformation he depicted took place in the postabolition US South.

Moreira asserted that across the ex-Confederacy, "the freedmen responded victoriously to the accusations of intellectual inferiority and prodigality that were hurled at them by the slavocrats."[21] Speaking three years after the final end of Reconstruction, the tenses he employed were significant: In the United States, "freedmen *worked and work today* under the direction of white supervisors," he told his audience, "and when they have saved a little money, they establish themselves as independents. Within four years," Moreira claimed, without specifying which timeframe he was referring to, "these prodigious men . . . deposited close to two million dollars in banks and in the same span of time . . . twenty thousand learned to read and write." Two facts suggest that Moreira was grappling with an important question that had the potential to undermine his generally sanguine—and chronologically vague—view of postemancipation history: To what degree did the end of US Reconstruction represent a reversal of progressive emancipationist policies?

First, his change of tenses and his emphasis that freed slaves continued to work—the implication being that the circumstances of their labor had changed significantly since the immediate aftermath of abolition—indicate that he may have been aware of a significant rupture in the history of the postemancipation United States. Using US government data, Rio's abolitionists tended to look at the decade of the 1870s as a whole and understandably used statistics from 1880 as their point of reference. The question of how quickly news traveled—and what sort of lags altered their perception of news from the United States—seems to be answerable only by speculation. What is clear is that collapsing the entire history of Reconstruction into an easily transmittable message was politically useful and that abolitionists grappled with the accuracy of this depiction, as they would do all the way through the 1880s.

Second, it is difficult to imagine Moreira giving encouragement to a multiracial audience of abolitionists, slaves, and freedpeople of color with the observation that former slaves continued to work under the supervision of their old masters. This assertion sat somewhat awkwardly alongside abolitionists' consistent claims that freedpeople had established a "rural democracy." Moreira sought to balance this problem out with a dramatic admiration of Black political power in the United States during Reconstruction:

> The Black, brutalized in captivity, having breathed the air of liberty gains in intelligence and becomes a lawyer, a doctor, and a priest; sitting on juries, he becomes a de facto judge, and he *dared* to occupy a seat in the Capitol in Washington where he *proposes*, *discusses*, and *votes* to reign over the destiny of the great American nation.[22]

In his shifting of tenses, Moreira may have been struggling with the potential long-term meaning of freedom in relation to what he was attempting to portray as short-term setbacks in the construction of a harmonious postemancipation society. His grammatical slippage reveals a possible lack of historicist confidence. Their ceaseless and totalizing propaganda about the United States suggests that Rio's abolitionists were quite nervous about the stability of the future they sought to usher in and that they were acutely aware of how malleable and unstable foreign examples were. But for political reasons, they tended to frame the pitfalls of progress not in flaws within the liberal view of the future but rather in the immense power of reactionary sectors in postemancipation societies to block, manipulate, and, in some cases, roll back reform. Pushing for progress required popular mobilization, even if the assumptions behind that mass political movement left many empirical tensions unaddressed. Abolitionists made it seem that life after emancipation was better for most people in the United States, while also asserting that the end of slavery let loose the potential for all ex-slaves to gain a degree of political power, even in a society so much more racist than Brazil's. These were remarkably alluring promises.

Yet they were still vague promises, and fragmented snippets of economic data did not make for a clear and politically useful narrative of what had transpired since the end of the Civil War and the abolition of slavery in the United States. A few weeks after Moreira's conference, on October 19, 1880, Joaquim Nabuco wrote to the US consul in Brazil, Henry Washington Hilliard, to inquire about the effect emancipation had on the United States. Nabuco and other abolitionists in the recently founded Sociedade Brasileira Contra a Escravidão—a more elite counterpart to the popular AGE—asked that Hilliard, a former Alabama slave owner and a Confederate veteran, offer "an enlightened opinion concerning the results produced, and which still loom, as a result of the immediate and total substitution of slave labor by free labor in the southern states of the Union."[23] Hilliard's response to Nabuco was a somewhat predictable narrative of the post-Reconstruction South. The Alabaman lamented that after the Civil War, "political considerations prevailed in resolving a profound social and economic problem. It was assumed after the war that the freed people of the South could not be entrusted to the authority of their former masters," and as a consequence, Hilliard explained, "measures were enacted to protect" freed slaves. Not only were freedpeople "granted complete legal equality[;] they were immediately given political privileges as well."[24] Like many embittered white southerners, Hilliard bemoaned the "spectacular anomaly" of ex-slaves exercising the franchise while masters were "deprived" of their political rights. He lamented the influx of "numerous adventurers" from the North who "incited in the colored race mistrust and hostility towards their former masters. Under such influence," he continued, the freedpeople "abandoned the plantations, where they were accustomed to work, and went off in search of work in the cities, taking up an errant and gainless life." This was the opposite of the story that abolitionists sought to popularize.

Hilliard continued, however, by pointing to the momentous transformation that had taken hold since the end of Reconstruction. "The blacks work well," this former Confederate officer reported, "with patience and loyalty, both on the cities and the plantations."[25] Cotton harvests had reached unprecedented levels.

Former slaves were setting aside small amounts of savings, "which in one state was calculated at many thousands of dollars." In Atlanta, an unnamed university for people of color was "attended by 240 students from 10 states and all 47 of Georgia's counties." In a predictable historical distortion that was striking only because of the frequency with which it was printed in Rio's Black press, Hilliard remarked: "The sounds, which rupture the tranquility of plantation life are the voices of a people voluntarily employed in an occupation which both enriches the plantation owner and improves the well-being of the sons of labor."[26] The historical lesson he offered to Brazil's elite abolitionists was thus: So long as political rights were not too eagerly bestowed, economic recovery and social regeneration arrived right on the heels of abolition. Hilliard recommended gradual and compensated emancipation over a term of seven years.

In the weeks following his correspondence with Nabuco, the US consul became something of a celebrity in abolitionist circles. The popular *Gazeta da Tarde* published news of their correspondence and noted its publication in another abolitionist newspaper, the *Gazeta da Noticias*.[27] In the *Gazeta da Tarde*'s flattering biography of the consul, the Black-owned and Black-run paper noted Hilliard's slaveholding past and participation in the war but informed its readers that when President Hayes initiated his "policy of southern forgetting and concord, the old confederate soldier" was welcomed back into political life.[28] Two thousand copies of the correspondence between Hilliard and Nabuco were quickly printed, and a banquet was organized in the diplomat's honor.[29] Bringing together the city's elite and popular abolitionist societies, the press advertised the gathering of the "Brazilian Abolitionist Family," a "solemn occasion" when Hilliard "who was once a slave owner, who was once a *sulista*, and who has practiced the sublime act of Abnegation, will counsel Brazilians to soon free themselves from ghastly slavery, the cause of the greatest misfortunes of the nation."[30]

At the banquet, Hilliard gave a careful speech. He insisted that his diplomatic position prevented him from speaking directly about Brazil's domestic policy; he would "only reiterate the grand principle" of antislavery.[31] He warned that the "challenge" of freeing one and a half million slaves required "a great deal of careful attention" but suggested that "the question [was] in the hands of true and able statesmen" and correctly pointed out that the emperor Dom Pedro II was "a deep student of history."

Hilliard presented his audience with very little of the detailed history he offered Nabuco—probably because the publication of their correspondence in the abolitionist press caused a minor diplomatic row. Slavocrats decried what they saw as a foreign diplomat's meddling in internal politics, speculating that this was North American vengeance for Brazil having recognized the Confederacy as a belligerent power.[32] Nabuco, writing under the penname Garrison in the *Gazeta da Tarde*, argued that the slaveholders' sensitivity to Hilliard's mild and, as Nabuco saw it, quite measured statement reflected their desperation in the face of a wave of antislavery sentiment.[33]

As the abolitionist movement gained steam, abolitionists solidified the broad outline of US Reconstruction that Moreira and Hilliard established. The historical analysis they propagated depicted federal policy to the southern states from Lincoln's death to the election of Hayes as a tragedy, one where corrupt opportunism by the victorious North and the Republican Party's well-connected business interests torpedoed progress in the South. In a rather jarring passage in Joaquim Nabuco's *Abolitionism* (1883)—a text some see as the manifesto of Brazil's abolitionist movement—Nabuco argued that after the Civil War, "the former slaves were, at that point, inorganic material, socially speaking, and for this reason, could only function in their first phase of political life as the instruments of speculative adventurers, such as the *carpetbaggers*."[34] The trope of the "perfidious carpetbagger" appeared regularly in Brazilian abolitionist literature and fulfilled a very specific political function. Abolitionists recast the challenges of Reconstruction that seemed so threatening to planters as the aberrational meddling of nefarious outsiders. The years after emancipation were tumultuous because a corrupt Republican Party—bereft of its martyr Lincoln—had sloppily intervened in the reconstruction of the postwar South. Once postemancipation labor relations returned to a laissez-faire state, this reading of history suggested, well-being increased both for masters and their former slaves, the latter of whom supposedly either worked on parceled-out bits of the old plantations or sought to make their fortunes on the western frontier. To assert that Brazil could mimic this progress, abolitionists developed a detailed, though far-fetched, scheme for how to transform the slaveholding Brazil of the *latifundia* into a rational economy and society driven to progress through the workings of economic liberalism.

In 1883, A. J. Lamoureux & Co. (a press owned by the editor of Rio's English-language paper *The Rio News*) published André Rebouças's *Agricultura nacional—estudos economicos: propaganda abolicionista e democratica*. Just over four hundred pages in length, *Agricultura nacional* was a compendium of articles Rebouças wrote between 1874 and 1883. He published most of these articles in the city's paper of record, the *Jornal do Commercio*, but they were reprinted across Rio's public sphere, and particularly in the abolitionist press, over the course of the 1880s. Usually appearing under the title of "Agricultura nacional," these articles drew on a wealth of transnational agronomic knowledge to popularize a modernist vision of a Brazil without slavery, contrasting the rural aristocracy of Brazil's slaveholding past with a technocratically planned and scientifically informed idyllic vision of a national future shaped by the democratization of the land and the modernization of the agricultural sector. This anthology, the *Gazeta da Tarde* noted upon its publication, would lend a "great advantage to those who undertake the study of economic science and [wish] to apply it to the social phenomena of our country. The principal merit of the book," Patrocínio's *Gazeta* stated, was "to place science within the reach of all."[35]

Rebouças began the compiled edition of *Agricultura nacional* by explaining what he saw as the engine of rural democracy: the *fazenda central*.[36] This was a curious choice, but it had its own logic. As part of a global process of industrial consolidation, planters in certain pockets of the Atlantic world—particularly in the French Caribbean and in Cuba—responded to (or were preparing for) the shock of abolition by establishing central processing plants to which freed slaves sold raw agricultural products, usually within the parameters of exploitative but negotiated economic and social relationships.[37] In northeastern Brazil, planters' experimentation with *engenhos centrais* in the struggling sugar industry since the middle of the nineteenth century led to a similar dynamic: The business of sugar refining was consolidated in the hands of a few families and firms, and in general terms, inequality and hierarchy continued to shape the economic relationships between mill owners, slaves, and freed tenant farmers.[38] At first glance, it would seem peculiar to argue that the key to creating a Brazilian yeomanry was to replicate the very institution that kept freed slaves in dependence to capitalists across the Atlantic world or to argue that a larger developmental project could succeed by utilizing the strategy that yielded only mixed results in the modernization of Brazil's northeastern sugar industry. Yet this was precisely why the program of rural democracy achieved the popularity that it did. Rebouças popularized the dream of making freed slaves into landholders along the lines of the United States' Homestead Act. This crucial innovation would be a departure from the lackluster history of planters' attempts to modernize both the production and the labor force of the *latifundia*. Abolition and the creation of small landholdings would give new promise to the innovation of centralized processing, making industrial agriculture the engine of social and economic regeneration.

A specific narrative of agrarian progress in the post-Reconstruction United States was central to the popularization of this image of the future. Building off Nicoláu Moreira's narrative of postemancipation agrarian life, Rebouças's propaganda popularized the alluring perception that an industrial yeomanry had blossomed in the Midwestern United States and that independent farmers existed in relationships of economic, social, and political harmony with an increasingly consolidating agricultural sector. In a classic physiocratic reading dating back to Quesnay and Jefferson, Rebouças saw the progress of the postemancipation United States as driven by a social impulse rooted in the life of agricultural production, a cooperative productivity that spurred the spirit of association undergirding a healthy civil society and a stable and democratic nation. "In a great number of the states of the American confederation," he quoted from an unnamed "admirable periodical . . . the farmers constitute themselves into associations, or companies, [known as] Granges."[39] These collectives "established banks to provide rural credit, factories to build machines and farming instruments; warehouses to store their goods [and] plants for the large-scale processing, export, and shipment of their products." Throughout *Agricultura nacional*, Rebouças portrayed agrarian life in the United States as a collective struggle of "small, associated landholders not against large landholders but against the abject and difficult condition of small rural farmers." Cooperative agriculturalists were supposedly banding together to create what could seem like a "nation within the nation" but what was in fact "a vital and substantial part of the nation, which finds in itself the strength and the direction which it needs to advance, without the humiliation and the tortures of feudal parasitism." The hope was that somehow in Brazil, a somewhat similar process—the replacement of the plantation with the yeoman farmer integrated into a modern capitalist economy via the *fazenda central*—could be the key to national renewal after emancipation.

Such a vision was, of course, nearly a political impossibility. Rifts between planters and the state had developed over the course of the 1870s, but the essential fact was that the *latifundia* was the basic unit of Brazil's economy, its social relationships, and, thanks to a rapidly expanding coffee economy, the source of most of the state's tax revenue. Abolitionists tried to frame rural democracy as a national development project, one that would carve small landholdings out of the Brazilian wilderness to create a new postemancipation future for Brazil. This argument—and the broader promise of land reform—became central to abolitionist politics over the course of the 1880s. In 1883, the reformist cabinet of Manuel Dantas proposed the most progressive abolitionist legislation in Brazilian history.[40] As abolitionists mobilized in unprecedented numbers behind the Dantas cabinet, holding rallies with thousands of people and engaging in mass manumission campaigns, the slogan of rural democracy became the engine of abolitionist mobilization. The *Gazeta da Tarde* wrote that abolitionist "democratic labors were twofold: to liberate the land and to restore Liberty to the African race.[41] On our standard," the paper declared, "it should read: Abolition and Rural Democracy." The Dantas cabinet fell in July. Patrocínio warned that without a viable program of land reform, the Brazilian "empire would be reduced to the Ireland of the New World," and rural democracy became for abolitionists the driving issue of the subsequent electoral campaigns.[42] At a "popular meeting" speaking to an audience of working people in the northeastern city of Recife on November 5, 1884, Joaquim Nabuco stood "for the first time, raising the banner of an agrarian law, the banner of building a rural democracy . . . the prophetic dream of André Rebouças."[43]

In Rio, Patrocínio lost in a landslide in his attempt to gain a seat in the Chamber of Deputies. Nabuco lost in the first round of the elections but was later seated to the chamber. The emperor chose the reactionary Liberal José Antonio Saraiva to head a new cabinet, and abolitionists went back to the strategies of street mobilization and slave resistance to continue the fight for emancipation.

The promise of agrarian reform resonated with the aspirations of numerous freedpeople, for whom conflict over rights to till lands worked under slavery was the central dynamic in the negotiation of freedom.[44] Both radical abolitionists like Patrocínio as well as modernizing liberals like Rebouças saw this transformative rationalization of the agrarian economy as the key to national and social regeneration. Ultimately, the question of emancipation was resolved more through resistance on the streets and flight from the plantations than by debate in the halls of government. It was as a unifying idea for the abolitionist movement that rural democracy—and the entire reading of history on which it was founded—had the greatest impact.

The historical example of the United States that was the bedrock of rural democracy was a flawed analysis from the start. But the essential cost of the abolitionist argument was not only that it promised a fantasy. The consequential problem was that the specific hope of land reform—and all the political ideas of republican society linked to it—was in many ways irrelevant. This was particularly the case in the city of Rio. The capital's slow and contentious process of abolition raised a whole set of observable and pressing problems about urban life. To the daily problems that Rio's abolitionists faced, the slogan of agrarian reform was only a tangential response. Questions of housing, vagrancy, public health, vocational education, and rights to the physical space of the city plagued the abolitionist program, as the process of emancipation itself seemed to be turning Brazil's capital into one of the teeming and fetid metropolises that so deeply concerned late-nineteenth-century social thinkers. Abolitionists and their foes were keen students of urban unrest in Europe and North America. Neither party had a parallel plan for "urban democracy."

When confronted with the problems of life in the city, abolitionists continually dodged the argument, arguing that the countryside was where a new postemancipation order could take shape. In an 1884 editorial in the *Gazeta da Tarde*, Dr. Ennes de Souza, a prominent abolitionist, professor of mineralogy at Rio's Escola Polytechnica, and frequent contributor to the paper, outlined a plan for development on the outskirts of the capital. Patrocínio remarked that de Souza's plan "advocated, in irrefutable terms, the convenience and the necessity of beginning a serious program of suburban settlement."[45] Drawing on the ideas shaping Rebouças's vision of a rural democracy, de Souza laid out an ambitious plan for drainage and land reclamation on a large swath of land running west from Realengo, then some thirty kilometers outside the city, to Campo Grande, some forty kilometers from the city center. This was precisely where ex-slaves from across the Paraíba River valley were setting up small farms. On plots of land far from the congested city, people who would otherwise flee to the capital could be established as the yeomanry abolitionists envisioned. There were already plans to set up an *engenho central* in the area, de Souza noted. The resettlement of families would be prioritized over that of single men, and by gaining a measure of self-sufficiency, Rio's growing proletariat could be transformed into a suburban yeomanry. This suggestion was a small-scale replication of Rebouças's plan for rural democracy, and it offered no practical answers to the problems of emancipation in the city of Rio itself.

Slavery's crisis in the final years of the 1880s destabilized Brazil's cities and roiled its countryside. Partially because planters viewed the monarchy as having permitted (or even abetted) the abolitionist challenge, Brazil's rural elites began to rapidly embrace the republican cause. As the republican challenge gained steam in the final years of slavery's crisis, Patrocínio tried to hold the republican and monarchist antislavery factions together. He echoed Joaquim Nabuco's exhortation that destroying slavery should be the "alphabet of Brazilian politics," superseding all other divisions within the abolitionist movement.[46] In April 1888—just weeks before slavery's final abolition—an election for minister of justice brought into focus a fracture in the republican movement that had grown steadily worse over the course of the abolitionist decade. Quintino Bocaiuva (the editor of Rio's *O Paiz*) was a prominent republican who increasingly saw in planter disaffection its route toward overthrowing the monarchy. He faced off against the Conservative Antonio Ferreira Vianna. After much coaxing from André Rebouças,

Patrocínio publicly backed Vianna. He was immediately expelled from the republican camp.

Days later, Patrocínio published a lengthy explanation of his political stance, entitled "Unloading My Conscience," on the front page of his new paper, *Cidade do Rio*. Announcing his excommunication and resignation from the republican movement, he reprinted an excerpt from an article in the *Gazeta Nacional* and explained that "people who did not know [him] well would through this article have an immediate understanding of the reasons why [he was] separating himself from the Republican Party, notwithstanding [his] belief in the Republic."[47] The cited article from the *Gazeta Nacional* was titled "Methods of Repression," and its point of departure was exactly the social question abolitionists had been struggling to answer for at least the entire decade and to which the plan for rural democracy—and the entire historical analysis within it—was supposed to resolve. Surely, it seemed that the revolution of having "one million men concentrated in a relatively limited area recover their freedom" would ostensibly require some sort of "stimulus to morality and prevention of perverse character." As a solution, the *Gazeta Nacional* had recommended that local authorities—under a federated republic—create "correctional colonies" in remote areas that would both discipline ex-slaves and "enlarge the communication network and the influence of the nation." The republican vision was thus a blend of Rebouças's ideas for agricultural colonies with fantasies of racial expulsion. Patrocínio's response was furious.

"Here the reader has," he wrote, "what the republicans, who fight me, wish for the future legislation of freed people." Like "the *senhor* Paulino de Souza," Patrocínio wrote, comparing his former allies to Brazil's most eminent slavocrat, these republicans "fantasize of imminent disturbances, work abandoned, vagrancy, and begging." These republicans preached democracy, liberty, equality, and fraternity "in the plazas and in the press" while keeping their "brethren" in the "saddest captivity." A republic by these republicans, Patrocínio continued, would be "the republic of Jefferson Davis," who he promised would "not have vengeance but will die crushed under the boot of abolitionists." "Let the pharisaic church of the Republic excommunicate me," Patrocínio declared; his "duty [was] to serve liberty, equality, and fraternity with actions and not only with words." He remarked that it "was an easy thing to judge the moneychangers in the temple of democracy" and signed his name on the front page of the paper.

Patrocínio remained a monarchist for the duration of the monarchy. After Princess Isabel finally signed an abolition decree on May 13, 1888, his commitment intensified. His break with the Republicans had been principled and ideological. Both he and Rebouças had built their entire abolitionist dream on a specific and established view of the relationship between rural society and social cohesion. Their interpretation of what had happened in the postemancipation United States—and their promise of what could happen in Brazil—rested on an only marginally updated version of the Jeffersonian ideal. The modern rationalization and technological innovation of the latter half of the nineteenth century seemed to have been connected to the yeoman idea in the United States, supposedly solving all the problems of a society after slavery. But where these abolitionists were part of a long intellectual tradition asserting that a harmony of individual interests bred stability, their planter foes had adopted a decidedly different and more current vision of republican thought. In their view, the perfection of human nature by the mechanisms of the state would instill self-discipline and consequently ensure the creation of a harmonious social arrangement. Through racialized vagrancy laws and immigration policies, they would realize this vision with a degree of uneven success. Eighteen months after abolition, on November 15, 1889, embittered planters allied with republicans and ousted the monarchy. Hours after the coup began, Patrocínio was a republican again. He would run for the constituent assembly in an attempt to save the new republic from planter republicans.

Forced to explain his political shifts, Patrocínio insisted that his only political allegiance was to the "grand social reforms which began on May 13, 1888," of which rural democracy was the centerpiece. Faced with the charge that he was no true republican, he adamantly refused "to enslave [his] country to a word, which is the glory of Switzerland but the shame of Peru."[48] In his view, there was nothing to prevent a faction of planters from perverting a republican government. "In the United States," Patrocínio pointed out, "abolition changed none of the prejudice or the greed of the former slave-owners, who forming the Democratic Party, until this day disrupt the life and the progress of the unfortunate race. Everyone knows that after abolition," he continued, "the North American planters continued to steal the labor of their ex-slaves."[49]

This departure from a decade of abolitionist propaganda was clearly the expedient political argument. So were the abolitionist narrative of history and the promise of rural democracy. Although their rhetorical choices created some inconsistencies and blind spots, Brazilian abolitionists were ultimately effective at rallying popular opinion and political resistance to destroy the hemisphere's oldest slave system. Abolitionists were remarkably good at making the idea that abolition equaled progress into a form of political common sense. The fact that in 1890 Patrocínio could say that "everybody" knew that the entire abolitionist history was an inaccurate picture of North American emancipation suggests that multiple counternarratives flowed through Rio's public sphere. Rio's abolitionists flooded those other narratives out by telling an alluring and aspirational tale of what had happened in the United States. Their rhetorical and ideological choices were part of one of the more peculiar moments in the interconnected history of slavery and abolition in the Americas.

## Notes

1. On the role of the *Gazeta* and of its editor José do Patrocínio in Rio's abolitionist movement, see Jeffrey Needell, *The Sacred Cause: The Abolitionist Movement, Afro-Brazilian Mobilization, and Imperial Politics in Rio de Janeiro* (Stanford, CA: Stanford University Press, 2020). For an explanation of how the *Gazeta da Tarde* was a key social resource for combating illegal enslavement and reenslavement—thus signifying its editors' deep social connections to and standing within Rio's community of the enslaved and the freed—see Ana Flavia Magalhães Pinto, "A *Gazeta da Tarde* e as peculiaridades do abolicionismo de Ferreira de Menezes e José do Patrocínio," paper presented at XXVIII Simposio Nacional de Historia, Florianopolis, Santa Catarina, July 27–July 31, 2015.

2. *Gazeta da Tarde*, "Beneficios da Abolição," February 2, 1881.

3. *Gazeta da Tarde*, "Beneficios da Abolição," February 4, 1881.

4. See Celia Maria Marinho de Azevedo, *Abolicionismo: Estados e Brasil, uma história comparada (século XIX)* (Annablume: São Paulo), 2003. For a broader exploration of this dynamic, see Micol Siegel, "Beyond Compare: Comparative Method after the Transnational Turn," *Radical History Review* (2005): esp. 68–77.

5. See Micol Seigel, *Uneven Encounters: Making Race and Nation in Brazil and the United States* (Durham, NC: Duke University Press, 2009).

6. Don Doyle, "Toward an International History of Reconstruction," in *Freedoms Gained and Lost": Reconstruction and Its Meaning 150 Years Later* (New York: Fordham University Press, 2021).

7. For an exploration of the reasons why a proslavery ideology on par with the US South's "peculiar institution" defense never developed in Brazil, see Barbara Weinstein, "Slavery, Citizenship, and National Identity in Brazil and the US South," in *Nationalism in the New World*, ed. Don Doyle, Marco Pamplona, and Barbara Weinstein (Athens: University of Georgia Press, 2006), 248–71.

8. See Needell, *The Sacred Cause*, chap. 4.

9. On Moreira's activism, see Needell, *The Sacred Cause*, 80–81.

10. Nicola Carula, "Nicoláu Joaquim Moreira e as questões raciais da imigração," paper presented at XXVII Simpósio Nacional de História, Natal, RN, July 22–26, 2013.

11. Assoçiacáo Central Emancipadora, "Suplemento á Gazeta da Tarde," *Gazeta da Tarde*, September 28, 1880.

12. *Gazeta da Tarde*, "1 de Janeiro 1862," January 1, 1881.

13. *Gazeta da Tarde*, "Suplemento," p. 1, col. 2.

14. Fogel calculates per capita income in 1860 at $141 in the northern states and at $103 in the slaveholding South but points out that the southern economy grew steadily.

Robert Fogel, *Without Consent or Contract: The Rise and Fall of American Slavery* (New York: Norton, 1989), 85, *passim*. Moreira's metrics (productivity per acre and per capita income) are somewhat different from the formula Walter Johnson shows was the typical method of measuring the plantation economy in the antebellum United States: dollars per hand per bale. For a thoughtful portrait of the South's economic dynamism, see Walter Johnson, *River of Dark Dreams: Slavery and Empire in the Cotton Kingdom* (Cambridge, MA: Belknap, 2013). For a comparison of the antebellum US South and southeastern Brazil showing that the southern economy was far more developed, productive, and dynamic, see Richard Graham, "Slavery and Economic Development: Brazil and the United States South in the Nineteenth Century," *Comparative Studies in Society and History* 23, no. 4 (1981): 620–55.

15. *Gazeta da Tarde*, "Suplemento," p. 2, cols. 1–2.

16. The debate over slavery's profitability and productivity as a form of labor is obviously quite far-ranging. For an argument specific to the US South emphasizing the institution's adaptability and modernity, see L. Diane Barnes, Brian Schoen, and Frank Towers, *The Old South's Modern Worlds: Slavery, Region, and Nation in the Age of Progress* (Oxford: Oxford University Press, 2011).

17. *Gazeta da Tarde*, "Suplemento," 2, col. 2.

18. *Gazeta da Tarde*, "Suplemento," 2, col. 2.

19. *Gazeta da Tarde*, "Suplemento," 2, col. 2.

20. *Gazeta da Tarde*, "Suplemento," 3, col. 2.

21. *Gazeta da Tarde*, "Suplemento," 3, col. 2.

22. *Gazeta da Tarde*, "Suplemento," 2, col. 2.

23. Sociedade Brasileira Contra a Escravidão, *Cartas do Presidente Joaquim Nabuco e do Ministro Americano H. W. Hilliard sobre a emancipação nos Estados Unidos* (Rio de Janeiro: G. Leuzinger & Filhos, 1880), 3.

24. *Cartas do Presidente Joaquim Nabuco*, 10–11.

25. *Cartas do Presidente Joaquim Nabuco*, 13.

26. *Cartas do Presidente Joaquim Nabuco*, 14.

27. "Um Documento Importante," *Gazeta da Tarde*, October 28, 1880; "Comunicação Honorosa," *Gazeta da Tarde*, November 3, 1880.

28. "Henry Washington Hilliard," *Gazeta da Tarde*, November 4, 1880

29. "Carta do Ministro Hilliard," *Gazeta da Tarde*, November 17, 1880.

30. "Banquete Abolicionista," *Gazeta da Tarde*, November 20, 1880.

31. "Discursos," *Gazeta da Tarde*, November 22, 1880. Nabuco used the penname Garrison in the abolitionist press over the course of the 1880s. Humberto Mayese Correa, "Joaquim Nabuco: Status, Stigma, Civilization, and Brazil's Place in the International Society," MA thesis, Universidade de Brasilia, 2019, 44.

32. Robert Conrad, *The Destruction of Brazilian Slavery, 1850–1888* (Berkeley: University of California Press, 1972), 142.

33. "Noticiario: Camara dos Deputados," *Gazeta da Tarde*, November 24, 1880.

34. Joaquim Nabuco, *O abolicionismo* (Rio de Janeiro: Centro Edelstein de Pesquisas Sociais, 2011), 111.

35. "Propaganda Abolicionista," *Gazeta da Tarde*, November 6, 1883.

36. Throughout this essay, *fazenda* and *engenho central* will be used interchangeably, depending on the commodity (coffee or sugar) under discussion. Rebouças used the basic concept of centralized production for a wide array of commodities.

37. For Cuba, see Rebecca Scott, *Degrees of Freedom: Louisiana and Cuba after Slavery* (Cambridge, MA: Harvard University Press, 2005), 114–20. For the French Caribbean, see Robin Blackburn, *The Overthrow of Colonial Slavery, 1776–1848* (New York: Verso, 1988), 502.

38. See Peter Eisenberg, *The Sugar Industry in Pernambuco, 1840–1910* (Berkeley: University of California Press, 1974); Eul-Soo Pang, "Modernization and Slavocracy in Nineteenth-Century Brazil," *Journal of Interdisciplinary History* 9, no. 4 (1979): 667–88.

39. André Rebouças, *Agricultura nacional—estudos economicos: propaganda abolicionista e democratica* (Rio de Janeiro: A. J. Lamoreaux, 1883), 3.

40. See Needell, *The Sacred Cause*, chap. 4.

41. "Abolição Immediata e Sem Indemnisação," *Gazeta da Tarde*, June 19, 1883.

42. "Abolição Immediata e Sem Indemnisação," *Gazeta da Tarde*, June 21, 1883.

43. Joaquim Nabuco, *Campanha abolicionista no Recife* (Rio de Janeiro: Typographia Leuzinger & Filhos, 1885), 47. This speech in the "*bairro popular*" was reprinted in the *Gazeta da Tarde*, December 15, 1884.

44. For an in-depth examination of this process in Brazil's northeastern sugar country, see Walter Fraga, *Crossroads of Freedom: Slaves and Freed People in Bahia, Brazil, 1871–1910* (Durham, NC: Duke University Press, 2016).

45. "Colonização Suburbana," *Gazeta da Tarde*, February 21, 1884.

46. José do Patrocínio, "Abolicionistas no seu Posto," in *Campanha abolcionista: coletânea de artigos*, ed. José Murilho de Carvalho (Rio de Janeiro: Fundação Biblioteca Nacional, 1996), 211.

47. "Desencargo de consciencia," *Cidade do Rio*, April 28, 1888.

48. "O Isabelismo," *Cidade do Rio*, May 1, 1889.

49. "Manifesto ao Eleitorado Fluminense," *Cidade do Rio*, September 9, 1890.

# Lessons from "Redemption"

*Memories of Reconstruction Violence in Colonial Policy*

*Adam H. Domby*

At the turn of the twentieth century, some white southern leaders were not just overturning African Americans' gains of Reconstruction as they instituted Jim Crow–era laws across the South; they were also emplacing on the landscape historical markers to commemorate the Confederacy. These monuments were physical manifestations of a distinct narrative about the Civil War era that conservative white southerners wanted propagated worldwide. As they dedicated these monuments, Confederate boosters told the world exactly what they wanted remembered about the past and what they intended these monuments to impart to younger generations. These monuments were physical embodiments of what scholars refer to as the Lost Cause, a memory of the past that glorified the Confederacy. The Lost Cause was a mythology that included other aspects (many of them fabricated), such as denying the centrality of slavery in bringing about secession. Confederate soldiers were recalled as devoted volunteers who should be ranked as among the most able warriors in history—only defeated because of overwhelming numbers. Lee was recollected as the perfect gentleman, reaching nearly saintly levels, in the hagiographic tales spun by Lost Cause boosters. It wasn't just the war that was remembered in a specific narrative fashion. In addition, remembering slavery as benevolent despite its being inherently violent, cruel, and premised upon terror was similarly crucial. But as important as myths about the antebellum era and the war itself was how former Confederates remembered the decade after the war. Among the key narrative aspects of the Lost Cause—especially in the early twentieth century—was celebrating the overturning of Reconstruction.[1] As Caroline Janney put it, Lost Cause proponents chose "to end the wartime narrative not with Appomattox but with the overturning of Reconstruction."[2]

The Confederates' depictions of supposed African American misrule during Reconstruction and attendant celebration of racial violence had real political consequences, both in and beyond the United States. As K. Stephen Prince has pointed out, "A white supremacist rewriting of Reconstruction was an indispensable corollary to the rise of Jim Crow."[3] By recalling emancipation and Reconstruction—and not slavery, oppression, disenfranchisement, or Klan violence—as the cause of racial strife in the South, the version of the past enshrined by former Confederates justified disenfranchisement of African Americans as the solution to racial problems. The story went that there had not been racial strife during antebellum times (a false understanding of the past) and that "the natural order of things"—that is, whites on top—left everyone happy. Only during Reconstruction had race relations been harmed, Confederate veterans claimed, so a disenfranchisement of Black southerners was simply a return to the "natural order of things" and was best for all. This depiction of Reconstruction was a fundamental part of the Lost Cause narrative. As Eric Foner has described it, "Along with a nostalgic image of the Confederacy, the idea of the Lost Cause rested on a view of slavery as a benign, paternalistic institution and of Reconstruction as a time of 'Negro rule' from which the South was rescued by the heroic actions of the self-styled Redeemers who restored white supremacy."[4]

While much has been said about the memory of Reconstruction in the South, southern white narratives of Reconstruction as a time of corruption and racial reversal spread far beyond the South.[5] As Foner and other scholars, including Marilyn Lake and Henry Reynolds, have pointed out, this depiction of Reconstruction not only "provided an intellectual foundation for Jim Crow" but also served as a "legitimation of colonial rule over nonwhite peoples in far flung places from South Africa to Australia."[6] Indeed, the Lost Cause version of Reconstruction was perhaps as influential internationally as it was nationally, spreading across the English-speaking world and helping justify colonialism and white supremacy in distant corners of the world. This Lost Cause narrative had an enduring international life, as procolonialism intellectuals used its account of Reconstruction to defend segregation, disenfranchisement, inequality, and apartheid from Australia to South Africa. At the turn of the twentieth century, tales of the post–Civil War South that blamed an unnatural forcing of racial equality and enfranchisement of Black southerners for racial violence served as a form of historical racism—a narrative of the past that justified racialism. Just as its parallel, scientific racism, still haunts the scientific community, historical racism remains alive in American and international popular memories, politics, and language to this day.

Turn-of-the-century Americans heard about Reconstruction from a variety of sources. Former Confederates and conservative politicians repeatedly used depictions of Reconstruction to encourage whites to vote Democratic and as a talking point to support the disenfranchisement of African Americans in the late nineteenth and early twentieth centuries. Arguing that African Americans' role in politics was a result of the machinations of northern whites during Reconstruction remained a crucial tool in defending Jim Crow and redirecting critiques of racial violence in the South. Reminders of Reconstruction's overturn were also used to threaten African Americans considering becoming politically involved and to justify violence.[7] For example, Alfred Waddell, a Confederate veteran, gave a speech in 1898 where he openly told a group of Democrats, wearing Red Shirts that harkened back to South Carolina's Reconstruction vigilantes, that they should "go to the polls tomorrow, and if you find the negro out voting, tell him to leave the polls and if he refuses, kill him, shoot him down in his tracks. We shall win tomorrow if we have to do it with guns."[8] This Lost Cause interpretation of Reconstruction was depicted in film with *Birth of a Nation*, while a group of historians trained by William Dunning wrote history books lending the narrative academic credibility. At the turn of the twentieth century, many, if not most, white southerners believed that the racial violence of Reconstruction had saved the South from equality and had assured white supremacy.

But this mythology spread beyond the South. Indeed, it spread beyond the United States. Though they may not have always realized it, framing racial violence during Reconstruction as necessary helped lay the groundwork for a larger international justification of oppression and segregation. Indeed, in discussing historical narratives of American Reconstruction that supported white supremacy and incited violence, we are not just talking about the South but about global systems of racial hierarchy and worldwide ideologies of white supremacy. In addition to convincing some white northerners not to interfere in southern race relations, these narratives were also exported to an international audience.[9]

For many memory makers, this narrative of Reconstruction was not just meant for white southerners to hear. For example, on a trip to Asia, the North Carolina industrialist Julian S. Carr bemoaned Reconstruction while addressing a crowd in Manila in 1916, announcing, "Take it from a Confederate soldier, the 5 years succeeding Appomattox from 1865 to 1870, were more horrible than the 4 years of bloody war." Though speaking in the Philippines, far from home, Carr still celebrated the notion that white North Carolinians had been able to "keep untarnished and unpolluted the red blood of the Anglo Saxon" thanks to the overturning of Reconstruction.[10]

Carr's message for an international audience was similar to the one he propagated to domestic audiences. Carr was perhaps the most popular and well-known speaker at Confederate memorial celebrations in North Carolina. Though he served only in the last few months of the war, he rose to become head of the United Confederate Veterans. An extremely wealthy philanthropist, Carr was also heavily involved in Democratic politics, helping fund white supremacist political campaigns and even running for the US Senate in 1900. He became notable again in the twenty-first century due to his role in 1913 at the University of North Carolina's dedication of their Confederate monument. There Carr gave a now infamous address in which he declared that Confederate monuments would remind future generations of how Confederate veterans overturned Reconstruction. He proudly told the audience how he "horse-whipped a negro wench, until her skirts hung in shreds, because upon the streets of this quiet village she had publicly insulted and maligned a Southern lady."[11] While this particular speech has frequently been quoted in arguments for changing building names and removing monuments, it was only one of many similar speeches he gave. Apart from his inclusion of how he himself participated in the violence, this speech does not stand out from other speeches given by Carr. In fact, justifying or even celebrating Reconstruction violence was a constant refrain in speeches given by Carr and other former Confederates.

Blaming Reconstruction as the cause of racial strife was a means to justify disenfranchisement and Jim Crow in the South. At the 1915 United Confederate Veterans Reunion in Richmond, Carr, as head of the North Carolina division of the UCV, told of how the "Southern soldier . . . was never so admirable, never so superb, as in that trying epoch" of Reconstruction, when they fought against the "multitude of remorseless and insatiable vultures . . . aptly stigmatized as carpetbaggers." According to Carr, carpetbaggers "set the slave to political rule above his former master," causing former Confederates to react violently. Carr recalled how he and other former Confederates "seized the reins of government, brought order out of chaos, established free government, and enthroned justice." His definition of free government and justice were not the same as most Americans would understand them today.

There is a reason Confederate monuments started appearing in front of courthouses after conservative Democrats gained control of southern governments. Without disenfranchisement and a memory of Reconstruction as a time of misrule, corruption, oppression, and criminality to justify a narrative of redemption through violence, there would have been little worthy of celebration in the early twentieth century for former Confederates. As a result of this seizing of power, Carr declared, during Reconstruction "the Southerner, the man who wore the gray, proved the metal of which he was made and he was even greater in the civic conflict" than he had been during the war. It was because of this accomplishment that he felt a white southerner could see himself as "the proudest man on God's footstool." Indeed, Carr even rejected that the Lost Cause had lost. Though he admitted that "for a time, she was beaten," that was no longer the case in 1915, because now the Jim Crow order was firmly established with whites in political control. Instead he contended that "is [the cause] not regained and more vital than it was the day South Carolina proclaimed the ordinance of Secession?"[12] For Carr, the success of "redemption" was vindication of the Confederacy's cause and of the justness of white supremacy.

Blaming Reconstruction instead of racism for later racial problems and presenting disenfranchisement as the solution was not limited to Americans. A ten-part series on "The Negro Question in the United States," published by the London *Times* from November 1890 through January 1891, detailed for British audiences what was supposedly causing racial strife in the United States. Three of the ten articles were devoted to recounting the period of Reconstruction and detailing Republican misrule. Written by British journalist William Laird Clowes, the very first column justified the use of "brute force" to keep African Americans from voting. Clowes acknowledged that South Carolina's white population had "seized power, in self-defense it is true, by fraud and violence, and it retains it by deception and intimidation," but like Carr he excused all of this.[13] The root of this need for intimidation, according to Clowes, was Reconstruction.

Clowes argued that the disenfranchisement of African Americans was necessitated in the present because of the ill-fated decision during Reconstruction to give fundamentally inferior individuals the ballot. He further asserted that once South Carolina whites had retaken control of the state, "the victors have not, upon the whole, abused their victory."[14] What exactly would have constituted abuse to the British journalist remains unclear—as the 1890s witnessed the highest number of lynchings in South Carolina in any decade from 1880 to 1940.[15] Clowes knew full well how common lynching was; he even detailed their frequency in his writings, but he attributed this to the danger white women supposedly faced from rape and to Black southerners' not accepting their place.[16] He accepted the weak excuses often given for lynching as reality.

This specific twisted memory of Reconstruction—full of specious tales of injustice against whites that meant "democrats were fighting for their liberty"—when paired with the depiction of whites creating prosperity after redemption justified undemocratic practices to Clowes's international audience.[17] Jim Crow–era racial hatred, violence, and discrimination seemed to Clowes to be the result of African Americans not "keeping [their] place" during Reconstruction and trying to take the natural rights of whites.[18] The arguments Clowes and others put forward were used to defend disenfranchisement of nonwhites both domestically and internationally in the years to come. Comparing the United States and "Hayti" to the supposed "fairly happy and contented" British subjects in Africa, Clowes found "the whole business is a fine illustration of the futility of introducing republican institutions to a country whose people are uneducated, untrained in affairs, and incapable of self-government."[19] Clowes's articles were later expanded into a book, *Black America: A Study of the Ex-Slave and His Late Master* (1891).

The defense (and at times celebration) of violence and oppression employed to maintain white rule was accepted by many international observers. While outright violence was not always viewed as laudable, many English observers nonetheless accepted it as necessary. Indeed, Clowes concluded that the only solution to end violence was to remove African Americans from the United States entirely. Clowes's writings in both the *Times* and other British journals provided some of the most widely circulated accounts of Reconstruction and contemporary US race relations outside of the United States at the end of the nineteenth century, making their way as far as Australia.[20]

Clowes's writings were clearly compelling to some readers. A London reviewer of his writings in 1891 concluded that "we must therefore look facts in the face, and when we do we must admit that the white man must be allowed to rule the South, if not by law, then by force or fraud." Although the reviewer acknowledged how "on the flimsiest of pretexts" an African American might find himself hunted by a mob and "even lashed to death by whips as cruel as any ever wielded by Legree," he nonetheless found Clowes's arguments compelling and decided that this was "not a more disgusting picture of human society" than "the same society under the heel of the negro and the white carpet-bagger whom he put in power in the Reconstruction era."[21] According to the historian Eric Weber, by 1900 efforts to portray southern race problems as the result of Reconstruction had been successful, and "Britons had largely accepted white Southern constructions of... Reconstruction."[22] British observers might not see violence as worthy of celebration—as Julian Carr wanted—but they were fully prepared to accept it as an unfortunate byproduct of whites being threatened by African Americans when supposedly unnatural equality was forced upon them. Both interpretations, however, served the purpose of justifying violence and supporting a racial hierarchy.

Not all British writers accepted this explanation of recent violence. In 1897, a writer for the *Guardian* concluded that much of the lynching—albeit not all—

was the "product of race hatred" and not entirely necessary.[23] A few writers even defended carpetbaggers. Upset that a Melbourne paper called recent arrivals from Canada carpetbaggers, one newly arrived Canadian defended southbound immigrants, writing to the editor that the term was "invented by chagrined and beaten slaveholders, and applied by them out of spite to the representatives of the victorious abolitionists who had gone south to take up their abode in ex-slavery states, where they were sadly needed."[24] He was one of few Australian commentators, however, who rejected the implication that carpetbaggers were bad.

In England, Sir Arthur Conan Doyle also failed to buy in, at least entirely, to the idea that the Klan was a good thing and critiqued Reconstruction violence. In the "Five Orange Pips," his villains were former Klan members, and Sherlock Holmes defined the Ku Klux Klan as a "terrible secret society... formed by some ex-Confederate soldiers [and] used for political purposes, principally for the terrorizing of the negro voters and the murdering and driving from the country of those who were opposed to its views." Holmes recounted to Watson that the Klan was opposed by "the United States government and [by] the better classes of the community in the South."[25] Yet Doyle's subtle jabs at efforts to disenfranchise Black Americans do not seem to have had much impact on English audiences, perhaps because they were in a work of fiction, and, besides, the Klan seemed so separate from contemporary England.[26]

Not everyone agreed with the Lost Cause narrative, and other counternarratives existed both domestically and internationally that recalled Reconstruction as a time of progress. Natalie Ring, for example, has written on how American liberals tried to create a "New Reconstruction."[27] At the request of the "colored citizens of Boston," Richard P. Hallowell published a pamphlet in 1903 entitled *Why the Negro Was Enfranchised*, which told a different narrative. Hallowell reminded readers how during Presidential Reconstruction African Americans were nearly reenslaved and noted the sacrifices of Black Union soldiers. He argued that "the facts of history" showed "that in the South *white* suffrage is comparatively a failure" and that the "fraud, persecution, terrorism, violence and murder" that Carr celebrated had actually served "as a potent weapon in their effort to degrade the negro to the condition of social servitude" rather than to save southern whites.[28] In these other narratives, violence, in other words, was a symptom or even the cause of racial strife, instead of the solution, as Carr presented it. As discussed in Matthew Stanley's essay in the present volume, Joseph Wilson similarly presented a narrative of Reconstruction that celebrated Black progress. Perhaps the most notable resistance to the Lost Cause narrative was W. E. B. Du Bois's *Black Reconstruction in America* (1935). Based on reviews, Du Bois's book does not appear to have gotten much international readership in the white procolonialism press. While Sergio Pinto-Handler argues in this volume that Reconstruction memory was used in Brazil to argue for emancipation, these alternative narratives of Reconstruction were largely dismissed by those English-speaking international audiences looking to justify colonialism and white supremacy.

Film was perhaps the most powerful medium for spreading a skewed sense of American history internationally. During the early twentieth century, the most accessible version of the white supremacist narrative of Reconstruction for those who lived outside the South was D. W. Griffith's *The Birth of a Nation* (1915). Advertisers often depicted the film as if it were a documentary. In Green Bay, Wisconsin, the film, which depicted the Klan as heroes who saved southern womanhood, was advertised as "a history lesson" with a reduced rate for "any school boy and girl."[29] In Pennsylvania, the *Wilkes-Barre Time Leader* noted how the "instructive" film showed "the mortal agony of four years of Civil War and eight years of more horrible Reconstruction."[30] African Americans objected to the film's historical inaccuracies and blatant racism, arguing it was not an accurate reflection of the past, but ticket sales failed to decrease.[31]

Despite some naysayers, the efforts of Lost Cause boosters to push their version of the past out to the world were wildly successful. *Birth of a Nation* was not just a hit in the United States but internationally as well. After achieving "the longest run of any attraction in New York," the film was brought to Australia, Canada, Brazil, and England.[32] In Australia, demand was so high that theaters, filled to capacity, lengthened the runs.[33] So popular was the film that an Australian film distributor changed the name of a different film to *The Curse of a Nation* in an attempt to trick potential viewers, leading to a lawsuit.[34] For most Australians, *Birth of a Nation* was likely their only exposure to Reconstruction, and as such they largely accepted the narrative it told. Not until 1938 did another film about Reconstruction apparently arrive in Sydney, when *The Texans* told the story of a noble former Confederate fighting against what one Australian described as "the most miserable men ever to appear on the American scene, the carpetbaggers."[35]

Historians have noted how narratives of Reconstruction were tightly tied to international affairs. As Mark Elliot and Samuel A. Schaffer have pointed out, memories of Reconstruction shaped American foreign policy during the late nineteenth and early twentieth centuries. For example, Woodrow Wilson's views on European rebuilding and peace treaties were influenced by his views that Reconstruction had failed because it was vindictive.[36] David Blight has noted that white southern views of American imperialism were often shaped by memories of Reconstruction.[37] The Lost Cause narrative of Reconstruction and an acceptance of the "white man's burden" combined to justify American imperialism abroad. On the other hand, Natalie Ring points out that scholars have overlooked how "American imperialism influenced the memory of the war and Reconstruction." Not only did understandings of the past influence American imperialism around the world, but the memory of Reconstruction also influenced international imperialism.

Though the creators of the Lost Cause Reconstruction myth were mostly concerned with the South, the impact of their narrative was worldwide. This recounting of Reconstruction was not just used to oppress African Americans in the South but was part of a larger international justification of colonial oppression.[38] Throughout the 1890s, international discussions occurred among imperialists about the impact of interracial interaction. While some theorists argued that "the lower race will always increase upon, ultimately degrade or dominate, the higher," others believed that "the weaker races disappear before the stronger through the effects of mere contact."[39] Clowes subscribed to the former school, but both philosophies supported policies of segregation and white supremacy in their own ways, as both assumed a superior and inferior race. Advocates for both interpretations assumed that a racial hierarchy was at least natural, if not necessary. Additionally, both views on the impact of races interacting excused violence as necessary to protect the white race. One theory was concerned about white degradation; the other feared that a supposedly inferior race would not accept their allotted place. Even those that disagreed with Clowes's contention that African Americans were an increasing threat to domestic tranquility given their increasing birth numbers often supported a racialized colonial interpretation of history. Indeed, the Brooklyn *Daily Eagle* argued that the African American population was actually decreasing and would eventually be supplanted "by members of the superior race" just as Native American, Australian Aboriginal peoples, and New Zealand's Maori populations appeared to be dwindling.[40] In this way genocides could be seen not as crimes against humanity but as caused by nature.

The *Eagle*'s turn to other countries was not surprising. Those engaged in discussions as to the nature of race relations frequently looked to other locations of interracial contact to support their arguments. Mark Elliot has pointed out that Americans looked at the "Negro problem" as similar to the "Indian Problem" in the 1890s. Indeed, the Dawes Act and the partitioning of Native American lands in many ways showed the influence of Reconstruction, in the way that Native

Americans had to "earn full citizenship by demonstrating their worthiness first" instead of being granted equality outright.[41] Reformers similarly hoped to use the lessons learned from their "success" with Native Americans to solve the problem of the color line in the South. But this was all part of a larger international discussion. Misrepresentations of African Americans, Native Americans, and, indeed, nonwhite peoples around the world were all used in creating racial views that supported both Jim Crow and Native American displacement.[42] At the same time, international observers used these examples to justify their own policies of racial discrimination and extermination. In turn, white southerners pointed out that the English had learned from America's mistakes, presenting these uses of southern history to justify colonialism as evidence that the overthrow of Reconstruction should be seen as a positive development.[43]

In Australia, Reconstruction became a key piece of evidence for both discriminatory domestic and immigration policies. Even before *The Birth of a Nation* premiered, Reconstruction was being used to justify racial policies in Australia. In 1892, in the midst of a debate about allowing Pacific Islanders, often derisively called "kanakas," to immigrate to work on Australian plantations, one Australian of European descent, John Maclean, suggested that these migrant laborers only be allowed to stay temporarily. Maclean felt that because the use of "colored races is both an economic and ethnological experiment," any migration should be temporary. He suggested rules requiring "the return of the kanakas to their island homes whether they desired to return or not." His racism was couched in paternalistic language, claiming that the laborers would learn to be civilized while in Australia and then take "an object lesson in civilized life" back home to other islanders.

At the core of Maclean's argument, however, was the danger race mixing ostensibly posed for white Australians, and the American South provided Maclean with a warning. Arguing that the "the United States have not yet paid the blood-cost of slavery in the Civil War of 1861" and that now "a war of the races has already begun," characterized by "lynchings and burnings alive of niggers guilty of offenses not unknown by white criminals," Maclean drew parallels to a potential Australian dystopian future. To Maclean the problems in the United States were caused not by white hatred of African Americans or the use of violence by whites. Instead, he believed that the Fifteenth Amendment had led African Americans to compete with whites. In essence, he used poor American race relations and racial violence, which he blamed on the enfranchisement of African Americans, to argue against the immigration of non-Europeans lest it "become a racial and social nuisance."[44]

Many British colonial leaders took the "lessons" of Reconstruction that southern whites spouted—that African Americans being put in places of power by well-meaning outsiders was a mistake—and found evidence to support their own paternalistic understanding of colonialism. Reconstruction and its memory served as proof for the British that colonies benefited from British management. Indeed, it is hardly surprising that the idea that "Reconstruction upset the natural order of things" was widely accepted by a British population that was itself engaged in oppressing Black, brown, and other nonwhite persons around the world.[45]

As one of the intellectual fathers of apartheid, the South African politician and author Maurice Smethurst Evans looked to outside examples for approaches to race relations. Evans used a memory of a disastrous Reconstruction, Clowes's research, and his own observations about poor race relations in the American South to justify continued segregation in his own homeland. In the aftermath of the Boer War, he saw a similar potential for problems that the United States had faced following the Civil War.[46] Declaring that "the white man must take up his burden" and rule, Evans felt Reconstruction proved equality between the races would inevitably fail.[47] Instead of equality, Evans advocated allowing "the election by qualified natives of a limited number of Europeans" to represent them.[48] While Evans's work was one of the first "thoroughgoing and broadly disseminated theor[ies] of segregation" and used Reconstruction to make his point, other colonial administrators were also looking at Reconstruction as a failure when considering how to govern South Africa.[49] In the minds of colonial administrators, avoiding the kind of violence Reconstruction had supposedly caused required segregation. Much like Carr, who claimed to be a friend of African Americans, Evans paternalistically saw himself as an ally to Africans and believed that by ensuring South Africa avoided equality he was helping avoid having nonwhites "terrorized into submission" as he felt was necessitated by Reconstruction in the American South.[50] Evans became so fascinated with the American example and with avoiding their "mistakes" that he wrote a book—complete with a chapter on Reconstruction—entitled *Black and White in the Southern States: A Study of the Race Problem in the United States from a South African Point of View*.

Evans was heavily influenced by William Pringle Livingstone, who had lived in Jamaica and written his own 1911 book on race in the United States. Livingstone was convinced that conflict was caused by a combination of factors, first among them efforts at equality. He argued that "mere contact does not produce race antagonism, which comes into play only where, along with the contact, there goes, on the part of the negro, an assumption of racial and social equality."[51]

Livingstone felt England had avoided the violence of America not because of superior character but because her Black population lived farther away from the majority of British citizens and, more importantly, because only whites held political power. Because they had never been promised the vote, the British Empire's nonwhite subjects across the world made no claim to equality, in Livingstone's view. He saw America's "[Civil] War Amendments," the resulting enfranchisement of African Americans, and an attempt to make the ideals of the Declaration of Independence real as the problem. The solution he derived for the American South was "to treat the negroes for the present as a distinct race on a lower scale of evolution." In essence, treat African Americans not as "citizens but subject" and undo Reconstruction.[52]

It was not just English speakers who looked to Reconstruction for lessons about race relations. Debates about how to interpret Reconstruction occurred elsewhere across the world, and Reconstruction's supposed "failure" also influenced the racial policies of other nations. Kate Ferris has found that in Spain some abolitionists viewed Reconstruction's failure as a sign of the white population not being reconstructed enough, while others argued that racial violence proved that democratic and republican ideals were a poor choice for Spain.[53] Scholars have noted how reports of lynching and racial violence were used to critique America's barbarous nature in both Europe and Latin America, but many international commentators also saw violence as proof of racial differences and of the dangers of too much equality.[54] In Cuba, for example, tales of Klan violence and lynching were used as warnings about the dangers of emancipation.[55] This study largely centers on sources in English, but additional work is needed on how Reconstruction was understood internationally, especially as Jim Crow took hold in the South. The widespread acceptance of a white supremacist narrative of Reconstruction helped lead other colonial powers to oppress populations, and thus these narratives were not only an American issue.

Back in the United States, some African Americans were also reading European colonizers' explanations of violence. In the aftermath of the Wilmington race riot, Howard University professor Kelly Miller, in an article in Washington's conservative *Evening Star*, declared that while whites should show more restraint, the more immediate solution was for African Americans to accept their second-class political status. He encouraged "retiring from the active field of politics and directing the energy which has hitherto dissipated over the political area into productive channels" by focusing on their "moral, mental, and material" improvement. Miller not only cited Clowes to explain why whites could not accept Black enfranchisement but he also examined the racial attributes of whites, arguing that political control "is the sphere in which the Anglo-Saxon race manifests its peculiar genius. Domination seems to be in the direct line of its destiny. The Englishman as clearly manifests his superiority over the Hindoo or the Chinese as the Roman did over the Gaul or the Briton."[56] Once again, inaccurate history was being used to justify white supremacy.

A white supremacist memory of Reconstruction proved a powerful force for supporting racism worldwide. As a parallel to scientific racism, these narratives represented a form of historical racism that buttressed white supremacy worldwide. The racial theories of Samuel Morton, Josiah Nott, and other early anthropologists worked alongside the historical narratives of Julian Carr, William Laird Clowes, and William Dunning to justify continued inequality.[57] The memory of Reconstruction was not just a passive story but was actively used to build and support the Jim Crow South and colonialism around the world. It remains alive today not just among hardcore neo-Confederates but among many less historically focused southerners as well. UDC-approved textbooks have had a lasting influence on school curricula, and thus many southerners still believe a Lost Cause narrative of Reconstruction.[58] Indeed, as Bruce Baker discusses earlier in this volume, even he used a dated textbook first written in 1917 that included UDC's talking points in 1980!

Today, this Lost Cause version of Reconstruction still shapes how people around the world understand the Reconstruction period and it often remains racialized. The way that "carpetbagger" spread as a derisive term is a clear example of how the international community accepted white southerners' explanations of Reconstruction violence. In 2018, Republican congressman Pete Olson rather racistly called his Democratic opponent Sri Preston Kulkarni an "Indo-American carpetbagger," presenting Kulkarni's ethnic background as evidence that he was not from Texas, despite the fact that Kulkarni grew up in Houston and is even descended from Sam Houston.[59] Sam Houston, it will be remembered, was not only the first president of the Republic of Texas but also one of the first two US senators from the state. Neo-Confederates often use the term "carpetbagger" to disparage those who disagree with them—even when they are southern born.

Outside the former Confederacy, the term is also still used. It was applied to Hillary Clinton, who, ironically enough, had moved from Arkansas to New York before winning the Empire State's senate seat.[60] This acceptance of carpetbaggers as villains can often be seen internationally as well. The term "carpetbagger" is still used as a pejorative in Canada.[61] After the 2001 coalition invasion of Afghanistan,

London's *Guardian* used the term to describe recent arrivals to Kabul, which it claimed was "awash with seasoned professionals, hopeful carpet-baggers, long exiled, educated Afghans wanting to help or to cash in, or a bit of both."[62]

Though clearly still alive, the memory of the Lost Cause continues to evolve. When modern-day neo-Confederates announce Confederate monuments have nothing to do with race or white supremacy, I cannot help but imagine the men and women who put them up rolling over in their graves. The originators of the Lost Cause, the men and women who erected monuments and fabricated stories about Reconstruction, would have disagreed. These monuments had everything to do with race and racial violence; indeed, that is why they put them up in the first place. Monuments proved the South was ruled by whites, and Confederate memory makers wanted the entire world to know it. They were proud of their beliefs in white supremacy. The monument builders were extremely successful in getting their message out. Many people worldwide listened to their tales, and the world was never the same because of it.

## Notes

1. For more on the growing importance of Reconstruction to the UDC, see Caroline E. Janney, *Remembering the Civil War: Reunion and the Limits of Reconciliation* (Chapel Hill: University of North Carolina Press, 2013), 269, 256, 275–76. See also Karen L. Cox, *Dixie's Daughters: The United Daughters of the Confederacy and the Preservation of Confederate Culture* (Gainesville: University Press of Florida, 2003), 37, 104, 106–10.

2. Janney, *Remembering the Civil War*, 275–76. In reality, the narrative continued beyond Reconstruction to explain racial violence occurring after Reconstruction as well.

3. K. Stephen Prince, "Jim Crow Memory: Southern White Supremacists and the Regional Politics of Remembrance," in *Remembering Reconstruction: Struggles over the Meaning of America's Most Turbulent Era*, ed. Carole Emberton and Bruce Baker (Baton Rouge: Louisiana State University Press, 2017), 19. For more on the use of this narrative to defend Jim Crow, see Adam H. Domby, *The False Cause: Fraud Fabrication and White Supremacy in Confederate Memory* (Charlottesville: University of Virginia Press, 2020); Cox, *Dixie's Daughters*, 106–10; Blight, *Race and Reunion: The Civil War in American Memory* (Cambridge, MA: Harvard University Press, 2001), 294–95; Edward J. Blum, *Reforging the White Republic: Race, Religion, and American Nationalism, 1865–1898* (Baton Rouge: Louisiana State University Press, 2005), esp. 1–3, 125–26.

4. Eric Foner, *Second Founding: How the Civil War and Reconstruction Remade the Constitution* (New York: Norton, 2019), xxii.

5. The two best works on the memory of Reconstruction are Bruce E. Baker, *What Reconstruction Meant: Historical Memory in the American South* (Charlottesville: University of Virginia Press, 2007); Carole Emberton and Bruce E. Baker, eds., *Remembering Reconstruction: Struggles over the Meaning of America's Most Turbulent Era* (Baton Rouge: Louisiana State University Press, 2017).

6. Foner, *Second Founding*, xxii–xxiii; Marilyn Lake and Henry Reynolds, *Drawing the Global Colour Line: White Men's Countries and the International Challenge of Racial Equality* (Cambridge: Cambridge University Press, 2008), 6, 49, 64–65.

7. For more on Carr, see Domby, *The False Cause*.

8. "A Northern Critic's View," *Atlanta Constitution*, November 21, 1898, 4.

9. For more on the acceptance of disenfranchisement in the North, see Blum, *Reforging the White Republic*, esp. 3.

10. Julian S. Carr, [Untitled speech from Manila, P.I.], in Folder 37a, "Addresses, Undated," Julian Shakespeare Carr Papers #141, SHC, University of North Carolina.

11. Julian S. Carr, "Unveiling of Confederate Monument at University, June 2, 1913," in "Folder 26: Addresses, 1912–1914," Julian Shakespeare Carr Papers #141, SHC, University of North Carolina.

12. Julian S. Carr, "Address of Julian S. Carr: 'The Confederate Soldier,' Reunion, Richmond, VA, June 2, 1915," 23, North Carolina Collection, University of North Carolina, https://archive.org/details/addressofgeneraloocarr.

13. "The Negro Question in the United States: I. The Black Belt," *The Times* (London), November 22, 1890, 16.

14. "The Negro Question in the United States: III. Reconstruction Era (Continued)," *The Times* (London), December 15, 1890, 4.

15. Equal Justice Initiative, "Lynching in America: Confronting the Legacy of Racial Terror," 3rd ed., https://lynchinginamerica.eji.org/report/.

16. Clowes, *Black America: A Study of the Ex-Slave and His Late Master* (London: Cassell and Company, 1891), 132–35, 141–42. For more on lynching and accusations of rape, see Crystal Nicole Feimster, *Southern Horrors: Women and the Politics of Rape and Lynching* (Cambridge, MA: Harvard University Press, 2009); W. Fitzhugh (William Fitzhugh) Brundage, *Lynching in the New South: Georgia and Virginia, 1880–1930* (Urbana: University of Illinois Press, 1993). For more on gender and political violence, see Glenda Elizabeth Gilmore, *Gender and Jim Crow: Women and the Politics of White Supremacy in North Carolina, 1896–1920* (Chapel Hill: University of North Carolina Press, 1996).

17. "The Negro Question in the United States: III. Reconstruction Era (Continued)," 4.

18. Clowes, *Black America*, 155. In 1895, Clowes continued arguing for disenfranchising African Americans. Eric Weber, "National Crimes and Southern Horrors: Trans-Atlantic Conversation about Race, Empire, and Civilization, 1880–1900," PhD diss., Duke University, 2011, 154.

19. Clowes, *Black America*, 203.

20. *The Age* (Melbourne), May 9, 1891, 8.

21. "New Books," *The Observer* (London), March 15, 1891, 7.

22. Weber, "National Crimes and Southern Horrors," 3.

23. *Guardian*, July 26, 1897, 7.

24. D. V. Lucas, "The Carpet Bagger," *The Age* (Melbourne), April 5, 1887, 6; see also *Argus* (Melbourne), March 28, 1887, 4.

25. Sir Arthur Conan Doyle, "The Five Orange Pips: Part Three," *Every Evening* (Wilmington, DE), December 16, 1922, 8. Doyle contradicted the assertions of Rose, who said the Klan only consisted of gentlemen.

26. Christopher Clausen, "Sherlock Holmes, Order, and the Late-Victorian Mind," *Georgia Review* 38, no. 1 (Spring 1984): 115.

27. Natalie J. Ring, "A New Reconstruction for the South," in Emberton and Baker, eds., *Remembering Reconstruction*, 173–202.

28. Richard P. Hallowell, *Why the Negro Was Enfranchised: Negro Suffrage Justified*, 2nd ed. (Boston: Geo. H. Ellis Co., 1903) 6–9, 11, 16.

29. "Special Attention," *Green Bay Press Gazette*, October 27, 1915, 2.

30. "'The Birth of a Nation' at the Grand Opera House an Indescribable Feature," *Wilkes-Barre Times Leader*, December 14, 1915, 17.

31. Lester A. Walton, "Colored Bostonians Aroused over 'Birth of a Nation' Film," *New York Age*, April 22, 1915, 6.

32. "Birth of a Nation Will Be Here to-Day," *Nanaimo Daily News* (Nanaimo, BC, Canada), December 1, 1916, 3.

33. "Theater Royal," *Sydney Morning Herald*, May 22, 1916, 2; "Birth of a Nation Will Be Here to-Day."

34. "The Birth of a Nation: Rival Picture Productions," *The Age* (Melbourne), May 24, 1916, 12.

35. "Film News of the Week: The Pioneering Days in America," *Sydney Morning Herald*, September 1, 1938, 28.

36. Mark Elliot, "The Lessons of Reconstruction: Debating Race and Imperialism in the 1890s," in Emberton and Baker, eds., *Remembering Reconstruction*, 165–66; Samuel L. Schaffer, "'A Bitter Memory upon Which Terms of Peace Would Rest': Woodrow Wilson, the Reconstruction of the South, and the Reconstruction of Europe," in Emberton and Baker, eds., *Remembering Reconstruction*, 203–22.

37. Blight, *Race and Reunion*, 252.

38. For more on Clowes influencing the larger debate, see also Douglas A. Lorimer, *Science, Race Relations, and Resistance: Britain, 1870–1914* (Manchester: Manchester University Press, 2013), 44. See also Weber, "National Crimes and Southern Horrors," 117–43.

39. *The Age* (Melbourne), May 9, 1891, 8; Mul., "Bishop Fowler Is Right," *Brooklyn Daily Eagle*, November 10, 1897, 7. The fear of racial and cultural degradation can be seen as a fear of "Reverse Colonialism." Stephen D. Arata, "The Occidental Tourist: Dracula and the Anxiety of Reverse Colonization," *Victorian Studies* 33 (Summer 1990): 621–45.

40. Mul., "Bishop Fowler Is Right," 7.

41. Elliot, "The Lessons of Reconstruction," 145, 147.

42. "A Race Problem in Australia," *Burlington* (VT) *Free Press*, June 3, 1891, 4.

43. "The Race Problem in Africa," *Charlotte News*, August 23, 1909, 4.

44. Jno Maclean, "To the Editor of the Herald," *Sydney Morning Herald*, June 15, 1892, 5. For more on Australian views of American race relations and Reconstruction, see Lake and Reynolds, *Drawing the Global Colour Line*, 138–43. Articles were appearing earlier still. See, for example, "Melbourne, Monday," *The Age*, June 23, 1980, 4.

45. Weber, "National Crimes and Southern Horrors," 120.

46. For more on Evans and his influence on American segregationists, see Elizabeth A. Herbin-Triant, "Southern Segregation South Africa–Style: Maurice Evans,

Clarence Poe, and the Ideology of Rural Segregation," *Agricultural History* 87, no. 2 (Spring 2013): esp. 173.

47. Maurice S. Evans, *Black and White in South East Africa: A Study in Sociology*, 2nd ed. (London: Longmans, Green and Co., 1916), viii, also 202–3, 231, 264, https://archive.org/details/in.ernet.dli.2015.48413.

48. Evans, *Black and White in South East Africa*, viii. He based his proposal also in part on examining New Zealand and the Maoris and modifying their system slightly (268).

49. Saul Dubow, "The Elaboration of Segregationist Ideology," in *Segregation and Apartheid in Twentieth-Century South Africa*, ed. William Beinart and Saul Dubow (London: Routledge, 1995), 150–52; Martin Legassick, "British Hegemony and the Origins of Segregation in South Africa, 1901–1904," in Beinart and Dubow, eds., *Segregation and Apartheid in Twentieth-Century South Africa*, 51.

50. Maurice S. Evans, *Black and White in the Southern States: A Study of the Race Problem in the United States from a South African Point of View* (London: Longmans, Green and Co., 1915), 53.

51. Evans, *Black and White in the Southern States*, v; William Pringle Livingston, *The Race Conflict: A Study of Conditions in America* (London: Sampson Low, Marston and Co., 1911), 18.

52. Livingston, *The Race Conflict*, 171–73.

53. Kate Ferris, *Imagining "America" in Late-Nineteenth-Century Spain* (New York: Palgrave Macmillan, 2016), 135–38, 142.

54. Axel Körner, "Barbarous America," in *America Imagined: Explaining the United States in Nineteenth-Century Europe and Latin America*, ed. Axel Körner, Nicola Miller, and Adam I. P. Smith (New York: Palgrave Macmillan, 2012), 146.

55. Kate Ferris, *Imagining "America" in Late-Nineteenth-Century Spain*, 134.

56. Kelly Miller, "The Negro Question," *Evening Star* (Washington, DC), November 14, 1898, 13.

57. For more on Dunning's international impact, see Lake and Reynolds, *Drawing the Global Colour Line*, 65, 70.

58. John Dittmer, *Local People: The Struggle for Civil Rights in Mississippi* (Urbana: University of Illinois Press, 1994), 12; Cox, *Dixie's Daughters*, 160.

59. David Dayen, "Texas Candidate's Radical Approach to Turning out Asian-American Non-Voters: Talking to Them (in 13 Different Languages)," *Intercept*, October 17, 2018, https://theintercept.com/2018/10/17/sri-kulkarni-congress-texas/.

60. Brian S. Briskie, "Narrating Democrats' Shameful Act," *Democrat and Chronicle* (Rochester, NY), December 30, 2008, 7A.

61. Daphne Bramham, *Vancouver Sun*, July 17, 2018, A5.

62. Polly Toynbee, "Was It Worth It?," *Guardian*, November 13, 2002, https://www.theguardian.com/world/2002/nov/13/afghanistan.comment.

# Remembering War, Constructing Race Pride, Promoting Uplift

*Joseph T. Wilson and the Black Politics of Reconstruction and Retreat*

## Matthew E. Stanley

For most of its existence, the first comprehensive history of Black soldiers in the United States has been sitting idle in the scholastic dustbin. Published in 1882, Joseph T. Wilson's *The Black Phalanx* is a voluminous account of Black fighting men in America from the Revolution through the Civil War. An African American Civil War veteran, Wilson was first inspired to pen his history during a Grand Army of the Republic encampment, and he ultimately drew on materials at public libraries in New York, Cincinnati, and Boston to record the "memories of the past" lest they be forgotten. Writing against the Lost Cause narrative emerging during the fallout of Reconstruction, and with the African American Civil War experience progressively ignored or devalued by white northerners and professional-class Blacks, *The Black Phalanx* combined "natural rights" tenets with identifiably Victorian notions of capitalist merit and civilization theory. The aim of Wilson's tome was straightforward: confirm Black aptitude, describe the endeavor for freedom, and give Black troops their proper place in the war's history. Though quickly surpassed in import and popularity by the works of the Black veterans William Wells Brown and George Washington Williams, *The Black Phalanx* is nevertheless part of a discourse that illuminates the competing and shifting but also occasionally reinforcing and intersecting intellectual-political models of Black radicalism and Black conservatism in the late nineteenth century. Indeed, Wilson's life and writings illustrate how African American Civil War veterans used war narratives to do two things simultaneously: underscore what W. E. B. Du Bois termed the "abolition-democracy" tradition of Reconstruction-era racial and economic justice and construct a new form of uplift rooted in conceptions of the "honor," "manhood," and "glory" of the race during the transition from a rights revolution to an era of "self-help."[1]

Wilson's path from radicalism to traditionalism was intricate and varying. A prolific political organizer and newspaper man in the post–Civil War Virginia Tidewater, Wilson was a founding member of the Norfolk Labor Association and the Norfolk Land Association and an officer in the Norfolk Union Monitor Club. Along with Henry Highland Garnet, he was also one of the authors of *Equal Suffrage: An Address from the Colored Citizens of Norfolk, Va., to the People of the United States*, a radical manifesto that demanded complete social and political equality and a full-scale military occupation of the South, in addition to urging "agitation" and organized resistance against recidivist Confederate veterans.[2] Wilson later served as editor of the *True Southerner*, the *American Sentinel*, and, eventually, the *Industrial Day*, advocating positions on the left wing of the Republican Party: land confiscation, firearms rights, free homesteads for former slaves, progressive taxation, and Black military occupation, often critiquing aggregated wealth and corporate capitalism.[3]

Yet the draining of Republican Party radicalism, the collapse of Reconstruction, and the failure of liberalism—civic rights without challenging property or capitalist markets—to subvert racial and class oppression in the postwar South led Wilson and others to look increasingly inward toward Black community, group reliance, shared decision-making, and "uplift-suasion" politics. His one-time insistence on inalienable rights and direct confrontation through grassroots political organizing lessened throughout the 1870s and 1880s relative to curbed Black opportunity and a hardening color line; uplift suasion grew as an alternative to the equal-rights demands of Reconstruction, especially among Black elites. Conceived of by late-eighteenth-century abolitionists, uplift had surged in the 1820s and 1830s and was once again ascendant, even as Black veteran authors and "historians of the race" used memories of emancipation and Black military service to elicit claims for unconditional equality and thwart (and sometimes reinforce) stereotypes regarding slave docility and Black pathology.[4] Shaped by a "racialized elite identity" characterized by "race progress" through class stratification, uplift suasion held that demonstrably positive Black behavior, often including individualized behavior, would undermine race prejudice. Conversely, negative Black behavior would confirm it. In fact, this strategy, not of confronting white supremacy's material and class foundations but of affluent or upwardly mobile Talented Tenths "persuading away racist ideas" while non-elite Black people were pressed to be "extraordinary," shifted the burden of upending racism away from the white oppressors and onto the Black oppressed.[5]

At the same time, intensifying US imperialism, first in the American West and then in Cuba and the Philippines, provided outlets for displays of national loyalty and masculinity, as well as new battlegrounds on which African American soldiers might "prove" their worth. Black volunteers sought to win equality and demonstrate their excellence through military service, which became the most obvious channel for demonstrating bravery and participating in patriotic rituals of violence sponsored by and for the nation-state. Moreover, Black women's clubs and individual activists increasingly called on Black men to confirm their manhood in order to both protect Black women and expose the mistakenness of white supremacy.[6] This connection between militancy and justice, between the cartridge box and the ballot box, led Wilson as editor to call for social transformation while intermittently urging formerly enslaved people to make the best of their condition.[7] His writings served two interrelated aims: They promoted race pride through the exploits of Black soldiers and defended the overall "conduct of the race"—conduct that, Wilson argued, merited greater inclusion into the American body politic. Precisely what the inclusion meant changed along with the course of Black politics.

Wilson's subtle tack from forthright resistance toward uplift, industrial training, and assimilationist gradualism in post-Reconstruction Virginia reveals how veterans' cultural work facilitated a larger transition within what Cedric Robinson terms the "Black radical tradition" from the universalist, postabolitionist politics of Frederick Douglass and T. Thomas Fortune to the more conservative, qualified, "nation within a nation" philosophy of Alexander Crummell and Booker T. Washington.[8] Yet this was no clear binary, and historians have often considered "Black thought" too narrowly, sometimes framing uplift and civil rights agitation as oppositional and mutually exclusive.[9] Wilson's writings contained both tension and overlap between radicalism and assimilation, between Western liberalism and "racial capitalism" (how capitalism relies on the construction and promotion of racial difference) and Black notions of community. John A. Casey Jr. rightly contends that Black veterans were in some sense marginalized by uplift politics because the veteran emphasis on violence and racism clashed with the emerging image of the African American middle-class professional—the representation of the Black businessman replaced that of the Black soldier.[10] But African American veterans adopted and promoted self-help, too. Through an impassioned defense of emancipation, Black soldiers, *and* racial uplift, Wilson's histories reveal the varied uses of emancipationist memory in Black politics, as well as how veterans both shaped and were shaped by this fluid discourse. His drift toward uplift suasion sheds light on both the friction among Black classes and the interplay between what Vincent Harding terms the "Great Tradition" of Black protest and Black Nationalism in the writings of Civil War veterans at the dawn of Jim Crow.

Joseph T. Wilson was likely born enslaved around 1840 near Norfolk, Virginia. Virtually nothing is known about his early years, except that he apparently escaped bondage in the mid-1850s, probably assisted by free dockworkers.[11] Wilson made his way to New Bedford, Massachusetts, a port town on the state's southern coast and the whaling capital of the antebellum world. A hub of antislavery politics and a haven for people who fled slavery, New Bedford was known as the "fugitive's Gibraltar."[12] Wilson left town in the late 1850s to work on a whaling ship, and word of the Civil War reached him while anchored in Valparaiso, Chile, in May 1862.[13] Arriving in New York from the South Pacific in August 1862, Wilson unsuccessfully attempted to circumvent the army's refusal of Black volunteers by enlisting as a "Spaniard."[14] Determined to become a soldier, he made his way to New Orleans, where Black militias had entered Union service when federals seized the city in April 1862. That fall he enlisted in the Second Louisiana Native Guards. Joining Company C of the Fifty-Fourth Massachusetts Infantry in December 1863, Wilson was wounded at the Battle of Olustee and would be physically disabled for the remainder of his life.[15]

It was as a veteran that Wilson left his biggest mark. Veteranhood was central to the Black postwar experience, as veterans disproportionately became civic leaders, often through the Republican Party, Equal Rights Leagues and Union Leagues, and the Grand Army of the Republic. For Wilson, the masculinized experience of battle—of "proving" oneself in combat and glorifying the race—were vital to claims for social equality.[16] Avowing that the Emancipation Proclamation was "a mere paper manifesto, impotent in power," it was Union soldiers and Blacks themselves, first in seizing freedom and then through military service, who made good on emancipation.[17] Wilson likewise maintained that Black demonstrations of attainment—a trial by combat—served to undermine racism first in the Union ranks, then on the Northern home front, and ultimately among conservatives abroad. Even in the Middle West, where conservative Unionist sentiment—which Wilson termed "semi-Unionist and Copperhead"—proved common, the exploits of Black regiments were instrumental in shifting popular attitudes.[18] The belief that the conduct of Black soldiers had led to tangible wartime decline in anti-Black prejudice would underpin his later emphasis on racial uplift.

Wilson's fluid social philosophies were shaped indelibly by regional politics. The story of Virginia's Lower Peninsula, the expanse of land between Richmond and Norfolk flanked by the York and James Rivers, is North America's oldest site of cash-crop economy and therefore an early setting of race making as structuring relations between and within social classes. By 1860, with this basic relationship between economic exploitation and racial hierarchy matured, the Lower Peninsula's population of thirty thousand was nearly 60 percent Black—four-fifths of whom were bonded—and that percentage multiplied during the war as previously enslaved people absconded to Union lines. Freedpeople struggled mightily to acquire land following emancipation. It became clear to the formerly enslaved and a handful of northern reformers that the overriding problem of Reconstruction was, as Wendell Phillips proclaimed, that "the black man has no capital."[19] Most whites refused to sell or extend credit. As renters, wage earners, and owners of the poorest and least productive land, recently freedpeople remained in various states of dependency even as Black leaders—a mix of free and formerly enslaved, native and transplant serving in a variety of local offices—fought to translate incremental economic gains into political power.[20] In the days and weeks after Appomattox, Norfolk's Black leaders began holding public meetings to outline their postwar aspirations and challenge the existing conservative Unionist white political structure. Endorsed by the Norfolk Union League and its Monitor Union Club (founded by the one-time Norfolk slave Dr. Thomas Bayne), such gatherings were Radical Republican auxiliaries, characterized by strident calls for reform. African American churches, meanwhile, became the nerve centers of Union or Loyal League political activity. One such convention, held on election morning, May 25, 1865, at the Bute Street African Methodist Church, saw perhaps one thousand citizens in attendance seeking to vote as "loyal men" under Virginia's 1864 constitution. After dividing themselves by the wards in which they lived, the crowd attempted to exercise their right to vote. When citizens of three of the four wards were denied and the slate of white Unionist candidates finished second in the city elections, Black leaders sought direct action. A subsequent meeting of two thousand African Americans and 150 white allies took place at Norfolk's Catharine Street Baptist Church on June 5 and led to the publication of a manifesto entitled *Equal Suffrage: An Address from the Colored Citizens of Norfolk, Va., to the People of the United States.*[21]

Wilson, having moved to Norfolk in 1864, met in committee with Bayne, Henry Highland Garnet, and several Black clergy to express their postwar expectations.[22] Drawing on issues raised at the June 5 assembly, Wilson, Garnet, and others championed the formation of labor and land associations to safeguard

Black workers and acquire economic power through land purchase, resulting in the founding of the Norfolk Labor Association and the Norfolk Land Association. The committee viewed Black labor as central to the current and future wealth of the United States and insisted that centuries of toil, along with military service, had given Black men title to social and political equality. They also understood suffrage as indispensable to the survival of Unionism and the Republican Party in the South.[23] Further, the committee urged freedpeople to "organize to resist" the violent white opposition that was sure to come, as the former "slaveocracy" would sell their power dearly. Committeemen promoted "agitation, discussion, and enforcement of your claims to equality" as weapons against white planters and revanchist Confederate veterans.

The second part of their message concerned economic rights, which the committee saw as necessary in order to safeguard political rights. They viewed land ownership as both critical to winning political power and the only path to long-term economic autonomy. As such, land associations aimed to foster Black land acquisition by "regulating fairly the price of labor." Despite Garnet's well-known inclinations toward Black Nationalism, the committee recognized that the rights of freedpeople depended on white support, if not formal interracial alliance based on shared political goals. Such goals meant appealing, variously, to both poor whites (through class themes) and elite white allies, including federal judge John C. Underwood, a noted abolitionist and land confiscation advocate. Combining the moral clarity of immediatist abolition with agrarianism and the producerist concepts of workaday trade unionism, the committee insisted that full civil rights were a matter of "justice, humanity, and sound political economy."[24] Signed on June 5, 1865, their declaration was read aloud and soon published in pamphlet form. Norfolk's *Equal Suffrage* manifesto was part of a broader strategy to create a progressive regional coalition beginning with a compact between the Hampton Union League, the Williamsburg Colored Union League, and the Norfolk Union Monitor Club, which had been organized in February 1865 with Wilson serving as secretary. Meanwhile, events between the summer of 1865 and the fall of 1867 drove reformers such as Wilson into increasingly radical stances, particularly on matters of economics and land.

Independent Black newspapers fused these policy debates with emancipationist memory. Mere weeks before the Norfolk meeting, in March 1865, Colonel D. B. White of the Eighty-Eighth New York Volunteers opened a Republican Party newspaper at the southeastern end of the Virginia Peninsula. Hampton's *True Southerner* was the first of its kind in the state. A city characterized by its "Emancipation Oak" and a crisscrossing of deliverance-themed streets—Grant,

Lincoln, Union, Liberty, and Hope—war and emancipation's diaspora had doubled Hampton's 1860 population as the municipality transitioned from a massive "contraband" camp to a locus of Radical Republican politics.[25] White's publication became the Black community's paper of record. Sponsored by the city's Union League, and with Wilson a frequent contributor, its editorials touted civil rights, railing against Black Codes and the restoration of political rights to former Confederates. Its readership consisted of soldiers, Northern aid workers, and freedpeople. The weekly broadsheet quickly became a key tool of Black politics in Tidewater Virginia and one of the most notable African American newspapers in the country.[26]

Wilson's tenure as editor of the *True Southerner* ran from the fall of 1865 through the paper's relocation to Norfolk the following spring. Its overriding aim was to promote civil rights and land reform through a defense of African American veterans and Radical Republican policies.[27] Combining a sweeping social and economic critique with advice for practical uplift, the weekly published political commentary alongside advertisements for firearms, livestock, agricultural implements, and printed articles on crop science and farming techniques. In this sense the gazette also facilitated working-class "self-activity," or struggling against oppression outside of formal institutions, and helped construct a Black political culture distinct from white Republicanism.[28] Building on Black Nationalist precepts and prefiguring the self-help of Booker T. Washington and Marcus Garvey, the paper highlighted injustice and underscored social renewal while simultaneously urging formerly enslaved people to make the best of their condition.[29] The *True Southerner* weighed the relocation of some Black people abroad alongside calls for extensive economic change and support for basic social improvements such as the Freedmen's Savings Bank and public schools.[30] Integrating what Ibram X. Kendi terms "uplift suasion" and "educational persuasion," Wilson recognized that many Black leaders believed that Black "ignorance" was the cause of white racism, and the white perception of Black people as intellectually inferior gave added cause to their desire for education.[31] As such, when Virginia's progressive 1868 constitution created the state's first public school system, Wilson proved instrumental in convincing Norfolk's city council to underwrite Black public schools.[32] It was a pragmatic and commercially savvy platform that appealed to a wide swath of African American class and social proclivities by insisting that transformational reform was consistent with long-standing American values.[33]

Yet as editor of the *True Southerner*, Wilson also sponsored the free-labor ethos and far-reaching planks expressed in Norfolk's "Equal Suffrage" manifesto.

He also sought to push Reconstruction's free-labor revolution further. In the context of the agrarian South and its recently emancipated labor force, this propagation entailed a new relationship between the federal government and its citizens based on the principles of equality and justice secured both economically and politically through the ownership of land. Indeed, the free-labor spirit that matured and radicalized during the 1840s and 1850s linked an individual brand of democracy with a species of landed communalism. This ideology imagined free homesteads (and the concomitant removal or absorption of Native people) as republican alternatives to the undemocratic and supposedly unmanly threat of fixed wage earning that was slowly emerging within industrializing northern cities. Free labor's most radical extension—its "semi-socialist idea"—promoted progressive taxation to fund public education, infrastructural improvements, and land reform. On the one hand, the prospect of "free land" represented a pointed break with pro-property liberalism that opened the door to challenges of other forms of ownership, either in man (slavery) or in production (capitalism). Reformers believed that landed proprietorship protected one's personal and political independence from "wage slavery" and other marketplace coercions, which then became the rationale for redistributing land to former slaves. On the other hand, the reality of Republican Party homesteading proved both classed and raced, favoring corporate firms over family farms and "redistributing" nonwhite land to white people.

Hoping for Republicans to make good on their semiegalitarian assurances, Wilson avowed that Virginia politics and culture had been dominated by "aristocratic [slaveholding] classes" who held labor in contempt as the mark of slavery.[34] As such, Wilson supported a land tax (replacing the antebellum tax on slave property) and progressive taxation on all annual incomes over 250 dollars.[35] He also backed Senator Charles Sumner's "common sense" clemency, under which "traitors should take a back seat in the work of restoration" and be received "slowly and cautiously back into the sovereignty of citizenship."[36] However, the free-labor promise that prosperity required only hard work and thrift perpetuated individualized notions of merit rather than historical and sociological explanations for poverty or the power imbalances and coercive possibilities within "freedom of contract." Free labor's ideal of continuous upward mobility for workers (rather than acknowledging the existence of a fixed wage–earning class with its own sets of political interests) prefigured Gilded Age social theories that both justified extreme material inequalities and underwrote popular support for eugenics, imperialism, and "natural" hierarchies of class, gender, ethnicity, race, and nation. Elements of free labor's utopian capitalism would permeate Black understandings of self-help.

As E. P. Thompson and Eric Hobsbawm demonstrate, peasants and proletariats often frame their radicalism through traditional imagery and familiar custom and language. Freedpeople were no exception. The *True Southerner* reported acts of terrorism against former slaves, insisting that white paramilitaries were the ones who had broken with political norms and the democratic promises of the so-called American tradition. Asking "Who Are Radical?," the editor concluded that the white Confederate "oligarchy" who looked to "annihilate an entire race of people" were the true extremists, leading Wilson and others to support martial law, censure President Andrew Johnson's amnesty toward former Confederates, and broadcast reports that former Confederates in Isle of Wight and Surrey counties were reenslaving their former property.[37] Aware that revanchists would not be convicted in civilian courts, the paper called for military tribunals composed of Union soldiers; the South, it said, needed to be purged and "burned clean."[38] Wilson and other Blacks in Norfolk concurred with the *New Orleans Tribune* that "up to this time, Emancipation has been a lie" and that military occupation by Black soldiers was "the only way to make Abolition a truth."[39]

The *True Southerner* also emphasized the relationship between class and racial hierarchy.[40] Denouncing the planter oligarchy, the editor maintained that workingmen should own their own labor and proposed political alliances between Blacks and poor whites in order to "vote down the old aristocratic party" that had formerly divided the two factions.[41] These possible allies—the "class of Confederate soldiers who never had any heart in the rebellion, but were compelled by circumstances to enter the army"—included deserters, scalawags, and nonideological Confederates, especially those with like-minded material interests.[42] In other words, this was a proposed class coalition. "What we desire is an equal, just, and republican government; a government that shall protect the helpless and bring to justice the guilty, whether rich or poor, black or white," Wilson affirmed in support of the Civil Rights Act of 1866, which he hoped would "obliterate political caste." Vastly overestimating the capacity of political liberalism and civic rights to upend the coercion of contract labor and the wage system, he avowed that legal equality would cause "the capitalist to lose his power to grind to dust the unfortunate and helpless. . . . The strong arm that wielded the hammer over the anvil will gather the fruit of his labor; he that toils in the field will gather its fruit for his own household."[43] For Wilson, there was a connection—if not an occasional contradiction—between demands directed at external audiences and internal advances from within the race; between political and economic assertiveness, militancy even, and self-reliance; and between knowing how to simultaneously press forward and take stock in and capitalize on existing, albeit limited, gains.

No issue better represented the conflict between the era's liberalism and calls for economic radicalism than the issue of land. Drawing on the injustices of slavery and the war experience, many freedpeople possessed a "Jacobin political orientation," in which "equal rights" meant the "right not to have a master at all." This racial empowerment stemmed from the recent war combined with popular claims for land redistribution or decommodification to foster a new form of egalitarian republicanism.[44] Countless formerly enslaved people expected land reform as a logical conclusion to emancipation. Most pronounced among rural Blacks who were born into slavery, this "peasant dream" of landed proprietorship, agrarian autonomy, industrial independence, and cooperative governance defied not only laissez-faire republicanism but also the small-producer ideal of the early Republican Party.[45] Yet leading Republicans, many eager to reenergize cotton production, overwhelmingly chose property over equality. They did so even as white planters nakedly exposed the limitations and contradictions of free labor by breaking contracts, failing to offer livable wages, refusing to rent (much less sell) land to freedpeople, and adopting nonemployment agreements for formerly enslaved persons who left their late owners. Industrialists in particular could not abide the possibility that Black radicalism in the South might unite with labor radicalism in the North. This rejection of land reform also involved white elites North and South imposing capitalist ideology (through various theories and strategies of self-help and merit-based mobility) onto a noncapitalist and largely propertyless proletariat, thus stabilizing the crucial place of freedpeople and their labor within the cash-crop marketplace and further integrating them into the national consumer economy. Though there would be no permanent working-class seizure of either the plantations or the factories, scholars since W. E. B. Du Bois have long identified the nonfulfillment of "forty acres and a mule" as central to the collapse of African American rights.

The land question being paramount to former bondspeople, the *True Southerner* extended its focus on the rights of labor to encompass questions of economic and agrarian justice. Wilson had participated in several Republican rallies in 1867 calling for land redistribution.[46] Other Black Virginians formed collectives, such as Hampton's Lincoln's Land Association, in order to acquire land cooperatively.[47] Opposing the reinstatement of "rebel property," Wilson lambasted the Freedmen's Bureau and its sole faith in wage savings (not the promise of land as a basic matter of justice but the promised *opportunity* to land through purchase for those individuals who ostensibly exhibited ample work effort, thrift, and worthiness). Wilson also decried white landlordism and deemed it a crime that lands lawfully seized by the federal government and improved by freedpeople during the war were returned to former Confederates so that they might exact rent from their former slaves. He warned that to seize freedpeople's newly won land and homes—their "castles of liberty"—was tantamount to the restoration of slavery. Any white southern property lost or abandoned during the war was an expected consequence of their having instigated a rebellion. "Want to know what became of your property?" he mocked white conservatives. "Your servants, by whose flesh and blood your property was obtained, have it, and we would to God they had more of it."[48] According to Wilson, the government's restoration of rebel land and the Freedmen's Bureau's negotiation of annual contracts between former slaves and former masters were akin to a "paternal lion" asking the lamb to reside with the wolves.[49] Supporting Norfolk's Land, Homestead, Settlement, and Labor Association, the *True Southerner* talked instead of a "homes for all" plank and a fundamentally new economic rearrangement in the postwar South.[50] Like Thaddeus Stevens, Frederick Douglass, and Charles Sumner, Wilson advocated confiscation as both just and lucrative.[51] While calls for land redistribution—and demands for economic equality in general—were an implicit rejection of both capitalist ideology and uplift suasion in that they did not require individual Black people to demonstrate their "respectability" or "worth" in order to attain greater material parity, Wilson and others nevertheless highlighted the "achievements of the race" in order to garner support for such policies.[52]

Driven by strident calls for structural social and economic change, the *True Southerner* continued to grow under Wilson's editorship, becoming the mouthpiece of Hampton's Union League and boasting over 6,200 regional subscribers in a city of roughly 15,000.[53] In late 1866, at the height of its circulation and influence, a white mob broke in to the newspaper offices, trashed the workplace, and destroyed the printing machinery. The publication never recovered. Although Wilson moved on to edit the short-lived *Union Republican* in Petersburg in 1867, the radicalism of his new publication (which also called for land redistribution) made it a target of white reactionaries, and he never matched his former influence as an editor.[54] Nevertheless, the *True Southerner* had captured the zeitgeist of the Black postwar Upper South and, in proposing economic radicalism, underscored one of the most polarizing and revolutionary questions of the immediate postwar era.

The zenith of the *True Southerner* paralleled increasing Black political power in Tidewater Virginia. Revolution met white reaction on Monday, April 16, 1866, as white men fired on a crowd of African Americans who were marching under the banner "The Ballot Box for All." Black veterans retaliated. Although the military declared martial law, white-on-Black attacks continued throughout the week, and no whites were ever charged.[55] The April 1866 riots proved a precursor to successful white counterrevolution, and reenfranchised former Confederates began to regain control of Norfolk's civic government in 1870. Although the appointed Radical Republican governor William H. Wells—a Michigan native maligned as "the prince of carpetbaggers" by his enemies—had supported Black rights and progressive taxation, his short tenure and ouster from power in the fall of 1869 by a coalition of moderate "True Republicans" and New Departure Democrats signaled a statewide Thermidor that crested with the end of military occupation in January 1870.[56] While several white Radicals and four Blacks, including Wilson, won election to the city council that year, conservatives gerrymandered the predominantly African American Fourth Ward, effectively ending Reconstruction in Norfolk as it was collapsing throughout Virginia.[57]

Wilson remained an active and loyal Republican, spurning the interracial and economically progressive Readjuster Party insurgency that swept across the state in the late 1870s. Organizing and speaking at Colored State Convention meetings, in 1875 Wilson decried new laws designed to disfranchise Black men for chicken stealing and other petty crimes.[58] Indeed, the civil rights project in the South was dimming by the time Wilson served as a representative on Washington, DC's Emancipation Monument committee in the spring of 1876. Having organized Norfolk's African American GAR Cailloux Post, he became by the late 1870s increasingly concerned with preserving the African American legacy of the war.[59] While he emphasized self-emancipation and stressed the role of Abraham Lincoln—the "white man's president"—as a reluctant liberator, Wilson nevertheless thought it necessary for "a grateful race" to offer a permanent monument to Lincoln as a testament to the "blood-bought freedom" of African Americans. Sculptor Thomas Ball's statue depicts Lincoln standing over a kneeling slave, suggesting the benevolent bestowal of freedom upon the bondsman—a white authority figure that appears to reencode the racial order of the plantation.[60] But rather than a purely racial-hierarchical relationship between master and servant, Wilson suggested that the slave be in the midst of "rising from the earth" to the level of the free man, anticipating "the full manhood of freedom."[61]

Meanwhile, the violent overturning of Reconstruction in the South, the "counterrevolution of property" in the North, and the failure of civic liberalism without economic radicalism steadily isolated southern Blacks and drove African American politics ever more inward. Although only forty-two years old at the time of his most notable publications in 1882 and still active on the veterans' circuit, Wilson was physically unwell when he attended the national Grand Army of the Republic encampment in Baltimore that year.[62] No longer organizing and unable to stand erect from old battle wounds, Wilson nonetheless authored a chronicle of emancipation, Black enlistment, and African American war memory—a literary vehicle that might reinforce the growing politics of uplift. He connected race progress to military service and, predicting that "the race will take care of itself," expressed self-reliance in addition to his past calls for civic equality. As the possibilities of Reconstruction faded, Wilson sought—and often struggled—to articulate a new synergy between confrontation, self-help, and uplift.[63] This overlap between accommodation and autonomy and integration and democratic first principles was both part and parcel of the broader debates and divergences within Black thought and political strategy—anticipating the theoretical rift between Washington and Du Bois.

By the early 1880s, a reinvigorated ideology of "race pride" facilitated new forms of Black autonomy in mutual aid societies, fraternal institutions, church activity, farmer associations, and labor organization, most notably through the Knights of Labor.[64] Faced with the issue of "readjusting" the state debt at a Black labor convention in Richmond in August 1875, Wilson had supported the creation of a "Laboring Men's Mechanic Union," calling for African American political "independence." Charging local white Republicans with corruption and claiming that Black voters had become "the political serfs of unworthy white leaders," Wilson lost the presidency of the convention to the former slave and "equal rights" advocate Joseph P. Evans. Yet the convention marked "a new stage in the evolution and articulation of black consciousness," and Wilson had heralded the trend of self-help and racial solidarity in the face of Jim Crow.[65] A new, more bourgeois generation who grew up after emancipation—"old enough to have experienced the duplicity and hostility of whites, young enough not to have seen themselves in terms of the 'Republican Ark'"—led the way, gravitating toward a "militant race pride."[66]

Published in late 1882, *Emancipation: Its Course and Progress, from 1481 B.C. to A.D. 1875* offered a comparative history of emancipation, a staunch defense of Black freedom in the United States, and an overview of Washington, DC's Freedmen's Memorial through the lens of uplift politics. Examining slave liberation from ancient Rome through Tsarist Russia, Wilson asserted that the War of the Rebellion became a revolutionary event of world-historical importance the moment US soldiers and enslaved people became a syndicate for freedom.[67] Bondspeople in particular proved an "internal enemy" who refused to be "laborers, producers, and factory operatives" for the rebel cause.[68] As such, Wilson maintained several fundamental points: that enslaved people, fully prepared for freedom in 1862, were agents of their own liberation; that prejudice and violence against freedpeople had not dissipated in the South; and that, despite continued hardships, the Black nation had made momentous advances since emancipation. Additionally, Wilson attacked "anti-emancipationist" Northerners, "particularly those in the West," who were loyal to the Union yet committed to racial exclusion; exalted bold Union policy makers such as Benjamin Butler and John C. Frémont for their early awareness of the need to "cripple and deprive" the white South of its greatest asset; and painted white Union soldiers—"free laborers of the North"—as critical agents of emancipation and Union military victories as essential in securing Black freedom.[69] He insisted that only then, pushed by ground-level slaves and soldiers, did the White House consider a formal emancipation measure. Indeed, *Emancipation* prefigured later Black Nationalist arguments by downplaying Abraham Lincoln's role as the "Great Emancipator." Wilson's self-emancipation premise anticipated the theses of Herbert Aptheker, Benjamin Quarles, Ira Berlin, and later social historians. Barbara Fields's assertion that "by the time Lincoln issued his Emancipation Proclamation, no human being alive could have held back the tide that swept toward freedom" might well have sprung from Wilson's pages.[70] Cultivated by veterans and civic leaders such as Frederick Douglass and Martin Delany, later buttressed by Black scholars including Carter Woodson and Du Bois, and conserved within Black educational and religious institutions, emancipationist memory became integral to African American folk narrative and oral and academic tradition, as well as a mechanism for racial "progress" during the depths of Jim Crow.

Assessing the "progress of the race" in the midst of Lost Cause construction and accelerating white reunion, Wilson no longer underscored the limitations and lost opportunities of Reconstruction, emphasizing instead the advancements of Black people and the "conduct of the race." Like Thomas Norris Jr. and others, Wilson used literacy and landholding statistics to prove that "progress" had occurred, despite the fact that African Americans continued to suffer from what Wilson termed "the curse of poverty and prejudice."[71] African American material scarcity—the "potent power of wealth"—was the freedpeople's chief obstacle. Rejecting his previous redistributionist position concerning land reform, Wilson increasingly suggested that hard work, frugality, and collective positivity were the best means by which to "wipe away all traces of two and a half centuries of slavery's debasement."[72] On some level, self-help ideology's focus on property ownership appealed especially to formerly enslaved people and Civil War veterans because it "evoked their collective hopes for land redistribution."[73] Written as the Black middle class was increasingly reluctant to remember the African American military experience, Wilson still felt that recognizing the historic bravery and dignity of the race could both rouse Black solidarity and galvanize a modicum of white support for equal civic rights.[74] Uplift as a means toward equality represented not so much a strategic illogicality as an attempt to fuse social demands with a new bourgeois call for assimilation and self-help often based on Victorian and capitalist values of thrift, respectability, and patriarchal authority.[75]

The same year as *Emancipation*, Wilson published *The Black Phalanx*, his magnum opus. This chronologically sprawling account reaffirmed Wilson's metahistory of a contest within society between aristocracy and "the people" and their "advancing spirit of freedom."[76] He attempted to reconcile Western history and Euro-American liberalism and capitalism with notions of Black community and self-organization, citing ancient Greece and Rome, Civil War England, and Revolutionary France as forerunners of a transhistoric march toward "Democracy," or self-rule.[77] Wilson interpreted the antebellum era as a conflict between "aristocrats," who happened to be southern slaveholders, and "democrats," who were primarily northerners. Borrowing from Republican ideology and Christian social equality theory, Wilson divided the antebellum era into two halves. He termed the decades after the Constitution (1790–1820) the era of "the consolidation of the Slave Power," climaxing with the Missouri Compromise. Despite great progress, Wilson argued, particularly in the form of the Northwest Territories and manumission in the Border South, the "slaveocracy" fortified its national authority, bringing even common whites under its material and ideological yoke. Two Americas soon developed, one democratic and progressive, and the other a "slave oligarchy" grounded in "feudal aristocracy." This Massachusetts–South Carolina binary framed the succeeding four decades. Terming the era between 1820 and 1860 "the consolidation of the people" under moral beacons such as William Lloyd Garrison and liberal nationalists including De Witt Clinton and William H. Seward, Wilson saw the period culminating in the triumph of Republican Party free labor in 1860.[78] This process, according to Wilson, combined public education, internal improvements, national markets, and the use of immigrant wage labor—"the brawny arms of Hans and Patrick"—with abolitionism.[79] The North's material advantage was evidence of its moral superiority.

Wilson viewed Black enlistment—the transformation of hundreds of thousands of men from an enslaved proletariat to armed agents of social metamorphosis, from property to person—as the war's single most radical outgrowth. This turn of events was both an offshoot of two centuries of antislavery resistance—Nat

Turner and John Brown writ national—and decisive in putting down the slaveholder's rebellion.[80] Defending the humanity and military capacity of African American soldiers, Wilson insisted that their contributions to the Union war effort were greater than commonly considered.[81] Both abolitionists and Black nationalists such as Martin Delany had seen military service as part of a broader racial uplift and "the first step toward the elevation of their race to full participation in American life."[82] Wilson further stressed the relative value of Black soldiers. Unlike white soldiers, who held no familiarity with the South's terrain and whose motivations for fighting ranged from desire for pay to fear of conscription to abstract ideology, Black troops possessed a righteous catalyst.[83] Enlistment altered the ideological complexion of the war for African Americans because military participation "linked *freedom* to the cause of the Union thus making the success of one the success of the other." The American flag, which "had been but a symbol of oppression to the black man," was "re-baptised" by the "life's blood" of William H. Carney and Andre Cailloux.[84] Most critically, Wilson argued that the feats and patriotism of the phalanx and the overall "conduct of the race" had given all Black people title to legal equality and that African Americans might buoy themselves through demonstrably manly and reputable behavior.[85]

Although *The Black Phalanx* proved groundbreaking, other studies of Black people during the Civil War soon followed. Wilson's work built on the abolitionist and USCT recruiter William Wells Brown's heavily anecdotal *The Negro in the American Rebellion: His Heroism and His Fidelity* (1867). Published over two decades later, and long after the collapse of Congressional Reconstruction, George Washington Williams's *History of the Negro Troops in the War of the Rebellion, 1861–1865* (1888) proved the most successful of the three. Williams had previously produced a two-volume *History of the Negro Race in America from 1619 to 1880* (1883), which came out only one year after both of Wilson's books and is often credited as the first history of African Americans in North America. Williams's uplift work eclipsed Wilson's both commercially and critically, in part explaining Wilson's neglect by later academics. Williams eventually became the subject of a full-scale biography by the historian John Hope Franklin and has been utilized by other Middle Period scholars, including David Blight.[86] Conversely, twentieth-century historians have drawn on Wilson's material but not given it standalone treatment. Although the National Archives archivist Sara Dunlap Jackson claims that "when *The Black Phalanx* appeared, it was welcomed as the most complete and accurate record of that part of the great struggles for liberty and the Union borne out by colored soldiers," scholars have only rarely employed it as a primary source.[87] In his groundbreaking *The Negro in the Civil War* (1953),

Black historian Benjamin Quarles called *The Black Phalanx* a "well-planned, but not always well-integrated study." Like so many nineteenth-century histories, the works of Wilson, Williams, and Brown are "padded with lengthy quotations from unacknowledged sources."[88] The historian Dudley Taylor Cornish felt similarly, stating that although *The Black Phalanx* was "very uneven," it contains more information than the works of Brown and Williams and is particularly useful in its "discussion of anti-Black prejudice within the Union army.[89]

Both Wilson and Williams appealed to race pride, trumpeting a new Black middle class of "representative men" and insisting that there was "room at the top" for those who strove.[90] Part racial preservation, part group promotion, and part bourgeois expression of "natural" hierarchy, "deserving" classes, and capitalist ideology, this notion of uplift sought to support independent (and largely bourgeois) Black political and economic activity—an aim furthered through middle-class histories of African American accomplishment. Turn-of-the-century self-help ideology often encouraged the assimilation of white ideas and values, prefiguring the assumption that the roots of racial (or any other) inequality lay less in structural and material disadvantage linked to capitalist exploitation than in the behavior, pathology, and cultural deficiency of the marginalized group in question. As Ibram X. Kendi asserts, this "uplift suasion," in which Black elites tended to police the "respectability" of the Black working class, was based on the problematic conviction that "every negro represented the race—and therefore that the behavior of every single Black person was partially (or totally) responsible for racist ideas."[91] One variant of this occurs in the pattern of white people turning individual African Americans into proxies for their entire race, which is one of the timeworn features of what Barbara J. Fields and Karen E. Fields term "racecraft."[92] For Wilson, the "phalanx" represented the race as a whole, and its feats were the achievements of all Black people, as well as testament to their worth.[93] That the "honor of the race" had been maintained by Black soldiers under every hardship and circumstance was evidence that Black people had earned equality.[94]

Steeped in masculinity tropes, *The Black Phalanx* proved a sweeping demonstration of race pride centered on cultural preservation and evincing the "honor" and "manhood" of the race.[95] Black Nationalism is a fluid concept, continuously refitted to suit contemporary needs.[96] As such, Wilson explored it as a means of reaffirming Black manhood in an era when Black men were increasingly subject to social and political emasculation through legal and extralegal violence, fraud, and coercion, as well as made "wage slaves" or "slaves by another name" (convict laborers) in the service of industrial mining, timber, and railroad profits. Touting the innate manhood of those now being exploited and debased in new and intricate ways, he contended that the "African race" was always particularly suited to warfare and "martial qualities," owing to a history of resistance.[97] "The Negro race . . . is the only race that has ever come into contact with the European race, and been able to withstand its atrocities and oppression," he explained. "All others, like the Indian . . . they have destroyed." Wilson avowed that the "American Negro," as "the only people able to cope with Anglo-American or Saxon, with any show of success, must be of *patient fortitude, progressive intelligence, brave in resentment and earnest in endeavor.*"[98] This particular fortitude, Wilson alleged, provided the bedrock of the success of African American soldiers.

Wilson combined his earlier calls for equal rights with racial uplift and self-help focused on notions of "civilization" and the "progress" of the race, or some version of what Manning Marable would later term the "capitalist road to Black liberation."[99] Such assumptions were influenced by utopian capitalist thinking, in which today's workers were tomorrow's owners (rather than a fixed and exploited class). They were also affected by Social Darwinism and eugenics, advocating as they did the separation of African Americans into superior and inferior classes and "an evolutionary view of cultural assimilation."[100] As Kevin K. Gaines illustrates, "Black elites claimed class distinctions, indeed, the very existence of a 'better class' of blacks, as evidence of what they called race progress."[101] Wilson's highlighting of the evolution, conduct, and pathology of the race, and his division of the world into "civilized" and "uncivilized" parts, tells a story about the 1860s, as well as the 1880s, and about the era's widespread belief that culture "reflected an individual's position in the class structure."[102] In one passage that rings particularly uncomfortably to modern ears, Wilson posited that while slavery had made African Americans pliable, docility was not their "natural" trait, and Black people could be "untrained" to be as active as other races who are "naturally quicker in temperament."[103] Here Wilson combined the moral urgency of rights language with assumptions regarding social rank that Kendi terms "class racism," or the belief—typically held by Black elites—that the long-term effects of white oppression had adversely affected the collective condition of nonelite Black people.[104]

*The Black Phalanx* concluded with an impassioned call for self-help. In one of its final passages, Wilson predicted, "In the time to come the race will take care of itself. Slavery is ended, and now they are striking off link by link the chains of ignorance which the servitude of some and the humility of all imposed upon them."[105] This was not simply a recitation of the meritocratic individualism of capitalism and white empire, as collectivism proved critical to the racial and ethnic self-help experience.[106] Nor did Wilson's Black Nationalism uphold group separatism as necessary owing to some ahistorical notion of the eternality and immutability of white supremacy. He was not a proto-Farrakhan. Rather, Wilson seemed to generally portray society as being in motion and often presented race as a historical phenomenon—if one undergirded by cultures of ritual and repetition—rather than an "external motor of history."[107] His position by 1882 combined race pride and uplift suasion, fusing greater cultural independence with social assimilation before the tightening legal and social constraints of Jim Crow. Wilson's self-help was also the product of an absence of other possibilities, espoused in replacement of and even *alongside* the equal-rights demands of the Black radical tradition.[108] Yet because they did not empower workers or threaten the basic hierarchy of either racial or class power, concepts of "self-improvement" and "respectability" would come to be supported by vast segments of the white community—first New South planters and industrial-era business elites who looked to maintain the profitability of the racial-labor hierarchy and later Movement Conservative and New Democratic leaders who highlighted African American "entrepreneurialism" as a substitute for large-scale redistributionist policies.

By the mid-1880s, Wilson was a fixture at Emancipation Day events in Virginia, where he linked the memory of the Civil War with a reinvigorated uplift politics.[109] Following Thomas Norris Jr.'s speech that highlighted racial "progress" indicators and urged African American men to vote their interests independent of white-controlled Democratic or Republican parties, Wilson prodded a Black crowd in Norfolk in 1885 to "unite and arise from the debris of slavery to the full enjoyment of manhood freedom."[110] Echoing John Mercer Langston and prefiguring Booker T. Washington, he espoused a brand of self-reliance, ostensibly pragmatic skills, and entrepreneurialism that had always existed in the free Black communities but was now reasserted in the face of interracial political collapse. Black poverty, Wilson suggested, was less a matter of racial capitalism, insufficient class-based interracial coalition building, or white reaction and violence than it was a failure on the part of Black people to adequately unify economically.[111]

Separatism was an understandable response to a hardening color line and the closing potential for a mass and interracial rights movement. African American business institutions often provided community-wide social services. Black economic solidarity bolstered a sense of community and frequently generated civil rights activism, especially when employed as an organizing tool (economic boycotts, etc.). Yet the entrepreneurial-consumer vision of Black owners employing upwardly mobile Black workers and serving a Black clientele through Black supply chains evaded questions about the social and legal fluidity of race (who is "Black" and who is not) and overestimated the efficacy—indeed, the very possibility—of economic segregation within an all-consuming and increasingly global capitalist market. Most critically, Wilson's model of a racially separate capitalism did not challenge the inequalities inherent to *all* capitalism. In measuring the "progress" of the race—the progress of the many—through the economic mobility of a few, it ignored the basic exploitation at the heart of owner-worker relations. It was, in other words, a social and economic philosophy that privileged the values and interests of the ownership class.

Wilson reiterated in prose form this combination of economic separatism, race pride, and rights claims. Written over the course of fifteen years and published in 1882, *Voice of a New Race* was a collection of poems and orations that nodded to Pan-Africanism and underscored manhood and dignity as claims to equality, capturing the zeitgeist of nominally free and aspirational African Americans in the postwar South. The freedom of the "NEW RACE" Wilson invoked was in part the freedom to express, mourn, demand, and self-determine. *Voice of a New Race* stressed mournful themes of requiem, solemn procession, and cities of the dead in order to venerate the military service of "Africa's noble sons" who had endured two and a half centuries of race-based slavery (which Wilson blamed upon both whites and "ignorant" Africans).[112] Although a stout defense of the Black past, Wilson's tracing of African and European history—"arts and sciences" flourishing in the Nile valley as "Saxon father, barbarians, were groping their way in ignorance"—also contained assessments of class and civilization that were quite expectedly influenced by prevailing white racial and cultural assumptions related to colonialism and capitalism.[113] While he continued to urge civil rights and racial equality, using the 1871 debates in Congress over Confederate amnesty and a federal civil rights bill to illustrate the eternal tension between "Democracy" and "Aristocracy," Wilson's suppositions about Black civilization and pathology—suppositions *informed by but not proportionate to* white capitalistic ideas regarding social merit, justified hierarchy, and Whiggish progress—betray the contradictions within self-help theory, the political limitations of the Black middle class, and the intellectual strains and philosophical incongruities inside Wilson's own political thought.[114]

In the wake of the Atlanta Compromise and preceding *Plessy v. Ferguson*, Wilson's death coincided with the codification of Jim Crow across the South. Once a stalwart Radical who had favored sweeping social and economic transformation, Wilson and other Black leaders turned ever more toward self-help after the collapse of Reconstruction and the capitulation of the Republican Party's small-producer ideal. White-on-Black political violence, abandonment by white allies, and the glaring inadequacy of civic rights devoid of economic radicalism in securing African American freedom surely led Wilson to his distrust of the sincerity, viability, or permanence of other interracial insurgencies (Readjusterism and, later, Populism) and reinforced his emergent "middleman" approach.[115] At the same time, increasing class stratification *within* the Black community further complicated the prospects of an insurgent Black working-class politics.

Market liberalism exposed—and still exposes today—the contradictions of capitalist democracy and the utter insufficiency of order, process, and legalism in either addressing how economic exploitation structures racial hierarchies or denting the material foundations of racial inequality in the United States. Yet Wilson and other "race men" were operating in a racially devolving political environment of unreliable allies and collapsing alternatives. Alongside political action, group solidarity, race consciousness, and so-called respectability, Wilson's 1882 writings contended that just as the phalanx had gained status through noble deeds, so, too, might future Black people. Those writings were also increasingly suggestive of ideas about social hierarchy and "civilization" common among the "Black bourgeoisie," sometimes contributing to notions of American exceptionalism.[116] Like white Grand Army of the Republic members who combined older millennial conceptions with newer Victorian social sensibilities, middle-class African American veterans often hawked a political vision through their memoirs, speeches, and institutions that attempted to satisfy both the memory of Reconstruction *and* the newer urgency of uplift suasion.[117]

Wilson's shift from direct confrontation to uplift—often pivoting between various messages—and his marrying of emancipationist memory and self-help reflected the multiformity of Black politics at the turn of the century, revealed the interplay and overlap between the Great Tradition and Black Nationalism, and betrayed how the popular writings of middle-class Black veterans both shaped and reflected broader social patterns during the high point of Civil War memoir. In this sense, Wilson was more than an ardent defender of the Black past and the legacy of African American veterans; he represented a transition in Black thought from the abolitionist tradition toward the self-reliance and Pan-Africanism that would crest in the "Booker T-ism" of the subsequent decade.[118] Promoting the exploits of Black soldiers—a "Black phalanx" that had earned social advancement through demonstrable bravery, manliness, and honor—was the ultimate synthesis of emancipationist memory and uplift suasion.

**Notes**

1. W. E. B. Du Bois, *Black Reconstruction in America, 1860–1880* (New York: Harcourt, Brace, and Co., 1935), 165, 289. Du Bois described the "abolition-democracy" as a vanguard of radicals and reform liberals, both wage earners and small-scale capitalists, who both identified slavery as a moral wrong and recognized the threat that slavery posed to both the labor movement and certain forms of capitalism ("free labor").

2. *Equal Suffrage: An Address from the Colored Citizens of Norfolk, Va., to the People of the United States. Also an Account of the Agitation of the Colored People of Virginia for Equal Rights. With an Appendix Concerning the Rights of Colored Witnesses before the State Courts* (New Bedford, MA: E. Anthony and Sons, 1865).

3. *True Southerner*, December 21, 1865; March 22, 1866.

4. John Hope Franklin, *George Washington Williams: A Biography* (Durham, NC: Duke University Press, 1998), 100–3; Kevin K. Gaines, *Uplifting the Race: Black Leadership, Politics, and Culture in the Twentieth Century* (Chapel Hill: University of North Carolina Press, 1996), 32. Gaines claims that Williams "glorified the egalitarian tradition of emancipation and radical Reconstruction" while also serving as a proponent of uplift. On uplift in the 1820s and 1830s, see Ibram X. Kendi, *Stamped from the Beginning: The Definitive History of Racist Ideas in America* (New York: Nation, 2016), 154–55.

5. Gaines, *Uplifting the Race*, xv. On uplift suasion, see Kendi, *Stamped from the Beginning*, 124, 294.

6. "'Civilization,' the Decline of Middle-Class Manliness, and Ida B. Wells's Anti-lynching Campaign (1892–94)," *Radical History Review* 52 (1992): 5–130.

7. *True Southerner*, November 24, 1865.

8. Cary D. Wintz, ed., *African American Political Thought, 1890–1930: Washington, Du Bois, Garvey, and Randolph* (New York: Routledge, 1996), 1–2. On the "Black radical tradition," see Gaye Theresa Johnson and Alex Lubin, eds., *The Futures of Black Radicalism* (New York: Verso, 2017), 141; Kendi, *Stamped from the Beginning*, 338–39, 508.

9. Gaines, *Uplifting the Race*, 2.

10. John A. Casey Jr., *New Men: Reconstructing the Image of the Veteran in Late-Nineteenth-Century American Literature and Culture* (New York: Fordham University Press, 2015), 131.

11. Bruce Levine, "In Search of a Usable Past: Black Confederates and Neo-Confederates," in *Slavery and Public History: The Tough Stuff of American Memory*, ed. James O. Horton and Lois E. Horton (Chapel Hill: University of North Carolina Press, 2006), 198.

12. Eric Foner, *Gateway to Freedom: The Hidden History of the Underground Railroad* (New York: Norton, 2015), 4; Adele Logan Alexander, *Homelands and Waterways: The American Journey of the Bond Family, 1846–1926* (New York: Vintage, 2000), 41, 125.

13. Pension Claim No. 78,530, Joseph T. Wilson, Fifty-Fourth Massachusetts Infantry, American Civil War, Record Group 15, National Archives and Records Administration, Washington, DC.

14. Joseph T. Wilson, *The Black Phalanx* (Hartford, CT: American Publishing Company, 1890), 63; Benjamin Quarles, *The Negro in the Civil War* (New York: Da Capo, 1953), 30–32.

15. Compiled military service record, Joseph T. Wilson, Private, Company G, Second Louisiana Infantry Native Guards, Carded Records Showing Military Service of Soldiers Who Fought in Volunteer Organizations during the American Civil War, compiled 1890–1912, Documenting the Period 1861–1866, Record Group 94, National Archives and Records Administration, Washington, DC.

16. Donald R. Schaffer, *After the Glory: The Struggles of Black Civil War Veterans* (Lawrence: University Press of Kansas, 2004); James Marten, *Sing Not War: The Lives of Union and Confederate Veterans in Gilded Age America* (Chapel Hill: University of North Carolina Press, 2011), 3.

17. Joseph T. Wilson, *Emancipation: Its Course and Progress, from 1481 B.C. to A.D. 1875, with a Review of President Lincoln's Proclamations, the XIII Amendment, and the Progress of the Freed People since Emancipation; with a History of the Emancipation Monument*, 2nd ed. (New York: Negro Universities Press, 1969), 138.

18. Wilson, *The Black Phalanx*, 264–65, 279, 286. On conservative popular opinion in London, see 394–96.

19. Timothy Messer-Kruse, *The Yankee International: Marxism and the American Reform Tradition* (Chapel Hill: University of North Carolina Press, 1998), 29.

20. Edna Greene Medford, "Land and Labor: The Quest for Black Economic Independence on Virginia's Lower Peninsula, 1865–1880," *Virginia Magazine of History and Biography* 100 (October 1992): 567–82.

21. Thomas C. Parramore, *Norfolk: The First Four Centuries* (Charlottesville: University of Virginia Press, 1994), 226–27. On the Union League, see Eric Foner, *Reconstruction: An Unfinished Revolution, 1863–1877* (New York: Harper & Row, 1988), 283–86; Michael Fitzgerald, *The Union League Movement in the Deep South: Politics and Agricultural Change during Reconstruction* (Baton Rouge: Louisiana State University Press, 1989); Richard Bailey, *Neither Carpetbaggers nor Scalawags: Black Officeholders during the Reconstruction of Alabama, 1867–1878* (Montgomery, AL: New South Books, 2010), 39–40.

22. General Affidavit of Thomas F. Paige, Pension Claim No. 78,530, Joseph T. Wilson, Private, Company C, Fifty-Fourth Massachusetts Infantry, Case Files of Approved Pension Applications of Veterans Who Fought in Volunteer Organizations during the American Civil War, Record Group 15, National Archives and Records Administration, Washington, DC.

23. *Equal Suffrage*, 3–4.

24. *Equal Suffrage*, 8–12.

25. University of Virginia, "Historical Census Browser," http://mapserver.lib.virginia.edu.

26. Workers of the Writers Program of the Work Projects Administration in the State of Virginia, *Virginia: A Guide to the Old Dominion* (New York: Oxford University Press, 1940), 136; Alexander, *Homelands and Waterways*, 161; I. Garland Penn, *The Afro-American Press and Its Editors* (Springfield, MA: Willey & Co., 1891), 174; Parramore, *Norfolk*, 227.

27. Donald Yacovone, ed., *Freedom's Journey: African American Voices of the Civil War* (Chicago: Lawrence Hill, 2004), 337; *True Southerner*, December 14, 1865.

28. George Rawick, "Working Class Self-Activity," *Radical America* 3 (March-April 1969): 23–31.

29. *True Southerner*, November 24, 1865.

30. *True Southerner*, January 4, 1866; Peter Rachleff, *Black Labor in Richmond, 1865–1890* (Urbana: University of Illinois Press, 1989), 38.

31. Kendi, *Stamped from the Beginning*, 503; Wilson, *The Black Phalanx*, 503.

32. Parramore, *Norfolk*, 236.

33. *True Southerner*, January 4, 1866.

34. *True Southerner*, November 24, 1865.

35. *True Southerner*, December 21, 1865.

36. *True Southerner*, December 7, 1865.

37. *True Southerner*, January 4, 18, 1866.

38. *True Southerner*, January 4, 11, 25, 1866.

39. *True Southerner*, January 11, 1866.

40. *True Southerner*, December 14, 1865.

41. *True Southerner*, November 24, 1865.

42. *True Southerner*, November 24, 1865.

43. *True Southerner*, March 22, 1866.

44. Alex Gourevitch, *From Slavery to the Cooperative Commonwealth: Labor and Republican Liberty in the Nineteenth Century* (New York: Cambridge University Press, 2015), 4; Steven Hahn, *A Nation without Borders: The United States and Its World in the Age of Civil Wars, 1830–1910* (New York: Viking, 2016), 289.

45. Hahn, *A Nation without Borders*, 289–91, 304.

46. Eric Foner, *Freedom's Lawmakers: A Directory of Black Officeholders during Reconstruction* (New York: Oxford University Press, 1993), 233–34.

47. Foner, *Reconstruction*, 106.

48. *True Southerner*, February 1, 1866.

49. *True Southerner*, December 21, 1865; January 18, 1866; February 1, 1866.

50. *True Southerner*, March 22, 1866.

51. Hahn, *A Nation without Borders*, 309; *True Southerner*, February 8 and January 11, 1866.

52. Kendi, *Stamped from the Beginning*, 231.

53. United States Census Bureau, "Population of the 100 Largest Urban Places: 1860," https://www.census.gov/population/www/documentation/twps0027/tab09.txt.

54. Yacovone, *Freedom's Journey*, 337; Penn, *The Afro-American Press and Its Editors*, 176.

55. Parramore, *Norfolk*, 224–26.

56. Patricia Hicken, "Henry Horatio Wells: The Rise and Fall of a Carpetbagger," *North Carolina Historical Review* 32 (January 1955): 52–80.

57. Parramore, *Norfolk*, 237.

58. Pippa Holloway, *Living in Infamy: Felon Disfranchisement and the History of American Citizenship* (New York: Oxford University Press, 2014), 73.

59. General Affidavit of W. F. Galt, Pension Claim No. 78,530.
60. Kirk Savage, *Standing Soldiers, Kneeling Slaves: Race, War, and Monument in Nineteenth-Century America* (Princeton, NJ: Princeton University Press, 1997), 89–128.
61. Wilson, *Emancipation*, 157–92.
62. Pension Claim No. 78,530.
63. Wilson, *The Black Phalanx*, 462.
64. Rachleff, *Black Labor*, 12.
65. Rachleff, *Black Labor*, 77–78, 168–69.
66. Rachleff, *Black Labor*, 94.
67. Wilson, *Emancipation*, 133.
68. Wilson, *The Black Phalanx*, 99–104.
69. Wilson, *Emancipation*, 62–64, 79–80, 44–45, 133.
70. James M. McPherson and William J. Cooper Jr., *Writing the Civil War: The Quest to Understand* (Columbia: University of South Carolina Press, 1998), 12.
71. William Blair, *Cities of the Dead: Contesting the Memory of the Civil War in the South, 1865–1914* (Chapel Hill: University of North Carolina Press, 2004), 141.
72. Wilson, *Emancipation*, 145–55.
73. Gaines, *Uplifting the Race*, 21.
74. Casey, *New Men*, 146; Wilson, *The Black Phalanx*, 462.
75. Gaines, *Uplifting the Race*, 4.
76. Gaines, *Uplifting the Race*, 227.
77. Wilson, *Emancipation*, 99–102; *The Black Phalanx*, 93–96.
78. Wilson, *Emancipation*, 106.
79. Wilson, *Emancipation*, 114, 121.
80. Wilson, *The Black Phalanx*, 200.
81. Philip S. Foner and George E. Walker, eds., *Proceedings of the Black National and State Conventions, 1865–1900* (Philadelphia: Temple University Press, 1986), 1:286. On the scholarly debate over Wilson's assertion, see Dudley Taylor Cornish, *The Sable Arm: Black Troops in the Union Army, 1861–1865* (Lawrence: University Press of Kansas, 1987), 288.
82. Cornish, *The Sable Arm*, xv.
83. Wilson, *The Black Phalanx*, 200.
84. Wilson, *The Black Phalanx*, 377–81, 460.
85. Wilson, *The Black Phalanx*, 220, 504.
86. William Wells Brown, *The Negro in the American Civil War* (Boston, 1867); George Washington Williams, *History of the Negro Race in America from 1619 to 1880* (New York: J. P. Putnam's Sons, 1883); George Washington Williams, *History of the Negro Troops in the War of the Rebellion, 1861–1865* (New York: Harper and Brothers, 1888); John Hope Franklin, *George Washington Williams: A Biography* (Chicago: University of Chicago Press, 1995); David Blight, *Race and Reunion: The Civil War in American Memory* (Cambridge, MA: Belknap, 2001).
87. Joseph T. Wilson, *The Black Phalanx*, 2nd ed. (New York: Arno, 1968), introduction.
88. Quarles, *The Negro in the Civil War*, 349–50.

89. Cornish, *The Sable Arm*, 317.
90. Rachleff, *Black Labor*, 94.
91. Kendi, *Stamped from the Beginning*, 373.
92. Karen E. Fields and Barbara J. Fields, *Racecraft: The Soul of Inequality in American Life* (New York: Verso, 2012), 279.
93. Wilson, *The Black Phalanx*, 219.
94. Wilson, *The Black Phalanx*, 88.
95. Wilson, *The Black Phalanx*, 25.
96. Gaines, *Uplifting the Race*, xvii. Gaines maintains that Black Nationalism tends to express "contemporary yearnings," including normative class assumptions and patriarchal gender relations. See also Sterling Stuckey, *The Ideological Origins of Black Nationalism* (New York: Beacon, 1972).
97. Wilson, *The Black Phalanx*, 108.
98. Wilson, *The Black Phalanx*, 96.
99. Manning Marable, *How Capitalism Underdeveloped Black America: Problems in Race, Political Economy, and Society* (Boston: South End, 1983), 227–28.
100. Wilson, *The Black Phalanx*, 289; Gaines, *Uplifting the Race*, 3. According to Gaines, emphasizing intraracial class difference was a critical aspect of racial uplift. On how capitalist logic grew within the Black middle class, see E. Franklin Frazier, *Black Bourgeoisie* (New York: Free Press, 1957), 37.
101. Gaines, *Uplifting the Race*, xiv.
102. Wilson, *The Black Phalanx*, 279; Marcus D. Pohlman, ed., *African American Political Thought*, vol. 4: *Capitalism vs. Collectivism: 1945 to the Present* (New York: Routledge, 2003), 296.
103. Wilson, *The Black Phalanx*, 420.
104. Kendi, *Stamped from the Beginning*, 155.
105. Wilson, *The Black Phalanx*, 462.
106. John Silbey Butler, *Entrepreneurship and Self-Help among Black Americans: A Reconsideration of Race and Economics* (Albany: State University of New York Press, 2005), 23–24.
107. Fields and Fields, *Racecraft*, 120.
108. Gaines, *Uplifting the Race*, xiv.
109. Blair, *Cities of the Dead*, 141.
110. Antoinette G. Van Zelm, "Virginia Women as Public Citizens: Emancipation Day Celebrations and Lost Cause Commemorations, 1863–1890," in *Negotiating Boundaries of Southern Womanhood: Dealing with the Powers That Be*, ed. Janet L. Coryell (Columbia: University of Missouri Press, 2000), 79.
111. Blair, *Cities of the Dead*, 141.
112. Joseph T. Wilson, *Voice of a New Race* (Hampton, VA: Normal School Steam Press, 1882), 36.
113. Wilson, *Voice of a New Race*, 36.
114. Wilson, *Voice of a New Race*, 13–22.
115. Butler, *Entrepreneurship and Self-Help*, 263.
116. Frazier, *Black Bourgeoisie*, 23–26.

117. Stuart McConnell, *Glorious Contentment: The Grand Army of the Republic, 1865–1900* (Chapel Hill: University of North Carolina Press, 1992), 237.

118. Even Frederick Douglass sensed the turning point in Black intellectualism, emphasizing internal economics and urging the creation and solidarity of "self-made men" of the Black race. Robert Jefferson Norrell, *Up from History: The Life of Booker T. Washington* (Cambridge, MA: Harvard University Press, 2009), 85.

# Fact, Fancy, and Nat Fuller's Feast in 1865 and 2015

*Ethan J. Kytle*

On April 19, 2015, eighty people gathered in Charleston, South Carolina, to recreate a remarkable feast held there 150 years earlier, in the final months of the Civil War. Shortly after the Union army occupied the city in early 1865, Nat Fuller—a recently emancipated Charlestonian and the city's leading chef and restaurateur in the late 1850s and 1860s—hosted what one local woman called "a miscegenation dinner." The elite resident complained to a friend that during that meal "blacks & whites sat on an equality, & gave toasts and sang songs for Lincoln & freedom."[1]

The 2015 reenactment of this meal, which has been dubbed "Nat Fuller's feast," was the capstone of Charleston's impressive commemoration of the 150th anniversary of the Civil War. The city's sesquicentennial had begun inauspiciously in December 2010, when Confederate enthusiasts paid homage to the state's decision to break away from the United States by throwing a much-maligned secession gala. Unlike that all-white affair, however, the bulk of the commemorative activities that followed over the next four and a half years were sober, reflective, and racially inclusive. Renowned scholars traveled to Charleston to deliver lectures on slavery, secession, the war years, and Reconstruction, while local groups marked the passing of key anniversaries, including the 1861 Confederate attack on Fort Sumter, Robert Smalls's dramatic 1862 escape, the 1863 assault on Battery Wagner, and the 1865 Decoration Day ceremony in what is now Hampton Park.[2]

The recreation of Nat Fuller's feast seemed to be an appropriate culmination of Charleston's Civil War sesquicentennial. It was the brainchild of the University of South Carolina scholar David S. Shields, who stumbled upon the story of the dinner while working on his 2015 book *Southern Provisions: The Creation and Revival of a Cuisine*. Shields immediately recognized the symbolic significance of a meal at which white and Black Americans broke bread together after a bloody war over slavery. "It's the first time an African-American has hosted (this kind of) mixed-race conversation," Shields later observed. "Here's a man who realizes that because of the abolition of slavery . . . there's going to be a new ground of social relations." What better way to mark the end of the Civil War anniversary commemoration, Shields and his collaborators asked, than by reenacting Nat Fuller's "hopeful act of racial reconciliation?"[3]

The commemorative feast was all the more fitting in light of Charleston's newfound reputation as a culinary hotspot. Since the early twentieth century, tourists have flocked to the city to gaze at its historic homes, wander its charming alleyways, and steal a glimpse of its beautiful gardens. But over the past decade, many visitors had also come to sample the shrimp and grits at Hominy Grill or the cornbread and pig's ear lettuce wraps at superstar chef Sean Brock's restaurant Husk.[4]

Having worked closely with local chefs, farmers, and scholars to help revive traditional Lowcountry cuisine, Shields enlisted Brock, the Culinary Institute of Charleston chef Kevin Mitchell, and the Gullah-Geechee specialist chef B. J. Dennis to recreate the 1865 dinner. Although the three culinary wizards were unable to locate the original bill of fare, they designed a menu based on Fuller's known repertoire of dishes and drinks. Mitchell agreed to play the role of the nineteenth-century master chef and host the event, while Dennis signed on to portray Fuller's protégé Tom R. Tulley. The College of Charleston historian Bernard E. Powers Jr. headed a committee that picked seventy-four guests for the feast—"a cross-section of modern Charleston in the religious, education, and government sectors" that, according to a press release, was chosen to mirror the diverse attendees of Fuller's 1865 dinner. Six additional guests were selected through an essay contest sponsored by the Charleston *Post and Courier*, which asked entrants to explain why they deserved a seat at the table, keeping in mind "the ideals of hospitality, culinary community and social justice embodied by Fuller and his feast."[5]

The festivities began at 6 PM with a cocktail reception at 103 Church Street, the former site of Fuller's acclaimed restaurant, the Bachelor's Retreat, which, Shields suspected, was the location of the 1865 meal.[6] A spring storm blew in just as guests arrived, but the weather didn't dampen the enthusiasm of the guests, who drank brandy smashes and persimmon beer and nibbled on benne tart shells with lobster salad and caviar, among other hors d'oeuvres. About an hour later, the celebrants walked a few blocks north and east in a procession led by a small contingent of Fifty-Fourth Massachusetts Infantry Regiment reenactors to McCrady's, the fine dining establishment that had put Sean Brock on the culinary map. There, in the second-floor Long Room, they enjoyed a lavish meal that included mock turtle soup, collard kraut, poached bass, squab with truffle sauce, and almond cake.[7]

At the end of the dinner, Shields invited the attendees to say a few words. Several offered toasts; one read a poem. Local historian Damon Fordham put the interracial dinner in the context of the recent murder of Walter Scott in North Charleston. "Nat Fuller said he wanted to have this dinner of reconciliation," Fordham remarked. "In light of the events of the past weeks, reconciliation is sorely needed in Charleston [today]."[8]

By all accounts, the reenactment was a resounding success, and it was widely publicized in local and regional newspapers, including the *Charlotte Observer* and the *Atlanta Journal-Constitution*. In conjunction with the event, the Lowcountry Digital History Initiative produced a polished online exhibition on Fuller's life and legacy, which included a biography of the chef written by Shields, accounts of the 1865 and 2015 feasts, and an interactive map of the locations in Charleston where Fuller lived and worked. Inspired by the story of Fuller's dinner, three other communities in South Carolina—Columbia, Greenville, and Clinton—hosted their own recreations.[9]

Nat Fuller's feast assumed even more meaning two months later, in the wake of the horrendous slaughter of nine African Americans at Emanuel African Methodist Episcopal Church in Charleston. One of those victims, Reverend Clementa C. Pinckney, had been among the eighty individuals who had come together to recreate the meal—a symbolic rejection, then and now, of the racial discord white supremacist murderer Dylann Roof hoped to sow. "Bringing people who were strangers of different racial and cultural backgrounds together at a common table has the power to lessen suspicion and enmity," insisted Shields after the shootings. "That was Nat Fuller's insight."[10]

But what if Nat Fuller's original reconciliation feast never actually happened?

I learned about the 1865 meal in late 2014, after the *Charleston Post and Courier* food critic Hanna Raskin wrote the first of a number of pieces on Fuller's feast.[11] I was immediately intrigued. My wife and colleague, Blain Roberts, and I were working on a book on the memory of slavery in Charleston. Fuller's reconciliation dinner seemed like it would be a great addition to our chapter on the emancipation celebrations staged by freedpeople and Union soldiers in 1865.

As I started to dig into the story, however, I was surprised to discover that there was not much evidence documenting the event. Indeed, all scholarly accounts of the 1865 meal—including three summaries that David Shields published in 2015, the year of the reenactment—can be traced to a single quotation found in Benjamin Quarles's 1953 classic *The Negro in the Civil War*. Describing the dramatically altered race relations in Charleston that followed the US army occupation of the city in early 1865, Quarles reproduced several lines from a letter written by a South Carolina woman he identified as Mrs. Frances J. Porcher. According to Quarles, Porcher told a friend that "Nat Fuller, a Negro caterer, provided munificently for a miscegenat [sic] dinner, at which blacks & whites sat on an equality, & gave toasts and sang songs for Lincoln & freedom."[12]

Unfortunately, Quarles employed neither footnotes nor endnotes in his study, and the book's bibliographic essay contains nothing that speaks to this letter or to Fuller's feast. But thanks to Google Books' search engine, I was able to track down the source of the Porcher quotation—the *Mason Smith Family Letters, 1860-1868*, an edited collection published in 1950—without too much difficulty. That book, in turn, led me to Porcher's original and complete letter, which is held in the manuscript collection of the South Caroliniana Library at the University of South Carolina in Columbia.[13]

Together, the original and published versions of the letter cleared up a number of questions I had about Fuller's feast and the woman who documented it. First, they revealed who Porcher, in fact, was. Quarles had attributed his Fuller quotation to Mrs. Frances J. Porcher, whom he described as a "white South Carolinian." But the header of the letter published in the *Mason Smith Family Letters* stipulated that it was written by Mrs. Franc*is* J. Porcher. Quarles had (perhaps inadvertently) altered the spelling of the author's first name from "Francis" to "Frances." As a result, Quarles—and all the scholars who relied on his account—mistakenly represented the letter as having been written by a woman named Frances J. Porcher, when it was actually written by Abby Louisa Porcher.[14] I subsequently learned that Abby Porcher was the wife of Francis James Porcher, a wealthy Charleston cotton and rice broker and Confederate officer who had signed the South Carolina Ordinance of Secession.[15]

Second, the two versions of the letter helped me narrow down when Fuller could have staged his feast. Although Quarles did not date the meal, David Shields claimed that it had taken place in late April 1865, the same month the 2015 reenactment was held. Yet Porcher's letter was dated March 29, 1865, indicating that the dinner could only have occurred between February 18, when the Union army occupied Charleston, and March 29. Third, and most significantly, the original and published versions revealed that Porcher had not written her letter from Charleston, after "having returned from her evacuation of the city," as Shields insisted. On the contrary, Porcher composed her missive in Greenville, South Carolina, where she had fled in 1862 with her mother, sister, and several other family members and where she remained until after the end of the war.[16]

The discovery of the letter's place of origin brought a new and more pressing question to the fore: How did a Confederate woman residing in Upcountry South Carolina—separated from Charleston by more than two hundred miles and a sizeable Union force—learn about Fuller's feast? Fortunately, Porcher's letter provided an answer to this new question, albeit a surprising one. Just a few lines before she mentioned the interracial dinner, Abby Porcher wrote, "We rarely see a paper except the Greenville Enterprise once a week, & sometimes an Augusta or Richmond paper of old date comes along." Secluded in the interior of a collapsing Confederacy, far behind Confederate lines, Porcher and her family struggled to keep up with developments in their hometown. "We are living in a strange way now," her mother, Caroline Gilman, had written from Greenville in late February or March. "Isolated, by the cutting off the R.R.s. we have only accidental communication with the outer world."[17]

The refugees' main source of news about life in Union-occupied Charleston, Porcher explained to her friend on March 29, was the *Greenville Enterprise* and the occasional newspaper published in Augusta or Richmond—Confederate cities that in late March 1865 had not yet fallen to the Union army. But even those southern papers, her letter suggested, did not have firsthand information about developments in Charleston. Instead, Confederate newspaper editors (and thus readers like Porcher) were forced to rely on the stories filed by northern correspondents in Charleston and published initially in northern or Unionist newspapers. "The Yankees['] accounts of the occupation of Charleston are so sickening to me," Porcher wrote, "yet there is a horrible sort of fascination in hearing about our dear old home, that impels one to read what they say." Next, she ticked off a list of disturbing tales of emancipated Charleston that captured her imagination, one of which was Fuller's feast:

> Gov Aiken is Provost Marshal, & I suppose has taken the oath. Laura Geddings is there, but her family can hear nothing from her. Nat Fuller provided munificently for a miscegenation dinner, at which blacks & whites sat on an equality, & gave toasts and sang songs for Lincoln & freedom. Miss Middleton & Miss Alston, young ladies of colour, presented a coloured regiment with a flag on the Citadel green, and nicely dressed black sentinels turn back white citizens, reprimanding them for their passes not being correct![18]

Unlike Quarles's short quotation, Porcher's full letter indicates that the Charleston lady had neither witnessed Nat Fuller's feast nor heard about it from someone who had. Instead, Porcher appears to have learned about it by reading a northern newspaper story that had been picked up and run by a Greenville, Richmond, or Augusta paper.

Could it be that the only shred of evidence we have to verify the much-celebrated meal is this third-hand account, a story gleaned from a story gleaned from a story written by one northern journalist? In a word, yes.

Charleston fell to the Union army on February 18, 1865. That day federal troops, most of whom were members of the Twenty-First United States Colored Infantry Regiment, marched into the bombed-out city where the Civil War had begun nearly four years earlier. Among the handful of journalists on hand to witness the historic occupation and the emancipation of Charleston's thousands of enslaved residents was *New-York Tribune* correspondent James Redpath. Over the next few months, the Scottish-born antislavery reporter documented the liberation of Charleston in a series of letters to the Republican daily under the penname "Berwick." Redpath's first dispatch was eight columns long and appeared in the *Tribune* on March 2.[19]

In this letter, Redpath chronicled myriad noteworthy events, including Black Charlestonians' enthusiastic reception of their African American liberators; northerners' pilgrimages to the holy sites of slavery, including John C. Calhoun's grave; and a grand dinner staged in honor of George Washington's birthday. According to the *Tribune* correspondent, that February 22 meal was held "at the house of a colored man" who was "noted . . . for being the chief of the class of caterers of Charleston." The host and caterer was Nat Fuller.[20]

We know very little about Fuller's early life. Born enslaved in 1812, he first appears in the written record in the 1850s working in Charleston's food service industry. Fuller landed what appears to have been one of his earliest catering gigs in 1853, providing "a sumptuous dinner" for the Moultrieville (today Sullivan's Island) town council's Palmetto Day celebration. "The table literally groaned with excellent and tempting viands and sparkled with choice wines," reported the *Charleston Courier* on June 23. "Mr. Nat Fuller was the caterer, a new hand at the bellows, but likely to prove an adept in business."[21]

The *Courier* was correct. Over the next few years, Fuller worked as a game vendor, importing turkeys, pheasants, green turtles, and venison for sale in Charleston's Fruit Market. But his main talent lay not in purveying food for other cooks to prepare but instead in preparing meals himself. By the end of the decade, Fuller had become the most accomplished caterer in the city, regularly staging the large banquets that were the mainstay of the profession there. The *New York World* proclaimed him Charleston's Delmonico in 1865. Almost a half-century later, the Charleston *News and Courier* noted that "the well-known negro caterer" had "kept a house of entertainment, which was a favorite resort during the fifties and up to the outbreak of the war with the gentlemen of the town who cared for a little cold bottle and a little hot bird." In the late 1850s and early 1860s, Fuller prepared banquets for the Medical Society of Charleston, the Society of Cincinnati, the Charleston Chamber of Commerce, the South Carolina Jockey Club, the St. Cecilia Society, and the Phoenix Fire Company, among many other groups. Francis J. Porcher was a member of these latter two organizations, and, as such, both he and his wife, Abby, were no doubt familiar with Fuller's formidable culinary skills.[22]

Surely some of Nat Fuller's distinguished clientele would have been surprised to learn that the man who hosted them—Charleston's top chef, as it were—was not a free man.[23] Yet most evidence suggests that Fuller did, in fact, remain legally enslaved up through the Civil War. By the mid-1850s, however, he lived as a de facto free person of color, a not uncommon state of affairs in antebellum Charleston. Faced with an 1820 law that prohibited private manumission in South Carolina—the measure stipulated that only the state legislature had the power to free an enslaved person—some bondpeople and slaveholders in the city forged creative workarounds. One means of circumventing the ban on manumission was trusteeship, a legal arrangement in which an enslaver sold a bondperson to a trustee or trustees, typically for a nominal sum of money, with the understanding that the enslaved individual was to be treated as if he or she were free.[24]

Nat Fuller, who was the trustee of a prominent Charleston businessman named William C. Gatewood, appears to have benefited from just this sort of arrangement.[25] Gatewood permitted Fuller to live separately with his wife, Diana Fuller, who was a pastry chef, and to operate his catering and food vending businesses on his own.[26] By 1860, Fuller had earned enough money through these ventures to make a $1,000 cash down payment on the building in which he opened his first restaurant, the Bachelor's Retreat. Since Fuller, as an enslaved man, could not legally acquire this property, Gatewood purchased it for Fuller as his trustee.[27]

Nat Fuller continued to live in virtual freedom and serve as Charleston's preeminent chef through the Civil War. Early on, he cooked at the Bachelor's Retreat, which was located at the corner of Church Street and St. Michael's Alley, in the heart of the city. By the end of 1863, Fuller had begun offering meals from his home at 25 Washington Street, between Charlotte and Calhoun Streets. This new establishment, which he named Nat Fuller's Eating House, was located near the city's northeastern railroad depot—and out of the range of Union artillery, which steadily bombarded lower portions of the peninsula in the latter stages of the war. On January 9, 1865, Fuller moved his restaurant next door on Washington Street to "a larger and more commodious house" that allowed him to better accommodate both diners and lodgers.[28]

Just one month later, as General William Tecumseh Sherman's army blazed a path through the South Carolina countryside, the Confederacy decided to abandon Charleston, bringing the Union's withering siege of the city to a close. Federal troops arrived on February 18. Four days later, on February 22, Fuller welcomed twenty gentlemen to his new Washington Street location to celebrate George Washington's birthday. The afternoon meal was arranged by Archibald Getty, a recently arrived Philadelphia merchant. Its guests included General J. D. Webster, chief of staff to William Tecumseh Sherman, as well as a number of other army and navy officers and northern merchants. Two Charleston Unionists joined them, as did three northern journalists—the *Boston Journal*'s Charles Coffin, the *Philadelphia Press*'s Kane O'Donnell, and James Redpath—each of whom subsequently published accounts of the meal. All of the attendees were white.[29]

Fuller treated his guests to a splendid affair, "probably the best that has been eaten in this lean and empty-bellied city since the blockade began," in Redpath's judgment. After dining on chicken, turkey, ham, rice, sweet potatoes, and apple pie, the guests offered "customary" toasts with glasses filled with champagne and "commissary wine." They paid respect to George Washington's memory, to the US army, and to Abraham Lincoln, reported Redpath. "Here, in the 'last ditch' of the Rebellion," one of the celebrants declared, "we love [Lincoln] for his fidelity, honor him for his integrity, and praise him for his steadfastness to our cause and principles." Toasts were offered to loyal southerners, to Black Union soldiers, and to the press. An army captain cheered peace, not the sort sought by Copperheads like New York Democrat Fernando Wood, he clarified, but "a peace founded on Liberty and Justice." Following the toasts, Redpath observed, the white guests were entertained by "a party of colored men" who performed "a comic song (of genuine negro humor)" and "a colored band," which "did credit to themselves as well as added much to the festivity of the assembly."[30]

Redpath sent his description of the Washington birthday celebration and of other moments from Charleston's liberation to the *New-York Tribune*, the most widely circulated newspaper in the country, which published them on Thursday, March 2. Similar accounts soon followed from Coffin and O'Donnell in the *Boston Journal* and the *Philadelphia Press*, helping disseminate news of the Washington birthday dinner—and the liberation of Charleston more generally—across much of the North. As was customary, especially for items published in the *Tribune*, a host of newspapers picked up and ran portions of Redpath's letter in the weeks that followed its initial appearance.[31]

By Tuesday, March 7, Redpath's dispatch had begun to make its way behind Confederate lines. That day, three newspapers in the Confederate capital—the *Richmond Dispatch*, the *Richmond Whig*, and the *Richmond Examiner*—published excerpts from it. All three papers offered healthy doses of negative commentary on the "moralizing" of the "crazy abolitionist correspondent" as well as much of Redpath's column itself. Neither the *Whig* nor the *Examiner* included Redpath's account of the Washington birthday dinner, but the *Dispatch*, which devoted three full columns to Redpath's letter, covered the feast at length. The Confederate paper featured a word-for-word rendition of the northern correspondent's description of the event, noting the renowned Black chef who had cooked the delectable meal, the toasts offered to Lincoln and liberty, and the song sung by a group of Black men.[32]

In the weeks that followed, Redpath's Charleston dispatch made its way deeper and deeper into what remained of the Confederate States of America. Between March 16 and March 29, portions of Redpath's letter appeared on the front pages of the *Yorkville Enquirer*, the *Augusta Constitutionalist*, and the *Edgefield Advertiser*. Although none of these newspapers included Redpath's account of the Washington birthday dinner, a newly founded paper produced in the South Carolina capital provided a short summary of the event that was drawn from Redpath's piece. "A letter in the New York *Tribune* shows the Abolitionists in Charleston to be in fine feather," declared the *Columbia Phoenix* on March 30. "They have had a dinner, provided by Nat Fuller, and drank to their own delight and to the confusion of the rest of the world."[33]

This *Columbia Phoenix* story bears a striking similarity to the tale of Fuller's feast penned by Abby Porcher just one day earlier and one hundred miles to the northwest. In Porcher's telling, Nat Fuller "provided" a "miscegenation dinner," in which white and Blacks ate together as equals and then toasted and sang songs for Lincoln and freedom. In the *Phoenix*'s telling, Fuller "provided" a "dinner" for "abolitionists"—inveterate supporters of miscegenation and social equality in the mind's eye of most white southerners—who then drank joyously. When you consider these stories' close resemblance alongside the fact that the *Phoenix* editors and Porcher each attributed their tale to a northern account of occupied Charleston, it seems clear that both parties were talking about the same Nat Fuller-hosted meal and were indebted to James Redpath's description of it.[34]

We cannot, however, trace Porcher's letter directly to the *Columbia Phoenix*, for the paper published its Fuller piece *after* the Charleston expat wrote her letter. The most likely scenario is that both the *Phoenix* editors and Porcher learned about the Washington birthday dinner from another southern newspaper that had reproduced Redpath's account, perhaps the *Richmond Dispatch* or the *Greenville Enterprise*. Porcher, after all, stated that she occasionally got her hands on "an Augusta or Richmond paper of old date," and the version of Redpath's story published by the *Richmond Dispatch* not only included a complete rendition of the Washington birthday dinner but also was entitled "A Yankee Picture of Charleston." Porcher may well have been echoing this title when she prefaced her discussion of Charleston's emancipation with the words: "The Yankees['] accounts of the occupation of Charleston." The other possibility is the *Greenville Enterprise*, which both Porcher and the *Columbia Phoenix* received. Unfortunately, there are no extant copies of the *Enterprise* from the spring of 1865. Regardless of the precise genealogy of either the *Phoenix*'s story or Porcher's, one thing appears certain: The Nat Fuller dinner described by Abby Porcher was, in fact, the Washington birthday celebration documented by James Redpath.[35]

But what of the toasts to and songs for Lincoln and freedom that Porcher mentioned? How did she get wind of them? Once again, the ultimate source seems to be James Redpath. Recall that the *New-York Tribune* correspondent reported that he and his fellow guests at the Washington birthday dinner gave a series of toasts, including those to Lincoln and liberty, and listened to a song performed by Black entertainers. Also recall that his account was subsequently reprinted in full in the *Richmond Dispatch* and that Richmond was one of three cities from which Porcher said she received newspapers.[36]

Other portions of Porcher's letter further demonstrate her debt to Redpath's reporting as well as to at least one other Unionist account that was reproduced in Confederate newspapers.[37] Porcher's assertion that "nicely dressed black sentinels turn back white citizens, reprimanding them for their passes not being correct" closely mirrored not only the sentiment but also some of the language employed in Redpath's initial *Tribune* column. "At every public building," wrote Redpath, "the tidy negro sentinels can be seen halting citizens, ordering them back, or examining their passes." This passage later appeared in the *Richmond Examiner* and *Richmond Dispatch*—the latter the same edition that included Redpath's account of the Washington birthday dinner. Porcher's story about Black women presenting a flag to an African American regiment on the Citadel Green, in turn, appeared in a handful of South Carolina and Georgia newspapers, including one from Augusta, another city from which Porcher said she received newspapers. Some of those papers attributed that anecdote to the *New-York Tribune*, others to the *Charleston Courier*, which by early March was in the hands of Unionist editors.[38]

Finally, Porcher's erroneous claims about former governor William Aiken—that he had been appointed provost marshal and had taken the oath of allegiance—seem to have been the result of jumbling together tidbits published in a variety of southern papers.[39] On March 6, the *Richmond Dispatch* printed a column titled the "Latest from the North," suggesting that Aiken was functioning in some official capacity in Charleston by helping distribute "supplies to the needy and destitute of the city." Five days later, the *New-York Tribune* printed a Redpath story stating that Aiken had been named a "first-class" Unionist by a group of "loyal" Charlestonians. On March 12, the *Augusta Chronicle* noted rumors out of Columbia that "Ex-Governor Aiken remained in Charleston, and has been made Mayor of the city by the Yankees." Reports of Aiken's role distributing food to the poor and his friendly relations with the occupying Union force eventually appeared in multiple southern newspapers. So, too, did stories asserting that "everybody [in Charleston] was to take the oath"—an act that, according to both Richmond and Augusta papers, was being administered at the office of the provost marshal. Aiken, in reality, had not yet taken the oath, and he never served as provost marshal in Charleston—a role focused on preserving law and order in occupied areas. Nevertheless, in light of the rampant speculation about the former governor's Unionist allegiances, his new role in postemancipation Charleston, and the duties of the provost marshal, it is easy to understand how Porcher might have gotten mixed up on these matters.[40]

Porcher's claims about Aiken were not, however, her only—or for the purposes of this chapter her most important—mistakes. Instead, her key error was mischaracterizing the Washington birthday celebration. After learning about that event from the *Richmond Dispatch* or another southern paper that printed portions of Redpath's letter, Porcher described it as "a miscegenation dinner, at which blacks & whites sat on an equality." Not a shred of evidence, however, supports this assertion. On the contrary, as all three firsthand witnesses to that February 22 meal—Coffin, O'Donnell, and Redpath—make clear, every one of Nat Fuller's nearly two dozen guests was white. The only African Americans that we know for sure were in the building that afternoon were the famed caterer, a group of singers, and a band.[41] Fuller's actual feast, in sum, was not a racial reconciliation dinner at all. Apart from the Unionist and emancipationist toasts, it was a rather typical Charleston affair in which a group of white gentlemen sat down to an elaborate meal cooked by a Black chef and then enjoyed the entertainment provided by Black performers.

How can we explain such a mistake? As with her misrepresentation of Aiken as provost marshal and her inaccurate supposition that he had taken the oath of allegiance, Porcher may have just been a careless reader. Or perhaps she was working from a fuzzy memory of the newspapers she had perused when Porcher finally put her pen to paper. Whatever the case, Porcher's characterization of Fuller's feast as a miscegenation dinner also betrays her fears about the post-emancipation breakdown of social barriers between whites and Blacks—fears she shared with much of the white South.

Terror gripped the Confederate citizenry as the Civil War ground to a halt in the first half of 1865. In June, white Charlestonians lobbied Union commanders in the city to shut down the Fourth of July celebration planned by Black residents because they believed that Lowcountry freedpeople planned "to rise in rebellion on the Fourth." This uprising, which tapped into the long-standing dread of slave rebellion, never materialized. Nevertheless, by the fall word had spread in sixty counties across the former Confederacy of a far more massive (though similarly fanciful) revolt planned for Christmas Day.[42]

Fear of servile insurrection was not the only thing that kept white southerners up at night. They were also haunted by the specter of race mixing and sexual violation—abominations that they were convinced would follow naturally with the end of slavery. On the eve of Abraham Lincoln's election in November 1860, one South Carolina congressman explained his recent conversion to the cause of secession as the result of his belief that Republican victory would bring "'negro equality,' 'final emancipation' & its logical results 'amalgamation.'" Such horrors loomed even larger as the close of the Civil War brought emancipation to cities like Charleston. Indeed, white South Carolinians' imaginations ran wild when they contemplated the "disgusting doings," in the words of one elite Charlestonian, in the cradle of secession.[43]

On March 18, 1865, Emma LeConte, of Columbia, South Carolina, noted in her journal that the residents of the state capital had received grim tidings from Charleston. "The city is garrisoned by negro troops who, unrestrained, perpetrate every barbarity, until at length their outrages reached such a pitch that their officers were obliged to interfere—thirty men were shot for violating women." The *Columbia Phoenix*, too, expressed concerns about race mixing in Charleston.

"Abolition there seems to be in full blast," reported the paper on March 21. "From the rumors which reach us, miscegenation is soon likely to follow, under the auspices of one of the Beecher family of the tender gender."[44]

Miscegenation—a new term for racial amalgamation that had been coined just the year before—was still on the *Phoenix* editors' minds a few weeks later, when they reproduced portions of James Redpath's account of the Washington birthday dinner.[45] In that column, the *Tribune* correspondent had also made reference to the beauty of Charleston's mulatto women, a comment that inspired a sardonic forecast from the *Phoenix*. It will not be long, predicted the paper, before the *Charleston Courier* will be filled with "the list of bridals between the two races, with copious detail of the marriage gifts, the *trousseau*, and full description of the costumes, *a l'Æthiopece et Barbarie*." A couple of months later, the *Phoenix* published a parody of a recent emancipation celebration in Charleston. "The whole affair terminat[ed] in a failure and Babel like confusion," claimed the author, "presenting a saturnalia or drunken fraternization between Yankee and negroes, never before exhibited to the world, and forming a reproach to a civilized community and a disgrace to the country."[46]

Anxiety about miscegenation in Charleston extended far beyond Columbia and lasted well into the fall. On March 26, the *Augusta Chronicle* reported that "Negro balls under the auspices of the military authorities who furnish guards for the occasion are advertised to take place nightly" in Charleston.[47] Five days later, Caroline R. Ravenel wrote from a plantation near Pendleton, South Carolina, that she had learned about a Charleston ball "at which the colored, Miss Susan Alston Pringle, Miss Adele Alston, etc., were the belles of the evening." "How does that make you feel, Belle?" Ravenel asked a friend. In October, Charlestonian Eliza Fludd told tall tales about the "outrages" that had taken place in her hometown since emancipation. "Mrs. Gen. Saxton goes to negro balls, and selects her partners for the dance from among the 'Gentlemen of color,' who form 'the sweaty throng,'" she insisted. "Mrs. Henry Ward Beecher, has a black officer or private in uniform to drive her out in a buggy every day with whom she chats and laughs in the most familiar manner." Just a few weeks earlier, the *New York World* had printed a story about a "most respectable colored man" in Charleston who challenged a white naval officer to what the paper styled a "miscegenation duel" after the latter had eloped with the former's daughter but returned to town without marrying her. That Black Charlestonian was supposedly Nat Fuller.[48]

Earlier in 1865, the refugee Emma Holmes wrote a telling summary of events in Charleston from her Upcountry refuge in Camden, South Carolina. Like Abby Porcher, Holmes kept track of developments in the occupied city by reading Yankee accounts in southern newspapers. In fact, four days after Porcher wrote about the Nat Fuller dinner, Holmes noted in her diary that she had gotten "hold of the last Camden *Journal*," which contained "extracts" from the *New-York Tribune* on the "doings in our beloved Charleston." Holmes's stories echoed Porcher's in numerous ways: She discussed "colored ladies" presenting "several flags," the provost marshal and oath-taking, and Black soldiers garrisoning the city and "insult[ing] the former masters by every petty way malignity can suggest." Holmes never mentioned Nat Fuller or his feast. But like Porcher and so many of their fellow white Carolinians, she could not stop thinking about the racial amalgamation that was sure to happen in emancipated Charleston. Even the idea of northern missionary work seemed suspect. "Yankee women are invited to hasten to come and enlighten the young ideas of Africa," she asserted, "no doubt with a similar result to their Beaufort experiment. O Heavens, the mind and heart sickens over the revolting thoughts—miscegenation in truth, & in our city!"[49]

Holmes's prediction that Yankee missionaries would soon go to bed with freedmen in Charleston, ultimately, was as groundless as the rest of the rumors and forecasts of racial amalgamation circulating across the southern countryside in 1865, including that of Nat Fuller's miscegenation feast. But collectively these falsehoods reveal an important truth about the South at the dawn of Reconstruction—a truth that highlights the real significance of Abby Porcher's Fuller story. Her March 29 letter did not document an extraordinary moment of interracial fellowship in the wake of a bloody civil war. Instead, it stands as evidence of the paranoia that plagued white southerners as they contemplated the end of slavery.

When I first began looking into Nat Fuller's feast, I had no intention of writing a chapter such as this one. My goal, instead, had been to learn more about the episode so that I might include it in the book on the memory of slavery in Charleston that I was coauthoring. What's more, like so many people who heard about the reconciliation dinner, I was enthralled. Abby Porcher's 1865 nightmare was our 2015 dream. I believed the story to be true. I still wish it were.

But, one might reasonably ask, who really cares that it is not? Put another way, why did I spend months chasing down and writing up the origin story of this unfounded rumor? After all, countless historical documents contain misrepresentations, half-truths, or outright falsehoods—none of which merit more than a footnote, if that.

Yet Nat Fuller's feast is more than just an inaccurate story buried in an old letter. And the 2015 reenactment turned it into something more than just evidence of Confederate fears about emancipation. The widespread interest in the story of Fuller's reconciliation feast generated by those recreations transformed the topic into something worthy of careful study and, as it turns out, refutation.

The popularity of Fuller's feast continued to grow after the 2015 reenactment. That fall, the online journal *Commonplace* published a roundtable on the (non)event and its very real reenactment. The story was subsequently featured in a Southern Foodways Alliance podcast. It also appeared in multiple books on southern food and culture as well as in lengthy pieces published by the *New Yorker* and the *New York Times*. In 2016, groups in New Orleans and Shreveport, Louisiana, staged reenactments inspired by the feast. The latter city hosted its second Reconciliation Dinner in February 2018.[50]

Meanwhile, between 2015 and 2018 Nat Fuller's feast also began to be incorporated into the historical narrative that Charlestonians share with the millions of people who visit "America's Most Historic City" each year. The itinerary for a March 2018 excursion to Charleston sponsored by the American Antiquarian Society, for example, included a talk on Nat Fuller by David Shields. And starting in 2017, Charleston visitors could also learn about Fuller and his famous meal from an hour-long walking-tour app. "Nat Fuller's Reconciliation Feast" featured narration by the chef Kevin Mitchell, who played Fuller at the 2015 reenactment in Charleston, as well as brief commentary by Shields. "At the start of Reconstruction, Nat used food as a way to bring people together," explained Mitchell early in the tour. "To transcend war and hatred and to gather them around a common table to break bread. . . . After two hundred years of African American bondage and suffering, what Nat did was truly revolutionary. It may have been just one meal, but that meal changed Charleston."[51]

Mitchell is wrong about the 1865 feast. It did not change Charleston one bit. The same, however, cannot be said about the 2015 reenactment, at least as of early 2018. Because of the reenactment and the interest it subsequently sparked, Nat Fuller's feast was by that point rapidly becoming part of the lore of the city, overshadowing the actual history of race relations in Charleston during Reconstruction and beyond, at least in the public eye. This was an unfortunate development. Although the city has long served as a mecca for historical tourism, Charleston tourism operators have tended to devote very little time to Black history or culture or to potentially controversial topics such as slavery and Reconstruction. The situation has begun to improve over the last few decades, but the city still has a long way to go toward fully and accurately remembering its past.[52]

Nat Fuller's feast, alas, does not help further this cause. I do not mean to suggest that we should ignore the story of the famed Black caterer. David Shields,

Kevin Mitchell, and others who have documented his pioneering exploits have done everyone interested in diversifying Charleston's historical memory a great service. But to continue to share the specious story of Fuller's reconciliation feast undercuts efforts to improve our understanding of the city's, and the nation's, past.

This was why I decided to go public with my research, reaching out to the Charleston *Post and Courier* food critic Hanna Raskin, who had covered the Nat Fuller reenactment for the paper, in the week leading up to the "Freedoms Gained and Lost" conference, at which I presented an early version of this essay. A few days before the conference opened on March 16, 2018, the *Post and Courier* published Raskin's column on my Fuller research as a front-page, feature story.[53]

Since I made my findings public in March 2018, it is worth noting that stories of the famed dinner have not circulated as widely in Charleston and beyond as they did in the three years following the 2015 reenactment. Although the tale continues to surface in print or digital publications on occasion, and at least one Charleston guide still recounts the tale on his tours, Nat Fuller's feast no longer appears destined to become a central feature in the city's public memory of Reconstruction or African American history more generally.[54]

In addition, David Shields now admits that Fuller's feast may not have happened the way he originally thought. As Raskin wrote in her 2018 story on the controversy, "Shields has conceded that his research was flawed," though he holds fast to the notion that Fuller hosted "a sit-down event where blacks and whites were together" at some point in early 1865. Shields no longer focuses on the feast he helped reenact—the banquet described by Abby Porcher—but rather on an alternative interracial meal (or meals) referenced in an unsourced newspaper clipping that someone emailed Shields after the 2015 event. It reads, "Charleston, March 12—The city's Black Boniface Nat Fuller reopened his old stand, the Bachelor's Retreat, and served gentlemen seated pell-mell with his colored brethren." Neither Shields nor I have been able to identify or date the newspaper that published this "squib," as he terms it, and Shields has not managed to reach the person who sent the clipping to him. Still, to Shields the squib is proof enough that Fuller forged "a new form of hospitality" in Charleston by seating Black and white diners alongside one another.[55]

This is certainly possible, but the extant evidence points to a different reading. On March 2, 1865, the *Charleston Courier* announced that "Nat Fuller, the well-known caterer . . . has resumed business at his old and well known stand, corner of Church Street and St. Michael's Alley, where he will be happy to meet and serve all who may favor him with a call." Shields's squib closely resembles this *Courier* notice, which was published at least ten days earlier and subsequently reproduced in other newspapers in South Carolina and Georgia. The squib's author appears to have made several minor alterations to the *Courier* text—substituting "Boniface," which was shorthand in the period for a hotel operator, for "caterer," "reopened" for "resumed," and "served gentlemen seated pell-mell with his colored brethren" for "serve all who may favor him with a call." Overall, though, the two pieces have similar wording, syntax, and content. When considered alongside the larger pattern of miscegenation rumors documented in this chapter, it is likely that the squib was the product of a southern newspaper editor who had read the *Courier* notice about Fuller's return to his old location and extrapolated what would happen when a newly freed caterer advertised that he was serving all comers. The idea that white and Black men dined together pell-mell at Fuller's restaurant, in short, appears to be yet another unsubstantiated story of life in emancipated Charleston rooted in southern white racial fear. That's not to say that it did not happen. But absent additional evidence, this alternative Fuller dinner is—like the feast reenacted in 2015—little more than unfounded speculation.[56]

It is worth remembering, too, that the sort of social integration Shields believes Fuller cultivated at his table was exceedingly rare, even in the postwar years that followed, when African Americans in South Carolina and elsewhere made significant political and legal strides. As the essays in *Freedoms Gained and Lost* illustrate, Reconstruction was characterized by remarkable racial progress in some realms but also by severe limitations on African American rights and opportunities in others. And one front upon which white Americans were unwilling to give any ground during and after Reconstruction was the racial segregation and exclusion that prevailed in dining rooms, eating houses, and similar public spaces. In the summer of 1866, for instance, Captain Campbell of the Shelton House, in Versailles, Kentucky, severely beat an African American man who had the temerity to sit down in the restaurant and order supper. White South Carolinians were also unwilling to serve Black customers or seat them alongside white ones, even after the state's Republican government outlawed discrimination in public accommodations and licensed businesses. Indeed, in the spring of 1870 seven Charleston restaurateurs were charged with violating the antidiscrimination act.[57]

African Americans' white Republican allies were only slightly more accommodating. After newly enfranchised Black men swept Republicans into office across South Carolina in 1868, white officials there "made no discrimination in their receptions, parties, balls, &c.," observed a *New York Times* correspondent called "Boise" in 1870. But after about a year, he added, "one by one the officials omitted to invite colored men and women, and now the races are separate." In an earlier column, Boise had noted that South Carolina governor Robert K. Scott chose not to invite a single African American person to the annual ball at the governor's mansion. Although the Pennsylvania-born Republican owed his office to the state's Black-majority electorate, he proved reluctant to challenge the racial mores of the day. Governor Scott "had not the courage to invite his colored friends to his entertainment," wrote Boise, much to the chagrin of Black South Carolinians and some of his fellow white Republicans. Ultimately, they pressured Scott into designating one night a week (Thursday) in which the governor's mansion would hold a reception open to all. The Thursday receptions seemed to be working "harmoniously," noted the *Times* correspondent, "except that scarcely any other than negroes are likely to pay their respects to the Governor."[58] During Reconstruction, in other words, Black South Carolinians were free, and African American men there and elsewhere had gained the right to vote. But those developments didn't mean that the state's white citizens, even Republican allies, were willing to drink, dine, or socialize with their Black neighbors.

Perhaps this was not the case at the Bachelor's Retreat. Perhaps Nat Fuller indeed created a space in which Black and white people came together to dine side by side. But if we are going to accept such a stunning claim—and to use it to recast what life was like in Reconstruction Charleston—we must insist on more evidence than an unverified squib, especially in the face of so much evidence to the contrary.

In the end, the story of Nat Fuller's racial reconciliation feast—whatever the iteration—does a disservice to the recovery of Charleston's African American history. In the process, it contributes to the general public's enduring ignorance of and misunderstandings about Reconstruction—shortcomings that this book aims to redress. The story, for one, belies the widespread resistance to social integration that persisted through the era. It also threatens to overshadow other examples of racial intolerance and discord, from the riot that erupted in Charleston on July 8, 1865, between white US soldiers, on the one hand, and Black soldiers and local freedpeople, on the other, to the white paranoia that gave birth to the idea that Nat Fuller hosted a miscegenation dinner in the first place. Third, Nat Fuller's feast eclipses *real* stories of progress during Reconstruction, including the biracial South Carolina constitutional convention that started at the Charleston Club House on January 14, 1868—an anniversary that passed without any public commemoration in Charleston in 2018.[59]

Finally, Nat Fuller's feast reinforces a paternalistic myth of interracial harmony that has thrived in Charleston since before the Civil War. This self-congratulatory tale has become even more prominent in the wake of the Emanuel African Methodist Episcopal Church massacre in 2015, to which residents—Black and white—responded with an admirable spirit of unity and forgiveness.[60] But such moments of genuine fellowship must not be used to paper over the racial inequities that have long plagued the city and persist to this day. Nor should they give license to swallow unproven feel-good stories like Nat Fuller's feast. As Charleston continues to mark the sesquicentennial of Reconstruction, the city must not linger on this fable of interracial bread-breaking, however comforting it is to us today, and instead focus on the postwar events that actually took place.

## Notes

1. [Abby] Louisa Porcher to Mrs. [William McKenzie] Parker, March 29, 1865, Smith Family Papers, South Caroliniana Library, University of South Carolina, Columbia (hereinafter SFPSC). An edited version of the letter can be found in Daniel E. Huger Smith, Alice R. Huger Smith, and Arney R. Childs, eds., *Mason Smith Family Letters, 1860–1868* (Columbia: University of South Carolina Press), 180–82.

2. On Charleston's Civil War sesquicentennial, see Ethan J. Kytle and Blain Roberts, *Denmark Vesey's Garden: Slavery and Memory in the Cradle of the Confederacy* (New York: New Press, 2018), 321–27.

3. Hanna Raskin, "Historian Releases Fuller Version of Nat Fuller Biography," Charleston *Post and Courier*, January 5, 2015, https://www.postandcourier.com/food/historian-releases-fuller-version-of-nat-fuller-biography/article_8c1f9669-0f18-52a4-be16-b0fe8435ef65.html; David S. Shields, "Nat Fuller's Feast," *Commonplace: The Journal of Early American Life* 15 (Summer 2015), http://common-place.org/book/nat-fullers-feast/; Kerry Diamond, "From Slave to Celebrated Chef: The Surprising Story of Nat Fuller," Yahoo.com, July 14, 2015, https://www.yahoo.com/lifestyle/from-slave-to-celebrated-chef-the-surprising-124093808331.html; David S. Shields, qtd. in Helen Schwab, "Feast Commemorates Nat Fuller: A Slave, a Star Chef, a Herald of Unity," *Charlotte Observer*, May 5, 2015, http://www.charlotteobserver.com/living/food-drink/article20275548.html; David Shields, "Charleston's First Top Chef," *Charleston Magazine*, December 2013, https://charlestonmag.com/features/charlestons_first_top_chefs; Nat Fuller Feast invitation, reproduced in David S. Shields and Kevin Mitchell, *Nat Fuller, 1822–1866: From Slavery to Artistry*, Special Collections, College of Charleston Library, College of Charleston, Charleston, SC (hereinafter SCCOC).

4. Kytle and Roberts, *Denmark Vesey's Garden*, esp. 167–95; Shields, "Charleston's First Top Chef"; Jane Mulkerrins, "A Food Revolution in Charleston, US," *Guardian*, October 12, 2012, https://www.theguardian.com/travel/2012/oct/11/charleston-food-gourmet-hotspot-barbecue.

5. Robert F. Moss, "The Nat Fuller Feast Opens a New Chapter in Charleston's Forgotten Culinary History," *Charleston City Paper*, April 29, 2015, https://www.charlestoncitypaper.com/charleston/the-nat-fuller-feast-opens-a-new-chapter-in-charlestons-forgotten-culinary-history/Content?oid=5142562; "Chef Kevin Mitchell to Channel Nat

Fuller in Re-Creation of 1865 Feast," *Cuisine Noir*, April 13, 2015, http://www.cuisinenoir mag.com/featured/chef-kevin-mitchell-to-channel-nat-fuller-in-re-creation-of-1865 -feast; Kinsey Gidick, "Historic Nat Fuller Dinner Menu Released," *Charleston City Paper*, March 19, 2015, https://www.charlestoncitypaper.com/Eat/archives/2015/03/19/ historic-nat-fuller-dinner-menu-released; Hanna Raskin, "Winners Chosen for Nat Fuller Dinner Essay Contest," Charleston *Post and Courier*, March 26, 2015, https://www .postandcourier.com/food/dinner-essay-contest-winners/article_cff38151-ac60-5a50 -8af9-fd66085fb4ed.html; Diamond, "From Slave to Celebrated Chef."

6. This building, located at the northwest corner of Church Street and St. Michael's Alley, was numbered 77 Church Street when Fuller operated it. See, for instance, advertisement, *Charleston Courier*, December 25, 1861, 2.

7. Moss, "The Nat Fuller Feast"; Schwab, "Feast Commemorates Nat Fuller"; Raskin, "Breaking Bread Together"; Nat Fuller Feast menu, reproduced in Shields and Mitchell, *Nat Fuller, 1822–1866*.

8. Raskin, "Breaking Bread Together"; Schwab, "Feast Commemorates Nat Fuller"; Damon Fordham, qtd. in John Kessler, "A Reconciliation Feast When City Needs It Most," *Atlanta Journal-Constitution*, April 25, 2015, http://www.myajc.com/news/state—regional/ reconciliation-feast-when-city-needs-most/riET2YdLvWHnqomwJXPZ9I/.

9. Raskin, "Breaking Bread Together"; Moss, "The Nat Fuller Feast"; Schwab, "Feast Commemorates Nat Fuller"; Kessler, "A Reconciliation Feast When City Needs It Most"; David S. Shields and Kevin Mitchell, "Nat Fuller's Feast: The Life and Legacy of an Enslaved Cook in Charleston," Low Country Digital History Initiative (hereinafter LDHI), April 2015, http://ldhi.library.cofc.edu/exhibits/show/nat_fuller. The LDHI exhibition was later revised to reflect some of my findings, such as Abby Louisa Porcher's authorship of the Fuller feast letter. "Nat Fuller Feasts in Columbia and Charleston Commemorate End of Civil War," *The State*, April 15, 2015, http://www.thestate.com/living/ article18515456.html; "Clinton's Nat Fuller Feast Demonstrates Racial Unity," GoLaurens .com, April 12, 1865, http://www.golaurens.com/news/item/20467-clinton-s-nat-fuller -feast-demonstrates-racial-unity.

10. David S. Shields, "Reflection," *Commonplace: The Journal of Early American Life* 15 (Summer 2015), http://common-place.org/book/reflection/.

11. Hanna Raskin, "Meal of History and Reconciliation," Charleston *Post and Courier*, December 23, 2014, https://www.postandcourier.com/food/meal-of-history-and -reconciliation/article_a2200b1e-fa8d-50a0-b90a-c2164f4fb285.html.

12. Benjamin Quarles, *The Negro in the Civil War* (Boston: Little, Brown, 1953), 329. For works that attribute some version of this quotation to Quarles's book, see Wilbert L. Jenkins, *Climbing Up to Glory: A Short History of African Americans during the Civil War* (Wilmington, DE: Scholarly Resources, 2002), 94, 245n66; David S. Shields, *Southern Provisions: The Creation and Revival of a Cuisine* (Chicago: University of Chicago Press, 2015), 125, 367n52; and David S. Shields, *The Culinarians: Lives and Careers from the First Age of Fine Dining* (Chicago: University of Chicago Press, 2017), 124, 131. For sources that attributed the quotation to Jenkins, *Climbing Up to Glory*, see Shields and Mitchell, *Nat Fuller, 1822–1866*, 3, 84n3; and Shields and Mitchell, "Nat Fuller's Feast," LDHI.

13. Quarles, *Negro in the Civil War*, 360; Porcher to Parker, March 29, 1865, in Huger Smith et al., eds., *Mason Smith Family Letters*, 180–82. The introduction to the *Mason Smith Family Letters*, which reproduced most, but not all, of Porcher's letter, explained that Alice R. H. Smith had deposited the original letters and typed copies of them at the South Caroliniana Library. I am grateful to South Caroliniana's librarian Graham Duncan, who helped me locate the original version of Porcher's letter. Arney R. Childs, introduction to Huger Smith et al., eds., *Mason Smith Family Letters*, xix. For the original, see Porcher to Parker, March 29, 1865, SFPSC.

14. This might have been a simple transcription error by Quarles. Or he may have overlooked the fact that married women were often identified by their husbands' names and thus made the change intentionally because "Frances" tends to be a female name and "Francis" a male name. Quarles also did not get Porcher's words quite right. For instance, he inserted the phrase "Negro caterer" into the quotation and transcribed "miscegenation" as "miscegenat." Quarles's description of Fuller was no doubt inspired by a footnote in the *Mason Smith Family Letters*, which described Fuller as "a well-known mulatto caterer." He also misspelled the name of a Black Charlestonian as "Middlen" rather than "Middleton." Quarles, *Negro in the Civil War*, 329; Porcher to Parker, March 29, 1865, in Huger Smith et al., eds., *Mason Smith Family Letters*, 181.

15. Arthur Gilman, *The Gilman Family: Traced in the Line of Hon. John Gilman of Exeter, N.H.* (Albany, NY: Joel Munsel, 1869), 191; "Francis James Porcher," in John Amasa May and Joan Reynolds Faunt, *South Carolina Secedes* (Columbia: University of South Carolina Press, 1960), 194.

16. Shields, "Nat Fuller's Feast"; Archie Vernon Huff Jr., *Greenville: The History of the City and County in the South Carolina Piedmont* (Columbia: University of South Carolina Press, 1995), 139–40; [Abby] Louisa Porcher to Anna Mason Smith, July 29, [1865], in Huger Smith et al., eds., *Mason Smith Family Letters*, 227–28.

17. Porcher to Parker, March 29, 1865, SFPSC; Caroline H. Gilman to Annie, n.d. [after February 17, 1865], Caroline H. Gilman Papers, South Carolina Historical Society, Charleston, SC (hereinafter SCHS). Gilman's undated letter mentions Sherman's army's occupation of Columbia, SC, which took place on February 17, 1865.

18. Porcher to Parker, March 29, 1865, SFPSC.

19. Berwick [James Redpath], "The Fall of Charleston," *New-York Tribune*, March 2, 1865, 1. On Redpath, see John R. McKivigan, *Forgotten Firebrand: James Redpath and the Making of Nineteenth-Century America* (Ithaca, NY: Cornell University Press, 2008).

20. Redpath, "Fall of Charleston." Although neither Redpath nor the other journalists who documented the feast explicitly named Fuller as the caterer in question, their accounts and other Fuller-related material collectively make it clear that he was the host. Redpath, "Fall of Charleston"; Kane O'Donnell, "Charleston," *Philadelphia Press*, March 3, 1865, 1; Charles Coffin, *The Boys of '61; Or, Four Years of Fighting* (Boston: Estes and Lauriat, 1844), 480.

21. South Carolina, Death Records, 1821–1965, for Nat Fuller, http://ancestry.com; "The 28th of June—Palmetto Day," *Charleston Courier*, June 23, 1853, 2.

22. Advertisements, *Charleston Courier*, January 18, 1854, 2; *Charleston Courier*, December 20, 1854, 3; *Charleston Courier*, June 12, 1855, 2; *Charleston Courier*, March 26,

1856, 2; "South Carolina," *New York World*, September 27, 1865, 8; "A Reminiscence of Timrod," Charleston *News and Courier*, December 20, 1903, 1. On catering in the nineteenth century, see Shields and Mitchell, *Nat Fuller, 1822–1866*, 38–40. "Medical Society," *Charleston Courier*, December 6, 1855, 2; "Cincinnati," *Charleston Courier*, February 23, 1857, 2; "Charleston Chamber of Commerce," *Charleston Mercury*, February 9, 1858, 2; "What We Are to Eat," *Charleston Courier*, January 19, 1857, 1; "The Phoenix Fire Company," *Charleston Mercury*, January 19, 1859, 2; "St. Cecilia Society," *Charleston Courier*, February 2, 1849, 3; "The Phoenix Fire Company," *Charleston Mercury*, January 19, 1859, 2.

23. The prominent role that Fuller played in Charleston's food scene in the late 1850s and early 1860s led several individuals at the time and later to mistakenly conclude that he was a free man. In 1859, Fuller appeared in *Charleston City Directory* as a free person of color, and a letter sent from Charleston the following year called the caterer a "free negro." A column published in the *New York World* in September 1865 claimed that Fuller had either been born free or manumitted before the war, calling him a "freeman not a freedman." Forty years later, the Charleston author John Bennett insisted that Fuller "was free," explaining that "he had bought himself from his master with his own earnings." Adding to the confusion about Fuller's status was the fact that in the 1850s and 1860s he paid both the city and the state annual capitation taxes, which were owed by free Black people of working age. It is likely that Fuller paid these taxes to reinforce the notion that he was a free man, since payment of these head taxes "had been accepted for decades as de facto proof of free status." *On the Eve of the Civil War: The Charleston SC Directories for the Years 1859 and 1860*, http://ancestry.com; "Charleston Correspondence," *Philadelphia Press*, April 23, 1860, 1; "South Carolina," *New York World*, September 27, 1865, 8; John Bennett, "'Slave Tags' for Tourists," *Charleston News and Courier*, May 3, 1903, 13; State Free Negro Capitation Tax Books, Charleston, SC, microfilm roll 2, 1855 and 1857, SCCOC; City of Charleston, Tax Book Free Persons of Color, 1862, 1863, 1864, microfilm roll 45/372, SCCOC; Bernard E. Powers Jr., email to Ethan J. Kytle, July 18, 2018; Michael P. Johnson and James L. Roark, eds., *No Chariot Down: Charleston's Free People of Color on the Eve of the Civil War* (Chapel Hill: University of North Carolina Press, 1984), 90n5.

24. Although the state legislature passed a law in 1841 that forbade the use of trusteeship to evade the emancipation prohibition, this practice continued through the Civil War. Bernard E. Powers Jr., *Black Charlestonians: A Social History, 1822–1885* (Fayetteville: University of Arkansas Press, 1994), 38–40; Marina Wikramanayake, *A World in Shadow: The Free Black in Antebellum South Carolina* (Columbia: University of South Carolina Press, 1973), 39–43; Larry Koger, *Black Slaveowners: Free Black Slave Masters in South Carolina, 1790–1860* (Jefferson, NC: McFarland, 1985), 45–68; Michael P. Johnson and James L. Roark, *Black Masters: A Free Family of Color in the Old South* (New York: Norton, 1984), 242; Johnson and Roark, eds., *No Chariot Down*, 90n5, 95–96n22.

25. "Death of William C. Gatewood," *Charleston Mercury*, February 28, 1861, 4; State of South Carolina, Charleston District, In Equity [1866]; Re Nathaniel Fuller v. Madeline M. Gatewood [1867], both in Fuller v. Gatewood Case Records, Simons & Simons Records, SCHS. David Shields concludes that Gatewood was not only Fuller's trustee but also his owner, but I have not been able to locate evidence to corroborate this claim.

Census records suggest that no enslaved person born in 1812, Fuller's birth year, was living in the Gatewood household in 1850 or 1860. In addition, Fuller's name does not appear on the list of eight slaves found in the official inventory of the estate Gatewood left after he died in 1861. Shields and Mitchell, *Nat Fuller, 1822–1866*, 6–7; *1850 US Federal Census—Slave Schedules*, http://ancestry.com; *1860 US Federal Census—Slave Schedules*, http://ancestry.com; Inventories, Appraisements, Sales, 1860–1864, vol. F, Charleston County, South Carolina Probate Records, Bound Volumes, 1671–1977, http://familysearch.org. I am grateful to Michael P. Johnson for alerting me to this last source.

26. State Free Negro Capitation Tax Books, Charleston, SC, microfilm roll 2, 1855 and 1857, SCCOC; advertisement, *Charleston Mercury*, January 2, 1860, 2.

27. Gatewood's widow testified in 1867 that all of the cash put down for this property was provided by Fuller, noting that her husband made the purchase for the Black caterer because "at that time" Fuller "was incapable in law of taking Estate in the said premises by reason that he was a slave." Re Nathaniel Fuller v. Madeline M. Gatewood [1867], Fuller v. Gatewood Case Records, Simons & Simons Records, SCHS.

28. "Notice," *Charleston Mercury*, October 9, 1860, 3; "Nat Fuller," *Charleston Mercury*, December 23, 1863, 2; "Good Cheer," *Charleston Mercury*, July 9, 1864, 2; "Turtle Soup and Wild Turkey," *Charleston Mercury*, September 9, 1864, 2; "Nat Fuller's Restaurant and Eating House," *Charleston Mercury*, January 11, 1865, 2. David Shields speculates that Fuller had been forced out of the Church Street location of the Bachelor's Retreat, observing that the property was put up for auction by its owner in March 1864. It is also possible that like many Charleston merchants and businessmen, he had decided to relocate north of Calhoun Street because of the Union bombardment. After all, just weeks after the Union army occupied Charleston, Fuller moved his business back to the Church Street location. Shields and Mitchell, *Nat Fuller, 1822–1866*, 47–49; "Estate Sale," *Charleston Mercury*, March 16, 1864, 2; Walter J. Fraser Jr., *Charleston! Charleston! The History of a Southern City* (Columbia: University of South Carolina Press, 1989), 264–67; "The Fuller House," *Charleston Courier*, March 2, 1865, 2.

29. Coffin, *The Boys of '61*, 480–81; O'Donnell, "Charleston"; Redpath, "Fall of Charleston." According to all of these accounts, the only African Americans on hand were those providing the meal and the entertainment.

30. Redpath, "Fall of Charleston." The description of the food consumed at the feast can be found in O'Donnell, "Charleston."

31. Adam-Max Tuchinsky, *Horace Greeley's New-York Tribune: Civil War–Era Socialism and the Crisis of Free Labor* (Ithaca, NY: Cornell University Press, 2009), 41; O'Donnell, "Charleston"; "Carleton" [Charles Coffin], "Occupation of Charleston," *Boston Journal*, reprinted in *Salem* (MA) *Register*, March 6, 1865, 2; "The Fall of Charleston," *Providence Evening Press*, March 3, 1865, 2; "The Fruits of Victory," *Illustrated New Age* (Philadelphia), March 7, 1865, 2; *Washington Evening Union*, March 7, 1865, 2; "Scenes in Charleston," *Xenia* (OH) *Sentinel*, March 17, 1865, 3; "Correspondence of the New York Tribune," *Ypsilanti* (MI) *Commercial*, March 31, 1865, 1.

32. No title, *Richmond Examiner*, March 7, 1865, 3; "From Charleston," *Richmond Whig*, March 7, 1865, 3; "A Yankee Picture of Charleston," *Richmond Dispatch*, March 7, 1865, 1–2.

33. "A Yankee Picture of Charleston," *Yorkville Advertiser*, March 16, 1865, 1; "A Live Yankee in Charleston," *Augusta Constitutionalist*, March 26, 1865, 1; "Latest from Charleston," *Edgefield Advertiser*, March 29, 1865, 1; "The Abolitionists in Charleston," *Columbia Phoenix*, March 30, 1865, 5. This *Phoenix* article is the only one I've located that names Fuller as the host of the Washington birthday meal. It is not clear how the *Phoenix* editors knew that Fuller had been the host for this feast, for Redpath never mentioned the chef by name. Perhaps, given their proximity to Charleston, they knew that he was "the chief of the class of caterers" in the city, in Redpath's words. Perhaps a Charlestonian who had relocated to Columbia after the evacuation of their hometown made the connection for them. (The same issue of the *Phoenix*, for example, reported that the "proprietor" of the *Charleston Mercury* now resided in Columbia, where he was planning to resume the publication of the firebrand paper.) Or perhaps they had picked up the *Tribune* story from another southern paper that had made the Fuller connection. "Charleston Mercury," *Columbia Phoenix*, March 30, 1865, 5.

34. Porcher to Parker, March 29, 1865, SFPSC; "The Abolitionists in Charleston." On white southerners' ideas about abolitionists and racial amalgamation, see Charles Dew, *Apostles of Disunion: Southern Secession Commissioners and the Causes of the Civil War* (Charlottesville: University of Virginia Press, 2002), esp. 55–58, 71, 79–81.

35. "A Yankee Picture of Charleston," *Richmond Dispatch*; Porcher to Parker, March 29, 1865, SFPSC; "Greenville Enterprise," *Columbia Phoenix*, June 21, 1865, 2. Although several issues of the *Augusta Daily Constitutionalist* included extracts from Redpath's Charleston dispatches, I have not located one that referenced the Washington Birthday dinner in the *Constitutionalist* or any other paper produced in Augusta. "From Charleston," *Augusta Daily Constitutionalist*, March 24, 1865, 3; "A Live Yankee in Charleston," *Augusta Daily Constitutionalist*, March 26, 1865, 1.

36. "A Yankee Picture of Charleston," *Richmond Dispatch*.

37. The exception to this rule is Porcher's comment that Laura Geddings was in Charleston, "but her family can hear nothing from her," which surely was an anecdote that came directly or indirectly from the Geddings family. Porcher to Parker, March 29, 1865, SFPSC.

38. Porcher to Parker, March 29, 1865, SFPSC; "A Yankee Picture of Charleston," *Richmond Dispatch*; No title, *Richmond Examiner*, March 7, 1865, 3; "From Charleston," *Augusta Daily Constitutionalist*; "The Courier Under Yankee Rule," *Tri-Weekly* (Newberry, SC) *Herald*, March 21, 1865, 1; "Latest from Charleston," *Tri-Weekly Herald*, March 23, 1865, 1. For the original versions, see "Presentation of a Stand of Colors," *Charleston Courier*, March 3, 1865, 1; and James Redpath, "From South Carolina," *New-York Tribune*, March 11, 1865, 1. None of these papers, it should be noted, said anything about "Miss Middleton" or "Miss Alston," the two "young ladies of colour" mentioned in Porcher's letter.

39. A *New York Times* article published on May 2, 1865, exposes the inaccuracy of these claims, reporting that on April 26 Aiken was arrested by the provost marshal in Charleston and conveyed to Washington, DC, because he refused "to take the oath of allegiance." "Our Charleston Correspondence," *New York Times*, May 2, 1865, 5.

40. "Latest from the North," *Richmond Dispatch*, March 6, 1865, 2; James Redpath, "From South Carolina," *New-York Tribune*, March 11, 1865, 1. I have not been able to locate

a southern newspaper that reprinted Redpath's anecdote about Aiken. "From Columbia," *Augusta Chronicle*, March 12, 1865, 1; "Latest from Charleston," *Tri-Weekly Herald*, March 23, 1865, 1; "Later from Charleston," *Augusta Daily Constitutionalist*, March 25, 1865, 3; "Interesting from the West," *Tri-Weekly Herald*, March 28, 1865, 1; "The Provost-Marshal's Office," *New York World*, March 2, 1865, 5. On the role of provost marshals during the Civil War, see Christopher Phillips, *The Civil War in the Border South* (Santa Barbara, CA: Praeger, 2013), 37–38. "From Charleston," *Augusta Chronicle*, March 10, 1865, 3; "Another Scene from the Performance in Charleston," *Richmond Dispatch*, March 14, 1865, 1; "From Charleston!," *Augusta Constitutionalist*, March 9, 1865, 3. The *Richmond Dispatch* story was written by James Redpath and published first in the *New-York Tribune*. James Redpath, "From South Carolina," *New-York Tribune*, March 10, 1865, 1.

41. See Coffin, *The Boys of '61*, 480–81; O'Donnell, "Charleston"; and Redpath, "Fall of Charleston."

42. "General Hatch Again," *National Anti-Slavery Standard*, July 28, 1865, 3; Dan T. Carter, "The Anatomy Fear: The Christmas Day Insurrection Scare of 1865," *Journal of Southern History* 42 (August 1976): 354–64; Leon F. Litwack, *Been in the Storm So Long: The Aftermath of Slavery* (New York: Random House, 1979), 426–30; Steven Hahn, "'Extravagant Expectations' of Freedom: Rumour, Political Struggle, and the Christmas Insurrection Scare of 1865 in the American South," *Past and Present* 157 (November 1997): 122–58. Hahn also documents concomitant rumors among freedpeople that mass land redistribution would take place over the Christmas holiday.

43. John Durant Ashmore, quoted in Charles B. Dew, "Lincoln, the Collapse of Deep South Moderation, and the Triumph of Secession: A South Carolina Congressman's Moment of Truth," in *Secession as an International Phenomenon: From America's Civil War to Contemporary Separatist Movements*, ed. Don H. Doyle (Athens: University of Georgia Press, 2010), 107; Eliza B. Fludd to [Mrs. Jolliffe], October 24, 1865, Eliza Burden Fludd Papers, Rubenstein Library, Duke University, Durham, NC.

44. Emma LeConte, diary, March 18, 1865, in *When the World Ended: The Diary of Emma LeConte*, ed. Earl Schenck Miers (1957; Lincoln: University of Nebraska Press, 1987), 80; "Favors," *Columbia Phoenix*, March 21, 1865, 6. The Beecher in question was probably Colonel James C. Beecher's wife, Frances, who had been announced as acting principal of the newly opened and interracial Morris Street School. "The Schools," *Charleston Courier*, March 14, 1865, 2.

45. Two editors from the Democratic *New York World* newspaper coined the term "miscegenation" in their 1864 hoax pamphlet, which aimed to undermine Abraham Lincoln's reelection campaign by falsely portraying Republicans as proponents of race mixing. The new term soon supplanted "amalgamation" as the most common way to refer to interracial relations. Alex Lubin, *Romance and Rights: The Politics of Interracial Intimacy, 1845–1954* (Jackson: University of Mississippi Press, 2005), 7–8; Mark E. Neely Jr., *Lincoln and the Democrats: The Politics of Opposition in the Civil War* (New York: Cambridge University Press, 2017), 107–9.

46. "The Abolitionists in Charleston." Portions of this story were reprinted in the *Tri-Weekly Herald*, April 4, 1865, 1. "Charleston—Burial of Slavery," W. H. S. to Editor, *Columbia Phoenix*, n.d, *Columbia Phoenix*, May 10, 1865, 3.

47. "Press Agents Dispatch," *Augusta Chronicle*, March 26, 1865, 3. This article was reprinted as "Interesting from the West," *Tri-Weekly Herald*, March 28, 1865, 1.

48. Caroline R. Ravenel to Isabella Middleton Smith, March 31, [1865], Huger Smith et al., eds., *Mason Smith Family Letters*, 187–88; Fludd to Jolliffe, October 24, 1865. Fludd likely confused Mrs. Henry Ward Beecher for her sister-in-law, Frances Beecher, who spent time in Charleston in 1865 because her husband, James C. Beecher, was a Union officer assigned to the area. "The Schools," *Charleston Courier*, March 14, 1865, 2; "Memorial-Day Texts and Suggestions," *Homiletic Review* 39 (May 1900): 431; Leslie A. Schwalm, *A Hard Fight for We: Women's Transition from Slavery to Freedom in South Carolina* (Urbana: University of Illinois Press, 1997), 169–70; "South Carolina," *New York World*, September 27, 1865, 8.

49. Emma Holmes, diary, April 2, 1865, in *The Diary of Miss Emma Holmes, 1861–1866*, ed. John F. Marszalek (Baton Rouge: Louisiana State University Press, 1979), 429–30.

50. *Commonplace: The Journal of Early American Life* 15 (Summer 2015), http://common-place.org/book/issue/vol-15-no-4/; Tina Antolini, "A Charleston Feast for Reconciliation," Southern Foodways Alliance, June 17, 2016, https://www.southernfoodways.org/a-charleston-feast-for-reconciliation/; Ashli Quesinberry Stokes and Wendy Atkins-Sayre, *Consuming Identity: The Role of Food in Redefining the South* (Jackson: University Press of Mississippi, 2016), 200–3; Michael Twitty, *The Cooking Gene: A Journey through African American Culinary History in the Old South* (New York: Harper Collins, 2017), 256–57, 324; Lauren Collins, "America's Most Political Food," *New Yorker*, April 24, 2017, https://www.newyorker.com/magazine/2017/04/24/americas-most-political-food; Ron Stodghill, "In Charleston, Coming to Terms with the Past," *New York Times*, November 15, 2016, https://www.nytimes.com/2016/11/20/travel/charleston-south-carolina-past-slave-trade-history.html; Ann Maloney, *New Orleans Times-Picayune*, October 17, 2016, http://www.nola.com/food/index.ssf/2016/10/leah_chase_honored_documentary.html; "See Who's Invited to Reconciliation Dinner of Shreveport," *Shreveport Times*, August 3, 2016, http://www.shreveporttimes.com/story/life/community/2016/08/03/see-whos-invited-reconciliation-dinner-shreveport/88033792/; "Nominations Open for Reconciliation Dinner Hosted by Centenary College," *Centenary College News*, November 21, 2017, https://www.centenary.edu/news-media/story/nominations-open-for-2018-shreveport-reconciliation-dinner-hosted-by-centenary-college/; Reconciliation Dinner Shreveport Program, February 24, 2018, http://www.reconciliationshreveport.com/wp/wp-content/uploads/2018/05/Reconciliation-Dinner-Program-2018.pdf.

51. Mayor Thomas Stoney claimed that Charleston was "America's Most Historic City" in 1924, and the city continues to lay claim to this title today. Kytle and Roberts, *Denmark Vesey's Garden*, 180; "Excursion to Charleston," http://www.americanantiquarian.org/excursion-charleston-0; Hanna Raskin, "Following in Nat Fuller's Footsteps with Detour and Kevin Mitchell," Charleston *Post and Courier*, June 5, 2017, https://www.postandcourier.com/blog/raskin_around/following-in-nat-fuller-s-footsteps-with-detour-and-chef/article_96791b48-4649-11e7-97c8-f71536216945.html; "Downtown: Nat Fuller's Reconciliation Feast," Detour app, https://www.detour.com/charleston/breaking-bread. This tour became unavailable in mid-2018 when Detour, the company that produced it,

was purchased by Bose. At the time of the purchase Bose announced that it was "actively looking for a partner to host the Detour content," but as of July 2021 there was no sign that a new host has been secured. Sarah Perez, "Bose Acquires Andrew Mason's Walking Tour Startup, Detour," *TechCrunch*, April 24, 2018, https://techcrunch.com/2018/04/24/bose-acquires-andrew-masons-walking-tour-startup-detour/.

52. See Kytle and Roberts, *Denmark Vesey's Garden*, esp. 167–349.

53. Hanna Raskin, "Expert: 1865 Meal to Unite Blacks, Whites Likely Myth," Charleston *Post and Courier*, March 13, 2018, https://www.postandcourier.com/food/expert-meal-to-unite-blacks-whites-likely-myth/article_7c1d2ab8-21a5-11e8-8cea-239d19b2fce6.html. I had previously shared my research with David Shields and the LDHI's co-director, Mary Battle, in 2015. Ethan J. Kytle, email messages to David Shields, July 27, 2015 (2 messages); September 2, 2015; September 14, 2015; Ethan J. Kytle, email messages to Mary Battle, September 1, 2015; October 23, 2015.

54. "Celebrating Black History Month," February 3, 2020, https://blog.eatclub.com/influential-african-american-chefs; review of Undiscovered Charleston tours, https://www.tripadvisor.com/Attraction_Review-g54171-d17735805-Reviews-or10-Undiscovered_Charleston-Charleston_South_Carolina.html. It is not clear precisely what caused Fuller's feast to fade in popularity over the past few years. While Raskin's front-page article in the *Post and Courier* likely had something to do with it, the change may also reflect recent developments in Charleston's culinary scene, including the closure and sale of McCrady's Tavern, which included the Long Room that hosted the 2015 reenactment. Hanna Raskin to Ethan J. Kytle, email message, September 1, 2020.

55. Raskin, "Expert"; David Shields to Ethan J. Kytle, email message, March 13, 2018.

56. "The Fuller House." For reproductions of the *Courier* notice, see "From Charleston!," *Augusta Constitutionalist*, March 9, 1865, 3; and "From Charleston," *Edgefield Advertiser*, March 15, 1865, 2. For other examples of the use of the term "Boniface," see "A Governor's Hotel Bill," *Manufacturers' and Farmers' Journal*, May 17, 1855, 1; and "Snubbed," *New York Herald*, June 22, 1869, 6.

57. Aaron Astor, *Rebels on the Border: Civil War, Emancipation, and the Reconstruction of Kentucky and Missouri* (Baton Rouge: Louisiana State University Press, 2012), 139; Eric Foner, *Reconstruction: America's Unfinished Revolution, 1863–1877* (New York: Harper and Row, 1988), 370–71; Joel Williamson, *After Slavery: The Negro in South Carolina during Reconstruction, 1861–1877* (1963; Hanover, NH: Wesleyan University Press/University Press of New England, 1990), 286–87.

58. *New York Times*, January 25, 1870, 2; *New York Times*, February 6, 1869, 2; Peggy Lamson, *The Glorious Failure: Black Congressmen Robert Brown Elliot and the Reconstruction in South Carolina* (New York: Norton, 1973), 108–9.

59. A historical marker commemorating this event was unveiled two months later, in March 2018, during the "Freedoms Gained and Lost: Reinterpreting Reconstruction in the Atlantic World" conference that helped generate the essays published in this book.

60. Stephen O'Neill, "From the Shadow of Slavery: The Civil Rights Years in Charleston," PhD diss., University of Virginia, 1994, esp. 6–143; Steven Estes, *Charleston in Black and White: Race Relations and Power in the South after the Civil Rights Movement* (Chapel Hill: University of North Carolina Press, 2015), 15–17; David Remnick,

"Blood at the Root," *New Yorker*, September 28, 2015, https://www.newyorker.com/magazine/2015/09/28/blood-at-the-root; Abigail Darlington, Paul Bowers, and Derrek Asberry, "Charleston Strong: A Rallying Cry in a Time of Mourning," Charleston *Post and Courier*, June 17, 2016, https://www.postandcourier.com/archives/charleston-strong-a-rallying-cry-in-a-time-of-mourning/article_6523db63-66cd-577a-a73b-7c3def9badoc.html.

# Acknowledgments

This book is the product of so many people we hesitate to try to thank anyone lest we miss someone. But an attempt must be made, so we apologize to anyone we forget.

Our chief debt is to the contributors, whose research and writing we are proud to showcase here. We are especially grateful to our authors for the efficiency and readiness with which they responded to suggestions for revision.

*Freedoms Gained and Lost* would not have happened without the Carolina Lowcountry and Atlantic World Program at the College of Charleston, which was the lead sponsor of the 2018 conference that led to this volume. The conference attracted forty amazing historians ranging from graduate students to leading scholars in the field and ran as a kind of seminar, allowing for fruitful critique and suggestions. It was a model of scholarly collaboration.

This book is better because of the participation of Alison McLetchie, Vernon Burton, Thavolia Glymph, James Oakes, Heather Cox Richardson, Brian Kelly, Bernie Powers, Nicole Turner, Jason Young, Blain Roberts, Joseph Rizzo, Sarah Gardner, Kathryn Dungy, H. Paul Thompson, Warren Milteer Jr., David Gleeson, Fionnghuala Sweeney, John Bardes, Blake Scott, Julia Eichelberger, Pippa Holloway, Rachel Donaldson, Urshula Barbour, Deloris Pringle, Melissa Ooten, Amanda Bellows, Rebecca Shumway, Niels Eichhorn, John Quist, Jonathan Daniel Wells, Wallis Tinnie, Angela Riotto, Bruce Cole, Lady Cole, Jon Hale, Edwin Breeden, Michael Allen, Eric Foner, Kate Masur, Billy Keyserling, Samuel Flores, Alton Barber, Jennifer Kosmin, Rodell Lawrence, and Michael Boulware Moore, among others.

On the organizational front, numerous people ensured that the 2018 conference went off without a hitch. Those providing key administrative and logistical support include Sandy Slater, Carl Wise, Scott Teodorski, Alexandra Bauer, Lauren Nivens, Ehren Foley, Edward Breeden, Bambi Downs, Andrea Evans, and Jillian Clayton, among others. Dean John White as well as the College of Charleston's library and facilities staff made sure things went smoothly, and Charleston lived up to its reputation of hospitality. The College of Charleston administration and faculty, especially the Department of History, wholeheartedly supported the conference, and a platoon of volunteers ensured it ran smoothly. Our thanks go to Colby Causey, Cory Bradley, Emily Jaskwhich, Jamie Rardin, Susannah Haury, Ashley Hollinshead, Lacie Rinehart, Jamie Mansbridge, Grace Hall, Greg Garvan, and Zalirah Cooper.

Beyond the confines of the seminar rooms and lecture halls, two additional elements significantly broadened the conference's reach and influence. Aaisha Haykal of the Avery Research Center for African American History and Culture and Mary Jo Fairchild of the College of Charleston's Addlestone Library created a beautifully curated exhibition informed by cultural heritage objects from repositories across the South and showcasing the documentary heritage of Reconstruction and the postemancipation era in South Carolina and the Atlantic world. (The exhibition is digitally archived at https://speccoll.cofc.edu/freedoms-gained-and-lost/.)

The conference began with the unveiling of a historical marker commemorating the 1868 South Carolina Constitutional Convention. Edwin Breeden had worked closely with the South Carolina Department of Archives and History and City of Charleston authorities. Anyone who has had experience working on such public memorials knows how much effort and commitment goes into their creation.

Working with Fordham University Press has been a delight. Andrew Slap and Fredric Nachbaur made this process as smooth as imaginable. Given the circumstances of the pandemic through which we have all been living, that is no small achievement. We are grateful, too, to the anonymous peer reviewers for the generous-hearted, constructive critique that allowed us to make significant improvements to individual essays and to the volume as a whole.

Finally, we must thank Janet, Megan, Zoë, Oliver, Jennifer, Lexi, and the rest of our families for supporting us throughout this process.

# Contributors

**Bruce E. Baker** is Reader in American History at Newcastle University. He is the author of *What Reconstruction Meant: Historical Memory in the American South* (2007) and co-editor of *After Slavery: Race, Labor, and Citizenship in the Reconstruction South* (2013); he has also written several other books and articles covering Reconstruction, labor history, lynching, and the cotton trade.

**Adam H. Domby** is an Associate Professor of History at Auburn University, having previously worked at the College of Charleston. He is the author of *The False Cause: Fraud, Fabrication, and White Supremacy in Confederate Memory*. In 2018, he won the John T. Hubble Prize for the best article in *Civil War History*. He received his PhD from the University of North Carolina at Chapel Hill.

**Don H. Doyle** is Emeritus Professor of History at the University of South Carolina. He is known for his numerous books, including *Faulkner's County: The Historical Roots of Yoknapatawpha* and *The Cause of All Nations: An International History of the American Civil War*. He is currently working on an international history of Reconstruction.

**Brian K. Fennessy** received his PhD in history from the University of North Carolina at Chapel Hill and is now a visiting assistant professor at the University of Richmond. His current project is on former Confederates who joined the Republican Party during Reconstruction.

**Michael W. Fitzgerald** is Professor of History at St. Olaf College. He is the author of *The Union League Movement in the Deep South*, *Urban Emancipation: Popular Politics in Reconstruction Mobile*, *Splendid Failure*, and, most recently, *Reconstruction in Alabama* (2017).

**Hilary N. Green** is an Associate Professor of History in the Department of Gender and Race Studies at the University of Alabama. She is the author of *Educational Reconstruction: African American Schools in the Urban South, 1865–1890* (2016) as well as articles, book chapters, and other scholarly publications.

**Ethan J. Kytle** is Professor of History at California State University, Fresno. His latest book, coauthored with Blain Roberts, is *Denmark Vesey's Garden: Slavery and Memory in the Cradle of the Confederacy* (2018). Dr. Kytle's work has also appeared in the *Journal of Southern History*, *American Nineteenth-Century History*, the *New York Times*, the *Atlantic*, the *Washington Post*, and the *Oxford American*.

**Simon Lewis** has been teaching African and Third World Literature at the College of Charleston since 1996. A former long-time director of the Carolina Lowcountry and Atlantic World (CLAW) program at the College, Dr. Lewis is the coeditor of three volumes of essays in USC Press's Carolina Lowcountry and Atlantic World series: *The Fruits of Exile: Central European Intellectual Immigration to America in the Age of Fascism*, *Ambiguous Anniversary: The Bicentennial of the International Slave Trade Bans*, and *The Civil War as Global Conflict: Transnational Meanings of the American Civil War*. He is also the author of two monographs on African literature and numerous refereed articles primarily on South African writers. He was recognized in 2021 with a Governor's Award in the Humanities from South Carolina.

**Holly A. Pinheiro, Jr.** is Assistant Professor of African American history in the History Department at Furman University. He has published articles in *Jeronimo Zurita* and the *Journal of American Nineteenth-Century History*. He is currently finalizing his monograph *The Families' Civil War: Northern African American Soldiers and The Fight for Racial Justice*.

**Sergio Pinto-Handler** holds a PhD in Latin American History from Stony Brook University. His research examines abolitionism in nineteenth-century Rio de Janeiro. He is currently a Visiting Assistant Professor of History at St. Olaf College.

**Shannon M. Smith** is Associate Professor of History at the College of Saint Benedict and Saint John's University in Minnesota, where she teaches courses on the Civil War and Reconstruction in American culture, gender and race in US history, and protest and rebellion. She holds a PhD from Indiana University and a master's degree from the University of Nevada, Reno.

**Felicity Turner** is currently Associate Professor of History at Georgia Southern University; she received her PhD in history from Duke University in 2010. Her research has been supported by postdoctoral fellowships from the Maurer School of Law, Indiana University, Bloomington; the University of Wisconsin Law School; and the United States Studies Centre at the University of Sydney, Australia.

**Samuel Watts** is a PhD candidate and teaching associate at the University of Melbourne. He is currently completing a dissertation entitled "No Masters but Ourselves: Black Reconstruction in the Deep South City," and his research focuses on the politics of race, gender, and everyday spaces in the nineteenth-century American South. He is the cofounder of *ANZASA Online*, a blog dedicated to highlighting new research in American history, culture, and politics.

# Index

Abbott, Richard H., 177n4
abolition, US Civil War and, 196, 209n38
abolition-democracy, 249, 270n1
abolitionists, 117n24, 229n1. *See also* Rio de Janeiro, abolitionists and Reconstruction in
Aboriginal peoples, 240
activism, 36n53; Alabama public schools and, 48–49; civil rights, 2, 23; civil rights and Black, 101–2; intimidation and, 108–9; social equality, postwar aspirations and, 12, 250, 253–61
Adams-Onis Treaty (1819), 53n5
Afghanistan, 244–45
African Americans: without guarantee of freedoms, 4, 43, 98, 101; population in South Carolina, 212; slavery and mental competency of, 126–27. *See also* bodies, Black; police officers, African American; slavery; women, Black
*After Appomattox* (Downs), 30
"After Slavery" project, 21
AGE, 218, 220
*Agricultura nacional—estudos economicos* (Rebouças), 222–23, 224
agriculture: FTA-CIO, 26; the Grange and, 82, 87, 224; production, 217–18; racism and, 82–84, 91–92; reform, 225; without slavery, 222–23
Aiken, William, 280, 286–87, 299nn39,40
A. J. Lamoureux & Co, 222
Akerman, Amos, 171, 174
Alabama: *Black Prisoners and Their World, Alabama, 1865–1900*, 95n30; Colored Mass Convention of the State of Alabama, 39–40; *Reconstruction in Alabama*, 94n26; voters registered in, 45; West-Central, 79–80. *See also* public schools, in Alabama; self-defense, racial empowerment and
*Alabama* Claims, 193, 201
Alabama Constitution (1868), 40, 42
Alabama Constitutional Convention (1867), 41–42, 45, 46
Alaska, 183, 193
Alcorn, James Lusk, 172
Alfonso (King of Spain), 193–94
Alfred, John, 170
Allen, James M., 29
Allen, William H., 190
Alley, James, 107, 108, 110
Alston, Adele, 280, 288, 299n38
amalgamation, with emancipation, 287. *See also* miscegenation
American Medical Association, 123
American Missionary Association, 40, 46–49, 51
*American Sentinel* (newspaper), 250
"America's Most Historic City," Charleston as, 301n51
amnesty, reconstructed rebels and: Amnesty Act and, 160, 161, 171, 173–75; citizenship and, 160, 172, 175–76; Democrats against, 165–66; Enforcement Act and, 171–72; Fourteenth Amendment and, 160–62, 167–71, 175–76; political ambitions and, 160, 162–66; selective, 172–73; social networks and petitions for, 166–69; Southern white elite empowered by, 169–71; support for, 11, 159–60
Amnesty Act (1872), 160, 161, 171, 173–75
Antoine, C. C., 60
apartheid, 233, 242

Aptheker, Herbert, 262
Army, US: in Charleston, 278–79, 281; federal bounties and pay frequency, 145–47, 150, 152–53; in Kentucky, 99–103, 106, 112; with racism, 145–47, 151–53; USCT, 10–11, 143–54
arrests: of DeSaussure, William, 64–70; KKK, 89; of Officier Fédéral, 61–64; records, 60, 72n33
Asians, 7, 176, 196
assassinations, 84, 88, 89, 95n40, 196, 216. *See also* murders
Atlanta Exposition Address (1895), 51
*Atlanta Journal-Constitution* (newspaper), 278
*The Atlantic* (magazine), 6, 21
*Augusta Chronicle* (newspaper), 286, 288
*Augusta Constitutionalist* (newspaper), 284
*Augusta Daily Constitutionalist* (newspaper), 299nn35,38
Australia, 233, 239, 240, 241
Austria, 192

Babbitt, Bruce, 18
Bachelor's Retreat restaurant, 277, 282, 291, 293, 295n6, 298n28
Badger, Algernon, 68
badges: police, 67, 69, 75n80; slave, 66–67
Baggett, James, 162, 166
Baker, Bruce, 14n1, 20, 32n1, 244
Ball, Thomas, 260
Ball, W. W., 28
Ballard, Bland, 111–12
Barber, William, 22–23
Barnes, Jake, 22
Battle, Mary, 302n53
Bayne, Thomas, 253
Beck, James, 174
Beecher, Frances, 300n44, 301n48
Beecher, Henry Ward (Mrs.), 288, 301n48
Beecher, James C., 300n44
Bennett, John, 297n23
Berry, Lawrence S., 39, 43

Biden, Joseph R., Jr., 7
Bigelow, John, 187, 191, 192
Billings, Walter P., 83, 88, 94n26
Bingham, John, 163
*The Birth of a Nation* (film), 234, 239
*Black America* (Clowes), 237
*Black and White in the Southern States* (Evans, M. S.), 242
Black Codes, 64, 255
Black Decree, 192
Black Nationalism, 252, 265–67, 269, 274n96
*The Black Phalanx* (Wilson, J. T.), 12, 249, 263–66, 269–70
*Black Prisoners and Their World, Alabama, 1865–1900* (Curtin), 95n30
Black radical tradition, 251
*Black Reconstruction in America, 1860–1880* (Du Bois), 238–39, 270n1
Blair, Frank, 174
Blair, Henry, 50, 51
Blair Education Bill, 48, 50, 51
Blight, David, 30, 239–40, 264
*Blyew v. United States*, 101–2, 115n14
Bocaiuva, Quintino, 226
bodies, Black: criminalization of, 131; racism and medicalization of, 127–28, 131–32; regulation of, 61, 68, 152; slave badges and, 66–67; war, racism and, 153. *See also* lynchings
bodies, white armed, 84
Boer War, 242
Boise (reporter), 292–93
Bolivia, 193
Booth, John Wilkes, 182, 187
Bose, 301n51
*Boston Journal* (newspaper), 283
Bradford, C. A., 41
Bradley, Joseph P., 115n14
Brant, Charles, 152, 157n59
Brazil, 185, 212, 213, 229nn7,14, 239. *See also* Rio de Janeiro, abolitionists and Reconstruction in
Brock, John C., 146

INDEX  311

Brock, Sean, 277
Brooks, James, 165
Brown, John, 264
Brown, Joseph E., 163, 165, 172, 173
Brown, William Wells, 249, 264, 265
Brundage, W. Fitzhugh, 40
Bryant, Lawrence, C., 27
Buck, Alfred E., 41
Buckley, Charles W., 41
Burritt, Loren, 152
Burton, Vernon, 20, 24
Butler, William F., 101, 262
Butler Emigration Bill, 51

Cailloux, Andre, 264
Caldwell, Tod, 168–69
Calhoun, John C., 128, 281
Campbell (Captain), 292
Canada, 182–84, 192–93, 205, 238, 239, 244
canes, 67–68
CAPS. *See* Community Action Programs, War on Poverty
Carney, William H., 264
Carolina Lowcountry and Atlantic World (CLAW), 1, 8, 14n1, 16n27
carpetbaggers, 20, 60, 222, 235, 238–39, 244–45, 260
Carr, Julian S., 234–36, 237, 238, 242, 244
Carraway, John, 41, 42
Carter, Dan, 20, 33n17
Cartwright, Samuel, 127
Casey, John A., Jr., 251
Castelar, Emilio, 203–4
Celia (enslaved woman), 138n2
Census, US, 93n6, 100, 128, 145
"A Century of Lawmaking for a New Nation," 21
Céspedes, Carlos Manuel de, 197–98
Champion, Justin, 30
Charleston, North Carolina: as "America's Most Historic City," 301n51; as historically separate from South, 58; sonic texture of, 68; US Army in, 278–79, 281

*Charleston City Directory*, 297n23
*Charleston Courier* (newspaper), 281, 286, 288, 291–92
*Charleston Daily News* (newspaper), 64
*Charleston News and Courier* (newspaper), 28, 282
Charleston Police Department, 71n10; African Americans in, 58–60, 64–65, 68–69; with arrest of DeSaussure, William, 64–70; arrest records, 60, 72n33; with metal badges, 67, 75n80
Charleston *Post and Courier* (newspaper), 277, 278, 291
*Charlotte Observer* (newspaper), 278
children: Creoles of Color, 42; infanticide, 121, 130–37; slavery and, 215
Chile, 182, 193
Chincha Islands War, 193
Chinese Exclusion Act, 176
Choctaw County, 85, 93n4, 94n26
*Christian Recorder* (newspaper), 146–47, 150
"Chronicling America," 21
*Cidade do Rio* (newspaper), 227
*Cincinnati Commercial Tribune* (newspaper), 105
*Cincinnati Gazette* (newspaper), 106, 107
citizens: ideal, 138n3; militia, 198
citizenship: with amnesty for reconstructed rebels, 160, 172, 175–76; freedom and, 3, 40; race and, 6; veteran rights and, 101, 112
*Citizens United v. Federal Election Commission*, 24
civil rights: without federal judicial intervention, 9–10, 98–99, 102, 111–12; social equality, postwar aspirations and, 254–55
Civil Rights Act (1866): Black activism and, 101–2; Black testimony without, 9–10, 98–99, 102, 111–12; lynching trial, 107–12; terrorism and, 102–12
Civil Rights Act (1964), 23

civil rights movement (Second Reconstruction), 22; activism, 2, 23; CAPS, 25; erosion of, 24; "for those who hope," 8, 17; historians and, 18, 30–31; legislation, 7, 83; Penn Center and, 24–25; as Radicals' Reconstruction, 17, 25–27; ratification process and, 41; Reconstruction influencing, 24–25; Southern Popular Front and, 25, 26
Civil War, US: abolition influenced by, 196, 209n38; democracy and, 183–84; pensions, 145, 151–52; with USCT and loss of freedom, 153–54
Clarke County, 85, 93n4, 94n26
class: racial hierarchy and, 257; racism, 266. *See also* elites
Claver, Pedro, 215
CLAW (Carolina Lowcountry and Atlantic World), 1, 8, 14n1, 16n27
Clinton, Bill, 18, 22
Clinton, De Witt, 263
Clinton, Hillary, 5–6, 244
Clowes, William Laird, 236–37, 240, 242, 244, 246n18
Coates, Ta-Nahisi, 6, 7
Coffin, Charles, 283, 286
Cole, Charles W., 149, 150
Colored Mass Convention of the State of Alabama (1867), 39–40, 41
*Columbia Phoenix* (newspaper), 284, 285, 287–88
Columbia University, 17
commemorative spaces, 18–19
*Commonplace* (journal), 290
Community Action Programs (CAPS), War on Poverty, 25
Confederates: monuments, 232, 235, 245; Sons of Confederate Veterans, 1; Unionists with disenfranchisement of ex-, 177n3, 179n30. *See also* neo-Confederates
congressional amnesty, 28
constitutional convention in New Orleans (1866), 58–59, 63

"The Conversation" blog, 21
Corley, Simeon, 28
correctional colonies, 227
Corwin, Arthur, 209n38
court system: civil rights without federal intervention, 9–10, 98–99, 102, 110–12; infanticide and, 130–37; mental competency, gender and race with, 129–37; US Supreme Court, 7, 24, 68–69, 101–2, 268; white supremacy and, 107–8, 110–11, 131–33, 137–38; women convicted by juries, 138n2. *See also* infanticide
Cox, Hannah, 134
Cox, Neri, 121
Cox, Samuel, 186
Creoles, 47, 53n5, 61–62, 169, 184, 195, 197
Creoles of Color, 40–46, 48–50, 53n5
Crittenden, John A., 108, 111
Crittenden, Richard, 107, 108, 110–13, 118n32
Crosby, Peter, 69
Crummell, Alexander, 251
Cuba, 183, 184, 213, 251; with citizen militia, 198; Guáimaro Assembly and, 198–200, 203; Liberation Army and, 197–98; Lincoln and, 195–96, 197, 205; slavery and, 194–200, 203, 209n38; Spain and, 197–98, 202–5; US and, 194–95, 200–4, 209n38, 243
Cummings, Kate, 57
Curtin, Mary Ellen, 95n30

*Daily Eagle* (newspaper), 240
Dantas, Manuel, 224–25
Davis, Henry Winter, 186
Davis, Jefferson, 227
Dawes, Henry, 159–60, 164
Dawes Act, 240–41
*Declarations of Dependence* (Downs), 30
Delany, Martin, 262, 264
delegates, racial makeup of, 41
De Lhuys, Drouyn, 192
demobilization, of USCT, 150–53

democracy: abolition-democracy and Du Bois, 249, 270n1; rural, 212, 214–15, 218–19, 223–28; US Civil War and, 183–84

Democrats, 95nn28,40, 234; with elections and state violence, 96–99, 104–5; with electoral fraud, 95n48; against public schools, 44; against reconstructed rebels, 165–66; South Carolina Progressive Democratic Party, 26; with voting, 89, 91

Denmark Vesey Conspiracy, 1–2

Dennis, B. J., 277

DeSaussure, Louis, 66

DeSaussure, William, 64–70

Desdunes, Rodolphe, 68

desegregation, education, 19

De Souza, Ennes, 226

De Souza, Paulino, 227

Desverney, Frank, 65

Detour, 301n51

Dew, Warren, 84, 86, 88–89, 92–93, 94n26

Digital History Initiative, 278

digital technologies, 18, 21

Dill, Solomon, 28

*Diseases of the Mind* (Rush), 123

disenfranchisement, of ex-Confederates, 177n3, 179n30

Domby, Adam, 12, 19, 213, 179n30

Dominican Republic, 182, 183, 193

Douglass, Frederick, 251, 259, 262, 275n118

Downs, Greg, P., 3, 7, 29–30

Doyle, Arthur Conan, 238, 246n25

Drane, George, 97

drapetomania (running away), 127

*Dred Scott* decision, 7, 175

Du Bois, W. E. B., 7, 21–22, 30, 258, 262; on abolition-democracy, 249, 270n1; *Black Reconstruction in America, 1860–1880*, 238–39, 270n1; on freedom and Reconstruction, 3; Washington, Booker T., and, 50, 261

duel, miscegenation, 288

Dulaney, W. Marvin, 60

Dunbar-Nelson, Alice, 61

Dunning, William, 234, 244

Dunning School, 3, 5, 17–18, 20, 60; neo-Dunning School, 5

Durden ferry confrontation, 86–87, 94n26

economy: Freedmen's Savings Bank, 255; freedom and, 10–11, 143–45, 147–48, 153–54; infrequency of pay, 145–47, 150, 152–53; North and South per capita income, 229n14; pay disparities, 146–47; plantation collapse and, 81–82, 92; slavery and, 216–18; white power militias and, 103

Ecuador, 193

*Edgefield Advertiser* (newspaper), 284

education: Blair Education Bill, 48, 50, 51; desegregation, 19; Freedmen's Bureau and, 46–47; freedom and, 9; HBCUs, 52; illegal, 41, 42; Jim Crow and, 50; land sales and, 42; with Reconstruction in textbooks, 20; right to, 40, 42–43; state-funded, 42, 46, 47, 49; textbooks, 20, 33nn16,17,20, 244; Washington, Booker T., and, 51. *See also* public schools, in Alabama; schools

educational persuasion, 255

elections: fraud, 95n48; Lincoln and, 287, 300n45; lynchings with, 97–98, 102, 107, 109–12; state violence with, 96–99, 104–5; violence with, 234, 260; voting, 45, 51, 89–91, 171–72, 236, 253, 260

elites: amnesty and Southern white, 169–71; Black, 266; Creoles, 61, 184; white, 108, 118n33

Elliot, Mark, 239, 240

Elliott, Robert, 175

emancipation: amalgamation with, 287; environmental implications of, 93n2; prohibition with trusteeship, 282, 297nn24,25; racial uplift and, 270n4. *See also* freedom

*Emancipation* (Wilson, J. T.), 261–62
Emanuel African Methodist Episcopal Church, 278, 294
Emerson Institute, 47, 48
Enforcement Act (1870), 171–72
*Equal Suffrage* (Garnet, Wilson, J. T., et al.), 250, 253, 254, 255
eugenics, 256, 266
Eutaw rally, 78, 85–86, 88, 94, 94n26
Evans, Joseph P., 261
Evans, Maurice Smethurst, 242
*Evening Post* (newspaper), 204–5
*Evening Star* (newspaper), 243

factionalism, racism and, 179n29
families: children, 42, 121, 130–37, 215; marriage and, 64, 215; USCT with homes and, 148–49
Farnsworth, John, 163–64, 165, 174
Favre, Jules, 187
*fazenda central*, 223, 224, 231n36
federal bounties, US Army and, 145–47, 150, 152–53
Federal Elections Bill, 51
Fennessy, Brian, 27–28
Ferrer, Ada, 209n38
Ferris, Kate, 243
Fields, Barbara J., 262, 265
Fields, Karen E., 265
Fifteenth Amendment, 2, 24, 99, 102–4, 241
Fifty-Fourth Massachusetts Infantry Regiment, 252; reenactors, 277
films, racism in, 234, 239
firefights, 78, 86, 95nn30,40
*The First Reconstruction* (Gosse), 35n40
Fish, Hamilton, 183, 200–3, 204, 205
Fitzgerald, Michael W., 80, 94n26
"Five Orange Pips" (Doyle), 238
Fleming, Walter, 60
flood victims, 95n28
Fludd, Eliza, 288, 301n48
Fogel, Robert, 229n14
Foley, Ehren, 14n1

Foner, Eric, 2–3, 5, 7, 22, 27, 30, 161; on Lost Cause, 233; NPS and, 18
Food, Tobacco, Agricultural & Allied Workers Union (FTA-CIO), 26
Foote, William Henderson, 76n92
Fordham, Damon, 278
Fordham, James, 60, 65, 69
foreign policy, US: with expulsion of European imperialism, 183–84; memories of Reconstruction violence influencing, 239; principles of, 11
Forrest, Nathan Bedford, 19
Fortune, T. Thomas, 251
"forty acres and a mule," 258
Foster, Gaines, 20
Fourteenth Amendment, 24, 28, 137; amnesty for reconstructed rebels and, 160–62, 167–71, 175–76
France, 181, 183–92, 193, 205
Francis (King consort of Spain), 194
*Frankfort Commonwealth* (newspaper), 102, 107–8
Frankfort riot (1871), 100, 106, 109, 112
*Frankfort Yeoman* (newspaper), 106
Franklin, John Hope, 264
fraud, elections, 95n48
Frazier, Evelina, 121–23, 129–30, 133
Fredrickson, George, 2
Freedmen's Bureau, 41, 42, 46–47, 49, 51, 259
Freedmen's Savings Bank, 255
freedom: African Americans without guarantee of, 4, 43, 98, 101; citizenship and, 3, 40; as dangerous, 128–29; economy and, 10–11, 143–45, 147–48, 153–54; education and, 9; emancipation, 93n2, 270n4, 282, 287, 297nn24,25; forms of, 3–4; gained and lost, 68–70, 98–99, 110–13; gender, race and, 10; labor and, 3; lost and regained, 13; lost for USCT, 144–45, 147–48, 153–54; myth of, 1; rebirth of, 2; Reconstruction and, 3. *See also* infanticide; state violence, Black freedom and

INDEX 315

Freedom Road Socialist Organization, 22
"Freedoms Gained and Lost" conference, 302n59
*Freedom's Lawmakers* (Foner), 27
free people, taxes for, 297n23
Frémont, John C., 262
French Opera House, 61–62, 64, 70
Friendly Brothers, 83
FTA-CIO (Food, Tobacco, Agricultural & Allied Workers Union), 26
Fuller, Diana, 282
Fuller, Nat: with Bachelor's Retreat restaurant, 277, 282, 291, 293, 295n6, 298n28; with birthday celebration meal for Washington, George, 281, 283–85, 296n20, 299n33; as celebrated caterer, 281–82, 283–84, 287, 291–92, 302n54; as de facto free person, 282, 297n23; evidence documenting feast by, 278–86; legacy, 293–94; with miscegenation duel, 288; with Nat Fuller's Eating House, 282–83; with real estate purchase, 282, 298n27; tour, 290, 301n51; trusteeship and, 282, 297n25. *See also* miscegenation feast

Gaines, Kevin K., 266, 270n4, 274nn96,100
Galt, John, 128
*Galveston News* (newspaper), 212
Garfield, James, 163
Garnet, Henry Highland, 250, 253, 254
Garrison, William Lloyd, 263
Garvey, Marcus, 255
Gatewood, William C., 282, 297n25, 298n27
*Gazeta da Noticias* (newspaper), 221
*Gazeta da Tarde* (newspaper), 212, 214–16, 221–25, 229n1
Geddings, Laura, 280, 299n37
gender. *See* mental competency, gender and race with
Germany, 192
Getty, Archibald, 283
Gilman, Caroline H., 280, 296n17

Gilmore, William, 96, 108
Glidden, George, 127
Glorious Revolution, Spain and, 197
Gosse, Van, 35n40
Gough, Jerry B., 27, 28
Grand Design, Napoleon III and, 185, 186, 187
the Grange (Patrons of Husbandry), 82, 87, 224
Grant, Ulysses S., 89, 181, 183, 188–92, 199, 201, 215
Great Britain, 182, 185, 198, 201, 239; Canada and, 192–93; with racism and US, 236–38, 242
Great Tradition, Black Nationalism and, 252, 269
Greeley, Horace, 80
Green, Hilary, 9, 27
*Greensboro Patriot* (newspaper), 134
*Greenville Enterprise* (newspaper), 280, 285
Gregory, Ovide, 41
Griffin, Albert, 41, 44
Griffith, D. W., 234
Grissom, Eugene, 134
Gross, Kali, 141n24
Guáimaro Assembly, 198–200, 203
*Guardian* (newspaper), 237–38, 245
guerrilla fighters, 84, 100, 193

Hahn, Steven, 30, 80, 92, 93n1, 209n38, 300n42
Haitian Revolution, 1, 193, 213
Hall, David, 147, 148
Hall, Jacquelyn Dowd, 25, 31
Hallowell, Richard P., 238
Hamilton, J. G. de Roulhac, 3
Hampton Union League, 254–55
Harding, Vincent, 252
Harlan, John Marshall, 96, 106–7
Harmon, Henry S., 143–44, 145
Harper, R. D., 41
Harrell, Starkey S., 167
Hayes, Rutherford B., 132, 221, 222

HBCUs (historically Black colleges and universities), 52
Heath, Edward, 59
Henderson, Eliza, 133
Henderson, Hamish, 31
Higginson, Thomas Wentworth, 24
Hilliard, Henry Washington, 220–23
historians: at Dunning School with white supremacy, 18; role of, 30–31
historically Black colleges and universities (HBCUs), 52
historical racism, 12, 233, 244
Historic Brattonsville, 19, 33n13
history: curriculum reform, 18; LDHI, 295n9, 302n53; revisionist, 18, 19, 20, 21; "We're History" blog, 21. *See also* memory, historical; Reconstruction, international history of
*History of the Negro Race in America from 1619 to 1880* (Williams, G. W.), 264
*History of the Negro Troops in the War of the Rebellion, 1861–1865* (Williams, G. W.), 264
Hoar, George, 175
Hobsbawm, Eric, 257
Hodges, A. G., 105
Hogarth, Rana, 127
Holden, William W., 165–72
Hollings, Ernest, 18
Holmes, Emma, 288–89
Holmes, Oliver, 138n3
Holt, Thomas, 40
homes: USCT with family and, 148–49; Woodrow Wilson Family Home, 19–20
homestead provision, 28–29, 223
hope, 8, 17, 31
Horton, Gustavus W., 41, 47
Houston, Frank, 136
Houston, Sam, 244
Howard, Jacob, 163
Hoyle, Henry Carpenter, 148
Huger Smith, Daniel E., 279, 296n13
Hume, Richard L., 27, 28

"I Have a Dream" speech (King), 23
indigenous populations, 147, 176, 240–41
*Industrial Day* (newspaper), 250
infanticide, 121, 130–37. *See also* mental competency, gender and race with
insanity: legal proof of, 124–25; menstruation and, 123–25; murder and temporary, 202; pregnancy and, 124–25, 134–35; puerperal, 125–26; race and, 133–34; US Census and, 128. *See also* mental competency, gender and race with
intellectualism, Black, 275n118
Internet Archive, 21
intimidation, 108–9
intraracial class difference, racial uplift and, 274n100
Ireland, land reform, 29
Irish-American Fenians, 193
Isabel (Princess of Brazil), 227
Isabella II (Queen of Spain), 193–94, 195, 197
Ivey, Thomas, 84, 88–89, 92, 94n26

Jackson, Lucy, 89
Jackson, Sara Dunlap, 264
Janney, Caroline, 232
Japanese Americans, 7
Jarvis, Edward, 128
*Jasper Weekly Courier* (newspaper), 133
Jefferson, Thomas, 224
Jervis, Charles, 152
Jim Crow: dismantling, 24; education and, 50; white supremacy justified with, 60, 234
Johnson, Andrew, 159, 161, 166, 188, 191, 257
Johnson, Harry: lynching of, 97–98, 109–12; military duty of, 108; trial for murder of, 107–12
Johnson, Henry, 151
Johnson, Samuel, 17
Johnson, Sarah D., 135–36, 142n35
Johnson, Walter, 229n14

INDEX 317

Johnson, William B., 149
Jones, Lewis, 20
Jordan, Wayne, 67
*Jornal do Commercio* (newspaper), 222
*Journal of Negro History*, 61
Joyner, Charles, 20
Juárez, Benito, 184, 187, 188–90, 192
Juárez laws, Roman Catholic Church and, 184
judicial intervention, civil rights without federal, 9–10, 98–99, 102, 111–12
juries, women convicted by, 138n2

Kelley, William, 163
Kellogg, William, 175
Kelly, Hugh, 135
Kendi, Ibram X., 255, 265, 266
Kennedy, James B.., 173
Kentucky, 115n16; Black testimony in, 10, 98–99, 101–2, 104, 107, 110–12; US Army in, 99–103, 106, 112. *See also* state violence, Black freedom and
King, Martin Luther, Jr., 23
KKK. *See* Ku Klux Klan
Knights of Labor, 261
Ku Klux Klan (KKK): arrests, 89; Black testimony and, 110–11; in film, 234, 239; Historic Brattonsville and, 19, 33n13; leadership, 20–21; militias, 103; murders by, 80, 83, 84, 93n4, 171; paramilitary activities and, 78, 80, 84, 92, 103; racism, 102–6, 238; supporters of, 246n25; terrorist acts, 78, 83–84, 88; violence, 79, 92, 173–74. *See also* white supremacy
Ku Klux Klan Act (1871), 80, 105–6
Kulkarni, Sri Preston, 244
Kytle, Ethan, 21, 22, 40, 302n54

labor: freedom and, 3; Knights of Labor, 261; upward mobility and, 256–57
Lamar, Lucius Quintus Cincinnatus, 173
land: "forty acres and a mule," 258; reform, 28–29, 223; sales and education, 42;

social equality, postwar aspirations and, 250, 253–54, 256, 258–59; tax, 256
Langston, John Mercer, 267
Latham, Albert, 147, 148
LDHI (Low Country Digital History Initiative) exhibition, 295n9, 302n53
LeConte, Emma, 287
Lee, Robert E., 144, 147, 232
LeFeber, Walter, 183
legislation, white supremacist, 111–12
Leslie, Preston H., 96, 107, 111
Lewis, James, 60
Lewis, Patrick A., 103
Liberation Army, Cuba and, 197–98
Lincoln, Abraham, 104, 182, 186, 187, 203; Clinton, Hillary, on, 5–6; Cuba and, 195–96, 197, 205; elections and, 287, 300n45; legacy, 262; propaganda and, 215–16; with re-birth of freedom, 2; statue, 260; support for, 283, 284, 285
Lincoln's Land Association, 258
Livingstone, William Pringle, 242–43
Logan, John, 163, 174
Logan, Nathaniel, 150
Longstreet, James, 169
López, Narciso, 198, 200
Lost Cause, Reconstruction and, 12, 213, 232–34, 236, 238–40, 244–45, 249, 262
Louisiana Purchase, 53n5
*Louisville Commercial* (newspaper), 97, 104, 106, 109, 111
*Louisville Courier-Journal* (newspaper), 99
Loving Brothers, 83
Low Country Digital History Initiative (LDHI) exhibition, 295n9, 302n53
loyalty oaths, 41, 159
lynchings: with elections, 97–98, 102, 107, 109–12; murder trials, 107–12; number of, 115n16; prosecutions, 98; to protect white women, 236; racism and, 237–38
Lyons, Richard, 195
Lyons-Seward Treaty, 195

Machado, Eduardo, 199
Maclean, John, 241
manhood, Black Nationalism and, 265–66
manumission, 1, 224, 263, 282
Maori people, 240
Marable, Manning, 22, 266
marriage, 64, 215
marronage, 1
Marshall, Anne E., 99
Martí, José, 196, 204–5
Martinet, Louis, 68
*Mason Smith Family Letters, 1860–1868* (Huger Smith), 279, 296n13
Masur, Kate, 7, 30
Matthews, Letha, 132
Maximilian I (Emperor of Mexico), 181–82, 184–90, 192
Maynard, Horace, 175
McCrady's Tavern, 302n54
McKaine, Osceola, 26
medicalization, of Black bodies and racism, 127–28, 131–32
memory, historical: as conflicted, 5; digital technology influencing, 21; Du Bois on truth and, 7. *See also* miscegenation feast; Reconstruction violence, memories of
menstruation, insanity and, 123–25
mental competency, gender and race with: African Americans, slavery and, 126–27; court system and, 129–37; freedom and, 10; with freedom as dangerous, 128–29; infanticide and, 121, 130–37; with medicalization of Black bodies and racism, 127–28, 131–32; menstruation and, 123–25; pregnancy and insanity, 124–25, 134–35; race and insanity, 133–34; racism and, 121–23
Meridian riot (1871), 80
Meriwether, W. A., 109–11
Merritt, Keri Leigh, 27
Metropolitan Police Act (1868), 62
Mexico, 181, 183–92, 207n22
Middleton (Miss), 280, 296n14, 299n38

migration, with population changes, 100–1
military, US: excellence through service in, 251–52; Fifty-Fourth Massachusetts Infantry Regiment, 252, 277; strength of, 184. *See also* Army, US; United States Colored Troops
militias: Cuban citizen, 198; Valley Rifles, 96–98, 103, 105, 107–10, 118n32; violence, 112; white power, 103–9
Miller, Kelly, 243–44
Miller, William L., 146
miscegenation (racial amalgamation), 296n14; coining of, 288, 300n45; fears, 64, 288–89
miscegenation (Nat Fuller's) feast: with birthday celebration meal for Washington, George, 281, 283–85, 296n20, 299n33; evidence documenting, 278–86; legacy, 293–94; mischaracterization of, 286–87, 291; Porcher, Abby Louisa, and, 279–82, 285–89, 291, 295n9, 296nn13,14, 299n37; Redpath and, 281, 283–86, 288, 296n20, 299n40; reenactment of fictional, 12–13, 276–77, 289–90; Shields and, 276–78, 290–92, 297n25, 298n28, 302n53; tour, 290, 301n51; white guests only at, 286–87
Mitchell, Kevin, 277, 290–91
*Mobile Daily Register* (newspaper), 39, 41–42, 45–46
Mobile *Register* (newspaper), 83, 94n26
Monroe, James, 183
Monroe Doctrine, 183–87, 189–90, 193, 200
Montesquieu, 215
monuments: Confederate, 232, 235, 245; Reconstruction Era National Monument, 18–19; Silent Sam, 19
Moore, Michael Boulware, 14n1
Moore, Roy, 22
Moore, Thomas, 150
Moral Monday movement, 22–23
Moredock, Will, 33n17
Moreira, Nicoláu Joaquim, 215–19, 223, 229n14

Moret Law, slavery and, 203–4
Moret y Pendergrast, Segismundo, 203
Morris Street School, 300n44
Morton, Samuel, 244
murders, 69; assassinations, 84, 88, 89, 95n40, 196, 216; by Democratic bands, 95n40; at Emanuel African Methodist Episcopal Church, 278, 294; by KKK, 80, 83, 84, 93n4, 171; by lynching, 97–98, 102, 107–11, 115n16; with temporary insanity, 202; women accused of, 138n2, 141n24

NAACP, Penn Center and, 24
Nabuco, Joaquim, 220–22, 225, 226, 230n31
Napoleon III (Emperor of France), 184, 185–87, 190–92
Nat Fuller's Eating House, 282–83
Nat Fuller's feast. *See* miscegenation feast
*Nationalist* (newspaper), 41, 44, 46
National Negro Congress, 26
National Park Service (NPS), 18, 19
Native Americans, 147, 176, 240–41
*The Negro in the American Rebellion* (Brown, W. W.), 264
*The Negro in the Civil War* (Quarles), 264–65, 278–79, 296nn13,14
"The Negro Question in the United States," 236
neo-Confederates, 244–45
New Confederacy, 22
Newman, William, 105
*New National Era* (newspaper), 130
New Orleans, 58–59, 63, 68
New Orleans Massacre (1866), 59, 63
New Orleans Police Department: African Americans in, 58–64, 68–69; arrest of Officier Fédéral, 61–64; arrest records, 60, 72n33; integration of, 59, 63; racism and, 63–64
*New Orleans Tribune* (newspaper), 59, 257
Newton, Alexander Heritage, 149
*New Yorker* (magazine), 290

*New York Times* (newspaper), 21, 173, 190, 290, 292–93
*New-York Tribune* (newspaper), 281, 283–84, 286
*New York World* (newspaper), 281, 288, 297n23, 300n45
New Zealand, 240
Norfolk Labor Association, 250, 254
Norfolk Land Association, 250, 254
Norfolk Union Monitor Club, 254
Norris, Thomas, Jr., 267
*North American* (newspaper), 132
North Carolina. *See* Charleston, North Carolina
the North, per capita income, 229n14
Nott, Josiah, 127, 244
NPS (National Park Service), 18, 19
Nye, James, 175

Obama, Barack, 6, 18, 22, 31
O'Donnell, Kane, 283, 286
Officier Fédéral, arrest of, 61–64
Oldfield, John, 60, 75n80
Oliphant, Mary C. Simms, 20, 33nn16,17
oppression, violence and, 237
Orr, James L., 29

Pacific Islanders, 241
paramilitary activities, 78, 80–81, 84, 92, 103, 173
pardons, commuted sentences and, 141n25
Paterson, Orlando, 1
Patrocínio, José do, 214, 215, 223, 225–28, 229n1
Patrons of Husbandry (the Grange), 82, 87, 224
Patton, Robert, 162, 165
pay disparity, USCT, 146–47
Peabody Education Fund, 48
Peckham, Albert A., 147–48
peculiar institution defense, of slavery, 129, 176, 229n7
Pelletan, Eugène, 187
Penn Center, 24–25

per capita income, South and North, 229n14
Pernell, Jacob, 151
Peru, 182, 193
*Philadelphia Press* (newspaper), 283
Philippines, 234, 251
Phillips, Wendell, 200, 253
Pickens, Samuel, 82
Pierce, Gorrell, 20–21
Pinckney, Clementa C., 278
Pinheiro, Jr., Holly A., 2, 10, 11
Pinto-Handler, Sergio, 239
Pius IX (Pope), 184–85
plantation collapse, 79
plantation collapse, economy and, 81–82, 92
*Plessy v. Ferguson*, 7, 68–69, 268
"Poisonous Doctrines," 39
Poland, Luke, 174
police officers, African American, 9; in Charleston, 58–60, 64–65, 68–69; in leadership roles, 57, 60; in New Orleans, 58–64, 68–69; in other Southern cities, 59, 68, 69; with public performance and spectacle, 70. *See also* Charleston Police Department; New Orleans Police Department
politics: of hope, 31; reconstructed rebels and, 160, 162–66; Reconstruction and global, 4–5; state violence, Black freedom and, 98–99, 104–7
populations: African Americans in South Carolina, 212; changes with migration, 100–1; data, 114n10; indigenous, 147, 176, 240–41
Porcher, Abby Louisa, 279–82, 285–89, 291, 295n9, 296nn13,14, 299n37
Porcher, Frances J., 279
Porcher, Francis James, 279, 282, 296n14
Port Royal Experiment, 19
*Post and Courier* (newspaper), 302n54
Powers, Bernard E., Jr., 14n1, 16n27, 277
pregnancy: infanticide and, 121, 130–37; insanity and, 124–25, 134–35
Prim, Juan, 197, 202

Prince, K. Stephen, 233
Pringle, Susan Alston, 288
prosecutions, lynchings, 98
Proudhon, Pierre, 214
Pryor, William S., 106
public performance, spectacle and, 70
public schools, in Alabama: activism and, 48–49; creation of, 39–40, 50; Freedmen's Bureau and, 46–47, 51; with freedom and citizenship, 40; with right to education, 40, 42–43; tuition-based, 43–44; whites as barriers to, 39. *See also* education
puerperal insanity, 125–26

Quarles, Benjamin, 262, 264–65, 278–79, 296nn13,14
Quesnay, François, 224

Rable, George, 78
race: citizenship and, 6; concentration data for 1870, 90; of delegates at Alabama Constitutional Convention, 41; French Opera House seating and, 61; insanity and, 133–34; with legacy of Reconstruction, 5; violence, 85–86, 88, 235, 245n2; *Voice of a New Race*, 268. *See also* mental competency, gender and race with
racecraft, 265
racial amalgamation. *See* miscegenation
racial empowerment. *See* self-defense, racial empowerment and
racial hierarchy, class and, 257
racial uplift, 270n4, 274n100. *See also* uplift suasion
racism: agriculture and, 82–84, 91–92; Alabama Constitutional Convention and, 41–42; class, 266; factionalism and, 179n29; in films, 234, 239; at French Opera House, 62; KKK and, 102–6, 238; lynchings and, 237–38; with medicalization of Black bodies, 127–28, 131–32; mental competency and, 121–23; New

INDEX 321

Orleans Police Department and, 63–64; scientific, 233, 256, 266; US Army with, 145–47, 151–53; as US export, 236–39, 241–44; voting and, 45. *See also* Ku Klux Klan
Radicals' Reconstruction, 17, 25–27. *See also* civil rights movement
Rapier, James, 170
rascality (stupidness of the mind), 127
Raskin, Hannah, 278, 291, 302n54
Ravenel, Caroline R., 288
Ravenel, Henry W., 57, 70
Rebouças, André, 214–15, 222–26, 228, 231n36
Reconstruction: amendments, 2; civil rights movement influenced by, 24–25; digital technologies and, 18, 21; education and textbooks on, 20; global politics and, 4–5; Lost Cause and, 12, 213, 232–34, 236, 238–40, 244–45, 249, 262; misunderstanding of, 6–7; NPS and, 18, 19; Woodrow Wilson Family Home and, 19–20. *See also* civil rights movement; Rio de Janeiro, abolitionists and Reconstruction in; Third Reconstruction
Reconstruction, international history of: Canada and, 192–93; Cuba and, 183, 184, 194–205; with expulsion of European imperialism, 183–84; with foreign relations and projection of American power, 11, 181–83; with France and Mexico, 181, 183–92; Irish-American Fenians and, 193; Maximilian I and, 181–82, 184–90, 192; Monroe Doctrine and, 183–87, 189–90, 193, 200; Republicans and, 186; slavery and, 181, 187, 188, 192, 194–200, 209n38; Spain, 182–83, 185, 193–95, 197–98, 202–5
Reconstruction Acts of 1867, 40
Reconstruction Amendments, 2, 9, 13, 23–24, 173
Reconstruction-era constitutions, 16n29, 43, 50

Reconstruction Era National Monument, 18–19
*Reconstruction in Alabama* (Fitzgerald), 80, 94n26
Reconstruction violence, memories of: carpetbaggers and, 235, 238–39, 244–45; Confederate monuments and, 232, 235, 245; elections and, 234; foreign policy and, 239; Lost Cause and, 12, 232–34, 236, 238–40, 244–45; "The Negro Question in the United States" and, 236; racism and, 236–38, 241–44; white supremacy and, 233–34
Redpath, James, 281, 283–86, 288, 296n20, 299n40
Red Shirts, 30, 78, 234
Reed, Robert, 86–87, 89, 92, 94n26
Reeves, Bass, 76n92
reforms: agriculture, 225; history curriculum, 18; land, 28–29, 223, 224
Renfroe, Steve, 80, 83, 89
*The Republican Party and the South* (Abbott), 177n4
Republicans: with control, 50; with elections and state violence, 96–99, 104–5; international history of Reconstruction and, 186; as main enemy of American people, 22; Monroe Doctrine and, 186; for public schools, 44; with voting, 90
"Rethinking Why There Are So Few Unions in the South" (Simon), 17
Revels, Hiram, 170
reverse colonialism, 247n39
Rey, Octave, 60, 68
Rice, Samuel, 170
Richmond, James, 151
*Richmond Dispatch* (newspaper), 284, 285, 286
*Richmond Examiner* (newspaper), 284, 285
*Richmond Whig* (newspaper), 284
rights: to education, 40, 42–43; equality and, 169–71; veteran, 101, 112; voting, 236, 253, 260; of women, 29, 136–37. *See also* civil rights

Ring, Natalie, 238, 240
Rio de Janeiro, abolitionists and Reconstruction in: agriculture without slavery and, 222–23; correctional colonies and, 227; with demands of planters, 213–14; economics of slavery and, 216–18; Hilliard and, 220–23; with positive narratives of US, 11–12, 212–19, 221–22, 225, 228–29; rural democracy and, 212, 214–15, 218–19, 223–28
*River of Dark Dreams* (Johnson, Walter), 229n14
Roach, Joseph, 96, 110
Robbins, William McKendree, 142n35
Roberts, Blain, 21, 40, 278
Robinson, Adrian, 86, 94n26, 95n30
Robinson, Cedric, 251
*Rockport Democrat* (newspaper), 133
Roland, George, 151
Roman Catholic Church, 184–85, 193
Romero, Matías, 186, 188–91
Roof, Dylann, 278
Roosevelt, Franklin D., 26
Ross, George, 151
Rousey, Dennis, 60
running away (drapetomania), 127
rural democracy, 212, 214–15, 218–19, 223–28
Rush, Benjamin, 123, 127, 128
Russ, William Adam, Jr., 177n4
Russia, 183, 193, 205, 261
Ryan, Paul, 6

Santovenia, Emilio, 195
Saraiva, José Antonio, 225
Sawyer, Frederick, 175
Scarborough, Leah, 130–31
Schaffer, Samuel A., 239
Schenck, David, 135
Schofield, John M., 189, 191–92, 208n29
"The School Question" (Griffin), 44
schools: Black public, 255; clandestine, 41, 42; Freedmen's Bureau, 41, 42. *See also* public schools, in Alabama

scientific racism, 233, 256, 266
Scotland, 29, 31
Scott, John, 175
Scott, Rebecca, 209n38
Scott, Robert K., 293–94
Scott, Walter, 278
*The Second Founding* (Foner), 2
Second Reconstruction, 2, 17, 22. *See also* civil rights movement
Sedgwick, William, 124
self-defense, racial empowerment and: Democratic voting turnout from 1872 to 1874, 91; Dew and, 84, 86, 88–89, 92–93, 94n26; Durden ferry confrontation, 86–87, 94n26; KKK, terrorism and, 78, 83–84, 88; plantation collapse and, 79, 81–82, 92; race concentration data for 1870, 90; racial violence and, 85–86, 88; racism and agriculture with, 82–84, 91–92; with transcendence and resilience, 78, 84; voting and, 89–90; West-Central Alabama, 79–80
Serrano, Francisco, 194, 197
Serwer, Adam, 6, 7
Seward, William H., 208n29, 263; with international history of Reconstruction, 182–92, 193, 205; Lyons-Seward Treaty and, 195
*Shelby County v. Holder*, 24
Sheridan, Phil, 59, 188–89, 191–92
Sherman, John, 162
Sherman, William Tecumseh, 283, 296n17
Shields, David, 276–78, 290–92, 297n25, 298n28, 302n53
Shrewsbury, George, 65
Sickles, Daniel, 201–2, 204
Silent Sam monument, 19
Silkenat, David, 29
Simms, William Gilmore, 33nn16,17
Simon, Bryant, 17
slavery, 43, 222–23; "After Slavery" project, 21; in Brazil, 212, 213; children and, 215; Cuba and, 194–200, 203, 209n38; economy and, 216–18; fears about

INDEX 323

ending, 287–88; *Gazeta da Tarde* against, 229n1; international history of Reconstruction and, 181, 187, 188, 192, 194–200; in Kentucky, 100; manumission upholding, 1; mental competency and, 126–27; Mexico and, 188, 192; Moret Law and, 203–4; peculiar institution defense of, 129, 176, 229n7; profitability and productivity as form of labor, 230n16; Spain and, 194, 203, 204; supporters of, 128–29

slaves: badges, 66–67; terrorism against former, 257

Small, Robert, 276

Smith, Alice R. H., 296n13

Smith, D. Howard, Jr., 107–8

Smith, Fanny, 132–33

Smith, Howard, Jr., 118n32

Social Darwinism, 266

social equality, postwar aspirations and: activism and, 12, 250, 253–61; Black Nationalism and manhood with, 265–66, 267; with Black public schools, 255; civil rights and, 254–55; class, racial hierarchy and, 257; through excellence through military service, 251–52; labor, upward mobility and, 256–57; land and, 250, 253–54, 256, 258–59; uplift suasion and, 250, 252, 255, 259, 265, 267, 269–70; voting rights and, 253

social networks, amnesty petitions and, 166–69

Sociedade Brasileira Contra a Escravidão, 220

Sombart, Werner, 17

sonic texture, of urban spaces, 68

Sons of Confederate Veterans, 1

the South, per capita income, 229n14

South Africa, 242

South Carolina: African American population in, 212; delegates and median wealth, 28

South Carolina Constitutional Convention (1868), 16n27, 17, 26–28, 31, 32n1, 293

South Carolina Progressive Democratic Party, 26

South Caroliniana Library, 279, 296n13

Southern Historical Collection, 21

Southern Negro Youth Congress, 26

Southern Popular Front, 25, 26

*Southern Provisions* (Shields), 276

Spain, 193, 195, 201, 243; Cuba and, 197–98, 202–5; Dominican Republic and, 182, 183; Glorious Revolution and, 197; slavery and, 194, 203, 204; Tripartite Alliance and, 185

Spanish–South American War, 193

spectacle, public performance and, 70

Speed, James F., 104

Stanley, Matthew, 238

state-funded education, 42, 46, 47, 49

state violence, Black freedom and: Civil Rights Act and, 101–12; civil rights activism and, 101–2; civil rights without federal intervention and, 9–10, 98–99, 102, 111–12; with elections, 96–99, 104–5; Frankfort riot, 100, 106, 109, 112; gains and losses, 98, 110–13; migration and, 100–1; politics and, 98–99, 104–7; with testimony, 10, 98–99, 101–2, 104, 107, 110–12; US Army and, 99–103; Valley Rifles militia and, 96–98, 103, 105, 107–10, 118n32

Stepan, Nancy, 1

Stephens, John W., 171

Stevens, Thaddeus, 25, 163, 165, 259

Stewart, William, 162, 174

St. Helena Island, 24

Stoney, Thomas, 301n51

Storer, Horatio, 123–24

stupidity of the mind (rascality), 127

subscription fees, digital technology, 21

Summers, Mark, 30

Sumner, Charles, 175, 256, 259

Supreme Court, US: *Blyew v. United States*, 101–2, 115n14; *Plessy v. Ferguson*, 7, 68–69, 268; *Shelby County v. Holder*, 24

Swayne, John H., 115n14

Tabbs, Hannah Mary, 141n24
Talented Tenths, 250
taxes: for free people, 297n23; land, 256
Taylor, Edmund H., Jr., 96
Taylor, William, 96, 97, 110
Tennessee, 3, 16n29
terrorism: acts of, 78, 83–84, 88; Civil Rights Act of 1866 and, 102–12; against former slaves, 257; Ku Klux Klan Act, 80, 105–6; resilience and transcending, 78; at *True Southerner*, 259. *See also* Ku Klux Klan
testimony, Black: without Civil Rights Act, 9–10, 98–99, 102, 111–12; on lynchings, 110; right to give, 101–2; white supremacy and, 10, 98, 104, 107, 110–13
testimony, white, 109
*The Texans* (film), 239
textbooks, 20, 33nn16,17,20, 244
Third Reconstruction, 17, 22–23
Thirteenth Amendment, 24, 100
Thompson, Bob, 88
Thompson, E. P., 257
Thompson, Robert (judge), 109
Tindall, George, 20
Tinker, William, 197
transcendence, with resilience, 78, 84
treaty population, 53n5
Trent Affair, 182
*La Tribune* (newspaper), 62
Tripartite Alliance, 185
*True Southerner* (newspaper), 250, 254, 255, 256, 257, 258–59
Trump, Donald, 7, 13, 33n13
trusteeship, 282, 297nn24,25
truth, Du Bois on historical memory and, 7
tuition-based schools, 43–44
Tulley, Tom R., 277
Turner, Jack, 85, 94n25, 94n26
Turner, Nat, 263–64
Turner, William V., 39, 43

Underwood, John C., 254
unemployment, USCT veterans, 150–52
*Union Republican* (newspaper), 259
United States (US): Census, 93n6, 100, 128, 145; civil rights without judicial intervention, 9–10, 98–99, 102, 111–12; Civil War, 145, 151–54, 209n38; Cuba and, 194–95, 200–4, 209n38, 243; Mexico and, 188–89, 207n22; "The Negro Question in the United States," 236; with racism as export, 236–39, 241–44; Rio de Janeiro and positive narratives of Reconstruction in, 11–12, 212–19, 221–22, 225, 228–29; Supreme Court, 24, 68–69, 101–2, 268. *See also* foreign policy, US; military, US
United States Colored Troops (USCT): Civil War pensions and, 145, 151–52; demobilization of, 150–53; disabilities and injuries, 150–51, 152; with economy and freedom, 10–11, 143–44; federal bounties and pay frequency, 145–47, 150, 152–53; freedoms lost, 144–45, 147–48, 153–54; home and family concerns, 148–49; with illness and death, 149–50; lengthy tenures for, 147, 149; pay disparity and, 146–47; racism and, 145–47, 151–53; unemployment and, 150–52
University of Alabama, 42
University of North Carolina at Chapel Hill, 19
"Unloading My Conscience" (Patrocínio), 227
unnamed Black woman (beaten by Julian Carr), 235
*Uplifting the Race* (Gaines), 270n4
uplift suasion, 250, 252, 255, 259, 265, 267, 269–70
urban spaces, 9, 61, 64, 68
USCT. *See* United States Colored Troops

Valley Rifles militia, 96–98, 103, 105, 107–10, 118n32
Valmaseda (General), 199
Vance, Zebulon, 174
veterans, Black: disabilities and injuries, 150–51, 152; with rights of citizenship,

101, 112; testimony from, 110; with unemployment, 150–52. *See also* United States Colored Troops
Vianna, Antonio Ferreira, 226–27
violence: against abolitionists, 117n24; agriculture and, 82–83; with elections, 234, 260; KKK, 79, 92, 173–74; militia, 112; oppression and, 237; racial, 85–86, 88, 235, 245n2; White League, 91. *See also* Reconstruction violence, memories of; state violence, Black freedom and
*Voice of a New Race* (Wilson, J. T.), 268
voting: Democrats with, 89, 91; Enforcement Act and, 171–72; Federal Elections Bill, 51; racism and, 45; Republicans with, 90; rights denied, 236, 253, 260. *See also* elections
Voting Rights Act (1965), 7, 23, 24

Waddell, Alfred, 234
Walcutt, Howard, 109, 110, 112
Wallace, Louisa, 131–32
Wall Street crash (1873), 81
Warmoth, Henry, 62–63
War on Poverty, 25
Warren, Edward, 130
Washington, Booker T., 50, 51, 251, 255, 261, 267
Washington, George, birthday celebration meal for, 281, 283–85, 296n20, 299n33
Washington, Henry: lynching of, 96–98, 109–12; military duty and elite status of, 108, 118n33; trial for murder of, 107–12
Waterbury, Maria, 51
Weber, Eric, 237
Webster, J. D., 283
*Weekly Anglo-African* (newspaper), 151
Welles, Gideon, 191
Wells, William H., 260
"We're History" blog, 21
West-Central Alabama, 79–80
"What Happened to the Civil Rights Movement?" (Woodward), 22

*What Reconstruction Meant* (Baker), 20, 32n1
*Whig* (newspaper), 85
Whipper, William J., 8, 29
White, D. B., 254–55
White, Garland H., 149, 150
White League, 63, 78, 83, 87, 89, 91
white power militias, 103–9
whites: African American police officers and reaction of, 60; as barriers to Alabama public schools, 39. *See also* women, white
white supremacy, 23, 251; agriculture and, 82–83; Black testimony and, 10, 98, 104, 107, 110–13; court system and, 107–8, 110–11, 131–33, 137–38; Dunning school historians with, 18; Jim Crow and justifications for, 60, 234; justifications for, 236–39, 241–44; KKK, 19–21, 33n13, 93n4, 246n25; legislation supporting, 111–12; Reconstruction violence and, 233–34; White League and, 63, 78, 83, 87, 89, 91
*Why the Negro Was Enfranchised* (Hallowell), 238
Wiggins, Robert V., 39, 43
Wilberforce, William, 215
*Wilkes-Barre Time Leader* (newspaper), 239
Williams, George Washington, 249, 264, 265, 270n4
Williams, Kidada, 40
Williamsburg Colored Union League, 254
Williamson, Joel, 20
Wilson, Henry, 164
Wilson, Joe, 18
Wilson, Joseph T., 20, 238; activism of, 12, 250, 253–61; *The Black Phalanx*, 12, 249, 263–66, 269–70; *Emancipation*, 261–62; excellence through military service and, 251–52; legacy of, 249–50; as *True Southerner* editor, 254, 255, 256, 259; *Voice of a New Race*, 268. *See also* social equality, postwar aspirations and

Wilson, Woodrow, 26, 239
women: accused of murder, 138n2, 141n24; rights of, 29, 136–37. *See also* mental competency, gender and race with
women, Black: insanity and, 133, 134; with prison sentences, 131–33, 137–38; protection of, 251
women, white: insanity and, 133–35; lynchings to protect, 236; mental competency of, 135; without prison sentences, 131; puerperal insanity and, 125–26
Wood, Fernando, 283
Wood, Marcus, 1

Woodrow Wilson Family Home, 19–20
Woodson, Carter, 262
Woodward, C. Vann, 22, 23
*The World the Civil War Made* (Downs and Masur), 30
*The World Turned Upside Down* (Hill), 37n77
Wright, Gavin, 26–27
Wright, George C., 115n16

*Yorkville Enquirer* (newspaper), 284

Zambrana, Antonio, 199

Reconstructing America
Andrew L. Slap, series editor

Hans L. Trefousse, *Impeachment of a President: Andrew Johnson, the Blacks, and Reconstruction.*

Richard Paul Fuke, *Imperfect Equality: African Americans and the Confines of White Ideology in Post-Emancipation Maryland.*

Ruth Currie-McDaniel, *Carpetbagger of Conscience: A Biography of John Emory Bryant.*

Paul A. Cimbala and Randall M. Miller, eds., *The Freedmen's Bureau and Reconstruction: Reconsiderations.*

Herman Belz, *A New Birth of Freedom: The Republican Party and Freedmen's Rights, 1861 to 1866.*

Robert Michael Goldman, *"A Free Ballot and a Fair Count": The Department of Justice and the Enforcement of Voting Rights in the South, 1877–1893.*

Ruth Douglas Currie, ed., *Emma Spaulding Bryant: Civil War Bride, Carpetbagger's Wife, Ardent Feminist—Letters, 1860–1900.*

Robert Francis Engs, *Freedom's First Generation: Black Hampton, Virginia, 1861–1890.*

Robert F. Kaczorowski, *The Politics of Judicial Interpretation: The Federal Courts, Department of Justice, and Civil Rights, 1866–1876.*

John Syrett, *The Civil War Confiscation Acts: Failing to Reconstruct the South.*

Michael Les Benedict, *Preserving the Constitution: Essays on Politics and the Constitution in the Reconstruction Era.*

Andrew L. Slap, *The Doom of Reconstruction: The Liberal Republicans in the Civil War Era.*

Edmund L. Drago, *Confederate Phoenix: Rebel Children and Their Families in South Carolina.*

Mary Farmer-Kaiser, *Freedwomen and the Freedmen's Bureau: Race, Gender, and Public Policy in the Age of Emancipation.*

Paul A. Cimbala and Randall Miller, eds., *The Great Task Remaining Before Us: Reconstruction as America's Continuing Civil War.*

John A. Casey Jr., *New Men: Reconstructing the Image of the Veteran in Late-Nineteenth-Century American Literature and Culture.*

Hilary Green, *Educational Reconstruction: African American Schools in the Urban South, 1865–1890.*

Christopher B. Bean, *Too Great a Burden to Bear: The Struggle and Failure of the Freedmen's Bureau in Texas.*

David E. Goldberg, *The Retreats of Reconstruction: Race, Leisure, and the Politics of Segregation at the New Jersey Shore, 1865–1920.*

David Prior, ed., *Reconstruction in a Globalizing World.*

Jewel L. Spangler and Frank Towers, eds., *Remaking North American Sovereignty: State Transformation in the 1860s.*

Adam H. Domby and Simon Lewis, eds., *Freedoms Gained and Lost: Reconstruction and Its Meanings 150 Years Later.*

www.ingramcontent.com/pod-product-compliance
Lightning Source LLC
Chambersburg PA
CBHW032026290426
44110CB00012B/695